In Memory of England

A Novelist's View of History

PETER
VANSITTART

JOHN MURRAY
Albemarle Street, London

To Joan Carnwath
Valued friend, marvellous hostess: novelist and biographer

© Peter Vansittart 1998

First published in 1998

Reissued in paperback in 1999
by John Murray (Publishers) Ltd,
50 Albemarle Street, London W1X 4BD

The moral right of the author has been asserted

A catalogue record for this book is available from the British Library

ISBN 0-7195-5747 X
Typeset in 11.5/13.5 Adobe Garamond by Servis Filmsetting Ltd
Printed and bound in Great Britain by
St Edmundsbury Press Ltd, Bury St Edmunds, Suffolk

Contents

Introduction

Several impulses lie behind this book. One was a sentence in John Major's speech to the 'Britain and the World' conference in March 1995: 'We are attached to our sovereignty and our national institutions.' Then there were the proposals that year to induce a sense of Britishness in schools. In some they provoked fury or contempt, but made me ponder both 'Britishness' and 'Englishness'. What would be taught? I began jotting down incidents, achievements, the trivial and the momentous, which gave me some sense of Englishness, necessarily merging into Britishness, which became this book. My first jotting was about a schoolmaster who wrote of his pupil, Winston Churchill, that he lacked ambition. I relish oddities and exceptions, like those lively or enigmatic figures in the margins of medieval books, carved on misericords, grinning from corbels. They balance the sententious, rancorous or momentous. They have place.

Again in 1995, Tony Benn replied to a *New Statesman* questionnaire: 'I don't believe in Englishness. I'm a socialist.' I then read that Brussels had granted British farmers permission to grow trees on set-aside portions of their land. Here was a minor signpost on a road barely imaginable in my youth, though in the Cuban Missile Crisis of 1962 I had realized that, for the first time in two centuries, Britain had no world role.

Britain might indeed disintegrate, England become a historical curiosity, remote as the Second Reich or the Golden Age of Spain. National sovereignty, with its moss-bound institutions and methodical selfishness, was being denounced as a pernicious obstacle to wider concepts of work, taxation, education, employment, progress. An old-timer, I had doubts whether an international society of mass-media, instant information, endlessly multiplied visual images, would much alter the regions in which many had their being, those of loneliness, fear of death and loss of beauty; private griefs, sexual and intellectual frustration, child abuse, urban gangsterism, power-hunger and irrational impulses, the unending human transience. The myths and illuminations by which we have hitherto lived can be as starved in a global studio as in a rural slum.

History, like science, fertilises the imagination, though it has often been unimaginatively taught. My own history teacher, however, has blazed within my mind since he showed me, rather ruefully, an observation by Lord Bryce: 'A clever man may teach geometry, or natural history, or Latin, to good purpose without being proficient in these subjects. But to teach history, one must have made history a study and must know something about things which are not to be found in any schoolbook.'

I was soon reading of a seamstress employed in the Tower to stitch back the heads of executed noblemen, before burial. What was her title? Was her job hereditary, like that of the Paris executioner? Had she really existed? No text book mentioned her, but if she was only imaginary, she yet remained unforgettable.

That gracious Brussels permission to grow trees seemed telling. From 1740 to 1914, Britain had felt herself supreme, issuing her own terms to Europe, usually acquisitive, sometimes ruthless. Relegation thus holds some cyclic element of retribution, and henceforward many traditions must be discarded: they are probably complacent, anti-social, or fraudulent. History, Tolstoy claimed, would be excellent matter, if only it were true! He could have added that it had been almost wholly written by men.

But none of this is an excuse for abandoning History. In 1995, Peter Prager, a Jewish teacher, described his invitation to tell Bristol pupils of his experience of Nazi persecution. 'When I asked the children, "How many of you have heard about the persecution of the Jews?", nobody had – not even the ones who had seen *Schindler's List*. It must have gone right over their heads: they saw it as a Hollywood film.' A 1995 survey among 1,600 pupils aged 11 to 14 discovered that 39 per cent identified Churchill as a song-writer. In the same year, Nina Preston wrote to *The Times*: 'I recently mentioned Samuel Johnson to two of my granddaughters, one a Cambridge graduate, the other reading Social Anthropology at London University. In both cases the reply was "Who was he?" When I tackled their mothers, they told me that modern teaching no longer includes the eighteenth century – there's no time.' In 1996, a 15-year-old boy asked an *Independent* reporter, apropos of Schubert, 'Why would we want to learn about people who are dead?', while many RAF recruits were reported to be ignorant of the Battle of Britain.

The Classics are virtually excommunicate, yet the Graeco-Roman dimension has been a lively precaution against over-optimistic estimates of human nature. Raymond Asquith wrote to John Buchan that if only Englishmen had known their Aeschylus a little better, they would not have hustled about the world appropriating things. Plutarch and Seneca, filtered through Shakespeare, warn against bland acceptance of fate, authority, the over-rational.

Classics, of course, have no monopoly of pertinent stories, and any age can learn from a French provincial governor, François de Montmorin, replying to King Charles IX: 'Sire, I have received an order from Your Majesty directing me to kill all Protestants in my province. I respect Your Majesty too much to believe that this order is genuine. But if, which God forbid, it should indeed be, I respect Your Majesty too greatly to feel it in my power to obey it.' Courage, dignity, wit and humanity in a handful of words.

English history, if still taught, could benefit from new technology – graphic images, coded visual footnotes, intricate cross-references, flashpoints of revelation, co-ordinated particles of fact, multiple and far-ranging analogies. My generation was probably fed with too many unrelated facts, too few conclusions, though for me the facts were vivid enough. What of the charge that these facts of History were simply Whiggish or élitist decoration, smothering a brutal, best-forgotten past and adding further temptation to emasculate Britain, 'heritaged' into a collection of theme parks, trapped in parochial mementos and moribund, pretentious institutions sustained by tourism and Brussels grants?

I hope to demonstrate that our past is more than an inert irrelevance or a conspiracy against civilisation, and has had some share in what Luigi Barzini has called the only art worth learning but which can never be wholly mastered, the art of inhabiting the earth.

I

England in Language

. . . I try to write lucidly
that even I
Can understand it . . .
Poems, at least
Ought not to be phantoms

D.J. Enright

I remain, Sir, your humble and obedient servant, which you know, and I know, is a damned lie.

1st Duke of Wellington

If the study of History has been largely perfunctory, the English language is now threatened less by foreign imports, often useful or stimulating, than from within, by slovenly chat-masters, ill-educated journalists, commercial fraudsters, literary pretenders with self-indulgent verbal inflation, and self-appointed committees of public safety demanding political correctness. All share ignorance or contempt for the marvellous resources of English.

English is older than cathedrals, tougher than dragoons and commandos, as flexible as music; and it underpins every variety of English behaviour which here follows – pugnacious, elegiac, lyrical, vindicative, ironic, subtle, hypocritical, unctuous, plain-speaking, romantic and nonsensical. It expresses my main theme, a certain continuity of spirit persisting despite class, regional and ethnic divisions, Scandinavian, Teutonic and Norman invasions, overseas expansion, perhaps the drift into Europe with its promises of new codes, images, horizons. It cemented considerable national cohesion through organic institutions, some pride in achievements, reprehensible dislike of foreigners, the advance of civilised manners. Though preliminary to the narrative, this chapter therefore is not tangential, but vitally engaged with it. Language was the energy within the development of distinctive law, politics, literature, it was crucial in the Reformation,

5

excitingly vigorous in the King James Bible, the dialectical arguments of the Republic, the papers of the Royal Society. It shines in Shakespeare, Gibbon, Swift, Johnson, Dickens, remains solid in the American Declaration of Independence and Lincoln's Gettysburg speech. Throughout, however, it has been refreshed from below, by street slang, sailors' bawdiness, rebels' pleas at the Bloody Assizes, by children's rhymes and music-hall repartee.

Rather forbiddingly, a former Cabinet Minister, Virginia Bottomley, remarked in 1995 that our greatest software product is the English language. It is spouted at international conferences, declaimed in world theatres, travestied at presidential inaugurations, manipulated by priests, lawyers, salesmen, officials, howled by wild singers for multi-national audiences. In Britain it is studied in hot classrooms and brooded over in lonely bedrooms by readers of Donne and Pope, Joyce and Patrick White, Emily Dickinson and Ben Okri. It easily withstands the subsidised rivalry of Gaelic and Welsh. Subtle, it has also the infinite resources of simplicity. Henry James, though seldom indulging in simplicity, told Edith Wharton that the two most beautiful words in English were 'summer afternoon'.

Words, grooves into time, make the most signal human tools. They can defy, through poetry, nonsense, humour, the laws of physics, logic, public opinion, common sense, good taste and sworn evidence. He lies like an eye-witness, runs the Russian proverb. Through language, priests invent a god; then crouch in terror when, in one hot noon, the god speaks. Humans have achieved the marvel of distinguishing between *evening* and *night, culture* and *civilisation, image* and *symbol.* Nuance is all, and precision is an ally of nuance. J.M. Synge remembered Douglas Hyde, profound linguist, President of Ireland, being rebuked by a peasant for using 'gold' instead of 'golden' in a translation from Gaelic. 'Gold' was showy – like gold-capped teeth and Johannesburg watches: Rossetti's 'Blessed Damozel leaning out of the gold bar of Heaven' suggests a barmaid. 'Golden' is slower, more graceful, elegiac as Shakespeare's golden lads and girls.

Emerson praised language for resembling not houses or farms, but ferries. Like tools, like regalia, words have had both function and mystique, personality and magic. A cheerful Greek fantasist, Antiphanes of Berga, told credulous readers that in northern winters words froze, becoming audible only in spring, a notion stolen by Baron Münchausen. They were inextricably noosed in the live fabric of the universe, so that a curse could destroy an enemy, praise could amplify the soul, song ease it from the body.

Metaphor and simile were spells, overcoming the literal, exploring space, uniting apparent dissimilarities, evoking enchantment. An ancient Egyptian wrote:

> Heaven lets fall love of her
> as a flame falls in the hay.

Such powers were dangerous, especially when written. Writing, often a caste monopoly, had subversive tendencies and suspect origins. In *Phaedrus*, Plato mentions the god of writing appearing to Pharoah holding his invention, the hieroglyphic script. Pharoah begged him to destroy it, for it would ruin memory, and delude people into imagining that they knew more than they did. British Druids, credited by Caesar with knowing thirty thousand lines of verse, supervised an oral culture and clan memory. Their monkish supplanters encouraged literacy though wielding censorship. Medieval Europeans held writing to be the invention of a fallen angel, Penemue, and thus as morally ambiguous as Prometheus's gift of fire. The poor were ungrateful: as documents thickened, their blood seemed to thin. Literacy could liberate the mind, but also enslave the body. Laws concerning sexual relations, dating from the Kentish King Aethelbert (560–610), seem to be the oldest extant written English: '*Gif Man Maegbmon nede genimbeh: oam agende L. scillinga and eft aet bam agende sinne william Aetgebiege.*' Its ethos was unsatisfactory: 'If a man abducts a maiden, 50 shillings are owed her owner, and the man must purchase his consent.'

In the old, oral days, words fixed in certain positions with rhyme and rhythm united earth, sky and sea, in brilliant clusters of discovery, suggestion, mystery. Bards directed satire and obscenity against ghosts, ill fortune, cowards; and to the deformation of enemies. Lively mockery pervades Celtic literature from pre-Christian queens and heroes to the Ginger Man. Laughter possessed *mana*, spirit: it cleansed, it stimulated. In the Welsh epic *Y Goddodin*, young braves stride to battle behind a laughing leader.

Poets and praise-singers uttered wisdom, explosive phrases, incantatory genealogical lists; they kept communion with the dead, promulgated 'the soul', human essence, live core of personality. Genealogy linked chief and tribe with the powerful dead. Alfred the Great was named fiftieth in descent from Adam; Sir Thomas Urquhart, the translator of Rabelais, informed Oliver Cromwell that his ancestor Ourqhuartes was fifth from Noah. The Celtic bards replenished group morale and moral codes – a function not quite extinct, in the office of Poet Laureate. A BBC poll in 1995 to find the most popular English poem was easily won by Kipling's 'If', a compendium of social virtues. Such was the potency of words and music surviving in Celtic Ireland that Elizabeth I's government decreed death for Irish harpists.

The writer and don Malcolm Bradbury told *The Times* in 1995 that his literature students were losing literary standards:

> But the most noticeable thing is linguistic inadequacy: not knowing where words come from. When we lost Latin we lost a learning system in the use of language which gave a training in metre, the ode, the elegy, the epic, basic forms. We studied Wordsworth and Milton for their linguistic mastery. That is lost, and the result is a falsehood about the nature of creativity, which is that it all spouts from inside, that the right to self-expression matters more than how you say things: it is about empowerment, self assertion, identity formation, rather than a craft, a task, a training.

Words, like Troy, are constantly rebuilt. In early tennis the player might briefly rest, letting a servant throw in the ball, thus 'service'. 'Nice' is often cited to illustrate verbal movement: since the Tudors it has meant slender, unusual, fashionable, womanish, extravagant, bad-tempered, pleasant, disputable. The Elizabethan 'bully' was 'lover, sweetheart' – bully Bottom.

Some English words have died unlamented – '*blodwit*', '*outfangentheof*' – while others have drifted in from trade, Empire, scholarship, mass media. 'Buckminsterfullerene' is defined by Webster (1995) as 'a round, hollow, pure-carbon molecule with a structure similar to that of a geodesic dome'. Another American import is 'antsy', 'agitated', culled from 'ants in your pants'. At the end of the sixteenth century, Shakespeare had amassed more than thirty thousand words, though J.R.R. Tolkien allegedly maintained that he ruined traditional English. Now English regional sayings and epithets fade with the onslaught of standardised media and education: 'calm as a clock,' 'chanceways', 'timberhill' (staircase).

Literacy only partially replaces one strata of imagination with another. Rhymes can lift the horizon, unpin the sky, without disclosing all, as in 'Barley Bridge', with its hint of sacrificial horror:

> How many miles to Barley Bridge?
> Three-score and ten.

8

> Can I get there by candlelight?
> *Yes, if your legs be long.*
> A curtsey to *you* and a curtsey to you,
> If you please, will you let the King's horses through?
> *Through and through shall they go,*
> *For the King's sake,*
> *But the one that is hindmost*
> *Shall meet with a great mistake.*

No need to analyse. The unicorn, wrote George Barker, does not exist because it has something better to do.

Dr Arnold asserted that boys do not like poetry. He was wrong, though they do not always care to admit it. Many delighted in the old ballads, with their backward look at the deadly and strange.

> Oh, little did my mother think
> The day she cradled me,
> What lands I was to travel through
> What death I had to dee.

Ballad language is English at its starkest, showing life pared to the elemental; it is keen as the black wind or the pursuer's knife; nerves can still quiver as Pretty Polly wakes in cold moonlight and sees her lover digging her grave. Hers is a world of love threatened by blood-feud, ruthlessness, immoderate passions of the nut-brown maiden, handsome seducer, avenging husband, told with brutal economy. Voltaire wrote that the secret of being boring is to omit nothing. The wild battle of Flodden in 1513 was scraped down to an anonymous sentence:

> Beside Branxton is a brook; breathless they lie
> Gaping against the moon; their ghosts went away.

English developed from Teutonic language which eschewed shallow decoration, stripped experience naked, yielded forthright sensation, within a multitude of dialects imposed on a Celtic sub-strata, with Latin additions. Only among the Portuguese was there a common language when Alfred translated Boethius's *Consolation of Philosophy*, once called the last independent statement of Classicism. It suited a northern temperament, Christian but not mystical, neither wholly optimistic nor pessimistic, but resolute in an age of crisis and uncertainty. God seems not all-powerful, yet provides the hope necessary for survival. Alfred's vocabulary is significant in its terseness.

> Nothing is wretched save what people so think.

> Who can give laws to lovers? Love itself is a law self-sufficient.

> He who would have full power must first strive for power over his own mind, and not be unduly subject to his vices, and he must put away from him undue cares, and cease to bewail his misery.

The emphasis on 'undue' is already recognisably English, and Alfred fore-shadows one level of English prose, plain, strong, lucid. Langland had it four centuries later, and Malory, with his robust simplicity:

> And thus they fought till it was past noon, and never would stint, till at last they lacked wind both, and then they stood wagging and scattering, panting, blowing, bleeding, that all that beheld them for the most part wept for pity. So when they had rested a while they yeded to battle again, tracying, racying, foyning as two boars.

'For the most part' is a realistic touch.

Preaching to Edward VI, Hugh Latimer maintained vigorous outspoken-ness: 'Peers of the realm must needs be, but the poorest ploughman is in Christ equal with the greatest prince there is.' He used English to nail down truths, not to blur, soothe or extenuate the gross. Shakespeare's prose rings like a hammer:

> This peace is nothing but to rust iron, increase tailors, and breed ballad-mongers.

> There's no more mercy in him than milk in a male tiger.

Walter Raleigh used a laconic, hard-edged style, observing that Death is 'he who puts into man all the wisdom of the world, without speaking a word'.

Plain English can outrage tender stomachs, encourage improvers, like musical cheap-jacks recording *Götterdämmerung* for mouth-organ. The Restoration producer Sir William D'Avenant amended Shakespeare's 'The devil damn thee black, thou cream-fac'd loon: where gott'st thou that goose-look?' to 'Now, friend, what means thy change of countenance?' He also incorporated Beatrice and Benedick into *Measure for Measure*.

It would have been dangerous to amend Dr Johnson, who could express the complex and the ephemeral with equal pith:

Like sour small beer, she could never have been a good thing, and even that bad thing is spoiled.

Tomorrow is an old deceiver, and his cheat never grows stale.

This language of common sense, energetic but imaginative, was often deployed by Wellington, who wrote no masterpiece but could improvise effective comment: 'A man may be born in a stable, but that does not make him a horse.' Dickens, even in private letters, peeled off such vivid phrases as 'all the chairs upside down as if they had turned over like birds and died with their legs in the air'.

Political English was traditionally neither whining, bland nor evasive, but delivered through what Boswell called the juiciness of the English mind. A fifteenth-century tirade assailed 'that sewer of treachery, sink of greed, charioteer of treason, coffer of vice, lie-maker, vilest of informers, most supreme slanderer, traitor to fatherland, Michael de la Pole, Earl of Suffolk'. A Scots pamphleteer mentioned that Charles I's bishops were 'bunchy knobs of papist flesh'. But few modern British politicians have quickened the language. Lloyd George once complained that Ramsay MacDonald used words as if they were sounds, not weapons. 'Ah, my friends,' MacDonald once mused, 'how easy it would be to listen to the milk of human kindness.' Lloyd George himself, introducing conscription in 1916, announced that 'Compulsion is simply organised voluntary effort', straining English to the limit. The socialist John Burns remarked that the Welshman's conscience was pure and unspotted because he never used it. Neville Chamberlain cannot have been using his ears when he came out with: 'It is the opinion of my committee that a further investigation should be undertaken, taking into consideration all those matters of which, in the opinion of the new committee, consideration should be taken.' John Major confused exhortation and logic: 'When your back's to the wall, it's time to turn around and fight.'

Officialdom flourishes on debased language, like dandelions in a neglected town. In 1995 the novelist Margaret Drabble unearthed from the Department of National Heritage: 'The Hereford and Worcester County Council, which has a long and well-established tradition of providing arts and cultural service through its static service points, has been investigating the feasibility of outsourcing through facilities management, that element of service.'

One frequent comment by Victorian school inspectors was that, though fluency was increasing, understanding of words was decreasing. Sensitivity to language preceded compulsory schooling. The poor could use racy or simple individualist speech. George Lovelace, a Tolpuddle Martyr, after being sentenced to transportation in 1834, wrote a poem ending:

> God is our guide! No swords we draw,
> We kindle not war's battle-fires.
> By reason, union, justice, law,
> We claim the birth-right of our sires:
> We raise the watch-word, Liberty.
> We will, we will, we will be free.

Edgell Rickword wrote in *The Spectator* in 1923:

As anyone who has heard both will remember, conversation in the ranks of the wartime Army was on a much higher level than that in the officers' messes, not because there were many literate men in the ranks, but for the opposite reason. Speech, with the illiterate, is their highest form of expression, and they put their best into it, till it rings like good money flung down. Those who live more remotely, the cultured, are apt to regard it as a necessary, but sometimes wearisome, system of exchange, for which leaden counters will suffice.

Language has its enemy within – jargon – which can easily become a political weapon. The Nazis called their murder squads 'Task Forces', Stalin's KGB was 'Certain Competent Organs', Heydrich's secret police were the 'Press and Information Service'. Allied prisoners-of-war and Asian conscripts, enslaved for the atrocious Siam–Burma railway, were performing what the Japanese termed 'Logistic Imperative', and the current Burmese military dictatorship of torture, murder, beatings, censorship entitles itself 'Infrastructure of the Modern State'.

Jargon soon shades into 'political correctness', the tyranny of mediocrities over each other, which revives the concept of heresy. Designed to enforce compassion, it invites ridicule. A Sixties British publisher condemned an author as 'highly prejudiced and emotional' for having called the Moors Murderers 'iniquitous'. A girl of four was removed in 1985 from loving foster-parents to the care of her criminal father, on Council assurance that he and his mate had been 'remotivated'. Within weeks he had slaughtered her. In 1988 D.J. Enright recalled a social worker reprimanding the BBC: 'We do not call it baby-battering, we call it non-accidental injury.'

Modern English has lately been embellished with 'prospects minimised' (dismissed), 'body count' (corpses), 'vertically challenged' (short), 'household companions' (pets), 'behaviour modification' (drugs), 'domestic executive' (housewife) and 'economically inactive' (unemployed). When 'immigrant' was denounced in the House of Commons in 1996, the Home Office obsequiously substituted 'A person from abroad who comes under immigration controls'. It all recalls French revolutionaries lopping steeples, for equality.

Once the Oxford University Press claimed to be the custodian of the English Language. Its 1995 American edition of the New Testament omitted 'darkness' (as a synonym for evil or ignorance) to avoid offending blacks; 'The right hand of God', to appease left-handers; and was reluctant to mention 'The Lord', an editor explaining that '"Lord God" doesn't cut it these days because we don't have Lords.'

Wittgenstein might say that philosophy is the battle against the bewitchment of our senses by language. But people of all persuasions throughout British history have been, if not bewitched, at least emotionally and intellectually sustained by language, less as rhetoric than in the measureless labyrinths of song, prayer, literature, conversation. Language, however, like democracy, does not survive unaided, and to be fair, gadgetry can assist as well as destroy. Pupils can learn too much from print, too little from observation – like the poet writing a vague ode to a lime tree, unaware that one existed in his own garden – but visual electronics have exposed, more vividly even than Blake, the webs and symbols of nature, the intricacies of rock and fossil, cell, germ, atom, the metamorphoses of plant and animal tissue. The text of *Richard III* can now be accompanied on screen by a map of fifteenth-century England, a diagram of the political situation, then examples of heraldry, costume, armour, architecture; the changed meanings of words; historians' attitudes to Richard, psychologists' attitudes to character; cross-references to painting, opera, abstract design; with dramatic analogies and amusing anecdotes. The danger lies in mechanical responses, passive reception of others' researches, the smothering of the text itself. The imagination can thrive by not knowing too much.

A disagreeable future for English is suggested by Professor Harold Bloom of Yale, who reported in 1995 that of twenty members of the Princeton

English Faculty, sixteen were specialising in Gender Studies, while the Director of American Studies at New York University had scrapped the study of classic novels in favour of discussion of comics. This might have pleased Heinrich Himmler, whose plans for Poland submitted to his employer in May 1940 included the dictum, 'Reading is unnecessary'. In England, a Report from the National Commission on Education in 1996 found 19 per cent of school leavers illiterate, some 15 per cent backward in literacy, and attested that reading standards had scarcely improved since 1945.

H.G. Wells's first story, *The Time Machine* (1895), had a chilling message, as visionary as any of Blake, Shelley, Tennyson, Yeats, in its forecast of England in AD 802701:

> I went out of that gallery and into another and still larger one, which at first glance reminded me of a military chapel hung with tattered flags; the brown and charred rags that hung from the sides of it I presently recognised as the decaying vestiges of books. They had long since dropped to pieces, and every semblance of print had left them. But here and there were warped boards and cracked metallic clasps that told the tale well enough.

2

Albion

In the early dayes of the King Arthur
Of which the Britons speken grete honour,
Al was this Lande fulfild of fayerye;
   The Elf Queene, with her jolly companye
   Daunced ful ofte in many a grene mede.

Anon.

   The son of the King of May
      Found a girl in a green dell,
   Of fruit, rich and plentiful,
      She allowed him his fill.

Anon.

Imagination, whether spiritual or national, is the most powerful thing in human affairs. Intangible itself, it moves bodies. Invisible itself, it changes visible civilization.

A.E. [George William Russell, Irish poet and Nationalist, 1867–1935]

A day's drive can reveal Stone Age middens, an artificial Bronze Age hill, an Iron Age fort, Pictish daggers and runes, a Roman brick, a Viking figurine, a stone cut with Ogham lettering, a Saxon church, suggestive place names – Glastonbury, 'Hill of Glass'.

A pit at Swanwick in Derbyshire of about 1400 BC, possibly a sacrificial cave, believed to lead to the Underworld, did seem to show tiny blood stains on a ruined column. Robert Graves, bugbear of academics, wrote of turf mazes, 'Troy Towns', trodden by centuries of English children: 'The discovery near Bosinney in Cornwall of a Cretan maze cut on a rock-face is of great importance. The ravine is one of the last haunts of the Cornish chough; and this bird houses the soul of King Arthur who harrowed Hell and with whom Bosinney is closely associated in legend.' The maze carried notions of the soul journeying through the perplexities of the after-life, of a

Mystery initiate's search for fulfilment, and of the traditional Quest, perennial symbol in Romance.

British pre-history is suggestively silent, peopled by nameless tribes founding a society reaching towards infinity. The cliff ramparts of Dun Aengus, a gigantic once-ovalled fortress overlooking the Atlantic, were considered by Sacheverell Sitwell the most magnificent monument to survive in Europe. 'Who were the enemy they expected to attack them, coming from open sea with the nearest landfall three thousand miles away, to invade the Arran Island off the west coast of Ireland? It is all a mystery.'

Most great names of long ago have gathered hearsay, hagiography, vilification, but little hard fact. Pre-Roman England, despite the evidence of language, coins, archaeology, folklore and monkish chronicles, is almost all imaginary, an era when the sacrificial blood of gods, chiefs, infants was needed to revive the dying sun and weapons, cauldrons, rings possessed *Mana*, and magic. The nut, like the salmon, signified wisdom. The land was no mere strip of dirt but lambent with hollow hills loud with music, enchanted stone circles and forests, sacred wells, talking birds, dragons, underworld presences. It was often remembered as *Albion*.

The Marxist historian Eric Hobsbawm has defined a nation as a people who share a common misconception as to their origins, and a common antipathy towards their neighbours. This seems true of England. Twelfth-century literary flattery of Henry II and the Plantagenet dynasty generated much fantasy, inventing a Trojan pedigree for Britain as Virgil did for Rome. Britain was connected with a venturesome though imaginary Trojan named Brut, and indeed Nicholas Brembre, a supporter of Richard II, was executed in 1388 for plotting to change London's name to Troynovant. Pope began an epic, *Brutus*, then abandoned it. Brut's Britain was 'Samothea', once ruled by Albion, a sea-god's son, his people descendants of the fourth son of the Biblical Japhet. Albion was thought to be derived from *Albus*, 'White' – possibly from Dover cliffs. James I, who coined *Great Britain*, a notion unpopular in England, boasted descent from Brut.

Only *Albion* survived this rigmarole, nostalgic symbol of a poetic or ideal England, small, valiant, pastoral, unpolluted. Drake's short-lived New Albion of 1579 was England's first American colony. William Warner published his *Albion's England* in 1580, wistful but unreadable.

Blake's Albion was a giant, representing a lost, etherealised realm, the huge celestial pulse of humanity, creativity, wisdom, a forgotten purity. *Visions of the Daughters of Albion* (1793) and *Jerusalem: The Emanation of the*

Giant Albion (1804–20) recall a vanished spiritual intensity and freshness of vision. Blake yearned for the reawakening of a society gone cold, over-rational, unclean. The London of waste, poverty, foundling babies, diseased prostitutes had long been drained of genuine feelings: it was a spiritual desert, crowded but empty, where lust was without love, art without impulse, and religion travestied by mechanical repetition. 'Jerusalem' must restore emotional, sensual and sexual powers atrophied by shame, or fear, or social oppressions.

William Morris possessed such yearnings. Surrealism, rejecting Greek scepticism and irony, Roman utilitarianism, linear time, upholding the instinctive and astrological, has links with Albion. In his anthology *Children of Albion: Poetry of the Underground in Britain* (1969), Michael Horowitz continues the theme of a rival and purer England.

Albion was rooted in a Celtic England which shared archetypes with all the world. The Celtic Rashin Coatie is one of more than three hundred versions of Cinderella. An Odysseus figure has been cherished by Hindus, Chinese, Sioux, and appears as the Celtic wanderers Bran, Brendan, Black Colin Campbell. The Celtic Vulcan was Gonfan, Tan, Tin: tinder, Tintagel. Cerridwen, Anna, Danaan was the universal Great Mother.

Robert Graves, of Irish, Scottish, Danish and German ancestry, dedicated his poetry to 'the Muse', the White Goddess, replica of Cerridwen and her Cauldron of Inspiration, which bred the baby Taliesin, supreme Welsh poet, fashioned from fruit, flowers, earth, and the ninth wave.

> Chief bard I am to Elphin
> And my homeland is that of the summer stars.

Graves maintained that when one is enthralled by the Goddess's strength in a true poem the hair stands on end, the eyes water, the skin crawls and a shiver runs down the spine.

Arthur, Gawain, Owain Glin Dwr are Albion's Sleeping Heroes, though the last was also historical. They await their second coming, akin to Charlemagne, Wild Edric, Harold, Drake, Monmouth; and to Kitchener, believed not to have drowned in 1915 but to live on, in the Orkneys, until he is needed in a renewed national crisis.

Other Albion heroes and figures included a Prometheus, Daedalus, Apollo, Demeter, Judas, Helen, Beauty and the Beast. Llyr, a wind god with three daughters, evolved into Lear, wracked in tempest, image of authority helpless within its own illusions, the blind leading the morally blind, and love causing worse than the hatreds it should dissolve. The Celtic Pluto, Gwyn ap Nudd, Lord of Cauldrons, ruled Annyn, the Underworld. The Celtic Theseus was Tristan: he volunteered to help Mark of Cornwall against the Irish king who every five years demanded three hundred Cornish boys, three hundred girls, for his service. Arthur and Peredur raid the Underworld; Bran is vulnerable in the heel, Llew Llawr in the hair; Morgan is fated to be heroic but die young. The Celtic Hecate, the Mala Lucina, waits balefully at crossways. Warned by an oracle against dethronement by a new-born child, Arthur slays all babies within reach on a May morning. He also kills his own son, near Hereford. An Irish belief lingers that a Whitsun-born child, destined to kill or be killed, can avert fate by strangling a bird. Arthur himself was sometimes seen as a bird-king, usually a wren.

Albion did have distinctive features, such as the stories of Jack and the Beanstalk, but shared with Western Romance such themes as tragic love, lost causes, quests, redemption, La Belle Dame sans Merci, love potions, and magic cauldrons of youth, illumination, poetry, from which no coward could drink – one of which Arthur stole from the Underworld. Such cauldrons or grails were known in Asia, in Greece, and by American Indians.

Arthur's repute extended throughout Europe. He is carved over the north door of Modena cathedral, glistens in an Otranto mosaic, is believed to await a summons to return, not only in Cadbury Hill but under Mount Etna. Before being idealised, even prettified, by Christian writers, Arthur had few moral traits. In one tale he, Lancelot and Gawain chance upon a castle, where their servant senses horror. Investigating, Lancelot finds three hundred corpses, oozing blood, after which the three pass the night in mirth.

Incestuous, adulterous, Arthur was a hero of a lost cause. In a stubborn refinement of wishful thinking, the defeated strive to represent catastrophe as psychological victory: Arthur, Baldur, Christ, Hamlet, King Lazar of Serbia have the last word as tragic heroes, images more poetic than those of coarser fellows who win battles, govern, march in triumph. He who loseth his life shall save it: the essence not only of religion, but of Tragedy.

Albion's pantheon is almost extinct. Few remember Lug and Mapona, Mannonon, Nodens of the Bright Hand. Old King Cole may be a smudged memory of a Welsh chieftain, Old Coel the Splendid. Tin, Tan may be embedded in St Anne's Hill. William Owen's *Book of Fairs* notes twenty-five on sites connected with 'St Anne', but held on the dates of ancient fire-festivals. Only Arthur and his retinue have continuing resonance. Milton contemplated an Arthurian epic. Tennyson, Masefield, Graves, John Cowper Powys, T.H. White attest to his manifold significance; also John Steinbeck, Henry Treece, Robert Nye, John Heath-Stubbs. Illustrations by Doré and Burne-Jones remain poignant. David Jones's *In Parenthesis* (1937) envisaged Romans and Arthurians merging with Welsh and Cockney tommies in the blood and horror, comradeship and expletives of the Great War.

Outside Albion, Arthur's reality is controversial. Field-Marshal Wavell considered Arthur was probably a grim figure in an unromantic struggle in a dark period. Geoffrey Ashe identified him with Riothamus, 'King of the Britons', commanding in Gaul against fifth-century Teutons and after battle 'summoned from human activity'. His name is associated with cults of wind and bear and, as a god, leader or symbol, with post-Roman Celtic resistance to Teutonic invaders.

Authority, Tennyson wrote, forgets a dying king. This is seldom altogether true. Stories continued, of an Arthur vanquishing a Roman Emperor and the Burgundians, freeing Britain, pursuing a supernatural boar through three worlds, enjoying three wives with identical names. At English royal funerals a statue might be carried painted with 'Arthur's arms', three golden crowns on an azure ground. Henry II, at his accession, reputedly received goodwill from Arthur in Avalon.

Nothing, Walter Scott mused, perhaps rather guiltily, is so easy to make as a tradition. Another new dynasty exploited the emotional appeal of Albion when the Welsh claimant Henry Tudor marched from Milford Haven to Bosworth under the banner of the Red Dragon of Cadwallader, and shrewdly named his elder son Arthur. The cult of Elizabeth Tudor as Gloriana, Virgin Queen may have stirred folk memories of antique goddesses of beauty, victory, fate.

Another early name for Britain was Clas Merddyn, 'Merlin's Enclosure'; Carmarthen is 'the Fields of Merlin'. Merlin is one more indestructible Albion character, a shaman at home in dream and reality, timeless seer, magician, alchemist, prophet, yet realistically vulnerable, betrayed by lust. He glimmers through poems by Spenser, Dryden, Wordsworth, Tennyson, Swinburne, Charles Williams. The thirteenth-century Robert de Boron regarded him as the Devil's son, conceived to overthrow Christ. Nikolai Tolstoy skilfully argues for Merlin as a sixth-century druid, a counter-Christ, ranging through Celyddon Forest and Hartfell Spa. In Catholic Europe Merlin remained sufficiently dangerous for his alleged prophecies to be proscribed by the Council of Trent (1546–63).

Celtic literature, the vital flavouring of Albion, rivals the Greek in antiquity and endurance. Celtic poets readily transmuted loneliness, fear, perplexity into the hush of reeds, a gleam of water, the leap of the wind, a bird's solitary flight, a song half-heard from the Other World. The motif of a land blighted by an ageing or impotent king and awaiting a saviour provided material for generations of music and literature. Albion, in whatever degree of reality, feasted on violence: legend and verse show southern Irish chieftains invading Ulster for honour and bloodshed long before Anglo-Norman confiscations and plantations. Tribes needed mockery of themselves and of enemies, what later societies called humour, to avert the jealousy of gods, of fate, of chiefs. A joke could placate a despot, humiliate a foe, chasten pride, unite a gathering. The bard noted incongruities, fleeting moods and colours, the ambiguity of sky, names, animals, the lure of the grotesque. Tacitus had described the Celts as devoted mainly to war and witty talk.

Transformations dominated early imagination. People became animals, plants, gods; slave girls wed princes, rags changed to riches. Mystery religions taught transformation rituals as stages towards illumination, salvation, Paradise. The phenomenon was given pre-eminent literary status in Ovid's *Metamorphoses*, where girls change to trees or reeds, a boy to a hyacinth. In Albion lore, a traveller may find a cave and reach the Underworld; have his life changed utterly by answering a riddle at a crossroads, encountering a stranger at a ford, or entering an uncanny tower. A queen is bewitched into a butterfly, a girl into a swallow. Celtic art seethes with limbs foaming into branches, serpents, waves; twigs becoming foliage, sun-rays, twirling patterns. Ripples, writhings, spirals, tendrils, circles, mazes are endlessly interlinked, cut onto torques, weapons, cauldrons. This fluidity of line matches mental gyrations which, unstoppable, translate rites and events to myth, thence to legend, then history, or literature: Cunebelinus becomes 'Cymbeline'. Boudicca's torque, twisted and golden, mirrors the flowing intricacies of Celtic verse. Celtic and Northumbrian line, curls of fancy and life-cycles, make what Louis MacNeice called the living curve which is breathlessly the same, reflected in the multiple transformations of young Arthur in T.H. White's *The Once and Future King*, in the cyclic images of Yeats, the visual puns of Dylan Thomas. It flows through the convoluted fantasies of The Book of Kells, the webs of Gothic allusion, the elaborate traceries of English Decorated: the surge of the Baroque, with its flames, wings, sensations of flight, has parallels to it; it is there in Hogarth's serpentine 'Line of Beauty'; it creates sinuous figures in art nouveau and in the early twentieth-century Scottish poets styled the 'Immortals'. It mimes botanical growths, interweaves invention and repetition, the headlong and stylised, the erotic and witty, its convulsions at odds with Classical formality, authority, clarity. Dark Age ornamentation was continuous celebration of existence, twisting and writhing, in all variousness, like larksong or the flight of swifts, from the days when bards, remembered as bird-men, wore feathered cloaks and chanted 'winged words', their song leaping skywards, their listeners, rapt, enchanted, also feeling themselves birds, able to peer into heaven.

A certain style, another 'Celtic line', curls throughout English history, easily exaggerated or parodied as in Shakespeare's Glendower and Fluellen. Spoilt by too exact definition, it has elements of wit, panache, defiance, swagger, oddity, as possessed by Wilde, Shaw, Yeats; and by Conan Doyle, romantic supporter of lost causes and staunch believer in the Other World.

In Gaul, British Celts were reputed dandies in dress and adornment, even in their behaviour in battle. Dandyism implies self-dedication, discrimination, a search for perfection, a visual and verbal liveliness that illustrates Albion and its legacy. Joyce's Dubliner – 'By the holy farmer, he never cried crack till he brought him as drunk as a boiled owl' – has not lost the vigour of an anonymous Dark Age poet seeing a hero 'snow-bright on one cheek, the other speckled red as a foxglove: one eye hyacinth-blue, the other black as a beetle's back.' Daffyd ap Gwilym shows a Cork scholar finding refuge in a monastery where the guests' bath is still soiled and 'as multitudinous as sea-shore sands or as fire-sparks or as dew-drops at May-morn or as the sky-stars were the lice and fleas gnawing at his feet'.

Everywhere, though seldom seen, hovered gods, sulky, mirthful, friendly or mischievous. The Other World, sexually casual, hazed with music, dancing, wine, was no remote elysium, the reward of piety and good works. Like love, it could not be won by storm. Chance was all. A crack appeared in the air, you passed through a shaft of light and found yourself transported into a dream realm. Your stay was seemingly brief, but on awaking you realised that centuries had passed. Pale gleams over a black tarn could denote it, mist at a ford open to reveal a bridge into it. A tremble of leaves at a windless noon, a sudden glow on a boundary stone, thin music carried down the wind, high keenings for battles long lost yet also triumphant could promise the Other World to a bandit, an abductor, while others, worthier, might vainly seek it for years. For all, it was real: one unreliable text suggests that repayment of earthly debts could be postponed until a meeting in the Other World.

Other World presences – Morgans, fairies, banshees, small folk – were the oldest Albion, spirits of pre-Celtic deities and peoples, far from what Kipling's Puck scorned as 'the painty-winged, wand-waving, sugar-and-shake-your-hand set of imposters'. Cautiously called Good Folk, Friendly Ones, Mothers, they might kidnap children, substitute changelings, seduce or injure humans, and were best avoided, though gifts could appease them. 'Cold iron' thrust into their dwellings would disperse them. Brooding, elusive behind the light, they would lament or shriek for their lost lands, and could foretell mortals' deaths. *A Midsummer Night's Dream* was in no Greek wood but in Albion, with metallic, sometimes uncanny glitter. Puck is residue of the British *pouca*, Cornish *bircca*, Irish *pooka*, no playful urchin but fateful, vengeful god shrivelled to a goblin: nimble, of uncertain mood, an erotic refugee from a vaster, disintegrated era. Such creatures are reminders of danger within beauty, a child's loneliness on a happy afternoon, the sudden, soundless rise of a flat head from motionless flowers. Bishop Richard Corbet (1582–1635), in his *Proper New Ballad* beginning 'Farewell, rewards and Fairies', ascribes their final departure to his own days, of the growth of Puritanism, towns, early industry, enclosure.

Albion, though flimsy and esoteric, had some historical substance. Celtic traditions suggest a certain sexual balance, wives allowed rights in divorce, and property. Albion's heroines – Grainne, Essylt (Isolde), Deirdre, Gwenhever, and unscrupulous, resolute Queen Mebd – were seldom swooning, slavish, or inert. Boys might receive early weapon-training from women, a suggestive parallel to Wotan's nine daughters, the battle-haunting Valkyrie. Tacitus adds that in distributing army commands, the Britons made no distinction between the sexes.

Roman proscription of Druidism did not suppress beliefs natural to Albion linking humans, the elements, nature, names, with mysterious codes to do with magic numbers, stars, bodily parts, thence to sickness and healing, luck and misfortune, sought or avoided with herbalism, charms, runes. A flower might have a ghost, the spectre of a rose, as might a sacked library or an abandoned road. There was still random awe at such phenomena as the Giants' Dance towering on Salisbury Plain, the stones, it was whispered, by some weird spell impossible to count. Albion could be tracked in covert shrines, haunted caves, wells secretly flower-strewn on dark nights when the mind expanded into tales of the Bear King, star voyages, uncanny hares and horses. It was in metals stored with magic, severed heads piled on ledges or fixed to spears, and a hand thrusting from water to receive a sword. A face might glimmer from a cloud, a birch or ash twig repel evil.

Christianity, particularly in its Celtic form, though finally destructive to Albion, absorbed much of it. Bran, who had voyaged to the far western Land of Promise, the Isle of Birds, Isle of Joy, Isle of Women, was easily adopted as St Brendan. In Albion's dream-mind, burial mounds were halls of the dead who, emerging at Hallowe'en, at All Souls', needed placating with fire, feasts, song. At such times, kinks even in the Christian year, the tremulous boundaries between the living and the Other World vanished, and people feared to glance behind them. Chance became grace.

A Celtic renown for occultism persisted into the Middle Ages. Welsh rulers like Llewellyn the Great were reputed wizards. Shakespeare's Owen Glendower, the historical Owain Glyn Dwr, respresented Merlin's Albion, claimed descent from Arthur and 'the rightful lords of Britain' and, like Arthur, mysteriously vanished after defeat.

Rome's withdrawal left dark legends of giants defeated by island gods after disloyalty to their own, and of twenty-eight marvellous cities abandoned to ivy, nettle, angry ghosts. Albion somewhat revived, but had to share much with invading Teutons and Scandinavians, ultimately overlords of 'AngleLand' east of the Dyke built by Offa to repel the Welsh and set a limit to their cattle-rustling, ambushes and castrations.

The newcomers also reverenced heroes and drinkers, and weapons; responded to tragedy as well as to trickery and sex and cunning; honoured names, loyalty, courage; abhorred treachery and cowardice. Almost all islanders of whatever vintage could accept a Viking lay:

> Cattle die, kinsfolk die,
> I too die the same:
> I know one thing alone that never dies –
> The renown of a noble name.

Here was the core of chivalry, refined by Islamic and, fitfully, by Christian culture, allegedly modifying gross masculinity.

Brutal in warfare, these invaders from mainland Europe, while respecting achievement and language, were suspicious of too high-flying boasts and argument. Beliefs about Odin, stemming from rituals doubtless hideous, became refined into a crude nobility which made the transition to Christianity less painful. In *The Lay of the High One* Odin, the Teutonic Wotan, Allfather, sacrifices an eye for wisdom; and, more mysterious and awesome:

> I know that I hung
> on the windy tree,
>   Swung there nights nine
> blade-gashed for Odin
>   Myself an offering to myself
> knotted to that tree:
> No man knows
>   Whither its root runs.
>
> None gave me bread,
> No man gave me drink,
>   I peered into the depths
> to draw up runes,
> with a roaring screech
> I fell to faintness.
>
> Well-being I won,
> also wisdom,
>   I grew and took delight in my growth.
> From a word to a word
> I was led to a word,
>   From a deed to another deed.

The Teutons may not have imported the Scandinavian belief in the destruction by fire of Earth and the Other World but, save for warriors, the latter was for them as dim as the Greek Hades, the Hebrew Sheol, unlike the sparking air and music of the Celtic Underworld.

Wotan the Bleeding God, Thor, Frey, Tiw, Frigg displaced Celtic divinities, giving their names to days of the week. From place-names, the most popular seems to have been Thor, red-bearded thunderer and hammer-wielder. Earth was Nerthus, a mother-goddess. Another predecessor of the English Christ was the young, gentle Balder, betrayed by Loki, sly mischief god, the northern Hermes, who tricked blind Höder into killing him, though in a second coming he would survive the destruction of the gods.

Albion, mythical England, nursery England, with its green chapel, round table, great hunts and quests, survives only faintly; as a distorted memory of

Celtic and Pictish Britain, remains in and out of shadow. No prayers are offered to Nodens, the realms of Bro Erech and Logris have vanished. Geoffrey of Monmouth's seventy-six British kings are spurious, as are both Beli, the Virgin's brother-in-law, and Bladud, early air-man who founded Bath. Only a verse survives of King Cadfran, 'of all kings that ever were, the most civilised and the most celebrated'. Only literature gives glimpses of Albion: the dimly seen Taliesin and Aneurin and many anonymous bards set vivid, supple patterns reaching towards great medieval Welsh verse.

> Man's spirit, youth's years,
> Courage for combat:
> Swift stallion strong-maned
> Beneath fine young thighs,
> Buckler-broad, light
> On slender horse-cropper,
> Blades blue-glittering,
> Garment gold-ringed:
> Let bitterness never divide us.
>
> (Aneurin)

At Easter, none give flowers, fruit, eggs, candles to the fertility goddess Eostre, Lady of Spring. It is a country of miracle and make-believe, of Shakespeare's 'Nothing is but what is not'. Bede mentions a monk, Dryhthelm of Melrose, returning from the dead; others talk of St Alban, after execution, carrying away his own head, St Kenthelm chatting to a wise salmon. Historical figures were swiftly enveloped in Albion. Wild Edric, pre-Conquest landowner, leader against the Normans, deserted to Duke William and was never forgiven; he remained Britain's equivalent of the 'Wandering Jew', still alive after centuries, unable to rest because of treachery – the unforgivable crime in a lawless society dependent on the sanctity of oaths, for which Dante placed Judas, Brutus, Cassius deep in Hell. Medievals still spoke of Edric, by then a demon of mines, leader of a subterranean Wild Hunt, lover of a fertility goddess, Godda, 'Godiva', with whom he might hunt the Shropshire hills. That he was nephew to Eric Streona, betrayer of the Saxon hero Edmund Ironside to the Vikings, redoubled his villainy, though in a further tale he, like Drake, like Kitchener, awaits his chance to defend England in a crisis. In the Bomere Pool in Shropshire a fish-god was believed to lurk, guarding Edric's sword.

Hereward, 'Dread Me', never to his face called 'The Wake' (cowardly), another resistance leader, was entangled in fantasy, overcoming a super-natural bear, rescuing a Cornish princess from a Pictish giant, Ulcus Ferreus, routing Cornish, Irish and Danish war-bands.

Shreds of Albion linger in remote countrysides. Some Welsh and Derbyshire wells are still decorated with flowers, on days once sacred. Nettles are occasionally called Devil's Aprons, Yorkshire yellowhammers may still be deemed unlucky – yellow denoting Satan, and Judas Iscariot. Edith Sitwell wrote of the Judas-coloured sun. The deformed, twins and red-heads were long thought to be particularly sinister, or unusually blessed: Weland the Albion smith was lame, like Vulcan: centuries later, Byron's limp suggested a glamour seductive, even diabolic.

3
Angle-land

Weland knew well enough what exile meant;
That hero suffered greatly.
Sorrow and longing were his companions,
Also winterset exile, when Nithhad
Enchained him, hamstrung a greater man;
Misfortune encompassed him.
   That passed away, so may this.

Deor [Anon.]

Racially mongrel, England was always part of Europe, open to intruders. Her widespread trade links are ancient: a bronze axe some 3,300 years old, excavated at Peterborough in 1994, resembles a design used in coeval Lower Saxony. Englishness, if it exists, compounds tradition and atmosphere, but scarcely race. Rider Haggard, High Victorian Englishman, had French, Danish, Indian, Jewish and Russian ancestors.

For some four centuries England was part of the Roman Empire. 'Saxon' England was within Canute's Scandinavian coalition; her Plantaganet kings ruled most of France, and English claims to the French crown were formally maintained until 1802. British kings ruled Hanover from 1714 until 1837. Britain helped finance and lead five European coalitions against a dominating power: Spain, France, Germany. She powerfully assisted the independence of the Netherlands, Greece, Belgium, Italy. In 1940 Winston Churchill vainly proposed a pooling of sovereignty with France.

English monarchs were Teuton, Scandinavian, Norman, Welsh, Scottish, Dutch, German. Medieval Continental priests held English bishoprics, offices of state, benefices. Hansa money backed Edward IV against 'the Kingmaker'. French troops fought for Henry Tudor at Bosworth, German mercenaries against the Scots, and East Anglian rebels.

From at least 1000 BC Celts were moving westwards, probably from around the Danube basin. They were never a single people, had distinct tribal differences; but most, quick in tongue and temper, witty and insolent in repartee, were gifted in arts, crafts, the 'superior lying' of poetry and, when it suited them, diplomacy. Though defeated by Rome, by England, they retained a pronounced identity, whatever their sometimes murderous clan differences. If they did domesticate the sheep, they affected English history more emphatically than had Rome. Their decorative art must have dazzled Europe – their jewellers had no superiors – and they could borrow as adeptly as they could invent. The Belgic coinage, the first in England, was adopted from Macedon. They brought Asiatic trousers, pioneered small wallets, soap, chain armour; and technical innovations in ploughing, harvesting, grinding, sawing and horse-shoes. Against the conquered, and against each other, they erected proud fortresses which, towering on stark crags, still haunt the imagination.

To romanticise them would be as misleading as to condescend to them as 'Ancient Britons'. Their god Teutates demanded blood from throats cut over a cauldron, the horned Cernunnos rejoiced in offerings of severed heads. Though liberal with women's rights they sometimes showed more reverence to pigs, so that tales of their princesses loving swineherds may call for re-interpretation.

In Britain, the Romans found Celtic peoples but not a Celtic State. Celts disliked towns, preferring a vigorous, quarrelsome regionalism. Some tribes welcomed Rome, others resisted. Like the British imperialists after them, the Romans manipulated client kings, collaborators, direct and indirect conquest, dangled offers of rewards, protection, citizenship.

The Celts made a famous revolt, early but serious, justified by exceptional Roman brutality, that of Boudicca, Albion heroine, in AD 69. In a ferocious onslaught her army sacked London, Colchester, St Albans, supplying a potent island legend. The second-century Roman Dio Cassius depicted her before her last battle haranguing her followers: 'On finishing, she consulted the will of the gods by letting a hare escape from the folds of her robe: it fled in what was reckoned a propitious direction, and the mob uttered a tremendous shout.' British witches were long credited with the ability to transform into hares: the unpopular Anne Boleyn was known to do so, as was, reportedly, a Lincolnshire villager in 1969.

As in British India in the nineteenth century, private wars, banditry, human sacrifice were eliminated and, from motives inextricably mixed, the overlords modernised communications, trade, mines, agriculture, and built palaces, forums, barracks, basilicas, hospitals, temples, schools, libraries, theatres. Little save legends, roads and town sites survived the Roman collapse, certainly not comfort. Winston Churchill wrote: 'From the year 400 to the year 1900, no one had central heating and very few had hot baths.'

At its best, whatever the bizarre behaviour of individuals, Rome's attitude to power was responsible, the greatest emperors – Trajan, Hadrian, Marcus Aurelius – more productive than Homer's capricious, amoral, childish gods. The Celts' saints revitalised culture, their monasteries were minor universities, but their kings tended to babble absurdities, fight unceasingly, build little. Roman buildings, the Roman Empire were intended to endure eternally, uninspired by fleeting glimpses of the Other World, for them a shadowy, dispirited abode.

The first Bishop of London was enthroned in 314, but Jesus was not *the* god, rather *a* god. Rural Celts remained loyal to Lug, Beli, Mapona, their magic more effective in woods, on hill-tops, by rivers than in crowded towns, where oriental mystery cults made headway. A Mithraic text translates as: 'And you saved us, having shed the blood that grants life eternal.'

Rome eventually failed to solve problems inherent in empires: how to treat subject peoples who, whatever they are given, must demand more; the burdens of unemployment, inflation, mutinous armies, trade imbalances, deforestation, disease, falling birth-rates among the governing class; now taxing too much and providing too little. Over-taxation crippled the morale of all classes, and unsettled the imagination. Jack Lindsay recognised that the *Dies Irae* contains metaphors from the vocabulary of tax-officials. Treasury officials changed participation in local government from a voluntary honour to a compulsory and expensive menace. Tax evasion became another art. Professor John Morris summarised: 'Rome fell because its great men would not pay for its defence. So did Britain.' Taxes went not on defence but in subsidies, public spectacles, and bribes to imperial pretenders and 'barbarian' enemies.

Throughout the Empire, debt-ridden, exploited citizens felt that a barbarian invasion would be, as in Cavafy's poem, 'a kind of solution'. In Britain, crisis erupted in 367 with the so-called 'Barbarian Conspiracy': a dimly-seen invasion of all regions south of the Wall by Irish, Picts, Scandinavians, Teutons, overwhelming the Roman order; government was restored, only after almost two years of chaos, by two Imperial generals, both Spaniards: Theodosius the Elder, and Magnus Clemens Maximus. Abroad a Roman Emperor was crushingly defeated in 378 by Gothic horsemen using stirrups for the first time in the West, making of man and horse a primitive tank. Thereafter, cavalry was dominant for a thousand years, acquiring the Christian and Islamic mystique of chivalry, allowing the male to ride rampant, dehumanising women into cult objects, purloining Albion's Round Table romances.

Maximus proclaimed himself Emperor in Britain in 383 and, with an army of Celts and Teutons, killed the Western Emperor Gratian. For five years he ruled Britain, Gaul, Spain, then triumphantly entered moribund Rome, only to be broken by the Eastern Emperor, Theodosius the Great, son of his old colleague.

Maximus's influence worked backwards, from history to Albion. He had demonstrated that Britain could be more than an off-shore appendage to Europe, creating a national icon of British troops swaggering into Rome. So mythology draped him as god–saviour, Universal Emperor, Macsen Wledig, married to the Celtic goddess Elen of Crossroads, subsequently conjured into 'St Helena', a reputed Balkan brothel-keeper, metamorphosed into the discoverer of the True Cross and, historically, the mother of Constantine the Great. This is a story at odds with chronology, facts, common sense, yet indispensible to British recovery.

More prosaically, Maximus had weakened native defences by removing troops to Europe. Rome, however, was in terminal decline. G.M. Trevelyan's sentence is ominous in its restraint: 'Before Roman Silchester was abandoned under Saxon pressure, an Ogam stone with a barbarous Celtic inscription had been set up in its streets.' 'Ghost town' first appears in English when King Alfred's chronicler applied it to post-Roman Chester.

The fifth-century Celts and Romanised gentry had a chance, risky but just possible, as a successor-State. The Emperor Honorius, for whom the 45th province was now an expensive liability, gave them formal permission to arm themselves. Soon Britain was denuded of all Roman forces. Alfred's *Anglo-Saxon Chronicle* added a pathetic postscript: 'In this year, 418, the Romans collected all the treasures that were in Britain, and hid some in the earth, so that no one afterwards could find them, and some they took with them into Gaul.' There seems, however, to have been no pronounced exodus: Romanised villas and cosmopolitan towns lingered on, making what they could of changing circumstances, striving for a defence policy of defiance or appeasement.

Some historians have called the levies against Constantine III – a tyrannical local pretender in Gaul – Britain's first national army. Constantine was betrayed by his minister Gerontius, named by Geoffrey Ashe as one of the few Britons to hold a key international position. Yet the great opportunity was unenviable.

Against invading Teutons – Angles, Jutes, Frisians, Saxons – Celtic Britain, without a fleet, had to improvise defence, strategy, supplies, though all was not hopeless. Considerable prosperity can be inferred until an outbreak of East Mediterranean plague in 443, and more systematic Teutonic settlement, rather than mere raids. The Celts made fierce counter-attacks, though after some twenty years many were in retreat from 'Great Britain', to Armorica, 'Little Britain', Brittany. From around 460 to perhaps 495, resistance was renewed and successful, culminating in a savage Celtic victory at an unidentified 'Badon', ascribed to 'Arthur' as earlier feats had been to 'Ambrosius Aurelianus', a pro-Roman leader. Arthur is associated with Celtic prowess in horsemanship.

Geoffrey Ashe insists that Celtic Britain was the most remarkable of the post-Roman successor-states. 'Few revolutions have been so persistantly under-rated. The British action was unique. No other Roman land did anything similar with lasting results. Only Britain managed to stand alone; only Britain produced a daughter civilization with the genius to create and the strength of will to repel invaders.' Final Teutonic conquest was delayed for over a century, the last significant Celtic counter-attack usually dated to 634. Cornwall surrendered last, Wales was left a secure Celtic fastness.

The cost in massacre, and eviction, remains controversial. No Teutonic tribe had over-all mastery, and enslavement would have been more profitable than genocide. Archaeology suggests considerable Celtic–Teuton interbreeding. By the late seventh century, Teutonic kingdoms in 'Angleland' were still competing for dominance, and the Celtic counter-attack was sustained, though no longer military. It was one of those examples of a lost cause redeeming itself by continuing the fight on the spiritual front. Celtic Christianity was soon rivalling Rome's and Byzantium's in Western imagination.

Many victorious Teutons were of imaginative fibre fresher than the corrupt and exhausted Empire knew; with exceptions, such as the Vandals, they wished not to destroy but to reinvigorate it. The Goths had their efficient Codex Argentelus legal system, Ostrogoths provided sensible government. Having conquered, the 'Anglo-Saxons', like their Viking cousins, revealed some architectural skills, a talent for firm but seldom despotic administration, the core of which still exists, and some sensitivity to popular feelings, shown in a dislike, rudimentarily democratic, of obsequiousness towards chieftains. Willing to enslave others, they rejected slavishness among themselves. They were not exceptionally insular. King Raedwald's Sutton Hoo burial ship, 82 feet long, was crammed with English, Byzantine and Frankish coins, jewels, artefacts.

Northerners shared the stubborn, laconic resolution enforced by long melancholic winters, forlorn landscapes, grim scarps and forests, dangerous seas, all dark with mystery, with ambush. This monotony they assuaged by summer raiding, family vendettas, some drug-induced mindless *berserk* rage, blood-brotherhoods, and lust. There was friendship too with gods, who themselves would perish, unable to escape the eye of time, inexorable *wyrd*, the three fates – goddesses spinning decrees beneath the World Tree and degenerating, in *Macbeth*, into the 'weird sisters' gibbering over their obscene cauldron.

The early English had in *Beowulf* an epic; Homeric, if less accessible than Homer. Their verse does not suggest loutishness but an obdurate, cavernous beat, an unfaltering instinct to survive against packed odds. 'That passed away, so may this.' This is not lugubrious, but determined. It is heard again in Pitt's praise in 1798, before the Battle of the Nile had turned the tide, of 'the virtues of adversity endured and adversity resisted, of adversity encountered and adversity surmounted'. The voice of the Old English *Wanderer* is unimpaired after twelve centuries: 'It is noble for a man to grip tight his soul's casket, hold his spirit fast, let his thoughts be what they may.' It can be found in the unflinching loyalty of the warrior Byrhtwold to his dead leader, his lost cause, in the tenth-century poem *The Battle of Maldon*: 'Thought should be harder, heart the keener, courage the greater as our strength dwindles.'

For Vikings and Teutons life might bring a few rewards, cruelly won; death, no rewards at all. Life was comparable to a sparrow, briefly finding refuge from a winter storm, then flying out into boundless night. Christianity might barely shift this dour pessimism, though it could tinge it with irony and a more clearly delineated after-life. Meanwhile, the anonymous *The Wanderer* opens:

> Who liveth alone longeth for mercy,
> Maker's mercy. Though he must traverse
> tracts of sea, sick at heart,

> – trouble with oars, ice-cold waters,
> the ways of exile, – Wyrd is set fast.

Slower, more brooding than Celtic verse, such lines contribute to the popular use of the word 'philosophical': they underlie much of Shakespeare, Tennyson, Kipling.

Unaware of dogmatism or legalism, confronted by the vast Roman wreckage and a future that discouraged idealism, the English trusted more to chance, pragmatism, spontaneous impulse in reaction to sudden opportunity, than to florid rhetoric, intellectual dexterity, extravagant claims, in a stoicism that was to survive their own defeat by the Normans.

Here is loneliness – the deserted wife, the lordless exile, the seafarer, the defeated, man upon earth under a sky hostile, indifferent or meaningless, at best confronted by imposed necessity. The need is for self-reliance and adaptability, a willingness to struggle, argue, accept whatever might transform the barren and wasted. The much-quoted response of King Aethelbert of Kent, influenced by his powerful Christian wife Bertha, to Augustine of Canterbury – an intolerant, perhaps intolerable, saint – and his Continental missionaries suggests a tone already 'English', acceptable to Henry VI and Archbishop Hooker, to Algernon Sidney, to Clem Attlee:

> I see you believe what you say, or you would not have come all this way to say it. But you must not expect me to renounce immediately the customs which I and the English have followed from one generation to another. So, go on talking; no one will interfere with you: and, if you convince us, well, of course, it follows that we will accept your message.

Augustine did found the first English library, at Canterbury in 596. Benedictine monasteries, tolerant, dedicated to agriculture, learning, hospitality, also supplied elements of moderation, good sense, a middle way between the extremes of asceticism and indulgence, acceptable to the island's evolution towards civilisation.

Christianity promised death as an enhanced life. An adroit ruler would also notice Christian Europe's superior agricultural techniques, ample resources of scholarship, respect for hierarchy. That earthly glories were contemptible, enemies should be embraced, the first would be last, might have required to be introduced rather delicately to King Aethelbert.

Mass conversions were usually shallow, dependent on royal wishes, or the result of clauses in peace treaties and in dynastic marriage bargains. In

England, the Cross could long be mistaken for Thor's hammer or a magic tool left over from Albion. 'Almighty' could be confused with 'Allfather', Odin. King Raedwald prudently kept altars to both Christ and Wotan. Moreover, the Roman missionaries, to their chagrin, indeed hatred, found a Celtic church already firmly established in Northumbria, Wales, Ireland. To Augustine, Celtic priests were virtual pagans or *heretics* – a new word which threatened the destruction of Christianity. Actual pagans must have grinned when he competed with Celtic monks in healing a blind man. He succeeded, but his delight may have been less for the blind man's restored sight than at his rivals' mortification.

The Celtic Church had already introduced the first British intellectual in European history, Pelagius, sometimes called Morgan (*c.* 350–420): downright, practical, sociable, serious but not solemn. He had read the Classical poets and the Christian Fathers and, more tolerant than many opponents, Lucretius. He opposed that other Augustine, North African intellectual, chiefly concerning human nature and sin. The contest was crucial, influencing a thousand years of Western attitudes to tolerance, good humour, observation. Augustine upheld a belief that Adam's sin had so contaminated his descendants that salvation was possible only through the Roman Church, and by the chance of Divine Grace. Original sin brought even babies to damnation, if they died before baptism.

Against this cheerless doctrine Pelagius argued, unsuccessfully, that man sinned not through Adam but through his own choice. Fate was not predestined, but was the result of personal error, weakness, perversity, which could be overcome by effort, fortitude, right judgement. Like Salvian, Rhineland radical, and the shadowy commentator 'Sicilian Briton', Pelagius waxed indignant over undeserved riches and poverty: all three suggesting an early British disposition to argue and grumble. 'Let us see', he wrote in *De Divitiis*, 'if the character of Christ has any resemblance to that of a millionaire.' He satisfied himself that it did not. He disliked State authority, spiritual tyranny, private property, sexual excess; was never refuted by Rome but, outmanoeuvred, was declared an 'enemy of Grace'. His Stoicism suggests that he had read Seneca, a long-living influence, and his teachings pervade many who have never heard of him but who recoil from dogmatic abstractions, and convictions that others are more evil than good. A moral descendant was E.M. Forster: 'I never had much sense of sin, and when I realised that the main aim of the Incarnation was not to stop war or pain or poverty, but to free us from sin, I became less interested.' Augustine might have retorted that war, pain, poverty were actually the result of sin. St Jerome was forthright about Pelagius: 'A dolt weighed down with Scots porridge.'

The Dark Ages were better lit than the adjective suggests. Welsh monasticism produced scholars, missionaries, administrators: St David, St Illtyd, Nennius, the ill-tempered Gildas. In the post-Roman reconstruction, Celtic monasteries were power-houses of literacy and craftsmanship, with notions of social responsibility stronger than those of much casual, decaying paganism. From the fifth to the eight century was an era of intellectual ferment, in the spirit of W.B. Yeats's belief that a man may show as reckless a courage in entering the abyss of himself as he does in battle.

Celtic saints – Brigid, Columba, Columbanus, Ninian, Aidan, Patrick – profoundly changed Britain and North Europe, as they taught and travelled. It was in this period that Irish monks settled in Scotland. Irish monasticism was particularly imaginative, quirky, humorous – Columbanus ordained against monks' giggles during Communion – disputative, fitfully ascetic. Its literature is sometimes claimed to have been influenced by Sufism, and certainly it delighted in lyricism, satire, learnedness. Its monkish asceticism probably owed something to the Desert Fathers in Egypt. Unlike the centralised Roman Church the Celtic, with autonomous monasteries more important than bishoprics, tended to regard the deposed gods as old friends on half-pay, and in its own rites permitted dancing. The Celtic–Teutonic ivory 'Franks' Casket' in the British Museum gives insight into current imagination, with carved illustrations of Norse epic, Roman legend and history, Biblical tales. Aware of life's imperfections, the Celtic Church did not brood overmuch on them. In Europe, Romans were outraged by the number of Celtic monasteries, and 'Irish' became a synonym for interference and unruliness.

Columbanus of Leinster (543–617) founded some fifty European houses, among them St Gallen – an effort so prodigious that at the founding of the West European Iron and Steel Community in 1950 he was hailed by Robert Schumann as the patron saint of those wishing to construct a United Europe. Columbanus himself wrote in 603: 'We are all joint members of one body, whether Franks or British or Irish, or whatever our race may be.' St Boniface of Devonshire, 'the Apostle of Germany' (680–755), a Benedictine working in Gaul and Germany, founding communities for both men and women, demanded that compassion should be shown to all Germans, because 'even they have the habit of saying "We are of one blood and of one bone".' He and others, Celts and English, christianised much of

Scandinavia, Holland, and Germany, for which he produced the first Latin primer. He was also councillor to Charles Martel, the Frankish king who saved France from Islamic Moors sweeping up from Spain, at a battle near Poitiers in 732. British missionaries became patron saints of Bremen, Münster, Deventer.

Conversion, literacy, debate seldom exorcised traditional magic. British Celts might cure cattle by water in which the holy Book of Durrow had been dipped, like nineteenth-century Zanzibarans ridding themselves of sickness by drinking liquor stroked by the Koran. In Christian England, an owl perched on a roof still betokened death.

Women were honoured in the Celtic Church. Saethryth and St Aethelburg were noted abbesses in Europe; Chelles was established by a Saxon nun; Bathild, a former slave, married Clovis II and founded or sub-sidised Gallic houses – as well as murdering nine bishops: Dark Age women of whatever persuasion could be formidable. Alfred's daughter indeed ruled alone as Lady of the English, doughty crusher of the Welsh and, allied with Northumbrian leaders, reigned in York as Lady of the Vikings. The names of these women retain the force of novelty, thanks to the impossibility of pronouncing them: Aetheflaed, Aelgifa, Aethelgeofa, Ealhswith.

Travel in the Dark Ages was extensive, and Italian influences were reviv-ing in England. Pelagius journeyed to Rome, Sicily, Carthage, Palestine, possibly Egypt. Benedict Biscop (born *c.* 689), founder of substantial monasteries at Jarrow and Wearmouth, reached Rome six times, returning with scholars, musicologists, craftsmen, glaziers, and books. He knew Latin and Spanish. St Wilfrid of Ripon was three times in Rome, whence he brought back two hundred books, a considerable library in those times. Through such personalities Britain gained Continental stature, though Celts still aroused hostility. The chronicler Ranulf Higden told an anecdote of the English scholar Alcuin of York who, asked by Charlemagne the difference between a Scot (Irishman) and a sot, replied 'Only the width of a table'.

Bede of Jarrow (673–735) had a range Goethean in its co-ordinated disci-plines. A theologian, he was affronted by Pelagius's cool dismissal of sin: no pietist, he would cite St Peter scourging an archbishop for timidity, and thus effect a king's conversion. He was moral philosopher, historian, natural sci-entist, musciologist, grammarian, cosmologist, geographer; he knew Latin, Greek, Hebrew. His History of the English Church was on a scale few in Europe attempted. The etymology of place-names attracted him. He popularised the BC/AD chronology. He was probably the first to begin English translations of the Bible, and was the only Englishman admitted to Dante's Paradise. He could quote Ovid, Sallust, Virgil, if only to prove the superiority of the Church Fathers. Alcuin would discourse on him to Charlemagne.

This cultural efflorescence was flawed by the Celtic–Roman rivalry developing a sharper cutting edge. The contest was between very different concepts of human behaviour, human nature, human needs. Rome had gathered astute, legalistic and sophisticated careerists into the vast administrative apparatus of the Church, impatient with the loosely-organised, theologically speculative and individualistic Celts. At the great conference at Whitby, before King Oswy of Northumbria, to decide the future of religion in England, Rome was represented by gentle, pious Cuthbert, who after death was absorbed into the Albion world of charms and miracles, and by the ruthless, sophisticated authoritarian St Wilfrid, administrator and diplomat of international standing, 'progressive', with all the potency and limitations of that many-sided word. 'To resist Rome', he asserted, 'is to combat the world.' The Celts had little experience of the State, small sympathy with the notion of heresy. Despite the great prestige of Brigid, Columbanus, Hilda, of Iona and Lindisfarne, they failed to convince the bemused Oswy, for whom Wilfrid cleverly exploited the role of Rome's leading spiritual asset, St Peter, as the guardian of Heaven's Gate. The Celts could summon no such Other World grandee, and Oswy, after consulting his council, the Witan, decided in 664 to yield the Pope 'jurisdiction over this realm of England'. Politically, Oswy's decision was more important than any made by Carausius or Magnus Maximus: it was England's first step towards status as a Great Power, with all the benefits due from closer ties with Europe. The moral results were less clear.

Small, warring Teutonic kingdoms dwindled to a few larger ones, all desiring a single national throne. Bede was now referring to the 'English' as one people, despite local differences in traditions, institutions, dialects. Now Northumbria, now Mercia, now Wessex held unstable supremacy. Under such 'Kings of the English' as Offa of Mercia (757–796), Egbert (d. 835) and Alfred (871–901) of Wessex, the land was further unified, more so than Ireland, Wales, Scotland, reducing the casualty lists from regional wars. Dynastic cultural and commercial links with the Continent were strengthened by trade and royal marriages. Charlemagne hailed Offa as 'the most powerful Western monarch', though the King held aloof from the Emperor's bloody crusades against Germanic and Slavonic pagans.

In 787 the English were challenged by a new seaborne force. Viking brutality is still remembered, mostly in bad films. Vikings praised 'the glorious murderer', yet respected Odin's sacrifice of his eye for wisdom: 'Better burden beareth no man abroad than wisdom. Better it is than riches in a foreign land.' Greek in its laconic good sense, acceptable to English temperaments, is 'Middling wise should each man be, never wise in excess'. Their devotion to chess suggests patience, deliberation, foresight, indeed cunning, attributes extending to a feeling for law and of resentment at despotism. The Norse Assembly, 'The Thing', was of 'freemen', thus excluding women and slaves: that in much Icelandic literature women were the more savage might have been a factor. Iceland's parliament adopted Christianity by majority vote in 930: medieval Sweden had, like Saxon England, an elected Monarch, and its peasants were allowed some political rights.

These peoples acquired discipline, loyalties, pragmatism: necessary for seafarers. Problems of over-population and food increasingly drove younger men to aggression during the eighth and ninth centuries. They ravaged not only Lindisfarne but Pisa; they reached Russia, Byzantium, Sicily, north France, 'Northmandy'. They founded Kiev. They built the first sizeable towns in Ireland, including Dublin; Nottingham, Derby, York, Lincoln were Viking centres.

They too were stoical. Little could be expected from gods who had no expectations for themselves. Fate was capricious – the wicked could prosper, the virtuous perish – yet it could be faced without fear or illusion, without cringing. Sons must inherit a Name untainted by cowardice. Rough good-fellowship was symbolised by the hard-drinking god Thor, at home in Valhalla or in a churl's hovel. Humour, often crude, relished the wily Loki, practical joker, dangerous friend.

No more than the Celts and English were the Vikings a single people. Danes and Norwegians fought each other savagely in Ireland. Their sagas, however, shared stories and values, affected British imagination down to the days of William Morris and Kipling, W.H. Auden and George Mackay Brown. London, indeed, was treated in 1912 to an imitation saga, *The Song of Aegir*, written by Kaiser Wilhelm II.

The saga-world was largely preserved by tolerant Icelandic bishops and the thirteenth-century Dane, Saxo Grammaticus, who presented the original version of *Hamlet*. Narration could be subtle, even complex, exploiting flashbacks, controlling inter-related plots. Characterisation is shrewd, seldom stereotyped, sex pleasant but seldom solemn or mindless. Karl Neri, in *Gautrik's Saga*, 'was so wise that you could nowhere find his match, all his plans turned out well, whatever the problem. He would never accept any gifts, for he was so mean that he could never bring himself to give anything in return.'

Ill-fortune is not magnified into Tragedy, nor crisis glamorised; the magical and fantastic are woven easily into the everyday; enemies are given their due, magnanimity is honoured, but realism is not overlooked. When a princess was captured by a monster, 'the King was dreadfully distressed by the news and had a search made for his daughter, but none could find trace of her, and soon people lost interest.'

'Dead words smell badly.' But Viking and Teutonic literature reverberates like axe-strokes, exposing brief vistas, beautiful or atrocious, baleful, or redeemed by comradeship, loyalty, and summer.

The Vikings respected their English enemy Alfred, with whom they had much in common. Yet very little of him is reliably documented. Part of his appeal was that, in leading resistance to the invaders, saddled with a cause apparently hopeless, he visibly defied Fate, and partially succeeded. He left one-third of England under Danish rule, 'the Dane Law', but imposed Christianity on his enemies.

Viking rule was not catastrophic in a troubled age which saw York held successively by Celts, Romans, Teutons, a ninth-century Dane, Halfdon, the Danish–Irish Ragnold, a Saxon earl, the Norman William. English respect for law, debate, literature, reputation, honesty, and – or so we like to think – its stubborn moderation, owes as much to the Vikings as to Teutons and Celts.

After Alfred's death his son Edward the Elder and his daughter Aethelflaed, the indomitable Lady of the English, then Aethelstan, 'King of earls, the Lord, rewarder of heroes', and Edgar, began the reconquest of the Danelaw and attempted sovereignty over Scottish and Welsh regions. At Brunanburh in 937 a dangerous coalition of Scots, Northumbrians and Irish Vikings was ferociously routed:

> Many a warrior lay there
> Star-stretched by spears, many a Northman and Scot
> Likewise stabbed above their shields.

Laws were enforced by governments of some acumen. A Petition of Right submitted to Edgar in 973 was quoted in the High Court in 1973.

Relative prosperity collapsed under renewed invasions from Denmark, most perilous during the reign of Aethelred II, the Redeless (960–81), so-named not for being 'Unready', though ready enough with other people's money, but for neglecting the *rede*, the counsel of the Witan. Since that advice once took the form of telling him to fast for three days and intone Psalm 3, 'Lord, how my enemies have multiplied', in order to stem Viking aggression, one has some sympathy for him. Unmartial, he attempted to appease the Danes by all means short of war. He introduced Dane-geld, England's first national tax: the invaders took the money and eagerly returned for more. Begun as a temporary expedient, the tax remained even when the Danish Canute ruled, until its abolition by Henry II in 1162.

Aethelred's later expedients finally wrecked his fortunes, notoriously a massacre of all Danes within reach which enfuriated King Sweyn of Denmark, a renegade Christian. Landing in England for revenge, his men in drunken merriment pelted to death with stones and sheep-bones the Archbishop of Canterbury. Aethelred's trusted confederate Streona betrayed him, forcing the Witan to eject Aethelred and enthrone Sweyn; who then died, leaving his son Canute to fight a popular English claimant, Edmund Ironside. Edmund perished after a further betrayal by Streona, in mid-battle, for which Canute, honourably ungrateful, executed him, to right-eous approval.

In Danish rule lay English redemption, since Canute turned out to be no racist despot. Anglo-Scandinavian instincts for positive but undogmatic leadership and a respect, rather grudgingly admitted by rulers, for tradi-tional rights, customs, rituals pagan and Christian, were undisturbed by him. Trials continued in public, with sworn witnesses, appeals to precedent, and the rudiments of a jury. In the Queen, Emma, was a merging of traits: English, Scandinavian, Norman. Widow of Aethelred and mother by him of Edward the Confessor, she married Canute.

The Romanist English Church had acquired considerable splendour, and a Benedictine monastic revival enjoyed royal support and the organising zeal of such leaders as the authoritarian Archbishop Dunstan, St Aethelwolde of Winchester, St Oswald of Worcester. The severe Aethelwolde, who 'cor-rected the foolish with rods' – someone attempted to poison him for his pains – encouraged the immigration of Continental monks experienced in husbandry, horticulture, crop-rotation, music, charitable services, education. The Winchester School was in the forefront of illumination, painting, cartography, drawing; carving in stone, wood, walrus and whale bone. Tenth-century and later English illuminated bibles and manuscripts were unrivalled in their gold and vermilion, their huge ornate capitals, their interplay of realism and fancy, setting precisely observed figures, their draperies full of movement, against the old Celtic and Northumbrian intricacies of agitated foliage, interlacings, dabs of fantasy and humour. Again, they are not wholly insular, with accretions from Greece, Carolingian Germany, Byzantium.

If Aethelwolde was stern, with Dunstan, statesman and national administrator, official intercourse was seldom amiable discussion between equals. After his death in 988 Dunstan swiftly became part of legendary Albion, as a priest–magician, grabbing the Devil by the nose with red-hot tongs to settle an argument – some poetic truth, here – and miraculously escaping disasters which, more realistic detractors alleged, he had himself craftily engineered, at the expense of rivals.

Under such guidance, lay and ecclesiastical, scores of churches with square and round towers arose: the scholar Harold Taylor has identified some four hundred, difficult to date but all suggesting English foundations. Bosham Church is believed to be the burial place of a daughter of Canute. Pre-Conquest England possessed some elaborate church organs, notably at Winchester and Sherborne Abbey. English and Celtic books, sculpture, engraved chalices, enamels, jewels, metal-work were popular throughout Europe. English women, and men, excelled in sumptuous draperies, robes, ceremonial trappings like the Durham stole owned by the Lady of the English, the embroidered linen of the unique Bayeux 'Tapestry', and the later, richly decorated *opus anglicanum* and *broderie anglaise*, with feudal and religious imagery woven into designs formal or naturalistic.

The English coinage was superior to the Norman, imitated in Scandinavia. Michael Grant judges: 'The heads on Offa's Canterbury silver pennies were more imaginative, varied and skilful in detail than any other European coin portraits for centuries to come.' 'Sixpennies' of Aethelred, from London and West Saxon mints, discovered at Roncevalles, imply considerable official and commercial liveliness.

The Normans, as conquerors, affected contempt for the English losers' hard-wrung achievements, contaminated, they felt, by Harold's perjury, worst of sins. Their propaganda was effective: to this day, many English believe their history began in 1066.

The pro-Norman Edward the Confessor was spared their contempt. He was patron saint of England until the Hundred Years' War, rather more than an honorary position in an era of prayer and miracle. Then Edward III, in debt to Genoese bankers, replaced him with their patron, the more aggressive St George, who was not to escape the attention of the supreme English ironist, Gibbon: he dismissed George as a dishonest bacon contractor, loathed by Christian and pagan alike.

Like Aethelred, Edward was long stereotyped as a pious weakling; the honorific 'Confessor', like Bede's 'Venerable', misleads. Edward appears a man of sophisticated values and methods who baffled, irritated, sometimes outfaced his clumsier English magnates, his strength that of a sapling in the wind. He awed many by his apparent saintliness, outraged others by what seemed a betrayal of them to outlanders. He too, with posthumous tales of miracles and healing, entered the lore of Albion.

Like another intellectual ruler, James I, Edward was an inordinate hunter. He founded Westminster Abbey, built in the latest French and Norman Romanesque. Also, he unwittingly set England on a significant double course by establishing himself at some distance from the City. A 'Good European', married to a Norman, preferring Continental tastes, manners, wit, more nimble, more inflected than those of the more stolid English, he surrounded himself with foreigners, particularly Normans, displeasing the powerful Godwin clan. Childless, Edward may have guaranteed the succession to the ambitious Duke William of Normandy, Harold may have seconded it in the Duchy after untimely shipwreck, but neither had the legal power to do this. It was the Witan's prerogative, but this grave body was approaching its last days, some of its members perhaps colluding with the hard, ever-alert Duke over the water, chaffing at a realm too small for his unremitting energies.

Reduced to essentials on the Bayeux Tapestry, 1066 was the year of four kings under the glare of Halley's comet: the enigmatic Confessor; the old-style Norse invader, world-ravager, Harald Hardrada; Harold II, son of Earl Godwin, betrayed by a Channel wind and over-impetuosity at Hastings; and the business-like William, who methodically exacted a Papal blessing on his adventure, and condemnation of Harold as a foresworn usurper. Thus commonplace theft, a profitable investment, was transformed into a crusade backed by God himself, an instance of psychological warfare. Prudently,

Duke William promised Norman, Flemish, Breton warrior–investors ample returns in English lands and dues.

As Harold was in Yorkshire, successfully grappling with the last serious Viking invasion, William landed in Sussex. After an exceptional and exhausting march south, the English confronted him 'at the gray apple tree'. William's more disciplined troops prevailing, the Royal English House was in the dust forever.

William I, never loved, but respected and feared, was far from Albion. He is unimaginable chatting to a salmon, or strolling on water in an off-hand way, or performing miracles:

> He had castles built
> And poor men he oppressed.
> The King was very stark
> And took from underlings many a mark.

He ruthlessly penalised rebellious Northumbria, confiscated much of Wessex for his New Forest; yet, like Canute, like Rome, he enforced laws reasonably just on both his peoples, on priest and layman, on his own family. He induced some sense of personal security, was never forgotten, but in death lay quite alone.

Whoever ruled, the mass of the populace remained English, grumbling, suspicious of authority, sceptical of 'winged words' from lords, but rebellious only if over-goaded by the rampantly unfair. They preferred the Crown to the baronage, one Devil being better than many devils. Tenacious of rights, however niggardly, they disputed boundary stones and bargained over marriages and field-strips with an unwavering obstinacy which would one day win them the right to vote, form unions, let women into Parliament, universities, the Law, the Church. They were still close to the earth, susceptible to lunatic prophecies, harassed by omens, famine, plague, God's wrath, and subject to visitations from the Other World. Meanwhile, lacking an Arthur, a Hengist, an Alfred, they acquired the characteristics of the defeated: dumb insolence, irony, deviousness, understatement. Their rule for good conduct was perfectly expressed by a foreign nun, the first recognised female dramatist and wholly unknown to them, Hrotswitha of Gandersheim (*c.* 932–1002): 'Blame not he who falls but he who fails to rise again.'

4

Merrie England

Love is plonte of hees most precious of vertues,
For hevene holde hit ne mighte, so hevy hit semede,
Til hit hadde of erthe y-Yoten hitselve.

Langland

The King is under God and the Law; for the Law makes the King and without the Law
there is no king.

Henry de Bracton

The Normans tended to despise the English as ale-sodden poor relations,
though they themselves were probably inferior in literacy and most arts,
only some eighty years from Odin, Thor and Balder. The Archbishop of
Rouen had a 'personal devil', Little Thor.

William established the strongest monarchy in Europe. He objected to
capital punishment – rulers need people over whom to rule – though his
alternative is unappealing to modern sensitivies: 'I also forbid that anyone
shall be slain or hanged for any fault, but let his eyes be put out and let him
be castrated. And this command shall not be violated under pain of a fine
in full to me.'

However they assessed him, the English may have grinned when, after the
great invader's death, his funeral was so delayed by factional disputes that his
over-corpulent body suddenly exploded. In much pain is much retribution.

Many Anglo-Danish laws were left unrevoked. English parish, shire,
manorial court continued, supporting traditional feeling for local government, neighbourhood justice, writs and charters. In turn, some English
institutions were transplanted to the Duchy by Henry I. If attention to
popular rights was often mere lip-service, this can be better than no service.
'The Norman Conquest', Professor Barlow concluded, 'was almost more
important for what it preserved than for what it created.'

The early Norman rulers attracted few affectionate anecdotes, though

William Rufus's reaction to the death of a Pope has Wellingtonian pith: 'God rot him who cares a damn for that!' As a vast and inviolate bureaucracy was lacking, the distribution of power could be variable, according to circumstance and personality; monarchs, prelates, lay magnates circled round each other, forming cabals, switching alliances, claiming privileges, uneasily aware of the Wheel of Fortune, but quarrelling sometimes to the death, or staging hypnotic ceremonies of reconciliation, the Kiss of Peace, before fashioning new patterns in ruthless, sometimes demented, pursuit of land, treasure, self-esteem, sexual peacocking.

Relations with Rome were necessarily complex, with a Pope who believed he was Vicar of Christ himself, and the Anglo-Normans increasingly becoming more united, self-regarding and wary of Italians. 'What need had Englishmen to receive the Will of God from the Pope of Rome?' an Archbishop of York asked Henry I. 'Had they not the guidance of Scripture?' At home, Church and State remained in profitable alliance, monasteries training literate and financially adept clerics for the Royal administration. The Church was, doubtless had to be, more political than spiritual, though the latter, a powerful weapon, was reserved for crisis, as in the Becket quarrel.

Changes were occurring. Clerical celibacy was ordained from Rome in 1074, but not obeyed hurriedly. As late as 1450 John de la Berc, Bishop of St David's, was refusing to countenance it, as he relied heavily on dues from priests' wives. Marriage became a sacrament only in 1215, the presence of a priest at the ceremony not hitherto having been essential.

The Saxon aristocracy was virtually extinguished; local communities were disturbed; many Bretons, recouping from the Hastings enterprise, settled in Essex. The English themselves remained largely anonymous, submerged in a political entity now contracting, now enlarging, but at its broadest sweep embracing Normandy, Brittany, Poitou, Gascony, Aquitaine, the vassallage of Toulouse, and with vital commercial links with Flanders. Stone churches and castles arose on the land; sombre and massive structures, on hill, by river-mouth, at crossways now dominated, as if the land's troubled dreams had grown visible.

Royal promises, charters, favours were granted, notably during financial shortages. Henry I promulgated a Charter of Rights, doubtless reassuring though with no immediate or sensational outcome. Lawyers, however, docketed it for use against weaker rulers in changed circumstances. Another Royal edict is a telling summary of medieval government: 'Henry, King of the English, to his faithful members of the Church at Winchester, Greeting. I order you to hold a free election, but nevertheless forbid you to elect anyone except Richard my clerk, the Archdeacon of Poitiers.'

Henry, 'Fine Scholar', Rufus's younger brother, cruel in a cruel age, imprisoned his elder brother Robert for twenty-nine years, blinded two granddaughters, possibly connived at Rufus's death. He was generous to art, and his achievement of perhaps twenty-five bastards was not surpassed in English Royal annals. He married his daughter Maud (Matilda) to the Holy Roman Emperor, and briefly considered joining England to the Empire to secure her rights. On Henry's death, these rights were successfully disputed by his nephew Stephen, ensuring almost two decades of destructive civil war that ended with Stephen's death and the crowning of Henry II, Plantagenet, Maud's son by her second husband.

Reputedly descended from a she-devil called Melusine, thoroughly Albionesque, Henry II (1154–89) was a great European personality: King of England, Duke of Normandy and Brittany, married to the tempestuous Eleanor of Aquitaine, largest landowner in Europe, divorced Queen of France, who had roughed it with crusaders in Palestine, crushed a rebellion, helped Provençal poets. Albion fantasies of Rome and Troy were revived in Geoffrey of Monmouth's mythic epic *Historia Britonum* and the opportune discovery of the bones of 'Arthur and Guinevere' at Glastonbury.

The King's mercurial relations with Eleanor, his tantrums with Archbishop Becket over clerical privileges, his campaigns against his sons, enlivened courtly Europe. Deeply flawed, tirelessly energetic, he was an Arthurian avatar, glittering in success, tragic in failure, passionate, vile-tempered, indomitable, dramatic. In one tale, at the rock of Lechlavar he was cursed by a witch; his followers fled, recalling Merlin's prophecy that on Lechlavar a king would perish. Henry jumped onto it, cheerfully declaiming: 'Who will now have any faith in that liar Merlin?'

In physique, personality, lapses of judgement, in erratic fatherhood, Henry resembled Churchill; and, though a French-speaking, international magnate, had elements recognisably English. Both men had complex simplicity, a mixture of bumptiousness and generosity, crude humour and irony, insensitivity and loyalty, pettiness and romantic exuberance, melancholic introspection and public panache, a fascination with violence and doughty achievements in the arts of peace. A confrontation between them would be explosive but inconclusive, each striving not for the last word, but the first. Often rash and inflexible, Henry could sometimes be managed by those he trusted and respected – rather few. He could be headstrong, prudent, vindictive, magnanimous, within an afternoon; and, by evening, thirty miles away, have forgotten the lot. Without literary gifts, he could use full-blooded language from an imagination now soaring, now sinking. When he captured Helias de la Flêche, the Count complained that this was a fluke: he would escape, and remedy it. Henry's response has probably been toned down. 'You do? You clown, you! Do you imagine I care what you do? Go away! Get out! Sod off! Do as you please!' Restless, forever interfering, few English rulers were less oppressed by *wyrd*, by self-doubt, by others' opinion. He had some psychological acumen; appreciated the propaganda value of religion, though his theological interests were scanty. Dying in defeat and disillusion, surrounded by jabbering clerics, the old man could still speak roundly: 'If the priests and clerks would not have me cast out, rejected, excluded, they must leave me in peace. Either their argument is false, or no man can be saved.'

To keep power, he appreciated the need for a spectacular and well-timed gesture: all Gothic Europe heard of him submitting, in penalty for Becket's murder, to a public whipping – probably not of the fiercest. His impetuosity could flare in less imposing spectacles: he is recorded, having been crossed in argument, as hurling down his cap, flinging off his clothes, and chewing straw, 'as if squatting on a dung-hill'.

That Archbishop Becket became England's most popular saint and martyr owed much to shrewd manipulation of news by the French King, Henry's enemy, together with the discovery of worms and lice in Becket's underclothes, veritable proof of sanctity. His canonisation was a coup for the Lords Spiritual to rival the temporal monarchy's when Edward the Confessor was canonised in 1166. Becket's attitude to Church and State was vehemently debated around Europe. A theatrical character, tenacious of his rights and beliefs and both charismatic and irritating, Becket was posthumously venerated not only at Canterbury but in Bologna, Saragossa, and particularly in Scandinavia.

Diplomatic tact was uncharacteristic of Henry II. Diplomacy requires smiling evasions, sly nuances, deadly rebuffs exquisitely delivered. Frequently begged by Royal emissaries for support against Becket, Pope Alexander II would reply: 'We are glad the King is so good. May God make him even better!' Henry, most powerful western monarch, was determined, without suave nuance or finesse, to reconstruct England after the turbulent rule of Stephen, 'who did no justice'. He proved more legal reformer than avenging warlord. Becket's claim for 'Benefit of Clergy' – that priests (in practice, all literates) were owed legal privileges denied to the rest – offended his sense of order, his prerogative, his conviction that kings should be masters in their own realm with no rival law from Church or baron, and that strong government was popular government. Becket's murder, however, secured the privileges of 'criminous clerks': long after the Reformation Ben Jonson, 'clerk' by his ability to recite the 'neck verse', escaped hanging for killing an actor, Gabriel Spencer, in 1598, authority having to content itself with branding him on the thumb.

Henry's law-giving, nevertheless, was to extend throughout the English-speaking world. His centralising instinct, and anger with the regional aristocracy, made him support and strengthen traditional Common Law through Royal justice, assisted by more systematic use of juries and implemented by travelling judges responsible to Westminster. Henry and his advisers tidied up a conflicting mass of Frankish, Viking, English and Norman procedures and verbal haziness: verdicts would be reached after research into 'case-law', appeals to jury, laborious argument. Juries had already helped compile Domesday Book, inspect disputed boundaries, discuss doubtful reputations. Chroniclers reported the Kings of Castile and Navarre, in dispute, resorting to one of Henry's courts. Appeals to the judgement of God, by Ordeal or Battle, decayed.

Richard Lionheart, Henry's son, scarcely visited England while King; though a far-famed international celebrity, he was an expensive liability, over-taxing England for his campaigns in France and Palestine; the English ransom-money paid for his release from captivity helped finance the fortifications of Vienna, which twice debarred the Turks.

Medieval England and Europe held values decidedly masculine. With literacy still rare, sworn loyalties cemented male relationships and properties; fighting was the ultimate sanction. Cowardice and desertion, involving betrayal of comrades, were thus abhorred; 'Honour', revered in Islamic and Christian society, was idealised in the Knights.

The cult of chivalry was romanticised centuries later by such novelists as Walter Scott, and Conan Doyle in *Sir Nigel* and *The White Company*, as well as by the early Boy Scout movement, with its outdoor practicalities, its insistence on Loyalty, Courtesy, Piety. Professing loyalty to Woman, subservient and chaste, Knights could be brutal to their wives and concubines, vindictive in martial triumph, and decidedly rapacious. In tournaments, outlets for ferocity during peace, champions would arrange to avoid fighting each other, would expect appearance money, demand 'transfer fees' from wealthy promoters. The great William Marshal, Earl of Pembroke, prospered mightily in partnership with Roger de Gaugi, winning ransom and armour from a hundred and three opponents in ten months; and married the second richest heiress in England. He was renowned throughout Europe as the epitome of chivalry; of magnanimity, courage, loyalty. Beginning as a landless knight, he served four English kings, as guardian, adviser, warrior and, from 1216 to 1219, Regent for the young Henry III. His moral prestige vied with his wealth. 'The most loyal man and true I have ever known, in any country where I have been,' said King Philip Augustus of France, wily schemer against Richard Lionheart.

To moderns, and particularly from a feminist standpoint, the Earl appears a pot-hunting élitist, time-serving grabber, moral pedant, hearty and unimaginative, a conformist careerist dedicated to preserving the static chivalric mould. But this is to impose the present on a past where oaths, lineage, numbers, stars, colours, goblins, shadows had powers quite different, provoked Other World links, often through heraldic symbolism, ornate ritual, fantasies of costume and armour – a live linnet in a golden cage surmounting a helmet. Grandeur such as William's, comic today, helped ease society through much squalor, peril, and fear.

The lot of north European women could be unenviable. Burgundians drowned discontented wives in mud. Charlemagne's consort died at twenty-five, having borne nine children. In the wake of Charles the Bald's unremitting prayers for children, his wife produced eleven. To counter accusations of promiscuity, queens might have to tread red-hot ploughshares. Aquinas, even Abelard, dutiful to Aristotle, thought women inferior, while the ungracious Tertullian had raged that a woman was a temple built upon a sewer. The Church rated fornication as less sinful than tithe-avoidance, and wives could legally be 'beaten with feet and fists'. On the other hand, baronial objection to the ex-Empress Maud (Matilda) in the twelfth century was as much due to her abrasive personality as to her gender. Edward III's queen, Philippa of Hainault, in his absence helped rout the Scots in battle: Richard II's love for his Bohemian wife was famously tragic – in grief at her death he destroyed their favourite palace, at Sheen.

A constitutional difference between England and France was that no French princess could inherit the crown, 'because of the imbecility of the sex'.

Elsewhere, much remains obscure. Medieval chroniclers were men, seldom greatly concerned with women's routine; and further down the social scale, the annals of the poor were not yet written by the poor: for serf, villein, small peasant, the werewolves may have howled and the dead walked.

In France and the Iberian peninsula, great provincial feudatories could overshadow the Crown. The Empire and Italy were divided between competing states. Scottish kings usually died violently; no consistent overall sovereignty existed in Wales or Ireland.

Norman purposeful capability was asserted in the Domesday Book. It was not a survey or census of all England; it omitted Winchester, London, Durham, Northumberland; yet, completed in a year, it was a remarkable feat, needing the co-operation of educated and experienced English officials. One motive was the more efficient collection of Danegeld.

It was not unique. Franks and Normans had made similar compilations, though more laboriously, less comprehensively. The English scarcely appreciated this, recognising the grip it gave the Treasury on lives, goods, animals, and unofficially abused it as 'Domesday', associated with the grim Last Judgement. For seventeenth-century republicans it still symbolised an instance of alien tyranny. It has been employed quite recently to settle rights of property, franchise, boundaries, even the ownership of an old tree.

To quarrel with a King capable of such an achievement, though it was frequent, required daring. Froissart thought the English difficult to govern. Typical enough was the exchange between the towering Edward I, 'Longshanks', and his Constable and Earl Marshal, Roger Bigod, Earl of Norfolk, who resented being ordered to campaign in Gascony: 'By God, Sir Earl, thou shalt either go, or hang.' 'By the same oath, Sir King, I will neither go nor hang.' His forecast was correct.

If the monarch was tactless, mischievous and erratic, like John, or incompetent like Edward II, rash and unpredictable like Richard II, the great landowners would intervene, sometimes terribly. Yet in its determination to preserve the rights of 'all free men', a term taken from the Coronation Oath of the Holy Roman Emperor, Magna Carta was not democratic. It excluded serfs and villeins, and Froissart's conjecture that England possessed more of these than anywhere else has been supported by the Cambridge medievalist H.S. Bennett in his calculation that in 1300 more than half the population were 'unfree'. Plague might hasten the decline of serfdom by increasing labourers' value, but everywhere the poor were forced to think with their knees, though English serfdom was less rigid than Continental. The Great

Charter, a temporary shock to the harassed King John, 'Lackland', was in keeping with contemporary charters in Spain and Hungary but scarcely affected feudal England. Pope Innocent II annulled it, though subsequent kings sometimes confirmed it. With all technically free following the final abolition of feudal tenures in 1641, seventeenth-century lawyers re-examined the Charter, using it against the Crown with radical impetus.

A new and obnoxious poll tax might arouse a massive popular revolt – it has happened as recently as 1990. In 1381 peasants from Kent and Essex invaded the huge and chilling Tower of London, murdered the Chancellor and Treasurer and, following the killing of the rebel leader, Wat Tyler, by the Lord Mayor, almost encompassed the massacre of the boy king Richard II, and his retinue. Richard's bravery, and insincere promises, saved the day. Several hundred hangings followed. High-handed expropriations, doubtfully legal, certainly unfair, did eventually cost Richard II his life. Unusually, he appears to have thought himself superior to both English customs and constitutional restraints. If he really claimed 'the laws of England are within my own breast', he was reverting to traditions of Rome, not of Britain.

From Wat Tyler and Jack Cade to Monmouth, the sporadic English rebellions were ill-organised, lacking the demented savagery of the French *jacquerie* outbreaks and the German peasant wars. They reacted to specific grievances for specific ends: resolute Tudor risings – the Evil May Day Riots, Kett's Rebellion, the Pilgrimage of Grace – were not apocalyptic but the result of goaded consciences, poisoned loyalties, long-held beliefs brutally outraged. Evil May Day victimised Flemings.

King and Council governed a population of some two millions, which went on increasing until the Black Death of the fourteenth century. Parliamentary origins are disputed: regional representatives may have set some precedents in giving witness for Domesday Book, and attending church councils. They were not unique: Iceland already had its Assembly; Philip the Fair's Estates-General, summoned in 1302, included urban delegates; Castile had elected municipalities; assemblies existed in Aragon and Leon; Sweden had a parliament that would soon include country gentry and merchants. In England, pursuing his quarrels with the artistic Henry III, weak yet stubborn, Simon de Montfort collected a Parliament in 1265, inviting not only Knights of the Shire but burgesses from towns supporting his anger at misgovernment.

Henceforward Parliaments had some place, though dependent on a Royal summons, usually only in a financial or political emergency. Parliament was forced to give formal assent to the depositions of Edward II, Richard II, Edward V, and indeed to Richard II's own revenge on the Lords Appellant, for 'treason', in 1397. The House of Commons was devised not to express common opinion but to obstruct or diffuse it. The Interests manipulated it: episcopal, monastic, territorial and, increasingly, mercantile. Less exclusive than the aristocratic Council, it was English enough in mingling florid pretentiousness with sober self-interest; its eventual objective was to induce Kings, later still the people, to do what they had no wish to do. The English always knew that politics consists of making a poor best of a bad job.

England did possess distinctive features; primogeniture ensured considerable social mobility, Anglo-Norman aristocratic younger sons having to seek status and property wherever they could, often with rising merchant families, titles being exchanged for wealth. Most Continental aristocracies, cherishing descent from gods and heroes, making social protocol almost a branch of canon law, were antipathetic to gainful toil, to 'trade'. Not greatly addicted to class-hatred, the English early developed, however, a concern for degrees of status: a sixteenth-century Mr Sprigg was listed as 'cloth-maker alias yeoman alias gentleman alias merchant'.

The English were not prone to over-revere lay or ecclessiastical authority. Their monarchs did not withdraw into Byzantine ceremonial and seclusion or, save Richard II in his last years, stand on hierarchic, stiff, ornate dignity. Palaces were open to all save known criminals and the blatantly diseased and unkempt. For propaganda, economy and palace cleansing, monarchs made well-advertised progresses through the Midlands and the south, benefiting from the hospitality, sometimes reluctant, of their nobles. Certain English stories, perhaps apocryphal but not misleading, are unimaginable elsewhere. William Penn was in audience with Charles II and, as a Quaker, kept his hat on; whereupon the King doffed his own. 'Brother Charles, why dost thou remove thine hat?' asked Penn. Charles mildly replied that it was the custom, in that apartment, for only one person to remain covered. Winston Churchill loathed whistling. His private detective, W.H. Thompson, was walking with him in Downing Street one day when they met a newspaper boy, whistling. Churchill ordered him to cease.

   'Why should I?'
    'Because I don't like it. It's a horrible noise.'
    'You can shut your ears, can't you?'

Thompson added that Churchill was as much amused as surprised and in the Foreign Office yard was still chuckling and repeating, 'You can shut your ears, can't you?'

An anonymous thirteenth-century English chronicler used imagery which a William or Henry would have understood, without actually applauding: 'Just as a ship cannot be saved from the perils of the sea without guidance from its oarsmen, so neither can any king govern his realm prosperously nor defend it from his enemies, without the help of his own subjects.'

The subjects would supply help without slavishness, with the wary scepticism and grousing reluctance which have preserved England from monarchical absolutism and the one-party state; from the army, the unions, the unrestricted rule of the City, bureaucracy. The individual could occasionally prevail, against odds. A twentieth-century Socialist minister, Arthur Henderson, spoke for this robust tradition: 'I do not mind a conscience, but I do object to an organised conscience.' The English great were always denied grandiose titles: society prospered on a refusal to be infantile. Their monarch was never 'Little Father', 'Shadow of God upon Earth', 'Light of the Aryans', 'King of Kings'. When Charles II, with unwonted pomposity, began: 'As Father of My people . . .', a Buckingham was on hand to murmur: 'The father of a great many of them, Sir.' Louis-Napoleon, admirer of British stability and moderation, of which he once planned a history, might have been embarrassed to learn that Chapuys-Monclaville, a member of the French Senate, had the Imperial bath-water bottled, as if it were the Waters of Jordan. No British premier has imitated Leonid Brezhnev, who awarded himself the Lenin Prize for Literature – though George IV, even in Wellington's presence, boasted of having led a charge at Waterloo.

Justice, Voltaire gibed, was invented to ruin the innocent; there is no need to idealise English Common Law, and few Englishmen were tempted to do so. One man dismissed Henry II's courts as mousetraps. The 1381 rebels burned legal documents, and slaughtered lawyers as gleefully as they did Flemish immigrants. Though Magna Carta and Common Law forbade torture, this could be used under Royal prerogative. Even in the eighteenth century, refusal to plead could entail 'pressing' with heavy weights, sometimes after the accused had been filled with water, until a plea was extracted. For Guy Fawkes, James I ordered: 'The gentler Tortures are to be first used unto him . . . and so by degrees proceeding to the worst – and so God speed your good work.'

Parliamentary impeachment and attainder, little more than sententious declarations of some great one's guilt, were closer to Roman Law. Throughout, Law could sanction slavery, burning of live people, gibbeting of children, imprisonment for debt and for possessing beliefs unacceptable to current fashion. A medieval Lord, resenting the Royal law courts, could often ignore them, intimidate juries, bribe officials, steal a poor man's home or impound his women, without fear of prosecution. Jacobean groundlings must have howled applause for Lear's groans to blind Gloucester: 'A man may see how this world goes with no eyes. Look with thine ears: see how yon justice rails upon yon simple thief. Hark, in thine ear: change places; and, handy-dandy, which is the justice, which is the thief?'

Behind the façade of impartiality might lie another reality, of vicious judges, rigged juries, hired witnesses, 'men of straw', and simple folk stupefied by legal jargon, coerced by legal attire. In English witchcraft trials a judge might promise mercy in return for a confession, but with fingers crossed, thus reserving the mercy for himself.

Nevertheless Common Law, dependent as much on sullen popular obstinacy as on Royal sanction, never quite succumbed to the subtleties of Henry VII and his servile 'Prerogative Courts' such as Star Chamber, to the overbearing Henry VIII, the hard impersonality of Thomas Cromwell, Walsingham or Strafford. Practical institutions, clumsy, often unfair, were always preferred to the inorganic and futuristic: *Utopia*, though written by an Englishman, was addressed to a people thoroughly unutopian. In testing times – involving Spain, France, Germany – when Continental institutions buckled, the British took the strain. The rich were never acknowledged to be immune from the Law, whether Prerogative or Common. Lord Suffolk was hauled before the King's Bench in 1498 for 'killing a mean person', though eventually pardoned. Lord Dacre was hanged for murder in 1541, Lord Stourton for murder at Salisbury in 1557, leaving a ghost to haunt the Cathedral. Like Stourton, Lord Ferrers was hanged with a silken cord, a peer's right, in 1760, for killing his steward. Horace Walpole reported that Ferrers went to Tyburn in his wedding clothes, and that 'there was a new contrivance for sinking the stage under him, which did not play well; and he suffered a little by the delay, but was dead in four minutes.'

Under Henry II the British Empire, as against the Angevin, began inauspiciously, in Ireland, when the deposed Dermot McMurrough, King of Leinster, rapist and tyrant, sought aid from Henry; who, never jibbing at territorial prospects, despatched Richard de Clare, 'Strongbow', on behalf less of McMurrough than of the Angevin dynasty. Inter-Irish antagonisms were already ancient: pre-Christian Ulster and Connaught had fiercely competed for cattle, for virile glory, and Irish leadership, in bouts enlarged into the Homeric by obsequious bards. Eleventh-century Ireland had long lost its monastic lustre: kings and bishops were mostly nondescript, culture was low, and the island, like late-Mogul India and nineteenth-century Africa, was ripe for domination barely disguised as alliances and treaties; for plunder, legal trickery, savagery.

A small 'Pale' of vigorous mainland freebooters was established around Dublin, a base for expansion. Henry also routed a rebellion led by his eldest son, received formal submission from the Welsh and from the Scots King, and then, in 1155, approval for his Irish policy from the first and last English Pope, Hadrian IV:

> You have shown Us your desire to enter the Irish isle to impose Law on its people and eradicate the weeds of vice . . . and to maintain the rights of the Irish Church whole and without loss . . . We therefore allow you to enter that island and there do all that pertains to God's Honour and Ireland's Salvation. May the people hail you with honour and revere you as their Lord.

Henry's son, John Lackland, summoned a conference of Irish chieftains, then wrecked it by his inability to resist the temptation to tweak their beards, a gesture believable in one reputed to have sought aid from Morocco by an offer to turn Moslem while in effect surrendering England to Pope Innocent III.

In a version of *apartheid*, Edward III's Statute of Kilkenny prohibited inter-racial marriage. By 1390 the Irish judiciary was reserved for Englishmen, and much of the land had been confiscated. Richard II's deputy, the Earl of March, was killed; cruelty and neglect wasted Irish resources. When Richard visited Ireland in 1394, he nevertheless promised a statesmanship not to be repeated until Gladstone and Parnell:

> Because that in our land of Ireland there are three kinds of people, the Wild Irish our enemies, the Irish rebels and the obedient English, it appears to us and our Council that, considering that the Irish rebels are perhaps so rebellious by reason of the grievances and wrongs done to them on the one part, and that redress hath not been made to them on the other part; and that likewise if they be not wisely managed, and put into good hope of favour, they

will probably join our enemies; wherefore, it shall not be any fault of ours that a general pardon be not granted them.

Richard's deposition extinguished precarious hopes of wise management and reconciliation.

In Scotland, while the Highlands remained Celtic, the Lowlands were an amalgam of Irish, Picts, Bretons, Normans, English, unruly nobles holding estates on either side of the Border, where cattle-rustling and banditry were endemic. Edward I, powerful and arrogant lawyer, a tall, intimidating presence, demanded the clear-cut, the orderly and unambiguous, hated the unsymmetrical and all unfinished business. He thus envisaged an island unified by laws, institutions, castles, the throne. He expelled some sixteen thousand Jews from England in 1274. Already 'Lord of Ireland', he revived dubious claims to Scotland, then enjoying an unusually peaceful well-being. His legal and military attempts were repulsed, and his son, the sport-loving, hedonistic, unwarlike Edward II, then suffered overwhelming defeat at Bannockburn in 1302.

Edward I illustrated less the medieval mind than one feature of the mind itself. Variously 'modern' he yet, when dying, commanded that his bones be carried by his son's army invading Scotland, implying faith in their magical powers. Similarly, Chinese today, versed in technology, physics, Marxist atheism, yet fear spirits, consult geomancers before building a new house, and appease the dead; a great Scottish scientist can be terrified of the dark. In solitude, many relapse into childhood.

In Wales, Celtic, but with some residue of the Roman Empire, Edward I was more successful. Anglo-Welsh antipathies had not abated. A chronicler complained of 'a dreadful and unendurable mass of Welsh . . . a raging mob', swelling a revolt against Stephen in 1140. Gerald of Wales, writing for Henry II, in his *Journey through Wales* described his people as avoiding drunkenness and gluttony, devoting themselves to national defence and care of horses and furniture, yet also as condoning plunder, not only of foreigners but of each other.

Repeating tales of Arthur and Albion, as propaganda, Edward enforced his rule over Welsh towns and ports, and by means of English plantations, bishoprics, castles, extinguished the chances of a Welsh State. He first imposed a totally English administration; having thus provoked renewed war in defence of Welsh laws he relented, allowing both laws to co-exist, not under Westminster but within a distinct Principality, guarded by resolute frontier lords. With boorish humour he beheaded Llewellyn ap Griffith, grandson of Llewellyn the Great, for refusing homage; then crowned the head with ivy and fixed it above London Bridge to fulfil a prophecy that Llewellyn would wear his crown in London.

Welsh administrators remained until Henry VIII's final Act of Union in 1526, which ordained English as the only official language. Native resentments smouldered throughout: French landed in support of the Welsh hero Owain Glyn Dŵr and his Scots allies; Welsh fought on both sides at Agincourt. A talkative people, they might have been perplexed by Katherine of France, widow of Henry V, dismissing the Welsh servants of her ill-fated second husband, Owen, ancester of the Tudors, with: 'They are the goodliest dumb creatures that I ever saw.'

The Welsh language was tougher to overcome, and, save for Chaucer, Langland and Malory, much medieval English literature seems inferior to Celtic. In the wake of Edward's shock-tactics, the speech of St David and Illtyd actually reached new splendours, comparable to any in Europe. Though English seeped into Welsh culture, it did not obliterate it. Welsh appetites remained lively, feeding on memories, grandly enlarged, of Llewellyn the Great and Owain; of famous quarrels, raids, loves, betrayals, tragedies and jokes. Welsh poetry remained bright, into the seventeenth century; no English lawyer could dislodge its sharp rhythms, startling compounds and juxtapositions, the sleight-of-hand imageries of a people fiercely independent yet not isolated. Christianity broadened the range of Albion with its Arthur, Kai, supernatural boar and magic towers: the Welsh lyrics suggest French courtliness, Daffyd ap Gwlym salutes Ovid, master of Metamorphosis and graceful eroticism. Professor Clancy notes the Welsh tone within the English of Smart's *A Song to David*, in Herbert's poem 'Prayer', in Crashaw, much of Henry Vaughan's lyric, and in Hopkins. Traditional Welsh verbal intricacies affected William Barnes, so admired by Hardy, and Dylan Thomas. In Clancy's translation, the fourteenth-century Gruffudd Gryg's *The April Moon*, as subtle and fresh as anything in contemporary English, begins:

> April moon, hideous hue,
> Mournful is your expression,
> Glassy coin, silver-coated,
> Stark moon, men would think you slain.
> Each day your dejected hue

You alter, face of anger,
Blushing before rushing winds,
Blue-grey before rain rages.
Pallid crust, sorry circle,
I languish, are you in Love?

Beneath lordly wars and tournaments, ritual ceremonies, intrigues and preenings, the common English round of hovel and tavern remained coarse and raucous, only grudgingly dedicated to the dignity and duty of honest toil. Casual, self-assured, wenching, scolding, boozing – 'booze' has been reckoned the second-oldest London word – people, not yet nationalist, were (save during wars) pledged less to England than to parish, county, manorial lord, united perhaps by religion, certainly by suspicion of those from the other side of the hill, let alone from overseas. A Venetian comment of 1500 remained topical for centuries: 'They have an antipathy to foreigners and imagine that these never come into their island but to make themselves master of it, and to usurp their goods.'

The England of Fashion – the phallic shoes of Richard II's courtiers enraged moralists – manners, cultural babble was still subservient to France, whence arrived Royal Tennis, probably originating in Italian street-games and formalised in Gallic cloisters: a French nun is said to have invented the backhand. In architecture, Edward III's leading mason was foremost in the emergence of native Perpendicular which, shedding the massed complexities of English Decorated, joined linear simplicity to aesthetics of light; little can rival the trim, lofty proportions of Gloucester choir, Norwich cloisters, Wells arches, the cool assurance of York Minister, masterful but not forbidding. Domestically, by the fifteenth century French and Low Countries brickwork had been imported, sometimes as ballast, to join English stone, timber, wattle and daub.

The élite read Latin Classics – Virgil, Ovid, Horace notably affected English literature – German and Breton Romance, sang Provençal *aubades*, listened to French and Flemish music. Native polyphony and instrumental virtuosity, however, were preparing significant additions to Western music. Chaucer, who travelled abroad in Royal employment, was imbued with Homer, Virgil, Ovid, French and Italian vernacular stories, Christian and pagan fable and allegory, though attentive to English gossip and popular life. Shakespeare omitted him from *Richard II*, where John of Gaunt complains of his nephew's modish court:

> ... there are fond
> Lascivious metres, to whose venom sound
> The open ear of youth doth always listen;
> Report of fashions in proud Italy,
> Whose manners still our tardy apish nation
> Limps after in base imitation.

From Italy would arrive not only gossip about sodomy and Papal scandal, but improved methods of banking and exchange essential for island independence. 'Lombards', with their quick-witted couriers, latest with 'the news', were resented as unscrupulous usurers, less vulnerable than the departed Jews, until Edward III, with even less scruple, coolly reneged on his debts. Yet some emotional parallel existed between Italian and urban English. The latter, loving tunes and bawdy verse, gaudy display, noisy crowds and processions, had dispositions somewhat operatic, until tamed by Puritanism. Also, the English were quarrelsome, litigious, prone to sudden violence. Lincoln, with a population of five thousand, held 114 murder trials in 1202. Not all would assent to the Italian proverb that the strongest on earth were the Pope, the Emperor, and the Good Loser.

Scholarship prospered throughout thirteenth-century Christendom, strengthened by the rise of Franciscan and Dominican friars. Early universities – Padua, Salerno, Bologna, Paris – were followed by Orleans, Montpellier, Salamanca, Cambrai, Prague, Cracow, Buda, Cologne, Pavia. Quarrels in twelfth-century Paris caused migration to Oxford, where further ill-will made many depart to Cambridge. The system of autonomous colleges was an English feature. At Paris the English, like the French, Normans, Picards, had their own quarter and, with Scots and Irish, sustained a name for rowdiness, irreverence, indecency. A favourite student song, 'Back and Sides go Bare', was bawled to a tune subsequently rearranged for 'All Things Bright and Beautiful'.

Matthew Paris of St Albans wrote and painted in Scandinavia; a thirteenth-century monk, William, reached China and saw printed money; Gerald of Wales was schooled in Paris, knew Rome, travelled through Europe. Michael the Scot, physician, mathematician and astrologer, was adviser to Frederick II at Palermo: he was reputed to possess the ability to fly, and gained unfavourable mention in Dante's *Inferno*.

A new tone, often at odds with received opinion, was audible in intellectual life. John Duns the Scot – 'dunce' – Oxford Franciscan, confronted Aquinas, the mighty Dominican, 'the Universal Doctor', debating the inadequacy of reason to prove the existence of God and the immortal soul; many rated him victorious. Another Oxford Franciscan, Roger Bacon (*c.* 1214–92), 'Doctor Admirabilis', was a mixture of Prospero and H.G. Wells, 'the English Faust'; natural philosopher, astronomer, astrologer, physicist, alchemist; his geographical speculations interested Columbus. He knew some Arabic and Jewish chemistry; worked on optics, and gunpowder; brooded over the possibility of flying, of power-driven ships, of diving machines, of poison gas. No mere scholastic, he felt theological debate distracted him from research. He held that the foundations of knowledge were placed, not in faith, miracles, Other World, but in mathematics.

The persistent spell of Albion enveloped Bacon in his own lifetime. Rumours sped through Europe of his use of natural condensation to throw a bridge from England to France, and of his invention of a double mirror to outwit both Satan and students, one surface revealing activities the world over, the other contenting itself with the ability to light candles. Students, however, not only lit candles with it, but would see their families ill or dying, so that they fled home. The Oxford authorities then destroyed the mirror, though not before two students, perceiving in it their fathers fighting, themselves quarrelled, fatally stabbing each other. In another legend, Bacon made a pact with the Devil, promising him his soul provided he could die neither in a church nor out of it. He abjured magic, destroyed his book of spells, and had the last laugh by making a cell in a church wall and dying there.

More soberly, Bacon saw his works proscribed as heretical, was twice imprisoned, once for fourteen years, a sentence energetically championed by Pope Nicholas III. Neither England nor Europe very visibly applauded his diagnosis of the causes of ignorance: the acceptance of statements without examining their sources, deference both to fashion and majority opinion, preference for the facile as against the laborious.

Oxford Franciscans had no awe of Continental Dominicans, the engineers of the Inquisition, which they were not allowed to introduce into England. John of Salisbury, classically-minded Bishop of Chartres, once secretary to Becket, adapted a moral treatise of Cicero to justify killing a cruel ruler, in terms which Pastor Bonhöffer might have approved. Anti-metaphysical, with tolerant common sense, he had no affection for Chivalry, grumbling that knights feasted daily but shirked hard work; but he also preached: 'Whoever he may be that is willing to suffer for his faith, whether he be little lad or grown man, Jew or Gentile, Christian or Infidel, man or woman, it matters not at all; whoever dies for justice dies a martyr, a defender of Christ's cause.'

Another English opponent of Aquinas at Paris, William of Occam, like John, strove to separate reason from exaggerated dogma; he felt the absolute authority of Pope and Church unjustified by scripture and good sense. No determinist, he championed free-will, may have influenced Wyclif. Bishop Roger Grosseteste of Lincoln (?1170–1253) was the first to translate Aristotle's *Ethics* into English. He and Bacon, John and William, pragmatic, independent, harked back to Pelagius, and provided a philosophical atmosphere rather than a school. In all this was a mode of inquiry, specifically English, in which certain mysteries could be left mysterious, perhaps not very important, unsusceptible to rational probings. Against this, politics, law, health, social morals were best not left to God, Fate, ancient writings, but were always urgent, challenging human will.

Though sharing Continental religious and feudal symbols, Gothic styles, England was developing in ways predictable in a defensible island. In the second half of the fourteenth century Wyclif, a Leicestershire rector, sturdily protested against wealthy and casuistical priestcraft, translated portions of the Bible (impairing ecclesiastical monopoly), favoured women priests, with effects reaching distant Bohemia. Himself married to a Bohemian, Richard II had much cultural prestige abroad, where English engraving, sculpture, ornamental alabaster and brass, painted murals, pewter and enamel, and illumination, commanded respect. Cross-currents seemed limitless.

Yet Richard was another Royal failure; responsive to painting and literature, cleanliness, fastidious meals and fashions, admired by Froissart for sensitive charm, patron of Chaucer, he was pacific in an aggressive age, but without the political skills needed to grapple with loss of empire, military defeat, greedy and irresponsible vassals and relations.

Wyclif had taught 'Dominion founded on Grace' – that priestly power should proceed from moral authority, not from wealth, arms, tradition, monopoly of the Latin Bible. England, however, distracted by internal unrest and 'Roses' clamour, played small part in fifteenth-century Europe's attempt to reform the Papacy, submit the Pope to international clerical

councils, so as to prevent religious and nationalist revolution alrea
threatened.

In 1300, England had not been so cosmopolitan since Roman tim
Gascons, Flemings, Germans, Italians crowded to such great trade fairs
Winchester. A hundred thousand foreigners might visit Becket's Canterbu
tomb in a single year. Pilgrims, students, merchants, emissaries, advent
ers swarmed to English ports, jostled on the roads. The English themselv
though most were legally bound to their manorial lord, might accompa
that lord in foreign wars, or venture overseas as licensed pilgrims, or as v
unteer crusaders. Chaucer's Knight fought in Lithuania (then a considera
empire), in Spain, Asia Minor, North Africa.

English pilgrims assiduously joined the multitudes tramping
Compostela, reputed burial place of the Greater St James. Little was kno
of James, nothing of any sojourn in Spain. Vera and Helmut Hell record t
'In the eighth century . . . St Beatus, who came from the Liébana Valley
Santander) . . ., was a theologian of European reputation, known to t
court of Charlemagne, a friend of Alcuin's.' This intellectual bravo, hos
to some current Christian–Moorish collaboration, wishing to impede Isla
'accepted as a fact the information in a corrupted list of the apostles' missi
fields that credited St James with Spain instead of Jerusalem (*Hispani*
instead of *Hierusalem* or *Hieroslyman*).' Henry VI licensed the departure
2,310 pilgrims in 1445.

Early medieval diplomats and courtiers travelled with considerable r
inues, a bishop or lesser nobleman with perhaps forty. Becket once took t
hundred to Paris: Edward I crossed the Channel with a thousand hors
Travel was no faster than in Roman days, though Richard II in crisis g
loped seventy miles through the night.

Fourteenth-century commerce, though interrupted by war and plag
was laying the foundations of a new England with its attendant inventio
varied employments, use of money, as the Angevin Empire collapsed a
the wars of reconquest failed. Normans and Angevins, increasingly confir
to England, small but profitable, had to develop a new identity. A grow
compound of English personality could be discerned. The spirit of perso
independence was common to almost all classes, strengthened by la
compelling 'free men' to own arms and train in them, at the expense
ball-games and gambling. Langland, in *Piers Plowman*, observed t

dependence among the poor, their need for self-esteem, for avoidance of
tronising charity and neighbourly espionage:

> Pitiful it is to read the cottage woman! Woe,
> Aye, and many another that puts a good face on it,
> Ashamed to beg, ashamed to let the neighbours know
> All that they need, noontide and evening.

An impression remains of people tough, often cussed, unconcerned with
s of empire, aristocratic defeats in France and the subsequent 'Roses'
nastic conflicts at home – unless these ravaged their crops; a people more
umbling than rebellious though, as in 1381, infuriated by unfairness, scep-
al of propaganda, suspicious of jargon-protected authority, ready to
rgain, unwilling to submit totally. Langland was more representative than
at Tyler; his *Piers Plowman* expresses love not of coercive law but of an
ential and classless goodwill, essential to unify society for security,
rmth, Christian love, humane understanding, a vision unlikely but not
possible. A Lebanese judge told V.S. Pritchett that the British were stupid,
ccessful not through brains but through 'character'. Wyndham Lewis
ote in 1948 that the English can be publicly robbed, fooled, ruined,
slaved, but cannot be *defeated*.

In an era of stinking middens and sharp, heaven-pointing spires, of tombs
ere one effigy showed the deceased fully clothed or armoured and another
e same as a fast-decaying corpse, of painted lords and steepled ladies,
mps and whores, mountebanks and hucksters, of sleek bishops and lepers,
pal legates and jewelled rapists, musical kings and highly educated bullies,
ry yokels and bellied merchants, of hangmen and lutanists; ugliness and
ualor existed within reach of woods and fields, beggars with crippled limbs
d famished eyes crouched at the gate of some earl with a year's revenue on
s back and fingers. Perpendicular churches dominated with calm assur-
ce villages where, it has been reckoned, it took two years to add one sur-
ving birth to the population.

Medieval England was underpinned not by decorated horses, heraldic
ns, unicorns and leopards, but by sheep, whose wool conditioned the
nest policy towards Europe. This animal served Europe well – England
tter – producing not only wool but meat, milk, parchment, felt, string,
ndle-fat, manure.

Burgundian Cistercians, early emigrating to the Pennines – named after
Albion god – founded sheep farms whose wool of outstanding excellence,

exported to eager north Italian and Flemish weavers, was England's ch
economic asset. Sheep farming extended over many spaces depopulated
the Black Death, and precipitated three centuries of landlords enclosi
common lands, not for the common good but for their sheep. It initiated
concern for the Low Countries' independence from Spain and France whi
persisted despite seventeeth-century wars with Holland and the Cit
rivalry with Antwerp. Britain was chief guarantor of Belgian independen
in 1830 and, ostensibly on her behalf, fatefully entered the Great War in 191

Though the proclaimed reason for the Hundred Years' War was the reco
ery of English supremacy in France – the lost lands, lost hopes, lost cause
the need to preserve the Gascon wine trade and Flemish wool markets w
more concrete. Edward III's nostalgia for the Albion of Round Tab
Guinevere's pledges and brocaded glove, chivalric rites, personal glory w
on the verge of being blown away with the introduction of gunpowder fro
China, and the disciplined application of an older technology: the hiss
Welsh long-bow arrows – significantly, a cloth-yard long – then the har
retort of guns, sounded a requiem for the flashing paladins.

Ghent's four thousand weavers and their clients looked for defen
against their feudal, outdated lords. England won the battles but lost t
war, and the weavers' own defeat at Roosebeke in 1382 increased Flemi
immigration to England, where export of raw wool changed to that of man
factured cloth. This, paying for the huge Perpendicular wool churches
East Anglia, influenced native architecture and comfort, class-attire, deco
tion – a fashion started for panels imitating the lines and folds of clo
hanging or stacked. It gave further opportunities for talented, ambitio
merchants, their lawyers and middle-men, who, from social and religio
motives, subsidised new churches, guildhalls, grammar schools. Unlike th
Continental counterparts, English aristocrats did not disdain to use th
acres for profit, and with the cloth revolution the pace of class-exchang
quickened. New titles emblazoned new riches, sometimes thrusting asi
the knightly but indigent, as observed sourly by Shakespeare's Richard II

> Since every Jack became a gentleman
> There's many a gentle person become a Jack.

For centuries, a solid tangle of inter-connections bound the English cla
system, particularly after the aristocracy lost its Norman exclusiveness, ev
unity. Oliver Cromwell sat in the Commons with eighteen relatives, socia

very varied. A downward social course was represented by John Bunyan, a tinker, descended from landowners who had prospered, then failed.

By the mid fourteenth century English was the official language, though as late as Henry VIII at least one abbey, Laycock, was still speaking Norman French. In churches, inscriptions no longer read '*Ici gist Henri de Aldryngton qui murast le VIII de August*'. More typical would be: 'Man com and see how schalle alle dede be.'

Chaucer was writing not only in English but in an English tone still apposite today: ironic, appreciative of human oddity, allergic to moralising but noting people's faults; tolerant, but indignant at blatant hypocrisy, deceit, cruelty.

This marked strand in English literature is as ineradicable as the fluid lines of Celtic and Northumbrian art. It avoids frills and unnecessary ornamentation, resides in clarity, briskness; usually (not invariably) humorous, ironic, sly or rollicking. It would be whimsical to categorise Wyclif, Thomas More, Skelton, Cranmer as anything other than English. *Henry IV* and *Bartholomew Fair* can be squeezed for Englishness in every line. Bunyan, Milton, Clarendon, Defoe, Johnson, Fielding maintained the tradition, and it is easy to add names from succeeding centuries.

To survive, people had to dig, hedge, plough, reap, brew, sew, pickle, cook, trap; pray, steal, meddle, entertain friars, peruse maps of Hell sold by streetwise frauds, daydream of Paradise, Jerusalem, and golden gryphons bearing Alexander aloft. The imagination, of Christendom and England alike, rarely troubled by Aquinas, Occam, Grosseteste, was cluttered with flakes of antiquity, unsystematically arranged. Famine stalked, the Plague Maiden rode, ague set in, the bailiff prowled, the baby died and the miller grinned. Millers, local monopolists, profiteering as in Chaucer, were considered insatiable lechers 'whose prowess', E.P. Thompson reflected, 'is still perpetuated in a vernacular meaning of the word *grinding*.'

Progress was not a pre-Renaissance ideal, as it drew people further from Eden, the Incarnation, Rome, nearer to death and Judgement. Village memories, tenacious of old wrongs, tragedies, jokes, untrained historically, easily degenerated into inaccurate proverbs and charms, tavern ditties bowdlerised but still foul, and seasonal mummeries. A few lines might have been salvaged from the blurred, gigantic wreckage of Classical literature – 'Men of Troy, trust not the Horse' – but, unrestricted by academic Time, illiterates would not have known or cared whether Ulysses, Arthur, Caesar had existed four hundred thousand, forty thousand or four hundred years previously. All history, as Croce would one day philosophise, was contemporary. Steven Runciman has recalled a feudal clan, boasting descent from David and Bathsheba, provoking irritation by continually referring to the Virgin as 'Cousin Mary'. Creative misunderstandings masqueraded as History. Italian peasants, deceived by a statue of Virgil standing on a book, revered him as a magician who could read through his feet.

In its mental images England was not English or even an island, but a small segment of Western imagination bounded only by sky and grave, Far Cathay and the Other World. In the fourteenth-century anonymous English masterpiece *Sir Gawain and the Green Knight* is to be found the primitive and courtly, blood-sacrifice and chivalric convention, horror and beauty, Albion and Christian England. The Suffolk Green Children emerging from beneath a Woolpit field, from a twilit underworld, partly resemble Tages, Etruscan Wise Child, springing from a furrow, teaching haruspicy, then vanishing. Peasants everywhere remained close to the earth, close to the Other Worlds; and perhaps most classes feared the dead staring on All Souls' Eve, and knew that on Midsummer Night they could leave the dreaming body and, like the Ghost in *Hamlet*, roam free until cock-crow; they might also wait in the church porch, to see the spirits of those fated to die within the year.

For William Blake the imagination was not 'a state', but existence itself. The medieval imagination seldom learnt from monks and schoolmen, more often from a painted saint, unusual cloud, dusky trees, flamboyant emblems on a passing banner, a distant tower seeming to turn with the sun. Symbols lay in sticks, stones, animals. Even earls and bishops knew that planets made music, imps lurked behind midden, shed or even scuttle, that women's souls were smaller than men's. Human lives drifted beneath an unseen or rarely seen pantheon of archangels and angels, devils and saints, magical relics and faraway princesses, all hung very loosely on the supremacy of God, Satan, Fate. The England of lawyers and clothiers was yet littered with chunks of Albion, alchemical yearnings, astrological portents, the difference between dream and daydream barely understood. The mind thrived not only on hopes of field-strips, even coins, but on much debarred from schoolroom texts. Christendom loved St Christina for piety, in defying her pagan father

66

over marriage: she was beaten, but smiled; she had her tongue slashed out, but flung it at the executioner and blinded him; she was hanged, strapped to a blazing wheel and, garlanded with snakes, weighted by a millstone, thrown into the sea; but reached Paradise triumphant. Women may have wept, men sighed or chuckled, over twelve adulterous wives refusing a stew in which floated their knightly paramours' genitals, preferring to die of starvation.

Richly illuminated bestiaries, stock medieval fare, disclose something of ancestral thought, with their hybrids and fantasies – unicorns, centaurs, gryphons, dragons, easier to describe than to discover. Richard Barber, a noted medievalist, judges bestiaries to have been most brilliant around 1250, peculiarly English, the Ashmole Bestiary with its lavish golds perhaps the most luxuriant. His translation of the Bodleian Bestiary discloses the way-wardness of free imagination: 'The monoceros is a monster with a horrible bray; it has the body of a horse, the feet of an elephant, and a tail like that of a stag. A horn of extraordinary splendour projects from the middle of its forehead, four feet in length, and so sharp that anything it strikes is easily pierced by the blow.'

All was still fluid as Celtic and Northumbrian art, a path into the sky. Devils could terrify but also amuse; one soubriquet for Satan was (like Fagin's) 'The Merry Old Gentleman'; another, more abstruse, more gnostic, 'The Wronged One'. For the oppressed, for the over-sophisticated, Hell could be a comfort, even a delight, as Beauty can yearn for the Beast.

'And it befell upon a day . . .' England remembered the doomed, sterile lovers, Classical and Celtic: Dido and Aeneas, Guinevere and Lancelot, Graine and Diarmid, Yseult (the Celtic Helen) and Tristan, and their avatars, Héloïse and Abélard. They responded to some deep-rooted hanker-ing for lost causes, the release of tears, satisfaction at another's plight. It made a baleful footnote to cults of success and complacency.

The Albion of Jack the Giant Killer, Godiva, Merlin, Herne the Hunter, Tom Hickathrift, Hynd Horn suffused medieval tales of youngest sons, pert jokers, ghosts and miracles, of Hugh of Lincoln, Fair Rosamund, Henry II, the Jealous Queen and the Maze, and the Witch of Yarrowford. The cycle of Robin Hood, master of trickery and disguise, enemy of chilly legality, was English to the core. He is a lament for lost freedom, lost woods, for wild youth and communal simplicity. His adventures subsume many heroes', in and out of Albion: Hereward, Eustace the Monk, Fulk Fitzwarin, Clym of the Plough, Adam Bell, and William of Cloudesley, the English William

Tell. He was a character in May Day rites with magic undertones, a
Professor J.C. Holt mentions Victorian railwaymen using chips of h
alleged gravestone to cure toothache.

Robin Hood has been classed as an archetypal mischief figure, essenti
to prevent social stagnation. He is also associated with the colour gree
often suggestive of the unearthly, ambiguous, drugged or forbidden: tl
Green Man, the Green Knight, stalked the edges of history, disruptiv
mocking.

'Hode' was an ancient name for Odin. In a fifteenth-century poer
Robin was 'the famous murderer'. Robert Cecil jeered at the Gunpowd
Plotters as 'Robin Hoods'. A verse of 1714 called him a murderous highwa
man, and 'hood' still denotes a criminal. Friar Tuck may derive from
Sussex priest and killer, Robert Stafford. Much of the outlaws' anti-Norma
radical sympathies appear to be the romantic inventions of writers lil
Walter Scott and Joseph Ritson, of a few traditions sentimentalised
ballads. Nevertheless, humorous, sardonic, resourceful, loyal, Robin h;
more rounded and varied personality than Arthur, the Irish Finn MacCo
the Indian Rama. He is an exemplar of decency, redresser of wrongs, nurse
hero, English as Betsey Trotwood, Becky Sharp, Archdeacon Grantle
Phileas Fogg and Sherlock Holmes. Holt, authority on medieval outlaw l;
erature, postulates Robin Hood not as myth but as historical personag
probably from bandit regions near York or Wakefield. Detached from an
clericalism, class conflicts and peasant subversiveness following agraria
changes, the legends may have been 'a yeoman's substitute for the knight
Arthurian romances'.

> Sir Roger of Doncaster
> By the Prioress he lay,
> And there betrayed gude Robyn Hode
> By their false play.

Christendom distrusted science: it had no biblical sanction, was too great
indebted both to pagan antiquity and to contemporary Jews and Arabs, wi
their suspect innovations such as the fork, algebra, 'Arabic' numerals (fro
India) and the concept of zero, anaesthetics – which might make women
childbirth forget Eve's sin – and regular baths (bath houses were associate
with brothels and vanity). The Roman Lucretius knew more about ator
than did all Plantagenet England. He, Democritus and Epicurus had elir.
inated gods from the workings of the universe, substituting atomic dete

minism. 'Material objects', Lucretius wrote, 'are of two kinds: atoms, and atomic compounds. No force can overwhelm them, their absolute solidity preserves them indefinitely.' Sin, prayer, divine retribution, Other World survival, were superstitious vanities. Until the Renaissance revival, students were confined to Grammar, Logic, Rhetoric; Arithmetic, Geometry, Astronomy, Music: useful, but over-academic. Girls were denied all of them. Ordinary congregations depended on priests barely literate who, gabbling from the Latin Bible, might be almost as ignorant of Latin as were their flocks. Rome's neglect of the English parish priest was dangerous, ultimately fatal.

Medicine was advancing in Salerno, Montpellier, Moorish Spain. Surgery was liable to be arraigned as a blasmphemous attempt to obstruct the Divine Will or improve on God's handiwork, though dissections took place in Italy in 1306. Erroneous Aristotelian doctrines of the Four Elements, the Four Humours, were very unhelpful; and the bloodletting which resulted from them could be murderous. Most English remained loyal to herbal bromides, charms, prayers: East Anglians swallowed live spiders against the Plague. Further relief out of church was apparently provided by drugs culled from broom, poppy, henbane, hemp, giving sensations of flight, luxuriant Other World visions, and self-delusions sufficiently grandiose to invite accusations of witchcraft.

Sickness allowed favours to none, the Wheel of Fortune was as potent as the Cross. A King of Portugal died of plague – so did Holbein; Henry IV's wasting disease was rumoured to be leprosy. Against plague, doctors were as helpless as their rivals, the priests. Images of St Roch, patron saint of the plague, might be paraded, red cloths and pigs' bladders soaked in oil be waved. Grotesque masks were donned to scare away the grisly visitor, and mirrors brandished so that it would flee its own ugliness. Pots were banged, weapons discharged towards the infectious east. Milk left in dishes might suck in plague imps. Dried bats and toads were left on boils, verses were recited above saffron and snakes' spines.

The new schools made small impact on such credulity. The fifteenth-century Polydor Vergil repeated a story, about Kentish men who reviled Thomas Becket, which confirmed many Continental misgivings about the English: when Becket, in disgrace, rode through Strood, the villagers, to show their Royalist anger, cut off his horse's tail. 'But for this profane and inhospitable act they covered themselves with eternal reproach, for it so happened that, by God's will, all the children of the perpetrators were born with tails, like animals.' Vergil acknowledged, however, that this mark of infamy vanished with the extinction of the guilty families.

Aquinas's 'Hell exists but none are in it' would have passed unheeded by those transfixed by visions of crowded hell-wains and scalding pits. They would have felt more kinship with John of Salisbury, who remarked that he abhorred nothing that made him drunk. To them the grave was both stinking horror and the gateway, if tithes had been paid, dues rendered, rites performed, to eternal happiness. This sufficed for the unmetaphysical English temperament, probably contented with Paul's promise to the Corinthians: 'It is sown a natural body, it shall rise a spiritual body.' English mysticism was upheld by the fourteenth-century nun Julian of Norwich, whose visionary *Sixteen Revelations of Divine Love* enclosed a shrouded, probably censored, early belief in which Jesus's concept of divinity embraced himself as 'Mother'. Most English, while not notably respectful of virgins, had heartfelt adoration for the Virgin. Robert Graves asserted that 'Merrie England' was actually 'Mary's England'.

More powerful than metaphysical conceits was the authoritarian tradition, sometimes becoming ruthless dogmatism, the logic of narrowness, running from both Saint Augustines and Wilfrid to Thomas More, Jane Grey, Mary I, to Knox and Laud. Opposed to them were long-forgotten Pelagius, sensible Wyclif, 'judicious' Hooker, and Elizabeth I, who defined theology as ropes of sand or sea-slime leading to the moon: 'There is but one Faith and one Jesus Christ, the rest is a dispute about trifles.' Trenchant towards moral exclusiveness, she observed to the Puritan Dr Laurence Humphries at Oxford in 1566: 'Master Doctor, that loose robe becomes you well; I wonder your notions should be so narrow.' Asked whether he was a Christian, Clem Attlee snapped: 'Accept the Christian ethic. Can't stand the mumbo-jumbo!'

The doctrine of the Trinity could never have absorbed English minds, and to that of Atonement, though it owed much to Anselm, Archbishop of Canterbury, they probably preferred Lionheart's rumoured retort to a reproach from a bishop: 'You advise me to dismiss my three daughters, Pride, Avarice, Lust. Well then, I relinquish them to the most deserving – my pride to the Templars, my avarice to the Cistercians, and my lust to the Bishops.' Richard's subjects, though loyal to his heroic legend, may also have chuckled at a report that the golden warrior had perished, hit by a frying-pan shot from a giant crossbow.

Catholicism had to discipline rambling, unco-ordinated beliefs floating on a groundswell of rebelliousness, scepticism, temptations from priapic paganism, ventilated by periodic licensed mockery of Church and State at carnivals, fairs, Feasts of Fools, communal saturnalia. These were bawdy reversals of status led by clowns, Boy Bishops, Lords of Misrule, freakish dancers in animal disguise imitating immemorial Transformation myths.

One stabilising axis was the parish church, a centre of worship, theatre, art, where the supernatural touched ground, carry-tale gossips crowded the aisle, petty thieves and pedlars gathered, children played, criminals sought sanctuary, animals wandered, old folk huddled at the wall. Professor Duby holds that medieval people were seldom alone, except the mad, 'marginal figures who were hunted down'. When freed from their labours, people crowded into markets, stews, taverns, sports gatherings, churches.

Since the Reformation, the prevailing atmosphere of English churches has been grey, soft or bleak, patched with Victorian stained glass, memorial brasses overlooked by Puritan ravages, a few regimental flags. Earlier, a church was a brilliant interplay of idealism and realism, awe and covert satire, tyrannical threats and elate promises, in words, gestures, colours, tinted sunbeams cutting through clouds of incense, and the familiar yet hypnotic monotony of Gregorian chant. Other World visions and moral shorthand were displayed in frescos, altar cloths, windows, statuary, all with depths of symbolism. Everything was something else, one's very name was an unseen cord attached to a guardian angel. 'East' could designate Heaven: 'North', Hell. Painted on a typical Wheel of the Five Senses are 'Taste', monkey; 'Touch', spider's web; 'Hearing', boar; 'Sight', cock; 'Smell', vulture.

In a church, people recognised the painter's brush as Luke; a centaur was the humanity and brutishness in man, a butterfly the soul; St Mark's lion was also Resurrection, through a belief that its roar could revive dead cubs; the pelican was Christ's self-sacrifice, since the bird was thought to feed its nestlings with its own blood. Willow betokened tragic love, as in Desdemona's song; yew, death; a snake, both evil and eternity; and a candle, immortality. The church itself meant the journey to Paradise; gargoyles – vicious, grotesque or comic, turbaned and glaring, scaled and mocking, obstacles on the way – might be racist caricatures.

Some six thousand English churches gave support to Chesterton's belief that, with the machine, men ceased to be masters of craft and merely became masters of other men. Clustered leaves, fruit, heads, decorated bosses, crockets, corbels, capitals and screens; birds like spoonbill and bittern, now almost lost, pelicans-in-their-piety, mermaids, bears and ragged staffs adorned pew-ends, misericords, fonts, pulpits. Golden flying angels holding up East Anglican roofs indicated an existence outside feuding, prying, back-biting, practical joking, but old resentments flickered in the carving of a cowled fox preaching to a goose. Memorial brasses reveal attitudes to children, class, pets, death; and the ascent of the professional classes and the decline of knights, traceable in sober robes, furs, ruffs, hairstyles, pens, ledgers, books, and in armour flaunting useless extravagance, florid unreality.

Small carved details, murals, painted screen panels – such imaginative touches helped provide relief from Break-Back Field, infant mortality, violence, the haggard drama at the gallows. Communal arts also embellished some sixty festivals of the Christian year, many inherited from Albion: Christmas, Candlemas, Easter, May Day, Whitsun, Midsummer, Lammas, Harvest, Michaelmas, All-Hallows, Christmas and many more, each with its emblems, carols, rituals.

The Reformation scraped off icons, smashed windows, beheaded statues, whitewashed the walls, crusading against idolatrous vanities, substituting an atmosphere, an imagination anchored to The Word, whether in sermon or printed books, necessitating an absence of graphic distractions. The shadowy, the half-glimpsed, the mysterious were dispersed by more clear-cut Old Testament alternatives, by vengeance and rewards, learned rhetoric, fearful analogies, and much painful logic. In 1599 the Mayor of Chester attacked the props used in the Mystery Plays there, causing 'the gyauntes in the midsomer show to be broken, and not to goe; the Devil in his feathers he put awaye . . . and the dragon and the naked boys'. As always, there was gain, in resplendent music, more trustworthy scholarship, less disorder; what were lost were the mediating reassurances of the Catholic priests, the robust, raggle-taggle jostle of loosely-organised communities, the profane delights of much church art. Yet not all of these were eliminated by reformers. A post-Reformation decorators' bill survives from Telscombe in Sussex: 'To renovating heaven and adjusting the stars, washing servant of the High Priest and putting carmine on his cheeks, and brightening up the flames of hell, putting a new tail on the Devil, and doing odd jobs for the damned, and correcting the Ten Commandments.'

Burford in Oxfordshire, 'Fort by the Ford' over the Windrush, most evocatively named of all rivers, like so many others has a past ample in its variety. A seventh-century conference there attempted to settle the date of aster, over which Celts and Romans were irreconcilable before the Synod of Whitby. Legends of a dragon suggest an eighth-century defeat of Mercia by Wessex under its dragon emblem. Among Lords of the Manor were the Conqueror's half-brother Odo, Bishop of Bayeux, who killed with a mace to avoid spilling Christian blood; King John, reputedly surviving as a were-wolf; Almaury of Evreux; Warwick the Kingmaker – a title apparently invented by one John Major (1469–1550) – who met Edward IV at Burford after victory at Mortimer's Cross; John Dudley, Duke of Northumberland, Jane Grey's father-in-law, Edward VI's Regent and father of Elizabeth's Leicester; and Speaker Lenthall, corrupt capitalist who courageously defied Charles I and, less successfully, Cromwell. Cromwell himself had three mutinous Levellers shot in the churchyard, one 'prisner' carving his name on the font: Anthony Sedley, 1649. The Stuart monument to Sir Lawrence Tanfield suggests his widow's regret that he was not buried somewhere grander, though the church's solid architecture has the dignity of restraint (she would have earned imprisonment in Venice, where boastful snobbery was a legal offence). The Rainoldes tomb seems a tribute to marriage as an affectionate pledge, rather than a mere property deal: 'I go to sleep before you and we shall wake together.' Charles II reputedly trysted Nell Gwynne at the Bull Inn; doubtless they did the same.

5

New Worlds

> Our souls, whose faculties can comprehend
> The wondrous architecture of the world
> And measure every wandering planet's course,
> Still climbing after knowledge infinite
> And always moving as the restless spheres
> Will us to wear ourselves, and never rest
> Until we reach the ripest fruit of all.
>
> Marlowe, *Tamburlaine the Great*

Reformation, Renaissance, Discoveries, transforming Christendom to Europe, subordinating *We* to *I*, gave the West, though still misleadingly Eurocentric in outlook, the chance to rethink religion and philosophy. The future was no longer retreat from Eden or Rome, but a dazzling promise. Sir John Hale has indicated that 'modern' was first used as praise in the sixteenth century. No century since the Roman Antonines could so cheerfully applaud Sophocles' *Antigone*: 'Beyond number are the world's wonders, but none more wonderful than man.' In the art of a Michelangelo, the human body could heroically flaunt itself and, thanks to burgeoning anatomy and physiology, men could find within it possibilities vast as the Pacific. Sanctorius's thermometer and proof by Servetus and William Harvey of the circulation of the blood ejected much antique nonsense about Humours and Elements.

A few thousand seafarers in ships smaller than most village churches altered the globe. Western authority, English imagination, were quickened by reports of vast empires toppled by a few-score whites with guns and horses, by travellers' tales of Golden Men ruling where gold lay in handfuls, glittering under huge equatorial suns. Prospero was a Renaissance Merlin, Caliban a portent, contemptible but ominous in his pathos. Henry VII declined to invest in Columbus but allowed ten pounds to a Bristol Italian, John Cabot, who braved the Atlantic with eighteen men, establishing Newfoundland, a stage in the fortunes of Bristol, a corner-stone of future Empire.

74

Technological advances and the study of matter tamed the role of chance and threatened to demote God from a capricious despot to an architect forced to retire after creating a flawed masterpiece. The objective could rule. A flower was no longer bound up with the Virgin's chastity, the sighs of Venus, the sickness of Love; a beryl ceased to signify domestic bliss, was merely rich in itself. Galileo's telescope discerned no goddess on the moon, a microscope would soon reveal titanic secrets from a broken rock, a smother of dust, from grass and bones. A sense of new time, new space spread from recently-exhumed Classical works, from physics and precise observation, all substituting analysis for faith, for the zodiacal, for the music of the spheres.

At first sight, much of this would seem Poetry's loss; but the new technology replenished literature with contemporary imagery. Here is Francis Quarles, cup-bearer to James I's daughter Elizabeth, the Winter Queen of Bohemia, chronologer to the City of London, father of eighteen, describing the needle of a magnetic compass as it

> First franticks up and down, from side to side,
>   And restless beats his crystall'd Iv'ry case
> With vain impatience; jets from place to place,
>   And seeks the bosom of his frozen bride;
>   At length he slacks his motion, and doth rest
> His trembling point at his bright Pole's beloved breast.

Print, with Venice and Holland publishing well-designed, free-spirited books, together with sonnet, madrigal and new drama, expanded readership, stimulated authorship, while the innovation of linear perspective in art disciplined the loose and sprawling at the expense of vigour and fantasy. Translation also expanded the mental range. National archives began, thin-blooded and detailed enemies of romance and 'If only', refuting the Golden Age, Albion, Camelot, Merrie England. The new individualism could look in mirrors – a Hamlet relishes the mirror – could indulge in written (sometimes published) diaries, journals, confessional verse, accounts, domestic descriptions, preparing for the Novel, in which sonorous but rambling epic and romance gave way to everyday moods, hazards, ambitions, loss, so that readers had less excuse to complain, like Trollope's Georgina Longstaffe: 'I suppose it's just the same with other people, only one doesn't know it.'

Throughout Europe, the Courtier was deposing the Knight. English and French sophisticates realised, through Castiglione's *The Courtier*, that conversation, ease of manner, social nuances could be art, literature becoming life, often self-conscious, facile, artificial, hypocritical, but also graceful, witty, both sexes in equality for feasting, dancing, music, discussion.

Mass-produced encyclopaedias, dictionaries, calendars, popular guides to cooking, crafts, social behaviour, fencing, botany, child-rearing, physics, etymology, medicine, biology, maps, filled the demands of wider-educated readers. They also stablised the authority, not only of authors and experts, but of governments, officials, polemicists: so not all was gain. The confining of imagination, garrulous but vivid, the bypassing of memory, once prolonged by necessity, threatened the spontaneous. With religious turmoil now savaging Europe the Classics, poetry, humanist treatises, rational scholarship, which had just found their way into print, were soon endangered by the surge of sectarian broadsheets, libellous invective, propaganda, weakening science itself. The astronomer Johannes Kepler noted even in 1634 that: 'So long as the Mother, Ignorance, survives, it is not safe for Science, the offspring, to divulge the hidden causes of things.'

The Reformation, aggressively masculine, showed scant interest in the hidden causes of things, and ended by reforming very little which would not have changed independently without the panoply of intolerant insults and religious wars and atrocities which convulsed sixteenth- and seventeenth-century Europe. Scottish yells for 'Jesus and No Quarter' echoed almost everywhere. The superstition of saints, miracles and altars was replaced by veneration of State, Fatherland, Empire, Army.

Beginning as a northern protest against clerical corruption, censorship, idolatry and extortion, the Reformation was a signal opportunity to restore more pristine attitudes, but was squandered in recriminations, then captured and tainted afresh by emergent nationalism throughout the West. What was missed by all sides was Michelangelo's great image on the Sistine Chapel ceiling of Man straining towards God – also of God stretching out towards Man; the idea, too, of God as impersonal, like love, creativity, electricity. In the Nation State, official religion was little more than a government department, most transcendentalism forgone. A bearded God was exhibited as the exclusive patron of each warlike country. 'The religion of Christ', Cardinal Mercier, Archbishop of Malines, could declare in fateful 1933, 'makes patriotism a law.' Renaissance rulers had no interest in Machiavelli's concept of a European Union of some fourteen states, as a tentative move towards peace.

Luther, 'buffoon of genius', used his mastery of language not only to translate the Bible but to vilify his opponents, stoke up German anti-Semitism, urge on destruction. He was appalled by the brutal popular radicalism he himself had unleashed: 'Therefore, let all who can, smite, kill and stab, secretly or publicly, remembering that naught can be more venomous, injurious or diabolical than a rebel.' Pope and Emperor, Henry VIII and Thomas Cromwell, would have no objection to that. 'Be pitiless,' a rival ranted, 'though Esau gives you fair words. Smite Pink Pank on the anvil of Nimrod.' Lutheranism submitted whole-heartedly to the secular State, sanctioning absolutism with its conscription, uniformity, violence: 'If constituted authority instructs you that Two and Two make Five, then you must believe it, even against your conviction.'

The English Reformation was not systematically planned but lurched forward in stages, led by Tudor monarchs, Privy Councillors, magnates and an obsequious Parliament, without much popular support, with rebellious anger in the north. Rumoured Papal antics appeared ludicrous, pagan, at best crafty, though the cynicism of the Medici Pope, Leo X, patron of Michelangelo, is almost refreshing: 'Since God has given us the Papacy, let us enjoy it.' The State expropriation of monastic lands was less for the foundation of grammar schools, hospitals, almshouses than to refill the Royal coffers and reward Royal supporters. It was condoned even under the temporary restoration of Catholicism by Mary I. More's sentence in *Utopia* was glumly topical: 'I can perceive nothing but a certain conspiracy of rich men procuring their own commodities under the name and title of the commonwealth.'

Cranmer's English Prayer Book, and the English Bible, gave people the chance to explore intoxicating visions, startling or judicious injunctions, some compelling stories, some history, some literary masterpieces, and much didacticism. Professor George Steiner writes of Tyndale's translation of the Bible: 'Beyond Shakespeare, it is William Tyndale who is the begetter of the English language as we know it ... no translation act, save Luther's, has been as generative of a whole language.' Moderate Anglicanism, obedient to the Crown, eschewed the fervid religious enthusiasm of the Calvinists. For such puritans the Bible was a spiritual citadel, dramatising conscience, belief, the Inner Light, bringing conviction of personal salvation. Sin could be surmounted by social activity, education, work, sexual restraint, avoidance of temptations.

The Old Testament prophets, in their demands for righteousness and social justice, were more potent than the pantheons of Albion and classicism. Internal drama could be optimistic, with Mr Valiant-for-Truth standing sentinel for honesty, self-reliant individualism; or pessimistic, overburdened by fears of sin and damnation, seeking protection in domestic tyranny (particularly over children) and spiritual arrogance, dividing humanity into Sheep and Goats, Elect and Damned.

Protestant removal of intermediaries – the Virgin, Saints, sacrament-dispensing priests, monks and nuns – could leave people lonelier, helpless before a harsh God of Judgement. The Bible, now freely available in the vernacular, could induce piety and neighbourliness or aid meditation, but also justify slavery, war and genocide. An ingrained Pelagianism secured England from lasting Calvinist determinism, the manic violence of Dutch and German Anabaptism, and wholesale persecutions. Wolsey, Cranmer, Edward VI's tutor John Cheke, Elizabeth and Burghley were reasonable and forbearing, relishing debate and ready to compromise, save with violence and rebellion.

A reputation for humane moderation formerly accumulated around Sir Thomas More, England's most venerated saint and martyr since Becket. He was renowned for genial humour, wit, courage: Anthony Kenny has called him our greatest story-teller between Chaucer and Shakespeare. He compressed Christianity into an aphorism, 'A man may lose his head and come to no harm', which he was given the opportunity to prove. In death he was supreme: stoical and amusing. Standards of twentieth-century liberalism are scarcely relevant, yet More's humour could too often be brutal, scatological, abusive, uncontrolled; his concern for poverty, injustice and victims of enclosures, unemphatic; his learning apt to be employed dishonestly. He was long an ineffective time-server, first to Wolsey, then to the King, once eulogising Henry VIII, at Caesar's expense, for some paltry military nonsense in France. His *Utopia* was little less authoritarian than Hobbes's *Leviathan*. He admired Plato's *Republic*, a society wholly controlled by a hard-working, selfless, civilised and remote élite. Still imbued with much medievalism, unlike Wolsey he was intolerant almost to fanaticism, hated freedom of conscience and expression for others, and could jeer at a condemned heretic. Burning, he asserted, was 'lawful, necessary and well-done'. As Lord Chancellor his policy was ruthless. Denouncing heretics, he considered that 'after the fire of Smithfield, hell doth receive them where the wretches burn forever'.

Like the large-scale capitalism then emerging, like any human movement, the Renaissance had contradictions and ambiguities. No unalloyed explosion of light, it had many hues, easily distorted or misunderstood.

It valued originality and mortal genius above medieval convictions that
Scriptures had finalised truth, that art should promote piety and that,
wever radiant the vision, it should never forget the skeleton and the
rm. The body, all too mortal, an unworthy casing of the soul, unwashed
months, had been a sermon against blasphemous self-vaunting, the
nity of beauty, and was more easily venerated when cowled and hooded,
noured, thickly robed, mitred or crowned. Now it arose in enthralling if
ually over-idealised nakedness.

Individuals who flinched at nothing, risking all, inspired Renaissance
ists and patrons to establish their being at whatever cost. Faust, sixteenth-
ntury German wonder-worker and hermeticist, also called Georg
lmstetter and Dr Sabellius, bartered his soul for infinite knowledge. The
ympians also returned, amoral but beautiful. Caxton hastened to print
nslations of Ovid, Virgil, Aesop, Trojan tales and Arthurian legend.
glish and Scottish university wits and literati at London's Inns of Court
died Classical republicanism, as an academic ideal. Plutarch, Plautus,
neca, Ovid, Homer were sources for Shakespeare and Jonson, while
zabeth was quoting Horace in her teens. In France, Montaigne applied
extensive Classical and contemporary reading, as well as his own experi-
ce, to the Essay: urbane, clear as glass, curious, often slightly amused, a
del for generations of English Humanists.

Classicism had much to disturb the orthodox. Pre-Christian acceptance of
exuality and cultured pederasty confused many moralists. Medieval
glish and Scots had burnt sexual deviants or drowned them, bound face to
e, and sodomy remained a capital offence for another three centuries. Now,
ong the courtly and well-read, romantic fraternities were initiated, often
volous, more eloquent than concupiscent, but detested by Puritanism with
concentration on family, restraint, work, devotion. Though Leicester and
alsingham had Puritan tastes, these had small influence at court until the
ual needs of James I were flaunted too ostentatiously.

Another cause of ferment among the orthodox was the New Science.
cho Brahe, a Dane, Copernicus, a Pole, Galileo, an Italian, and Kepler, a
rman, drastically altered cosmological thought and attendant philoso-
ies by exiling Earth from the centre to the periphery, and setting it to
olve round the Sun. Another Dane, Romer, calculated with fair accuracy
speed of light. Here too, England held its own. Gilbert of Chichester
s eminent in electro-magnetics, tutored Walter Raleigh and, with
omas Harriot, achieved international status as a mathematician. Both

were more modern than the celebrated John Dee who, like More, retain
many medieval concepts, though he corresponded with Kepler and m
have influenced Descartes. Newton's cosmology, founded on physics a
mathematics, was barely disputed until the age of Einstein. Napie
promulgation of logarithms had more European significance than Pa
Bulls, or the Field of the Cloth of Gold, even though logarithms themsel
were swiftly conscripted to help discover a date for the deposition of An
Christ, with which Newton too was concerned. Boyle severed chemistry a
physics from alchemy and astrology.

Science demanded objectivity, and Francis Bacon, after watching
parson tortured for alleged treason, recognised the usefulness of this meth
for anatomical studies; he also remarked on the fact that 'The heart of a m
who had his bowels torn out (the punishment with us for high treason) .
on being cast into the fire, leapt up at first about a foot and a half, and th
by degrees into a less height.' In a traditional tale, he was himself to di
martyr to the new spirit of scientific enquiry, after catching cold when tryi
to preserve a chicken carcass by stuffing it with snow.

No revolution is complete: Reformation bred Counter-Reformatic
with science came partisan recrudescence of the irrational. There was lit
disposition, save perhaps on the part of a few secluded groups like t
School of Night, which Raleigh attended, to accept the atomic theories
Democritus, Epicurus, Lucretius. Humanist sensuality, sceptical curiosi
exact observation, the Renaissance, had roots far back in the Middle A
and did not wholly discard the occult and astrological. Science, religion a
hermeticism could jostle within the same head. The Archbishop
Canterbury assured Elizabeth that she need not fear assassination wh
Virgo was in the ascendant. Dee, graduate of Louvain and Paris, with
beard 'white as milk', accused of encompassing Mary I's death by spells, w
one of Europe's greatest mathematicians. His chemical researches won h
invitations from the Tsar, which he refused, and welcome from Empe
Rudolf II at Prague. Rudolf was fascinated by the latest inventions, yet a
by ancient Mysteries, early surrealism, and expensive quackery. Patron a
of Brahe and Kepler, he loved delving into alchemy, clairvoyance, nec
mancy, as did Dee, Elizabeth's Astrologer-Royal who, expert in ciphe
signing himself 007, seems to have wished to reconcile science with t
supernatural, and made considerable personal profit in the process. Gali
did not disdain astrology, Blake and Kepler dabbled in it. Newton, p
foundest thinker in Europe, respected certain branches of alchemy, and t

magic properties of numbers, from which Pythagoras himself had not escaped. France, even in 1996, was reported as possessing more clairvoyants and astrologers than priests.

Culturally, the France of Rabelais and Montaigne, Ronsard and du Bellay claimed European supremacy, disputed in Spain and Italy. England, with the confidence of a new dynasty, new overseas opportunities, well-sited Atlantic ports, new North Sea fishing grounds, its carrying trade wrested from Hanseatic merchant combines, had considerable aspirations, though the Plantagenet and Lancastrian Anglo-French Empire had vanished forever. Wolsey had dreams of becoming Pope; Henry VIII, envying the modish and cultivated Francis I of France, made claims for the Imperial Crown. 'Bluff King Hal', though not appropriate to Henry's cold, selfish, perhaps nervous, temperament, was apt for his reputation abroad, as his swagger was indeed bluff. 'Squire Harry' Luther called him, contemptuously, though the Emperor Charles V thought England of sufficient importance to marry his heir, Philip, to Henry's daughter Mary Tudor. At her death Philip grandly offered to wed Elizabeth, whose execution by his wife he had helped prevent; but was refused.

Tudor courts remained indebted to foreigners. Rumours abounded about 'the murderous Machiavel', though Francis Bacon admitted, in the *Advancement of Learning*: 'We are much beholden to Machiavel and others that write what men do, and not what they ought to do.' Pietro Torrigiano, after breaking Michelangelo's nose in Florence, fled to Rome before coming to London to carve for Henry VII the realistic effigies of him, his Queen and the Queen Mother on their magnificent Westminster Abbey tombs. Henry VIII's Nonesuch Palace, with its painted towers, domes, pinnacles, reproduced the elegant embellishments of Francis I's Italianate Fontainebleau. The Earl of Surrey and Sir Thomas Wyatt adapted the sonnet from Dante, Ariosto and Petrarch, giving shape and economy to the looseness of much native verse. And if the Italian sonnet and madrigal, slightly modified, delighted the educated English, so did, through Inigo Jones, the genius of Vitruvius and Palladio. A more sinister Italian glamour filtered, as if through silks gorgeous but soiled, into the Jacobean 'revenge' drama of Webster and lesser writers, a lurid charade of incestuous ladies, homicidal princes, lustful cardinals, foppish braggards, bisexual connoisseurs of blade and poison.

In Europe generally, Fra Pacioli's *Treatise on Double Entry Bookkeeping* of

1494 had more profound effect than any single battle: this, and artillery, gold, silver, other minerals and raw materials from overseas, improved taxation and banking, underwrote the powerful, nationalistic monarchies who interpreted the examples of Classical tyrannies and slave-states to their own advantage, while leaving the problems of unemployment and inflation, like the hidden dry rot in a shining temple, to ministers who seldom understood or even recognised them. Rulers were now less free of popular restraint and ministerial opposition. The crusading spirit was dead, save as an excuse for aggression. Catholic France, Catholic Spain would seek alliance with Moslem Turks and compete to plunder Italy and control the Papacy; unpaid Spanish Catholic troops sacked Rome in 1527. Pope Sixtus IV, connoisseur of art, was involved in a plot against the Platonist Florentine, Lorenzo di Medici, the Magnificent, whose brother was indeed stabbed by two priests during the Elevation of the Host.

English history, however, was more than an import–export graph, the play of impersonal economic and geographical forces and the balance of classes. The Tudor usurpers, pacing stiffly through gorgeous, tapestried palaces to the descant of Italian airs and the elegant susurrations of French dances, yet seem within footfall of Albion, a muster of archetypes: Wicked Uncle Richard III overcome by the Virtuous Hero, and perhaps becoming entangled with the contemporary legend of the Babes in the Wood; the victorious Adventurer, swifly transformed to Jack, prudent and industrious, unconcerned with superannuated notions of chivalry and 'honour', on top of the Beanstalk. He is then succeeded by Bluebeard, whose tally of wives might have been peeled off an imaginary deck of playing cards: Wronged Queen, Witch Queen (with six fingers on her right hand), Sacrificial Queen, Ugly Queen, Guilty Queen, Fortunate Queen. (Bishop Stubbs remarked that an explanation, though not a justification, of Henry's need to shed them is given by their portraits.) Then the withered Boy King, incurably wounded, whom no Virgin Saviour could cure, and the Two Sisters, the Dark and Bloody, the Golden and Virgin, both in the lineage of heroines powerful but barren.

Lurid details patch a dream-like mosaic. Anne Boleyn's erratic and unexplained fits of laughter, eerily humourless; Lady Salisbury, defiant at sixty-nine, chased by sheriff and executioner round the scaffold – she was unlucky enough to be daughter of the Yorkish Duke of Clarence who supposedly met his end in a butt of malmsey; the Duke of Northumberland, dictatorial ruler of England, then, pelted with dung, stones, bad eggs, led through London, ready trussed for the axe; his daughter-in-law, Lady Jane Grey, Shadow ueen, Classical scholar chilled by over-piety, blindfolded, groping for the lock – 'Where is it? Where is it? What shall I do?' – onlookers marvelling at so slight a body should gush so much blood. Judge Morgan, who con- emned her, swiftly became deranged by a black shape haunting his bed, and ied in convulsions, gasping, 'Take the Lady Jane from me!' In keeping with is over-charged atmosphere was a legend of Jane Grey's reluctant killer, frus- ated, courageous, bigoted and tormented 'Bloody Mary', giving birth to a onster at Framlington Castle in Suffolk and smashing it against a wall.

The Court was a display of biological survival tactics, slowed by protocol r hastened by Royal caprice. Lord Paget defined his own tactics: 'Fly the ourt. Speak little. Care less. Devise nothing. In answer, cold.' Surrounded y bejewelled toadies Henry VIII, all in yellow, dangles the infant Elizabeth, elebrating her mother's slaughter. Never far from him are the scarlet Wolsey, the soberly but richly arrayed More, Thomas Cromwell, watchful black among the rainbow tints of pages, maids-of-honour, jesters, ambi- ous courtiers and young heiresses. The poet Lord Surrey translated into ords Holbein's portrait of the man who ordered his execution: 'glutted eeks sloth feeds so fat, as scant their eyes be seen'.

The English monarchy joined its Continental rivals in organising politics theatre: with smaller resources, it strove to achieve by display what it uld not by force. 'The ceremony', wrote Dr Rowse, 'that surrounded the nglish monarchy was greater than that of any Court in Europe: all foreign bservers commented on it. A Venetian ambassador was astonished to see e Princess Elizabeth kneeling before her father three times in the course f one interview. Anyone who came into the sovereign's presence knelt.' ourt routine was a live frieze of obeisances, fanfares, doffing of caps, formal lutations between elaborately decorated resplendents, together with urmurs, side-glances, covert signals in shadowy recesses.

Yet whatever the rigidities at the centre, social mobility quickened further nder the Tudors, though many were swift to invent more aristocratic pedi- ees. To establish kinship, irredeemably bogus, with an ancient Roman an, the patrician Caecilii, a plain Welsh soldier changed his name from ytyllt' to 'Cecil', his grandson finalising the achievement as Lord Burghley, ivot of the Elizabethan State, master of superb Burghley House in Iorthamptonshire. His son Robert became Earl of Salisbury, James I's chief inister, possessor of another Renaissance palace, Hatfield House. Burghley imself acknowledged that nobility is but wealth grown old. Trollope was

to write: 'Rank squanders money, trade makes it – and then purchases ra█
by regilding its splendour.'

Trade had its own codes: *Honour* was fading before *Honesty*. The Ci█
with its growing Puritan and anti-Court tendencies, liked to insist that █
combined them: 'An Englishman's word is his bond.' In *Hamlet* Polonius█
Cecil type, gives advice to Laertes bespeaking moderate Puritanism, insi█
ing on wariness in friendship, prudence in finance, unceasing self-contr█
restraint in personal expenditure, fidelity to personal being and moral sta█
dards. Such avoidance of decorative idleness promoted energies by whi█
Europe, with England in the vanguard, exercised sway throughout t█
world.

Extravagant, often tasteful ceremonial enhanced rather than disguised t█
ruthlessness it covered. The much-trumpeted English love of freedo█
sometimes vaunted by authority in rhetoric to disparage foreigners, usual█
meant not individual liberty but resolution to defend national ind█
pendence. Henry VII, triumphant through artistocratic treachery and t█
luck of battle, determined that English freedom would be monarchi█
supremacy, financing English naval power against Dutch and Baltic trade█
and curbing the aristocracy. A weak Crown had released years of cl█
anarchy. Throughout he ruled astutely, severely, though with what Bac█
called 'a kind of justice'. Abroad, popular assemblies were decaying:█
home, Parliament would be a useful registrar of Royal decrees, and for pe█
odic granting of supplies. Sagacious, unromantic, dryly humorous, Hen█
left his son a solvent Treasury, Cornwall and Wales quelled, Engla█
respected abroad and with a foothold in North America, the Crown mo█
powerful than at any time since the Plantagenets, as Wolsey was to reco█
nise: 'If the Crown were prosecutor and asserted it, juries would be fou█
to bring in a verdict that Abel was the murderer of Cain.'

Henry VIII's reign began, to raucous applause, with the execution of tw█
competent but exacting middle-class ministers who had followed th█
ruler's prescriptions to the letter but failed to take precautions against █
departure. Early years had a morning freshness in which the youthful Ki█
appeared an Albion hero: manly, chivalric, song-loving, generous. The spi█
is discerned in Hall's *Annals* for 1515, recounting a charade picturesq█
staged, but with some more substantial resonances:

> The King and the Queen accompanied by many lords and ladies rode to the█
> high ground of Shooters Hill to take the open air, and as they passed by the█

way, they espied a company of tall yeomen, clothed all in green with green hoods and bows and arrows, to the number of two hundred. Then one of them which called himself Robin Hood came to the King desiring him to see his men shoot, and the King was content. Then he whistled and all the two hundred archers shot and loosed at once, and then he whistled again; their arrows whistled by craft of the head, so that the noise was strange and great and much pleased the King, the Queen and all the company.

Then Robin Hood desired the King and Queen to come into the green-wood and see how the outlaws lived. The King demanded of the Queen and her ladies, if they durst adventure to go into the wood with so many outlaws. Then the Queen said that if it pleased him she was content. Then the horns blew till they came to the wood under Shooters Hill, and there was an arber made of boughs with a hall and a great chamber and an inner chamber very well made and covered with flowers and sweet herbs, which the King much praised. Then said Robin Hood, 'Sir, outlaws' breakfast is venison, and there-after you must be content with such fare as we use.' Then the King and Queen sat down and were served with venison and wine by Robin Hood and his men, to their great contentation.

Such are the perpetual façades of power, though almost to the end the Tudor era never quite lost this aura of green and gold, outdoor humours and human exuberance; but politically, within make-believe and deception, the political stakes were slowly raised. Henry VIII understood as concisely as his father that a usurping dynasty needed to protect itself from dangers real or imaginary: for his, two English kings, Henry VI and Edward V, had vanished in sinister circumstances, a third, Richard III, perished in battle against a pretender. Other pretenders and rebels followed. The sixteenth century saw the murder of two French kings; a Scottish Regent; a Scottish King Consort; Cardinal Beaton; Mary Stuart's favourite, David Rizzio; the Duc de Guise; the Huguenot leader Coligny; and William the Silent, Protestant leader of the Netherlands.

The English monarch at times ignored all law, as when Richard III hustled Hastings to the block without trial. Henry VIII had Buckingham, too close to the Blood Royal, beheaded for 'harbouring treasonous thought', like the twentieth-century President Moi of Kenya arresting a man 'for imagining the death of the President'.

In the wake of the Roses wars, the Crown established emergency rights through Prerogative Courts – Star Chamber, Council of the North, Council of Wales – which dodged Common Law and though popular in restoring order were, predictably, over-prolonged. Through obsequious parliamentary procedures, Impeachment and Attainder could, like later revolutionary procedures, very simply, for 'reasons of state', summarily remove any suspect, however high-born. A State Trial, following muffled examination by the Privy Council, which occasionally allowed acquittal, was further theatrical ritual, described by Macaulay as 'merely a murder preceded by the uttering of certain gibberish and the performance of certain mummeries'. Anne Boleyn was forbidden to call witnesses, submit evidence, or have legal defence. Her father, one of the judges, hastened to assent to her death. 'It is', she said afterwards, with another outbreak of laughter, 'but a little neck.' By the block, she spoke of her killer: 'A gentler and more merciful Prince was there never.' Earlier, Henry's servile courtiers threatened to crush Princess Mary's head 'like baked apples' if she refused acquiescence to his ill-treatment of her mother, Katherine.

An accepted maxim was 'Stone dead hath no fellow'. Thomas Cromwell declared that a single word was high treason. He was promoted Earl of Essex, then swiftly found himself in the Tower, vainly begging mercy from his master, who sensed conspiracy, detected atmospheric change, or simply felt tedium.

Henry burnt Protestant zealots, hanged Catholic monks, made the possessor of a picture of Becket, whose rich tomb he despoiled, liable to execution. After much political and doctrinal wrangling, the Elizabethan government secured a moderate compromise. 'Let it not be said', Elizabeth proclaimed, 'that our Reformation tendeth to cruelty.' There was cruelty, less publicised, less large-scale than under Mary. In 1575 Elizabeth personally insisted on the burning of two Anabaptists, who perished 'in great horror with roaring and crying'. But it has to be remembered that when Anabaptists seized power in Westphalia in 1533, they denounced Pope and Luther as two halves of the same bum, also monogamy, property, and all authority save their own, that of the Elect of God.

In some areas, State supremacy was flexible. Under Henry VIII, the Duke of Norfolk was scarcely alone in accepting French bribes. In 1614 Sir John Digby, ambassador in Madrid, discovered a longish list of British notables, headed by King James and his chief minister, receiving Spanish pensions.

The Tudor State attempted to legislate how people thought, prayed, worked, travelled, played: to enforce church attendance, what each class should wear and eat, and the numbers of servants it employed. It supervised the Church, press, theatre, trade, industry. Tillage Acts fined inefficient farmers, Poor Laws were framed against beggars. A law of 1545 on credit still remains. Dr Rowse writes: 'One is oppressed, one is almost stifled, by the completeness and intimacies of the controls.' This was more acceptable while Spanish, Scottish, Irish threats suggested crises, less so as dangers receded and Queen Elizabeth aged.

The prerogative courts were aimed at the 'overmighty subjects'; the State ruled humbler folk through Justices of the Peace and the country gentry, who tended to respect Common Law though they were harsh on recusancy and agitation against enclosures, rack-renting, and Poor Law; on crimes against property, and active disrespect. At Durham in 1592, five men were hanged for being 'Egyptians', gipsies; four more at Edinburgh in 1611. A Welsh striker was hanged in 1541; at least two poisoners were boiled alive. Holinshed, probably with fair accuracy, estimated 72,000 thieves hanged during Henry VIII's reign. Lacking a regular army and police – Italian mercenaries helped crush the Devonshire religious rebellion in 1549 – the government maintained itself as best it could. Sometimes, common sense and political acumen mitigated punishments. Northumberland, having defeated Kett's rebellion against enclosures, hanged the leaders but intervened for the foot-sloggers. 'Is there no place for pardon? Without pardon what shall we [the aristocrats] then do? Shall we hold the plough ourselves, play the carters, labour the ground with our own hands?'

No Tudor ruler or minister overturned the course of history, but several deflected or hastened it, and each ruler stamped the reign with the Royal personality. Of all English monarchs, Henry VIII is best known, probably the most popular and, for children, a fascinating nursery ogre:

> Bluff King Hal, full of beans,
> He married half a dozen Queens.

He was musician, poet, scholar of the new learning, champion jouster, patron, military commander, virtual founder of the Royal Navy despite the humiliation of watching the *Mary Rose* founder with all hands; he was tireless hunter, lover, diplomat; he was a theologican who had written (or at least signed), to his own satisfaction, a refutation of Luther perhaps outlined by More; he was the patriot who had, with Cranmer and Cromwell, creatures virtually his own creation, freed England from the Italian Pope; he was a prodigious builder – his father had contented himself with twenty homes, he increased them to sixty. Then his personal promise declined, through self-delusion, flattery, disease, into the grotesque. For Walter Raleigh, 'If all the pictures and patterns of a merciless prince were lost in the world, they might all again be painted to the life out of the story of this king', but the young Jane Austen wrote in 1791:

> The crimes and cruelties of this prince, were too numerous to be mentioned
> . . . and nothing can be said in his vindication, but that his abolishing reli-
> gious houses and leaving them to the ruinous depredations of time has been
> of infinite use to the landscape of England in general, which probably was a
> principal motive for his doing it, since otherwise why should a man who was
> of no religion himself be at so much trouble to abolish one which had for ages
> been established in the kingdom?

'Tudor Despotism' must be compared with conditions elsewhere: the Spanish were burying female heretics alive, merely beheading any males they had not burnt. In the New World, they were practising genocide. However, England's record in Ireland does not stand up to close scrutiny. No Tudor rulers visited Ireland (or their patrimonial Wales). For England, Ireland was progressively a mere source of cheap land and titles, then of cheap food and labour. In 1577 the Lord Chancellor of Ireland advocated extermination of the inhabitants, as savages. In the 1580 rebellion, Raleigh stands accused of ruthless slaughter of Irish, Spanish and Italian defenders of the Fort del Oro, Kerry. The poet Edmund Spenser, employed in Ireland, dealt out evictions, man-hunts, executions to those whom their fellow-Catholic Edmund Campion considered in 1585 to be 'very religious, hospitable, frank, amorous, useful, sufferable of pains infinite, very glorious – many sorcerors, excellent horsemen, delighted with wars, great almsgivers'.

Sir Richard Bynham, Governor of Connacht, had fought twice for Spain, and once against her. After the wreck of the Armada in 1588 he was merci-less to Spanish survivors and Irish alike, when more than forty Spanish ships were wrecked on the Irish coast: the Irish often plundered and stripped sur-vivors, killing some, or joining others against the common enemy. In Connemara, as in parts of Africa, people felt it unlucky to rescue the drown-ing, since this might offend the sea, deprived of its lawful prey, so the grandees choked to death in velvet capes and golden chains, imploring a God blind, indifferent, unnerved, or possibly Protestant. 'Certainly lamen-table,' King Philip commented.

Elizabeth spent more treasure combating Tyrone's rebellion than against Spain: three thousand Spaniards reinforced the rebels, and G.B. Harrison

alculated that Essex's sixteen thousand against Tyrone in 1599 was a
orce relatively larger and more costly than the British Army in France in
914. In 1601, years after the Armada, Spanish troops landed to assist the
evolt.

he English masses, working on farms, seething in urban streets, adjusting
o religious, agricultural, technological changes, lacked concern for much
eyond their own parishes. Largely excluded from politics until the nine-
eenth century, they were as they had long been: suspicious, gregarious,
rink-loving, stoical but never wholly resigned, and with their own sharply-
ointed humour. An angry countryman declaimed that it would be 'a good
urn if there were as many gentlemen in Norfolk as there be white bulls'.
F.C. Harrison has discovered a letter of a Kett rebel to a hated enclosing
andlord during the short, faction-ridden reign of Henry VIII's son, the
ntelligent but sickly, indeed doomed, Edward VI:

> Mr Pratt, your sheep are very fat,
> And we thank you for that.
> We have left you the skins,
> To pay for your wife's pins,
> And you must thank us for that.

here was still little national cohesion. In the Armada crisis of 1588 counties
vere more willing to defend themselves than eager to cross boundaries and
ally to defend England, though victory must have inspired some patriotic
ensations.

The sixteenth century had a crop of women with uncommon political
nd domestic power: a Lady Margaret Beaufort, Lady Suffolk; Bess of
Hardwick, who had four husbands, made herself her sovereign's richest
ubject, and built the stupendous Hardwick Hall. Shakespeare's women
eldom suggest the secluded, the dispirited, the abject: Margaret of Anjou,
Lady Macbeth, Portia, Rosalind, Beatrice, Cleopatra, Lady Hotspur,
Volumnia, Viola. By 1620 the Crown was ordering the clergy to condemn
he insolence of our women and their wearing of broad-brimmed hats,
ointed doublets, their hair cut-short or shorn'. Catholic women played a
onsiderable and courageous part in the Gunpowder Plot. The assured,
vittily purposeful repartee between Beatrice and Benedick suggests unusual
exual balance, in an age when decline of local wars increased the impor-

tance of domestic comfort, thus fortifying women's position and releasi
their creative energies.

Much was expected of Elizabeth Tudor, in England and in Euro
Opinions of her performance are as varied as those of her father's. Ja
Austen, at fifteen, was unenthusiastic: 'That disgrace to humanity, that p
of society, Elizabeth.' Elizabeth's contemporary, the Catholic Char
Arundel, derided her as 'the most monstrous and barbarous creature of H
sex that ever bore crown or sceptre'. Queen Victoria deplored her unkin
ness 'to my ancestor the Queen of Scots'. She has been dismissed as a figu
head for the policies of Burghley and Walsingham, or a puppet trapped
her class, her times, the impersonal drift of history. Yet State papers, the te
timonies of her ministers and enemies, her own writings, do not back
this interpretation. The girl who outfaced Queen Mary's deadly inte
rogators, in the Tower where her own mother had been beheaded, is unlike
as woman and sovereign to have been moved around like a chess-queen
hands not her own.

Robert Beale, stolid Clerk of the Council, acknowledged her 'gre
wisdom, learning and experience'. Pope Sixtus V in 1588 admitted: 'She is
great woman; and if only she were Catholic, she would be whol
unequalled . . . regard the excellence by which she rules; she is but a woma
no more than mistress of half an island, and nevertheless she inspires fear
Spain, France, in the Empire, in all.' For Cardinal Allen, a fervid support
of the Armada, she was an unjust usurper, 'the very shame of her sex, th
chief spectacle of sin'. A Papal Nuncio reported: 'The Queen of England
know not how, penetrates everything.' He could have mentioned the Tud
spy-system, perfected by Walsingham and his spymaster and chief 'rac
master', Richard Topcliffe. A.L. Rowse, after a lifetime of Elizabetha
studies, concludes: 'She was schooled in danger and discretion [and] he
on her course alone for forty-five years, in a world of distractions ar
dangers, full of treacherous currents and many threats to her life. True, sh
was wonderfully served: she saw to that.'

Whatever she was, her image was multitudinous. As Virgin Goddes
Astrea, 'Imperial Virgin', immaculate, inviolate, she echoed Diana, chill
receiving but seldom giving, backed by the tricky lustre of moonlight. Sh
was Gloriana; she was Fair Oriana, Beauty's Queen; she was Good Quee
Bess. But, daughter of that mother whose name she never uttered, she prob
ably appraised herself laconically, once reflecting: 'In being, not seeming, v
may wish the best.' At the extravagant theatricals presented by Leicester

Kenilworth, 'The Lady of the Lake' offered Elizabeth the lake itself, explaining that she had been guarding it since King Arthur. The Queen was ungrateful, tartly replying that she had supposed it was hers already.

One rather admires the mayor who, congratulating her on the Armada victory, observed that His Spanish Majesty had seized the wrong sow by the ear. She herself once said that a pregnant woman was worse than a sow. Bram Stoker, creator of *Dracula*, assumed that she was a man. Through pageantry, rhetoric and song, she was stiffened into an icon of national unity and pride.

European princes sought her: Philip, Anjou, Alençon, even Ivan the Terrible – a potentially alarming clash of spirit; but her marriage to anyone but Leicester, itself unlikely, is barely conceivable. Flirtatious but asexual, she must have had profound personal griefs. In old age, she kept by her bed the casket wherein lay 'his [Leicester's] last letter'. Some years later a courtier wrote: 'Her delight is to sit in the dark, and sometimes with shedding tears to bewail Essex.' Essex, Leicester's step-son, was the intemperate lover of her later years.

Certainly, Leicester's reply when rebuked for worldliness by a Puritan gives a hint of what she saw in him: 'I may fall in many ways and have more witnesses thereof than others who perhaps be no saints either.'

When in 1570 the Pope declared Elizabeth excommunicate, and thus open to murder or deposition, he must, as much as King Philip, have fuelled angry English nationalism, for which a Gloriana was a handy icon. He also condemned English Catholics to systematic mistrust and persecution. The Bull, nailed to the Bishop of London's gate, did not ingratiate: 'We do declare her to be deprived of her pretended title to the kingdom . . . We do command and charge all and every the noblemen, subjects, people, that they presume not to obey her or her orders, mandates and laws.' The kings of Catholic Spain and France nevertheless forbade its publication, being sensitive to Royal depositions.

In keeping with Renaissance times, the Queen's learning was formidable. She spoke four languages and read assiduously. She wrote poetry, speeches, prayers, dissertations, dedications. At thirteen she translated Marguerite of Navarre's *The Mirror of the Sinful Soul*, the next year, Catherine Parr's *Prayers and Meditations* – an international best-seller, Maria Perry reveals – into French, Italian and Latin. For her brother Edward VI she translated Ochino's *Sermon on the Nature of Christ*; and, at sixty, Boethius's *Consolation of Philosophy*, 'to riddle out for herself the various theories of divine foreknowledge'.

Her father's daughter, she was not study-bound but loved the hunt, dancing, music, theatre. Often pain-wracked, she was devious – or diplomatic; authoritarian; by modern standards, was frequently deficient in fairness and, towards her women, in even common decency. Grappling with a debased coinage, she strove, not wholly successfully, to retain the Crown's dues and properties; although, adroit casuist and circumlocutionist, she would withdraw with staged dignity when circumstances demanded. She lacked scruple in withstanding Catholicism, Puritanism, and Parliamentary claims. 'Freedom of speech', she informed the Commons in 1593, 'is granted, but you must know what privileges you have; not to speak everyone what he listeth, or what cometh into his brain to utter that; but your privilege is Aye or Nay.' That year, ageing and childless, she despatched a member, Peter Wentworth, to the Tower, quite unconstitutionally, for venturing a question about the succession and objecting to the constant intrusion of Royal authority. He died, unreprieved, in 1596.

Like most busy rulers, Elizabeth was too preoccupied with immediate urgencies to be far-sighted. Always impoverished, she had excuse enough for policies of caution, delay, dithering, when hesitation usually lost her little more than goodwill. Parliament wanted grand anti-Spanish campaigns in the Netherlands, a final reduction of Ireland, but jibbed at the requisite taxes. Elizabeth jibbed at waste, insecurity, financial carelessness. She denounced John Hawkins's first slaving expedition to Africa as 'detestable' and said it 'would call down the vengeance of Heaven'; but, seeing its excellent dividends, she invested in the second, one vessel inappropriately named the *Jesus of Lübeck*.

After the smoke of Mary and Philip, Elizabeth's reign still appears an outburst of sunlight, more matter for a May morning. Physical comforts also were improving, dread of famine receding. Even under Mary, a Spanish witness recorded: 'These English have their houses made of sticks and dirt, but they fare commonly as well as the King.'

A surge of new words bespoke some national confidence, enterprise, hazardous but profitable voyages, new inventiveness, writers plucking imagery exotic or descriptive, corresponding with New World marvels, scientific concepts and innovations, social change and cultural exchanges. 'I have frequent been with unknown minds,' Shakespeare wrote. The Danish critic Georg Brandes showed 5,642 different words in the Old Testament, less than a fifth of the number to be found in Shakespeare. A society remembered for its gleaming ruffs and ornate hats, ornamental dress, jewelled hands, plumes, scents, and curious pets, its show-off parades, rejoiced in the most novel literature in Europe, in drama using coarse but brightly-spun vernacular to counterpoint formal verse-structures, and giving Classical plots freedoms of time and character with a headlong panache that delighted socially mixed audiences and astounded or shocked scholastic pedants.

The State, with such moderates as Burghley, Leicester, Hooker, wished more to reconcile and heal than to swing the axe and light the pyre. Nevertheless, whoever reigned, human nature ruled: competitive, violent, selfish, anxious, doubtfully honest. Great music and literature, fine architecture and craftsmanship, already provoking Puritan scowls, could never entirely bandage the sores of the multitude. Smallpox stalked palace and slum; plague would close theatres and chase away the Court. London, Bristol, Norwich, York were not clean or well-lit, and humane Christian injunctions, though inspiring considerable personal charity, were disregarded in the larger scene. In *Christ's Teares over Jerusalem* (1593) Thomas Nashe complained that 'the rich disdain the poor . . . one occupation disdaineth another'. Treason executions remained extended torture, severed heads grinned from spikes, gallows loomed above thoroughfares piled with horse and human dung, scavenged by curs and magpies, thronged with cutpurses, cheapjacks, conmen, ruthless felons and 'sturdy beggars'. Mary Frith, model for Moll Cutpurse in Dekker's *The Roaring Girle* (1611), hated chickens, managed her own brothel, organised widespread prostitution, captained a robber street gang and, forerunning Jonathan Wild, 'fenced' stolen goods, then resold them to the original owners. Nor was rural England everywhere a daisy-chain pastoral of willing milkmaids and lusting but benign esquires, stout yeomen, Justice Shallows and dancing shepherds. It knew penalised vagrancy, religious persecution, enclosures, petty crime, rising prices.

By Elizabeth's later years, hopeful exuberance had declined. Catholic plots involving Mary Stuart, a continuing Spanish menace, doubts about the succession, growth of sombre Puritanism, failure of some overseas colonies and loss of famous captains, the beheading of Essex, and primitive superstitions linking the decay of the monarch with the fortunes of the community guaranteed no smooth inheritance for a new King.

Beginnings of Empire are never genteel. Backed by Papal mandate, Spain and Portugal had conquered much of Central and South America, Cuba,

Hispaniola; the English, with or without Royal permission, raided these and ventured further north. As early as 1483, furthermore, the Portuguese were slaving on the Congo, and Spanish Hispaniola was the first slave-based colony. England, Scotland, France, Denmark, later Holland, were joining the hellish slave-trade, substituting Africans for the exterminated Caribs and the many Mexicans and Mayans killed through overwork, disease, genocide. They had found such commerce already prospering in Africa, rulers colluding with Arab middlemen, happy to deal with Westerners who, with Papal blessing, instituted the Atlantic trade. Few humanitarian questions were asked at home. Africans too required constant replenishment: castration was inflicted as a punishment for disobedience by slave-owners who considered themselves envoys of Catholic piety, Protestant integrity. English Common Law was ignored in the greed for spices, sugar, gold, silver, skins. Colonialism would stimulate ship-building, trade in timber, metals, furs, fish, saltpetre, cloves, rum, damasks, tea, coffee, calico, rice, turkeys, tobacco, the potato, arms, leather: the export of cloth, spirits and trinkets.

English imperialism was not haphazard, but professionally organised by a composite of City and Royal finance, joint-stock and monopolist enterprise which subsidised ships, gave grants, and found easy avenues between licensed projects and piracy. Chartered companies planted colonies, built factories, fortresses, strategic harbours, their names tracing the global scope: Muscovy, Turkey, Levant, Virginia, Hudson's Bay, North West Passage, Barbados, Africa, Eastland. These were tough rivets of Empire, less romantic than they sounded. Granted the spices monopoly in 1600, the joint-stock East India Company had a future of world power. Colonies proved more than markets and sources of raw materials: they became outlets for Puritan dissenters, social idealists and misfits, missionaries, doctors, administrators, adventurers, criminals, and for novelists needing a change of scene or twist of narrative. Profits financed industrial and agricultural advance at home, great houses, political change.

Crucial to island fortunes, English naval power in the form of armed merchant ships allied to the variable strength of the Royal Navy enforced foreign policy in unofficial war with Spain in the Pacific, Atlantic and Mediterranean. English ships also carried troops to support the once Protestant, now Catholic, Henri IV; to reinforce the claimant to the Portuguese throne currently occupied by Philip; and to assist England's best customer, the Dutch Netherlands, also against Philip. Thus English and Scottish troops were landed in Brittany and Normandy, sacked Lisbon,

Corunna and, watched by Donne, Cadiz: they helped the Dutch sustain a three-year siege of Ostend. Leicester, who had lavishly overspent Elizabeth's subsidy, was, to her fury, offered the Dutch crown. The Earl, himself scarcely a Caesar, complained of one general, Sir John Smythe, in terms which veterans of the Boer War would have recognised: 'After the muster, he entered into such strange cries for ordering of men and for fight with weapons as made me think he was not well. God forbid that he should have charge of men who know so little as I dare say he does.'

'Barbary Pirates' from North Africa were able to raid the Channel and Irish Sea, camping in Dorset during the winter of 1624–5, and once briefly occupying Cork. There was not much to choose between them and the Elizabethan sea adventurers symbolised by Drake, El Draque, and his mixed characteristics. An 'upwardly mobile' entrepreneur and speculator, privateer, Royal commander against the Armada, he had Renaissance versatility: magistrate, Lord Mayor of Plymouth, Member of Parliament, military and civil engineer, lover of music, painter of wild life, always with an eye for the main chance. Like Philip II, 'he wove the interests of his God and country in one'. His address to Walsingham in 1587, 'There must be a beginning of any great matter, but the continuing unto the end until it be thoroughly finished yields the true glory', was elaborated in 1940 into a prayer which comforted Bernard Montgomery and, later, Margaret Thatcher. A biographer, John Sugden, acknowledges his Nelson-like cockiness, inventive initiatives, his affability and tact with subordinates, his clumsiness with equals and superiors, his inflexible hatred of Spain, and of almost all opposition. He cherished grudges as if they were the children he never had, excommunicated his ship's chaplain for mischief and, having given dinner and Holy Communion to his second-in-command, the gentlemanly Thomas Doughty, personally beheaded him for 'conspiracy'.

In a ship scarcely larger than an Onassis bathroom he sailed more than nine thousand miles round the world, going from Java to Sierre Leone without maps, throughout preserving his men from disease; which Anson could not, a century and a half later. Daring the Atlantic and the unknown Pacific, in 1599 he reached California, where he named the site of the future San Francisco 'New Albion'. Such feats expanded European consciousness; or, detractors would submit, by emphasising Eurocentricity, created a racial arrogance which boded ill. Nevertheless, Drake himself 'had a genuine respect for peoples of another culture and colour that was absent in so many of the great discoverers, in Columbus, da Gama, Hawkins.' Indeed, as

Sugden confirms, his popularity with blacks and Indians raised terror among the racially intolerant Spaniards. A black, Diego, was his constant companion at sea; California Indians besought him to remain as their king, and even after perilous ambush he refused to use artillery against natives. For the Spanish killing of one black boy he exacted savage and unjust revenge. Despite identifying Spain with Inquisition, absolutism, torture, the stake, he was courteous to Spanish prisoners, one testifying that he was 'sharp, restless, well-spoken, inclined to liberality and ambition, vainglorious, boastful, not very cruel'. Don Alonso de Sotomayor described him as 'very courteous and honourable with those who have surrendered, of great humanity and gentleness, virtues which must be praised, even in an enemy'. When Queen and Council left Armada victors to rot, unpaid and diseased, Drake was a founder of England's first naval charity, and pioneered welfare insurance at a time when the Treasury welcomed high casualties as a saving on wages.

Though Dr Johnson disapproved of him, Drake was recognisably English: obstinate, acquisitive, humorous, puritan, dedicated to his reputation and Name, to gold, England, God, probably in that order, though generous with his profits. Hearing of the disappearance at sea of El Draque, destroyer of five hundred Spanish ships, King Philip at last smiled: 'It is good news, and now I will get well.' He was wrong.

Europeans had respect for this England, upstart and aggressive, but little affection. They sniggered about 'Madame Leicester', gossiped about Elizabeth and Essex, professed horror at the execution of Mary Stuart and the grisly punishment of Catholic priests. Foreign visitors thought the English grossly chauvinistic (Dutch refugees, Protestant to the bone, were unpopular, particularly in hard times); too susceptible to outward appearance and fashions, most of which they purloined from abroad. William Harrison admitted, in his *Description of England* (1587):

> To-day there is none to the Spanish guise, to-morrow the French toys are most fine and delectable, ere long no such apparel as that which is after the high Almain fashion . . . and the short French breeches make a comely vesture that, except it were a dog in a doublet, you shall see, so disguised as are my countrymen of England.

Submission to foreign taste, sometimes abjectly, in what Arthur Koestler called 'the French 'flu', was continuous, from snobbery, connoisseurship, or ignorance. Most English court painters in the sixteenth and the seventeenth centuries were from abroad, the exceptions being the exquisite miniaturist Nicholas Hilliard and his followers, and William Dobson. Hilliard had trained as jeweller and goldsmith, as betrayed by his emphasis on linear design rather than modelling in the round. Charles I particularly delighted in a Hilliard jewel adorned with an enamelled miniature of the Battle of Bosworth. Did he wear it at Naseby?

The end of private warfare saw the castle, as aristocratic and cultural centre, abandoned in favour of the country house, and the foremost architects and decorators turned their attention to the latter now that ecclesiastical patronage and cathedral-building had ended. Unlike many foreign capitals, London never had a monopoly of culture. Olive Cook has noticed the first mention of 'architect', as artist rather than craftsman, then of 'overtime', in this bustling era.

The chimneys of the Great Houses – coiffed and knobbed, hooded, ruffed, coned, ledged, rimmed, pargeted or plain, patterned in diamond, lozenge, criss-cross, bristling with decorative unnecessaries: chimneys squat as petards, narrow as cannons trained on the noon sun, bulging like midget volcanoes: chimneys like a zed or Roman I: like tubs, stove-pipe hats, like judges, jurymen, brooding monks: chimneys ochred, black, slate-grey, blood-red: a jungle of shapes, at dusk becoming giant inert frogs, mitres, witches' hats, dim candy-twists, cowled shoulders, smudged pinnacles, tops of pagodas, even concertinas, symbols of this, reminders of that, an effort towards poetry – still fret the skyline, for pause and rumination.

Treasures from many lands accumulated within the houses. Burghley possessed a collection of Ming porcelain; lofty halls were hazed with candle-lit tapestries from Brussels, Arras, Mortlake, such as those behind which Hamlet heard the rat move. Leicester, a patron of Hilliard, and with whom Spenser missed his chance, left more than two hundred paintings, mostly well-chosen portraits, and a large library. William Harrison catalogued the contents of these houses:

> The furniture . . . also exceedeth, and is grown in manner even to passing delicacy: and herein I do not speak of the nobility and gentry only, but likewise of the lowest sort in most places of our south country that have anything at all to take to. Certes in noblemen's houses it is not rare to see abundance of arras, rich hangings of tapestry, silver vessel, and so much other plate as may furnish sundry cupboards to the sum oftentimes of a thousand or two thousand pounds at the least, whereby the value of this and the rest of their stuff doth grow to be almost inestimable. Likewise, in the houses of knights, gentle-

men, merchantmen, and some other wealthy citizens, it is not geason [rare] to behold generally their great provision of tapestry, Turkey work, pewter, brass, fine linen, and thereto costly cupboards of plate . . .

Old men told Harrison of an outstanding growth of chimneys, beds, pillows, and the change of kitchen ware from wood and pewter to silver and tin.

The great Tudor mansions could only function with the help of many servants. The Fussels, introducing Sir Hugh Plat's *Delights for Ladies* (1602), delineated the treatment of Tudor menials:

Sir John Harrington, that debonair courtier, translator of *Orlando Furiosos* [and pioneer of the watercloset], made his household servants pay 2d. for each failure, and the careless use of an oath cost the unfortunate another 1d. for each oath. These were heavy fines upon people whose annual earnings were counted in shillings rather than in pounds. A bed unmade after 8 o'clock in the morning cost another penny. A late dinner cost the cook 6d., and a dirty shirt on Sundays or a missing button cost the same.

An old saying held that England was a woman's paradise, a servant's prison. Thomas Platter, a Swiss traveller, noted in his diary in 1599 that English wives frequently beat their husbands.

The Great House, compact, self-sufficient fiefdom both dominating and protecting a considerable population, while exacting dues, ensuring church attendance, social decorum, country customs, dispensing justice and punishing horseplay, provided hospitality, charity, multiple employments, artistic and scholarly patronage, festivities of masque and drama, pageant, dance, music.

English music already had a long history. The pre-Conquest two-part gymel had survived and expanded, and from the twelfth century, in Christian and Moorish Spain and throughout Europe, polyphony was being experimented with, eventually becoming the exquisite accompaniment to the Renaissance. It remained unrivalled until the ascent of Italian keyboard music, song, ultimately opera. England did not lag far behind. Part-song, motet, fantasia, church chorale shuffled melody and counter-point, light and shadow with bewildering versatility. The church music of Tallis, Fayrfax, Taverner, Cornish, Gibbons and Byrd, with small organs and orchestras, reached much of England, from the Chapel Royal to St Albans, from York to Oxford, in successions of lamentations, credos, kyries, canticles, hymns, anthems. At Court and Country House the songs of Wilbye, Lawes, Morley, Campion, Dowland mingled spring delights and autumn elegies, love passionate or regretful; sung to harp, lute, and the clavichord, perfected under Elizabeth. Erasmus called England a nest of singing birds. With the 'English consort' of Bull, Holborne, Cooper, Byrd and others came, in F.E. Halliday's words, 'the golden age of English music, the only time in England's history, before the present, when it could be said that her composers were the peers of those anywhere else in the world. Byrd was only fifty in 1593, and in the next ten years led the way in every form of musical composition.'

Holinshed describes Henry VIII 'exercising himself dailie in shooting, singing, dansing, wrestling, casting of the barre, playing at the recorders, flute, virginals, in setting of songs and making of ballads'. English virginal music had high repute in Europe, and Henry's daughter Elizabeth I was a virtuoso on the virginals. Italian music floated through her palaces, where she employed the Venetian Bassanos, and Laniers from Rouen, as well as Dutch, German and Danish keyboard composers. There was dance music, with Anthony Holborne's pavans, galliards, corontos, Dowland's 'Mrs Winter's Jumpe' and 'Queen Elizabeth her Galliard', Gibbons's 'The King's Juell', and such anonymous keyboard melodies as 'My Lady Carey's Dompe'. Popular airs, ballades, catches were adopted and refined, making music an art genuinely national.

The lure of proud Italy never faltered. Particularly offensive to Tudor Puritans was a flesh-revealing dance, the *volta*, all twists and shakes; a picture survives of Elizabeth jigging with Leicester. A critic observed: 'The *volta*, which magicians brought from Italy, besides insolent and indecent movements, hath this misfortune, that a great many murders and miscarriages result.' From Italy also came the violin, slowly to replace viol and rebec: technical advances and enlarged range prepared for Henry Purcell (*c.* 1659–95), whose personal life is as obscure as that of the comparable genius, Inigo Jones; he died young, but with achievements on the scale of Shakespeare and Milton.

Always there lay, beneath the flood of words – printed accounts of Navigation Acts, Acts of Uniformity, Declarations of Indulgence, Grand Remonstrances, Solemn Leagues and Covenants, Humble Petitions of Advice, Bills of Right – what words can never fully identify, the possibility of the unattainable, glimmering yet distinct as a unicorn. It can gleam from a Giorgione, a Poussin; or from some detail in a lesser work of art: an ovalled face above a stiff, glistening collar, a flash of brocade, a cap pearled and tasselled, snow against sunset, a mask not blank but grinning on a chapletted, moonlit dancer, a small hand caressing a toy, a hound's moist eye, bearded features callous under black horns, a withered face on a child's richly-clad body, a dangling rose, jewelled finger, a sprig of thyme, a snatch of half-heard music of Morley or Byrd; and in George Herbert's attempted evocation: 'Church bels heard beyond the starres, the soule's bloude. / The Land of spices; something understood.'

Perhaps in gardens it was most understood, or at least accessible.

Gardens had profited from Crusades, as a result of which roses, iris, Solomon's seal, saffron, lily, rhubarb – used as a drug – were introduced or refined. Printed descriptions of Classical or Arabic gardens envisaged an ideal Garden, no longer larder or surgery but an aesthetic complex perfected by stone or green statuary, heraldic devices, tinted soil. Gardens could imitate tapestry, illuminated pages, mythological friezes and mosaics, with divisions of hedge, wall, shrub catering for the relaxed body and stimulated mind, for exercise and contemplation.

The sixteenth-century intellectual tenor demanded the formal and convoluted. English lords would hear, with envy, wonder, or incredulity, of some Burgundian nobleman sauntering through his Gardens of Love: rectangular hedges, beds shaped in diamonds, arcs, squares, circles for Courtly Love: soft blues and pinks overlapping for Tender Love: hard green spikes, black thorns and crimsons clashing in Passionate Love: tumescent roses balanced by deep-throated lilies, demure violets, for Married Love: tangled blacks, blood-reds, agonised purples within knots and mazes for Doomed Love. The rose suggested femininity and sexual joys, though thorns recalled pain and danger. In hawthorn were Hope and Christ's Passion; cherry expressed Divine Love, as in the Cherry Tree Carol; St John's wort, or Grace of God, exorcised Evil. Apple was a reminder of sin in Eden; oak leaf meant drunkenness; violet, loyalty; palms, conquest of death. Daisy, eye of day, was an image both of the sun and of deceit.

Old lore lingered, not yet wholly dead. William Turner, botanist, physician to Protector Somerset, praised 'the flowers of lavender which should be quilted in a cappe and dayle worn for all diseases of the head that come of a cold cause, and comfort the brayne very well.' Mr Gerard, 'Maister in Chirurgie' and supervisor of Burghley's ample gardens at Theobalds in Hertfordshire and in the Strand, catalogued 1,033 of his own plants, and sold roots of yellowhorn poppy which, 'when properly preserved with sugar, are exceedingly good for them that are withered with age'. Rather than a cap of lavender, he advocated that a garland of rosemary be put about the head, since 'it comforteth the brain, the memorie, the inward senses and comforteth the heart and maketh it merry'. Ophelia in her madness agreed with him: 'There's rosemary, that's for remembrance.' Her pansies symbolised thoughts; fennel, flattery; columbine, the deserted; bitter rue, Herb of Grace, protection from sickness.

Late Tudor and early Stuart gardens sparkled with sweet william, marigold, pansy; nasturtium and tobacco-plant from America, tulips from Asia. Francis Bacon, cold in human relations, loved double violets, gilliflowers, the scented heat of wallflowers. John Tradascent (*c.* 1570–1638) and his son, also John (1608–62), introduced many plants from abroad with which they stocked gardens for Robert Cecil, Buckingham, Charles I. By 1658, the Oxford Botanical Garden was divided for plants of the four known continents, advertising itself as complementary to the Ark, which had contained all the world's animals. 'You have the plants of this world in microcosm in our Garden.'

Tudor and Stuart gardens did not wholly banish medieval symbolism and heraldic conceits, which lingered within Renaissance interpretations of hermetic Mysteries, pagan voluptuousness, astrological codes, belief in the music of the spheres and the harmonious dance of the universe barely perturbed by Galileo's telescope or Baconian theories of space and existence. The synthesis was paralleled in the patchwork Renaissance surfaces and undercurrents of the new Theatre, for which gardens real, staged or imagined were suggestive settings for mock-pastoral comedies, introspective soliloquies, emotional harangues. Imagination was teased and diverted by stone or evergreen globes and astrolabes, pyramids, obelisks, naked figures fading at the ends of hedged alleys and avenues or brooding above arbours and mazes, with flower beds, in deference to rediscovered Classical forms, also Arabic geometry, cut into ovals, arcs, crescents, squares, circles, rectangles, stars and zig-zags, now elevated on balustraded terraces, now laid around urn or fountain in Italian-style sunken gardens. Here too, personal waywardness could sublimate fashion.

Fashionable Tudor gardens flaunted arbours for study, feasting, dalliance, play, 'escape from wearisome occupations'; topiary fashioned into peacocks, unicorns, centaurs; crescent moons honouring the Virgin Queen and Goddess; glossy bowling alleys, archery butts, artificial mounds, glittering fish-ponds, beehives, dovecotes, coppices, arches mottled with roses, draped with honeysuckle. Box hedging, or small fences striped in Tudor white and green, enclosed lavender, rosemary, violet, surmounted by a sculptured Venus or Hercules, or a sundial with its incised mottoes. One royal sundial had thirty ways of announcing time, also a mechanism by which the unsuspecting, expensively attired, examining these, could be abruptly drenched. The monastery bell may have been silenced, but the Renaissance obsession with time was catered for by the new public clocks and personal watches, which relegated the sundial to an ornamental role. As Hilaire Belloc put it some centuries later:

> I am a sundial, and I make a botch
> Of what is done far better by a watch.

The Austrian-born art historian Ernst Gombrich, when asked in 1995 whether the British had a strong visual sense, replied: 'They must have, because gardening is their greatest art. It is immensely widely spread, the interest in gardening and flowers. It is the most living art in this country, I think, and has been for a long time.'

Counter-Reformation wars, the prevalence of banditry and the danger of being taken for a spy did not obstruct the inclination of some of the gentry to travel, in anticipation of the eighteenth-century Grand Tour. Thomas More studied in Paris and Louvain; Philip Sidney studied music and astronomy in Venice, knew Genoa and Padua, Vienna and Prague, Frankfurt and Antwerp, witnessed the St Bartholomew Massacre in Paris and, serving under Leicester in the Netherlands, as perhaps did Ben Jonson, was killed at Zutphen. Men like Sir Richard Grenville and Thomas Arundel volunteered against the Turks. Arundel was created Count of the Holy Roman Empire for personally capturing an enemy banner, infuriating Elizabeth, and his own father, who was only a knight. 'My dogs shall wear no collar but my own,' the Queen raged and, despite their friendship, briefly sent him to the Tower. Milton was in Italy, as was Hobbes, who met Galileo there in 1636. Scattered like flakes of history are characters like the gentleman of Sens (Siena) described in Robert Burton's *The Anatomy of Melancholy* (1621) 'who was afraid to piss, lest all the town should be drowned': the physician caused the bells to be rung backwards and told him that the town was on fire, whereupon he made water and was immediately cured.

But on the whole, foreign wars and the religious divide fostered English insularity. Robert Ascham, austere but humane, tutor to Mary and Elizabeth, Latin Secretary to Edward VI, discovered in a single Italian town 'more liberty to sin than ever I hear tell of in our noble City of London in nine years'. James Howell's *Instructions for Foreine Travell* (1642) deplored such voyaging, as it 'oftentimes makes many to wander from themselves as well as from their country, and to come back mere mimics; and so in going to fare worse, and bring back less wit than they carried forth. They go out figures (according to the Italian proverb) and return ciphers.'

Mental travel on the flood of translations was effective compromise: North's *Plutarch*, Chapman's *Homer*, Florio's version of Leo Africanus' *History and Description of Africa*, as well as translations of Petrarch, Ariosto, Montaigne, the blazing lusty bulk of Rabelais, afforded depths of allusion and gave edge to blunt English humour.

But the Renaissance could only refine the Gothic and Reformation apprehension of Death, whose summons could itself be a form of wit, tripping Caesar in his glory, mocking statecraft, tilting askew the boastful crown, foreclosing on debts to vanity, disease, disillusion, the night. For Raleigh, bitter-sweet, 'Our mothers' wombs the tiring housese be, / Where we are dressed for this short comedy', but Shakespeare's Richard II, in a play outrageous to Elizabeth, was forced to humble himself before the deceiving nature of kingship:

> For within the hollow crown
> That rounds the mortal temples of a king,
> Keeps Death his court.

Cyril Tourneur wrote an Address to his mistress's skull, feeling, like many of his fellow-poets, melancholy beneath pageantry, beauty so fleeting, rosebuds to be so swiftly gathered. In funerary monuments as in poetry, the skull remained a favoured ornament, its pallid, taunting silence reducing trained eloquence to cackle and gibber, the more chilling as novelty, comforts, discovery, technics dissolved primeval certainties. Science, it now seemed, could acknowledge *Wyrd* more ruthlessly than any oracle, more coldly than the wavering reassurances of salvation and immortality. Puritans could, more dynamically than Anglicans, transmute dread of death into fresh certainties, methodically fortifying themselves with convictions of self-righteousness, of sin overcome. Their vision was often vengefully apocalyptic and as purposeful as Science itself, to be feared by crown and mitre alike.

Dr Johnson pronounced that poetry was a force able to call new powers into being. Classical themes were sharply renewed in Tudor and Jacobean theatres: power as appetite, responsibility, or destroyer: the thrills, limitations and urgency of individual choice: retribution exacted for pride: the sway of unconscious motives: the temptations of the repulsive, destructive, and mischievous: the resources of practical women, devoted yet independent, often ambitious: the sudden, unforeseen action demanded of the introspective: the impact of racial difference, the pledged word, unrestrained humour, and of 'degree' and 'commodity', reputation and Name. All converge in Shakespeare. Shrewd about behaviour, the frequent discrepancy between character and personality – 'I like not fair terms and a villain's mind' – he was less concerned with the scientific dimension being expanded by Copernicus, Kepler, Dee. The theological and intellectual range of the plays are adequate for one who mingled, on whatever terms, with sophisticates from the Court, the Inns of Court, the Universities. However, he seems obsessed not with current Western disputes but with individual necessity. The ruin of Richard II, an Essex, is self-induced and need be attributed to no historical trend. In whatever age, fraud can masquerade as piety, the charlatan as philosopher:

> In religion
> What damned error but some silver brow
> Will bless it and approve it with a test?

Ireland, the Armada, a Poor Law, are less potent for him than old beliefs in the inter-connectedness of matter under the eye of Providence: colours, stars, music remain woven into nature and the supernatural. But, like T.S. Eliot, he distinguished between information, knowledge, wisdom. Like Goethe, he knew that if you thrust your hand deep into the life around you, what you haul up will contain something of truth. Here, university polish was unnecessary. In *Henry VIII*, much history is ignored, the greatest lines are given to the losers, Wolsey and Katharine, victims of lost causes.

The dramatist Edward Bond observed in 1995: 'We badly abuse Shakespeare if we pretend he knows all the answers. He doesn't. He knows the questions.' Ibsen, Chekhov would agree.

Shakespeare was rooted in popular culture, with educated overtones: ballads, oral tales, slangy badinage from foul-mouthed tapsters, stage-hands, ostlers, 'liberal shepherds'. An easy wit is grounded less in stock Renaissance conceits, pedantic puns, scholarly references (though all recur) than in perception and listening, in the perpetual contrast between 'Might be' and 'Is', and the fusing of the hitherto unconnected. 'A sentence is but a cheverell glove to a good wit: how quickly the wrong side may be turned outward.' Cheverell is kidskin, notable for its pliancy: 'Here's a wit of cheverell, that stretches from an inch to an ell broad.'

As actor, writer, shareholder, of ambiguous social standing, Shakespeare knew, like Dickens, what life was about and, despite obligations to the box-office, often filled a play with more than audiences of very varied social groups could be expected to comprehend fully, thus (if inadvertently) ensuring vast posthumous attention. Any condescension to 'the man from Stratford' is, however, misplaced. Tudor grammar schools gave education more thorough and all-round than in many modern English academies. Between 1547 and 1603 a hundred and thirty-six grammar schools were founded, teaching English, Latin, sometimes Greek, arithmetic, though William Harrison complained (1587) that in some, 'poor men's children are commonly shut out, and the richer sort received', adding that most pupils studied little other than histories, tables, dice, and trifles . . . 'a lamentable hearing'. Grammar and arithmetic were important, but so was music. An adept pupil could sniff what was in the wind, what people might be behind their faces, also some difference between intellectual dross and lasting essences, between truth and illusion. The pragmatic common sense and scepticism about high-flying pretensions, so evident in Alfred, Chaucer, Occam, survived the exaltations of Renaissance and Reformation.

In *All's Well That Ends Well*, Lafeu remarks: 'They say miracles are past, and we have our philosophical persons, to make modern and familiar things supernatural and causeless. Hence is it, that we make trifles of terrors, ensconcing ourselves into seeming knowledge, when we should submit ourselves to an unknown fear.'

Psychologically astute within a considerable legacy of melodrama, Shakespearian theatre exploited native poetic irony, dissolving then reassembling the familiar Wheel of Fortune: Murder gains a crown which poisons the murderer, a prince revenges his father but loses all but his Name. To push even justice, integrity, virtue beyond reasonable limits is to become a nuisance. Face-values deceive; the Devil can possibly speak truth, a petty scoundrel fool a victorious hero.

> Strength by limping sway disabled,
> And art made tongue-tied by authority:
> And folly (doctor-like), controlling skill.

Shakespeare moralises only through others, allowing sympathy to both Richard II and Bolingbroke, Caesar and Brutus, Falstaff and Hal. Vision transpires from the oblique, together with visitations from extraordinary territories of sleep and dream. His personal attitudes can only be inferred, though they are unlikely to include anarchism, regicide, Puritan prudishness, and the dogmatism of ignorance. He has been treated as an acquisitive *rentier*, a pure poet forced into the theatre for money, a secret Catholic, a nationalist, a conservative, an anti-Semite, attractive fancy-man, lawyer or aristocrat concealing himself behind another's pen, even an Iraqi, Sheik Shabir. Feminists are having their say. A computer known to W.H. Auden discovered that he was Edward VI, dying aged 125, having also written all of Bacon and Ben Jonson, as well as *Don Quixote*.

The plays are not goads to action, in the way that *Uncle Tom's Cabin* stimulated Lincoln, but they provoke mature consideration of opposites so often proved identical, some wonderings about whether most friendship is feigning, most loving mere folly, and whether culture is much more than a misleading metaphor, existence itself devised by the wilful, the misleading, the cynical, or the ill-disposed. This imaginative existence is only nominally Christian, in Tragedy depending not on miracles or Grace but on human effort and choice, with traces of Seneca's Stoicism, tolerant but resolute and self-controlled. 'The very substance of the ambitious is merely the shadow of a dream.' Many are frustrated, but sometimes usefully so:

> We, ignorant of ourselves,
> Beg often our own harms, which the wise powers
> Deny us for our own good. So find we profit
> By losing of our prayers.

Shakespeare's inner restlessness continually extends the simple:

> Glory is like a circle in the water
> Which never ceaseth to enlarge itself
> Till, by broad spreading, it disperse to naught.

To the detriment of his own plays, watertight and airless, Voltaire hated 'details' in literature, but the Englishman's eye for a detail – Lear's button –

humanises Tragedy, bonds coarse reality to impulses spoilt by definition, to the life beyond words. Shaw insisted that to see *Richard II* is insufficient, one should be able to whistle it.

Audiences demanded originality of treatment, not of plot. Plots were available from the Classics, Italy, Albion, History. *Hamlet*, derived from a thirteenth-century Danish murder tale, was fleshed out, probably by Kyd, as a typical revenge play, raised to Tragedy by Shakespeare, and had a German counterpart, *Der Bestrafte Brudermord*. The British historical plays, taken from Geoffrey of Monmouth and Holinshed, he fashioned from the pioneer historical drama of Elizabeth's first publisher, John Bale.

Shakespeare's scholarship might have been inferior to Jonson's or Bacon's, but scholarship alone seldom unravels the mystery of people. In a single sentence he could delight the wits without numbing the groundlings; or, in a trifling snatch – 'For bonny sweet Robin is all my joy' – unite both. A modern German dramatist, Peter Hacks, asserts: 'We know a certain amount more about the world than Shakespeare did. We hardly know more about man, and we still do not know the half of what he knew about art.' Terence Tiller, journalist and poet, extracted from one line – 'They say the owl was a baker's daughter' – anthropological, mythological and historical allusions, indeed patterns, involving Athene, sacred and profane prostitution, fear of stepmothers; this, in a context of madness and death and some recall of garlanded ritual sacrifice.

Macbeth interlocks several circles of time and consciousness: Albion and Holinshed, the occult and the political, Christian conscience and pagan promptings. Historical facts are woven into the medieval Chain of Being: Duncan's murder, 'gainst nature, causes earthquake, tempest, animal cannibalism. Forked truths counter the deceptive precise, where nothing is but what is not. There are also Shakespeare's blatant compliments to James VI and I.

Those whose ancestors knew only Mystery plays and seasonal or guild mummery could now watch a legendary Celtic King or Roman hero unfreeze into a being as tangible as Burghley or Essex. They could perceive the chaos within Macbeth mounting as he moved through planes of being while remaining basically himself. 'Storm and Stress', *Sturm und Drang*, was appreciated in England before F.M. von Klinger coined the phrase in 1776. *King Lear* was hacked four-square from Albion, but far transcended it. Stock medieval types, 'humours', have become human, even minor characters make quiet asides and rejoinders sometimes more crucial than rhetorical set-pieces. All have more life than Grail heroes and Knights, usually one-dimensional, without unconscious demands or inexplicable perversities.

> In men, as in a rough-grown grove, remain
> Cave-keeping evils that obscurely sleep.

Marlowe, Jonson, Shakespeare disregarded Classical and French unities for looser innovations, stinging Voltaire to compare Shakespeare to a drunken savage, of power and grandeur but with a detestable form of witless vulgarity. 'Vulgarity', in its proper sense, was particularly appealing to the English, and indeed praised by Goethe; an immersion in total humanity, shared by Dickens, Hogarth, Gogol, Balzac, regardless of decorum. The tragic can include the farcical. That a drunken porter can intrude on a tense moment is one of the tricks of actual existence, natural as weather or a Royal yawn.

Pelagian free-will and English compromise oppose *wyrd*, inborn human traits, and vaulting ambition. Evil can be resisted, and failure is not always total. Richard II's kingdom drains away to a prison cell but music creates new sources of insight. Lear disintegrates in madness and loss, submitting to terrifying self-judgement: 'Who is it who can tell me who I am?' – an ironic comment on personal irresponsibility. Self-regarding, he has had a feeble notion of self. Yet he finally realises truths he should long have known:

> Take physic, pomp:
> Expose thyself to feel what wretches feel.

Hamlet was in Renaissance mode, university trained, with wit cultivated, apt, malicious, a bundle of possibilities at a court where Polonius out-matches any priest and the monarch has inklings of Divine Right, so attractive to James I. Self-aware, versatile, Hamlet has not discarded pre-Renaissance responses to incest, death, the supernatural. Like many English intellectuals, he recognises both the futility of war and that right action may entail killing. He times his revenge with a scientist's detachment. In him, human themes represented by Orestes, Antigone, Oedipus reach a stature perhaps rivalled only by versions of Odysseus revised for each generation, Tennyson and Joyce supplying startling but still plausible contrasts.

Absolutes are untrustworthy; no institution, however majestic, should be omnipotent; a Fool's quip can demolish authority, Reputation can be set at naught: 'Can honour set a leg?' Admiration for Shakespeare's achievements was never unanimous. A London headmistress, Jane Brown, banned *Romeo and Juliet* for her pupils in 1995, as too heterosexual. But Brown need not have the last word. Chekhov, whom Tolstoy begged to renounce play-writing, his plays being 'even worse' than Shakespeare's, admired Shakespeare, and *The Seagull* has poignant reminders of *Hamlet*. For Hazlitt (1817), 'Anyone who studies *Coriolanus* may save himself the trouble of reading Burke's *Reflections*, Paine's *Rights of Man* or the debates in both Houses of Parliament since the French Revolution.'

Danton, a Falstaff blended with Caliban, studied Shakespeare. Kemble's Company, in France in 1827, shattered much academic hostility and con-vulsed such youthful Romantics as Hugo, Delacroix, Berlioz, Dumas *fils*, de Vigny, Lemaître; and Gautier, described by the Goncourts as an amalgam of Falstaff and Mercutio. In the wake of the blood-drenched Napoleonic adventure, misinterpreted as romance – its hero was as romantic as a cannon – they saw in Shakespeare a sensational challenge to orthodoxy, questioning character, the stable ego, and simplistic motivation.

Seventeenth-century English travelling actors had taken plays, mostly Shakespeare's, as far east as Poland. The Thirty Years' War disrupted this, but then translations by A.W. Schlegel and Ludwig Tieck gave German drama-tists models of startling originality, Schlegel finding Othello a tragic Rembrandt, and Shakespeare 'a profound artist, not a blind, wild-running genius. He links together all that is high and deep in his being, and the strangest, indeed apparently most incompatible qualities exist in him peace-fully side by side.' Hamlet, as sensitive youth, emotionally wounded, already disillusioned, prefigured Werther and Wilhelm Meister. Pirandello put Shakespeare first, then Ibsen. Nietzsche's favourite poets were Hölderlin, Byron and Shakespeare, though his comment on the last is revealing: 'He presents you with so many strong men – rough, hard, powerful, iron-willed. It is in men like these that our age is so poor.' Hitler, however, at a dinner in 1942 honouring – inappropriate verb – Himmler, preached: 'The mis-fortune is that none of our great writers took his subjects from German Imperial history. Our Schiller found nothing better to do than to glorify a Swiss cross-bowman . . . The English, for their part, had a Shakespeare – but the history of his country has supplied Shakespeare, as far as heroes are con-cerned, only with imbeciles and madmen.'

In England, Gloriana had predeceased Elizabeth. The myth had faded, the foreign Stuarts were questionable assets and, though sharing a monarch,

England and Scotland remained separate, inimical states. James VI and I inherited a Treasury depleted by inflation and loss of Crown properties, an uneasy international situation, domestic religious tensions, unrest among lawyers and judges, and a Parliament filling with doughty personalities inclined to opposition.

His mental abilities outranged his physical appearance. Chattering, lecturing incessantly, clumsy, he lacked dignity. His legs tended to buckle, so that he had often to lean on a handsome favourite; his eyes rolled, his mouth slobbered, and his clothes, too obviously padded, invited ridicule. His nervousness was understandable. With a father blown up, his mother beheaded by English officials, some now serving him, he could scarcely affect disdainful insouciance to weapons, slights, crowds. He had already survived Scottish violence, conspiracy, pursuit, and would soon be confronted with the unparalleled Gunpowder Plot. On Twelfth Night 1623 the young members of Gray's Inn borrowed some small cannon from the Tower of London as part of their masquing; when they were fired the timid King James started from his bed, crying 'Treason! Treason!' He could sense more popular curiosity than acclaim. Few hated him, save English Catholics who had expected too much from the son of the martyred Mary; but many despised him, and resented not only his favourites but his intimacy with Gondomar, the Spanish ambassador, 'the Spanish Machiavelli', seemingly an unofficial member of the government. His greedy and indiscriminate sale of titles – with humour signally his own, he knighted a loin of beef, 'Sir Loin', at Hoghton Tower in Lancashire – and his judicial murder of the glamorous Sir Walter Raleigh dismayed the English. In brogue scarcely comprehensible he would refer to a monarch's Divine Right, which earlier monarchs must often have felt but knew better than to formalise. 'Kings', James informed Parliament in 1610, 'are justly called gods, for they exercise a manner of resemblance of divine power upon earth.'

Today he becomes more complex and interesting, like Aethelred II, John, Edward II, Richard II. William Harvey saw him as afflicted with 'incredible sadness'. His hatred of war, even drill, while causing him to neglect the Navy, preserved England from the nightmarish Thirty Years' War, despite obligations to his son-in-law, the Elector Palatine and King of Bohemia, who quickly lost his crown, with Spanish connivance. Earlier, James and Salisbury insisted on neutrality, and peace with Spain, resisting belligerent clamour from Parliament, unaccompanied by any readiness to grant the requisite taxes.

Raleigh had written that there are no religious wars, only civil wars. The Thirty Years' War, the first fully international contest since Roman times, was territorial in motive, with religious slogans, presided over by a Swedish 'Protestant Lion' allied to a French cardinal against the Catholic Emperor, whose foremost general, Wallenstein, was addicted to astrology, and with the Turks holding a watching brief. It spread disease, famine, even cannibalism throughout central Europe, with neurotic results for Germany which Bismarck was to detect. For ten years after 1650 Nuremburg allowed men two wives at once, in an attempt at repopulation. C.V. Wedgwood, the war's chronicler, thought the seventeenth century the unhappiest in western Europe until the twentieth, 'a time (like ours) in which Man's activities outran his powers of control'. Mercenaries left Britain to fight, often for Sweden; some of them were future Civil War commanders – Essex, Goring, Wilmot, the Fairfaxes, Prince Rupert – though Thomas Carew wrote unprophetically in 1632:

> What though the German drum
> Bellow for freedom and revenge, the noise
> Concerns not us, nor shall divert our joys;
> Nor ought the thunder of their carabins
> Drown the sweet airs of our tun'd violins.

King James had several weaknesses, one of which was for young men. Clarendon wrote of George Villiers, soon to be Duke of Buckingham: 'Never any man in any age, nor, I believe, in any country, rose in so short a time to so much greatness of honour, power, or fortune, upon no other advantages or recommendation than of the beauty and graciousness of his person.' James's other main obsession, for hunting, embraced a delight in fondling the steaming entrails of his victims, a trait scarcely enhanced by his aversion to washing, save for resting his finger-tips on a damp towel. More seriously, he prided himself on his 'King-craft', euphemism for political dissimulation, confidently assuring Parliament: 'This I must say for Scotland and may truly vaunt it. Here I sit and govern with my pen; I write, and it is done; and by a clerk of the Council I govern Scotland now, which my ancestors could not do by the sword.' Yet he was more tolerant and well-intentioned than many who despised him, and compares well enough with the thrusting Cecils and Howards, Cokes, Bacons, Pyms, let alone with a Richelieu, Tilly, Wallenstein – assassinated by an Irish mercenary – or Gustavus Adolphus.

He survives, however, more as a considerable curiosity than a great achiever. When he was in his turn eviscerated, for embalming, a witness attested that, on being opened, his head 'was so full of braynes as they could not, upon the openinge, keep them from spilling, a great marke of his infinite judgement.' Some could have thought of him as Malvolio, now in full charge, ashine with authority but stuffed with fears, bitterness, upstart pride. When his Abbey tomb was examined in the nineteenth century, near the body of that inveterate hater of tobacco lay, like a sardonic tribute from Raleigh, a workman's half-smoked pipe.

Outward show was undeterred by the misgivings of Parliament, the judiciary, Puritans and country squires. Rubens painted the baroque ceiling in Inigo Jones's Banqueting Hall in Whitehall Palace, thought by Roy Strong the greatest of all Europe's extant ceilings. It flattered the new inter-loping dynasty from the North, deceiving its exemplar into inflated notions of authority. With mechanical marvels and hypnotic collusion of per-spective, colour, movement, Inigo Jones, aided by such writers as Jonson, created the Masque, an extension of the Court, itself an arena for the monarch, excluding the people. Its flattering mythological correspondences added another layer of unreality.

The Masque was more pantomine than drama, ballet, opera, but with suggestions of each. Despite massive stage architecture and elaborate scenic mountains, lakes, woods, towers, pavilions, grottoes, its boundaries were as flimsy as those between Albion and the Other World: there was the same yearning for evanescence, the fascination of mortal flux. At a quaver from viol or lute, a shift of colour, statues would tremble into a dance, a bird speak verse. There was elision of light and sound, a transparency of effect flickering with quicksilver impressions – beautiful, bizarre, courteously erotic, eerie – combining to imply pagan impulses barely checked, a nostalgia for a golden past and chimerical future, restrained by the formalities of design, rhyme, metre. Science seemed locked into Magic, in Ovidian transformations of a cloud to a palace, a monster to a knight, courtiers to satyrs, prayers to doves, nixies to princesses. Fire and water, earth and air fused in greens, golds, scar-lets, vanishing at a technician's nod. A sun dropped flowers, gods murmured orders to sprites; nymphs, discreetly garlanded, trod galliards, pavans, alle-mandes, in time to tambourine and trumpet and the high, plaintive unwinding of a madrigal.

Scripts allowed topical allusions: in one Masque, Envy traipsed behind an angelic Presence, exquisite and omnipotent, clearly Buckingham. But mostly time collapsed, allowing a mermaid to chat with a courtier, the King to feel at home on Olympus. In such dreams, created to lead nowhere, and in the sylvan artificiality of the Cavalier lyric, the social élite could evade both personal premonitions and parliamentary rowdiness. A masque could repel the clamour excited by brute questions of law, monopoly, privilege, taxation.

Outside this enchanted realm was another magic. Wholesale witchcraft persecution erupted in the western world. Some thirty thousand English 'witches' are estimated to have been hanged between 1400 and 1716, witchcraft ceasing to be a capital crime only in 1736. Britain never matched the hysteria of Sweden, Germany, Switzerland, New England. English prosecutions, most numerous or most efficiently recorded in Essex, were as rigorous under the republic as under the monarchy. Matthew Hopkins of Manningtree, student of James I's indignant tract *Demonology*, Witchfinder-General after the triumph of parliamentary liberties, achieved considerable renown and awe. Parodying godliness, a McCarthyian prototype, he sent several score to the gibbet. One, still remembered, was John Lowes, eighty years old, the assiduous, gentle and much loved Rector of Brandeston for five decades. Hopkins, in the name of Christ, accused him of traffic with the Devil, tortured him into admitting that he had seen demons destroying ships; then, at Bury St Edmunds in 1646, forced him to conduct his own funeral service.

For some recent historians, English witchcraft has less meant pagan survivals superannuated by science than resentments and fears deriving from changed social relations. These left many villagers isolated from neighbours prospering on more diverse occupations, on enclosures, even on inflation. Losers could respond only with a muttered curse or angry gesture, too easily connected with the loss of a baby or cow, or with an inopportune storm. Old scores could be repaid, malice let loose, children denounce their parents and science, never to this day wholly comprehensible, be disregarded. At least in the seventeenth century 'science' was not used as one of their weapons by the witch hunters, as it was by some doctors and social workers when they persuaded themselves that they had discovered epidemics of child abuse in late twentieth-century Cleveland and elsewhere.

Astrology continues to appeal to dictators, Indian politicians, the White House; in 1620 it made John Metson fulminate:

Astrology is an art whereby cozening of knaves cheat plain honest men, that teacheth both the theory and practise of these cozenage, a science instructing all the students of it to lie as often as they speak, and to be believed no oftener than they hold their tongues; that tells the truth as often as Bawds go to Church, witches and whores say their prayers, or never but when the English nones and Greek Kalends meet together.

Under both Charles I and Cromwell, plain honest men annually bought thirty thousand copies of William Lilly's astronomical almanacs, a prodigious sale. These successfully predicted the rebels' victory in the Civil War, but neither Restoration nor Great Fire.

Few perhaps noticed the deeper historical currents: the Overbury poisoning scandal, involving some of the highest in the land, had not been a rare hiccough and was but too much apiece with Jacobean Whitehall, emotionally over-heated until the sobriety imposed by Charles I. *Macbeth*, *The Duchess of Malfi* reflected this, while *The Tempest* could arouse doubts about scholarship, masculine authority, overseas glamour. Deaths of European notables were frequently ascribed to poison. Science was not dispersing that curious human fascination with dissolution, loss, pain, the lure of decay. From such tainted air and shifting sands stepped Cornelia, in Webster's *The White Devil*, a play with much reference to poison, apposite in an age when old beliefs were stagnant, new certainties apt either to crumble or to justify resort to gun, axe, and the cup perilous.

> . . . here's a white hand;
> Can blood so soon be washed out? Let me see;
> When screech-owls croak upon the chimney-top,
> And the strange cricket i' the oven sings and hops,
> When yellow spots do on your hands appear,
> Be certain then you of a corse shall hear.
> Out upon't, how 'tis speckled! h'as handled a
> toad, sure. Cowslip-water is good for the memory:
> pray, buy me three ounces of 't.

Whatever the febrile imaginings at Court and in the playhouses, the City, profiting from prolonged Continental warfare, was studying economics as expertly as Antwerp and Amsterdam. Its capitalists were teaching money how to breed. From his financial experience in Holland, Sir Thomas Gresham founded the Royal Exchange in 1556, facilitating England's commercial dealings and itself a replica of the Antwerp Exchange, which by Stuart times it surpassed. In London in 1592, Duke Frederick of

Württemburg saw the Thames dense with shipping from France, the Netherlands, Sweden, Denmark, Hamburg 'and other kingdoms', and noted that Londoners were 'magnificently apparelled and extremely proud and overbearing'. Further off, the great mercantile companies were making the individualistic Raleighs, Drakes, Frobishers seem picturesque but out-dated.

England was also utilising her own natural assets, aside from cloth. Deep-coal mining had begun, often on the expropriated monastic lands, and at the Civil War trebled the output of all Europe; glass and lead production was vying with German; Kentish and Sussex iron expanded, William Camden having already recorded that Sussex was 'full of mines, all over it, and the incessant noise of hammering'. A German, Richard Cranich, had introduced superior mining techniques, supplying the raw materials for the English armaments industry, which would lead Europe in exporting artillery.

The Crown faced increasing demands, financial and administrative, but with a depleted Treasury and diminished revenues. In his *History of the World* Raleigh had submitted kings to moral censure and divine rebuke. There was soon gathering impatience with Royal restrictions, gestures towards reli-gious tolerance, the threat of taxes legal but novel. Capricious bestowal of trade monopolies – some seven hundred of them – on Royal supporters and favourites was an obstacle to commerce and manufacture. Prerogative Courts, formerly useful in restoring quotidian order, were now, by obstruct-ing Common Law, harsh weapons for a Crown faced with a restive Commons, more than usually reluctant to grant extra taxes without gains for itself and, more incidentally, for the public.

Charles I's efforts to sustain government free of parliamentary interfer-ence did not then appear as hopeless as they do now, when it seems clear to us that Divine Right can have had no future in an England of furnaces and deep mining. In *Sir Thomas More*, the Chancellor rebuked the Evil May Day rioters in terms no longer appropriate to England, though used daily by Habsburgs, Bourbons, Romanovs, Ottomans: 'For to the King, God hath His Office lent', an equating of law-breaking with blasphemy which would grate on City merchants, parliamentary lawyers, Puritan ministers.

For much of this period national prosperity was considerable, though without much benefit to the King, who saw that, while the nation was rich, the State was poor. His remedies were ingenious taxes based, for example, on old laws of knighthood and forest, and demands for religious uniformity.

Archbishop Laud cherished the magnificent English liturgy, Anglican ritual and order. He put stress on the sacramental, as opposed to the Puritan concentration on Scripture and preaching. He loved and restored churches, expelling idlers, vagrants, gossips, forcing parsons to attend to their jobs. Suave diplomacy, tactful manipulation, cultured query were not his way, but rather episcopal fines, imprisonments, threats. This provoked revolts in Scotland, and to meet them Charles was forced to summon Parliament, giving it the chance to assert itself once more. Laud could have learnt from a future Archbishop, Robert Runcie, who confessed in 1996 that, against ecclesiastical law, he had 'turned a blind eye' in ordaining known homosexuals. The phrase is English, originating with Nelson, and, as much as 'the letter of the law', assists civilisation.

Charles himself was a dignified private face in a stormy public place, his merits not political but domestic and artistic. The patron of Inigo Jones and Van Dyck, he built one of Europe's greatest art collections including pictures by Titian, Raphael, Veronese, Tintoretto, Rubens, Leonardo, and a choice assembly of miniatures. He tried to promote an English appreciation of sculpture, not complete even today and which would have ruffled Dr Johnson: 'Painting consumes labour not disproportionate to its effect; but a fellow will hack half a year at a block of marble to make something in stone that hardly resembles a man. The value of statuary is owing to its difficulty. You would not value the finest head cut upon a carrot.'

One parliamentary accusation levelled against Charles concerned his addiction 'to Mr Shakespere's witty comedies'. He planned a library for Cambridge, purchasing Arabic manuscripts for it. All this had scant popular appeal. Publicly, the King displayed his father's self-regarding argumentativeness without his wary intelligence, or Elizabeth's finesse, even in retreat. Attempting personal rule without Parliament, he relied less on his own talents than on the muscle of Laud and Thomas Wentworth, Lord Strafford, his Lord Deputy in Ireland. Strong-willed, Strafford was determined that, at whatever cost, he must rescue society for its own good by sustaining the monarchy. He used ministerial decree and prerogative courts as short-cuts through the rigmarole of Common Law, pig-headed juries, lawyers' wrangles. 'I am for *Thorough*, my lord, less than *Thorough* will not do.' Richelieu, Wallenstein, Gustavus Adolphus, Emperor Ferdinand would have agreed without further thought; unlike Charles, they possessed standing armies.

Racked by incurable disease, facing opposition from almost all quarters, even from within the Court, Strafford had little patience. Parliament, at last recalled after eleven years to vote funds with which to fight rebellious Scots, had less. Failing to impeach Strafford, the Commons declared him, by Bill of Attainder, guilty of treason – a witness testified that he had said in Council, 'You have an army here you may employ to reduce this rebellious kingdom'. The wording was ambiguous: it might have referred to Scotland, but could be interpreted as suggesting the use of an Irish army to subdue England.

Only one man could save Strafford: without the Royal signature, the Bill was invalid. For two days, enflamed by orators, preachers, agitators, immense and shouting crowds stood before Whitehall Palace, within which sat the harrassed little King, his wife and children, amongst them two future kings. He had pledged himself to save Strafford, his signature would betray his honour; but refusal to sign might well see the masses invading the Palace, destroying himself, the dynasty, the Crown.

Charles signed, preserving his reign, though not his conscience – as, at the end, he confessed. There was an appalling howl as Strafford, dark, bowed with sickness, climbed the scaffold on Tower Hill, muttering the Psalmist's warning against trusting princes. Black Tom, last defender of English sacramental monarchy, never entered folk-lore or Victorian legend to join Godiva, Streona, Hereward, Robin Hood, Herne, Richard III, Guy Fawkes. When Robert Browning's historical play *Strafford* was produced at Covent Garden in 1837, it closed after four nights. Today it would be less successful.

The republican Tony Benn, of whom Harold Wilson remarked that he immatured with age, said in a broadcast in 1996 that historical change comes from below. English history does not wholly confirm this, though it is true of the rise of trade-unionism, of the Peasants' Revolt, resistance to enclosures, Chartism; all, while failing, did ultimately affect social movement. Nevertheless, the Synod of Whitby, the Norman Conquest, Magna Carta, the Dissolution of the Monasteries and break with Rome, the execution of Charles I, Habeas Corpus, the 1688 Revolution, parliamentary Reform, the entry into the Great War were enforced from above, sometimes to popular dissent or indifference.

In origin the English Civil War was no mass movement; nor a simple conflict of old land against new money, laughing Cavaliers against stern Puritans. Many families were divided, like the landowning class itself.

Mercantile interests were less so, being largely for Parliament, not envisaging the later usurpations of army officers and presbyters, and the ascent of Levellers. Like primitive Christianity and early socialism, the conflict demonstrated that economics and self-interest are not invariably the conscious human motive. Personal loyalty to King or principle could determine choice. In the absence of conscription, the role of ambition, friendship, boredom, accident, temperament, bone-headedness, together with local issues, cannot be disregarded. 'I have no reverence for bishops for whom this quarrel subsists,' Sir Edmund Verney said, carrying the Royal standard to his death at Edgehill.

Fighting began reluctantly, tentatively. The first Parliamentary commanders were noblemen, more eager to rebuke than thrash the King, one of themselves. There were those like the Royalist volunteer and physician William Harvey who, in charge of the Prince of Wales and Duke of York during the battle of Edgehill, in Aubrey's words, 'withdrew with them under a hedge', to read; or like the Yorkshire farmer Charles Williams who, when the war ended, did not know that it had ever begun; or Lord Falkland, killed at Newbury, of whom people said that he had ceased to hate but had not yet learnt to love. Matthew Arnold reflected: 'For a sound cause he could not fight, because there was none; he could only fight for the least bad of the unsound ones.'

Cromwell himself was goaded towards republicanism only by Charles's intransigence and by the factionalism and incompetence of his own colleagues. More malleable and trustworthy than Charles, he fruitlessly experimented with constitutional devices until, tersely irritated, he accepted 'Protectorship' of the entire island.

In the war's several stages, bloodier and larger sieges and battles were eventually followed by executions, even massacres, though these should be seen in European perspective. From a population of some four and a half million, about 90,000 perished in battle, some 100,000 from related disease and famine. Germany, in the Thirty Years' War, lost perhaps eight million. Despite savagery inflicted on women after Naseby, civilian rights were respected to a degree which would have astonished Tilly and Wallenstein; mercenaries, paid by plunder, were not used.

Charles finally surrendered to the Scots, was then sold to the English. After a second outbreak of civil war and months of negotiation nullified by Royal deviousness, Commissioners from the Commons and Army assembled in Rufus's Westminster Hall to try the King for treason, not against the

Crown but against the People. Charles, soon reviled as Man of Blood, Beast of the Apocalypse, refused to plead and died on a scaffold outside Whitehall Palace with courteous dignity before a silent crowd which, after the axe fell, groaned eerily and was viciously dispersed by dragoons. It was reported that staples had been brought as a precaution against him struggling, but the officials misjudged their man, who himself gave the order – his last – to the axeman. Kipling was to inform Gilbert Murray that when being decapitated, a man usually belches slightly, with a clammy sound.

Was Kingship an organic, indeed animal, institution, rooted deep in psychological needs, or would science, reason, backed by military force, permanently extinguish archaism, magic, crude loyalty? Egalitarian soldiers and Levellers were imagining that Royal downfall would, or should, usher in Paradise, abolish enclosures, Property itself. Cromwell was, however, a staunch upholder of private property, rank, orderly society, rejecting dreams of absolute justice and freedom. To him, general religious tolerance meant tolerance of idolatry or indifference, equality was a chimera unjustified by the Bible and against the visible distribution of talents and moral worth. As politician and general, he was the amateur only slowly finding his natural gifts; he allowed mediocrities to improvise, experiment and manoeuvre until, his patience exhausted, he shoved them aside. He and Fairfax gave England its first professionalised army, truly a 'New Model'. Against ideological Army mutinies he tried exhortation, then bullets.

Cromwell was one of many small-time gentleman farmers, unambitious, domestically upright, devout, preferring experience and impulse to doctrinaire utopianism. Unlike many canting preachers, he did not seek revenge on life for its manifold temptations; he enjoyed bowls, hawking, and he bred horses. Extremists deplored the number of violins at a daughter's wedding. His favourite daughter was always Royalist. He had no ingrained hatred of kings, only a growing objection to a particular King.

In Ireland he succumbed to barely sane God-smitten ferocity, and in general showed that nationalism, like sex, can as brutally inflame a progressive as a stick-in-the-mud. He congratulated himself on avenging 'the most barbarous massacre that ever the sun beheld', by slaughtering several thousand soldiers and civilians at Drogheda and Wexford. Normally, he was quick-tempered when crossed, subject to depression, clutching Biblical texts which too easily became toxic slogans, strengthening his predilection to self-deception, to passing the moral buck. He excused his Irish atrocities: 'I am persuaded that this is the judgement of God upon these barbarous wretches.' Such premises were perilously akin to that of Divine Right. He remains England's solitary dictator, unrestricted by Parliament, public opinion, foreign powers, though never wholly independent of the City. Wily at manipulating the letter of the law while ignoring its spirit, to win a particular motion he once tricked the Commons by choosing not to remind them that calendar months were not lunar months. He was no manic leader inventing catastrophe to prolong his rule, though he may not have whole-heartedly agreed that dictatorship is justified only when it creates conditions for its own abdication. Certainly, under him three centuries of English global sea power began. The first of a series of maritime wars against England's trade rivals, the Dutch, was launched; the Spanish were attacked in the Mediterranean and in the West Indies, where Jamaica was seized in 1655. Thurloe, an impeccable civil servant, supplied him with an intelligence organisation surpassing the Tudors'.

His court, if self-righteous, sometimes vindictive, avoided sexual scandals, provocative favouritism, rumours of poison. English Catholics suffered no more, perhaps less, than under Laud, and in 1656, influenced by Antonio Carvajal, his Sephardic military grain purveyor and espionage chief, he re-admitted the Jews, though the City blocked his idea of founding a Jewish National Home: no more than Catholics were they allowed political rights.

The Republic, often underestimated for its administrative and intellectual achievements, like most revolutionary or parvenu regimes feared the uncertain, the slightly askew, and strove for sobriety. J. Howell's *Londonopolis* (1657) lists regulations about dung, dirt, coal, tavern behaviour, farm beasts in houses, street booths. 'They inquire about panders, bawds, witches, strumpets, common punks and scolds.' Modern republicans should not over-revere their predecessors – Howell continued: 'With regard to the law, it is so severe and so systematically ordered that nowhere in the world can it be more so . . . hence comes it that one can really go about at night unarmed and with purse at hand. The slightest theft is punished with death: even a youth of fifteen for his first crime or theft is hanged: a few months ago a lad was seen on his way to the gallows merely for having stolen a bag of currants.'

Theatres were closed, adultery made a capital offence, perhaps only nominally. Parliament legislated against 'unlawful meetings of idle and vain persons, for erecting May Poles and May bushes, and for using Moric Dances and other heathenism and unlawful customs, the observation whereof tendeth to draw together a great concourse of loose people.'

Beneath these sanctimonious rigours, like water under the ice, ran much of the old English hedonism of fairs and football, Robin Hood and Puck. William Dowsing of Laxfield, 'The Puritans' Hammer', roamed East Anglia, in six weeks ravaging a hundred and fifty churches, their altar-pieces, effigies, painted walls and glass, carved panels, smashing a thousand windows in one day. The Royal accumulation of paintings was sold to European collectors; Greenwich Palace, beloved by Henry VIII and Elizabeth, was stripped of pictures, cabinets, musical instruments, profane books, tapestries; became a biscuit factory. Exceptions occurred. Fairfax saved the Bodelian Library from demented troopers, and Cromwell himself became one of its benefactors. But improvers, planners, idealists are often grossly philistine. The Cromwellian Great Yarmouth municipality wanted to demolish Norwich Cathedral for stone to repair the harbour. A passage in Ecclesiastes, unacceptable to bigots, might have gratified those they were attempting to discipline:

> There is a just man that perishes in his righteousness, and there is a wicked man that prolongeth his life in his wickedness. Be not righteous overmuch; neither make thyself over-wise: why should'st thou destroy thyself? Be not overmuch wicked, neither be thou foolish; why should'st thou die before thy time?

Be not overmuch wicked: it is in the tradition of Wolsey, Occam, Henry II, and pre-Conquest Albion; a moderate reckoning of existence.

In Catholic Ireland, Strafford had eliminated internecine violence, reformed the Army, encouraged and personally financed an important flax industry; but, a harsh paternalist, lacked interest in the Irish themselves. Ireland was a problem to be solved, not a people to be fostered. Disorder, then rebellion, followed his departure. Cromwell ordained massacres of civilians and priests, some fifty thousand deportations to plantation slavery, further importation of mainland Protestants, withdrawal of remaining Catholic rights, and expropriation of one-third of the best land. C.V. Wedgwood mentions 'concentration camps' for Catholic priests on Arran.

By the late 1640s there was a garrulous hubbub of Presbyterian preachers, Independents, fringe thinkers, agitators and private soldiers abroad in England, many of them exceptionally literate and pledged to the Rights of Man long before Paine, Mirabeau, Jefferson. Women were seldom included, though they had staged a Peace March in 1643; Cromwell, even Lilburne, spent little time on their claims. The military debates, particularly at Putney, concerned with grievances about pay and conditions, were also fine exercises in constitutional theory, together with impatient outcries for root-and-branch revolution. Their spirit, together with that of Locke, pervades the American Declaration of Independence and the Constitution of the United States. Parliament, though it expropriated or over-taxed Royalist property, had no design to share it out wholesale.

Appealing not to Albion but to history, the Leveller premiss was that all land had been stolen from the English people by the Normans, and should now be restored, a belief that was later grafted onto Victorian Chartism. The Levellers' *Declaration from the Poor Oppressed People of England* (1649) demanded the abolition of 'that cursed thing called Particular Property, which is the cause of all wars, bloodshed, theft and enslaving laws that hold the people under misery'. In his clarion *New Year's Gift* the Leveller Gerrard Winstanley wrote: 'Therefore, you rulers, be not ashamed nor afraid of Levellers; hate them not; Christ comes to you riding upon these clouds; look not upon other lands to be your pattern; all lands in the world lie under duress; so does England yet, though nearest to light and freedom of any others; therefore, let no other land take your Crown.'

Richard Overton's indignant *The Hunting of Foxes* raged against wealthy republicans disowning popular liberties: 'We were before ruled by a King, Lords and Commons; now by a General, a Court Martial and the House of Commons; We pray you, what is the difference . . . We are only under the old cheat, the transmutation of names, but with the addition of new tyrannies for old.' Such Independents were suppressed – sometimes, as at Burford, by firing squads – but in subversive and idealistic annals were never forgotten.

Concepts of 'The Elect', 'The Saints', the supremacy of individual conscience and Inner Light, could strengthen a character of intellectual and moral independence, provide spiritual sustenance in a vale of tears. They were also a free gift to mediocrities and bullies. Few of Cromwell's awkward squad would be agreeable companions today. The ranting preacher Hugh Peters spat in the King's face, as Charles went to his trial. John Lilburne's disposition was such that, A.L. Rowse wrote, he would not accept even 'yes' for an answer. The presence of John Bunyan in the Army can never have reassured the officers. Bunyan was an enduring but not altogether endearing English, or northern, type, the type that will sacrifice all goods, all relationships, for his own truth. His wrath is alarming, his goodwill suspect, his theology deeply felt but narrow, sometimes preposterous.

Bunyan too had a telling and copious stock of language: 'Here will I spill my soul.' An unofficial preacher when the Restoration, reacting from Puritan buzz, forbade preaching on pain of 'stretching of the neck', he backed his 'either–or' creed with stubborn defiance, downright rudeness, threats of hell. A walking truth, he had a profound influence on British and American imaginations through *Pilgrim's Progress*. Such people remain grit in the machines, however well-oiled. It has been asserted that the most unwavering German resistance to Hitler came, not from intellectuals, Churches, universities, trade unions, but from Jehovah's Witnesses.

As a writer, Bunyan was no isolated beacon: literary and scientific groups were liberally spawned throughout the century – though this can be a captious guide to human happiness. Stalinism possessed more literacy, less great literature, than Tsarism, both using censorship and persecution. Napoleonic literature scarcely existed, though printers enjoyed full employment; when the Emperor was asked why his regime produced no poets, he advised his questioner to consult the Minister of the Interior.

English republican literature, if less exuberant than the Elizabethan, earnestly grappled with essentials. Though Donne had died in 1631, and such treatises as *The Necessity and Benefit of Washing the Heart* deserve no reprinting, much is still read and in some quarters enjoyed. As Secretary of Foreign Tongues Cromwell employed Milton, the aspirant English Virgil who, having discarded King Arthur as subject for epic, chose instead the Fall of Man. His prose titles between 1643 and 1665 illustrate a concern for the topical: *The Doctrine and Discipline of Divorce, Tractate on Education, The Tenure of Kings and Magistrates, The Ready and Easy Way to Establish a Free Commonwealth*. European political republicans read his *Defensio*, reaffirming his approval of the King's execution though probably disputing his plea, proclaimed elsewhere: 'Let not England forget her precedence of teaching nations how to live.'

Lilburne had no inhibition about wielding vigorous language against the Protectorate: 'All you intended when you set us a-fighting was merely to unhorse and dismount our old riders and tyrants, that so you might get up, and ride us in their stead.' Colonal Rainsborough's remark made in 1647, in the Putney Debates, though not widely known until 1891, is fixed in standard radical literature: 'The poorest he that is in England hath a life to live as the greatest he.'

Few European rulers, philosophers, future regicides would henceforward ignore the declaration of the English Parliament, in January 1649, that 'the People, under God, are the original of all just power; that the Commons of

England, in Parliament assembled, being chosen by, and representing the People, are the supreme power in this land.'

Phrases have powers. *Commons* begged many questions and was misleading in its associations, especially when translated. Few men and no women had chosen them, and none could know what the *People* either thought or wanted. Not until the nineteenth century did Grey, Peel, Disraeli realise what Louis-Napoleon well understood: that the masses are not bloodthirsty haters of property, religion, government – though they might, as Burckhardt put it, apropos the French revolutionaries, wish to be new owners of stolen goods.

The Lord Protector's death was followed by two years of incoherence under his son, Tumbledown Dick, who was to die a country gentleman, harmless and unmolested, in 1712. Finally, instead of King Jesus despatched by God and descending from clouds, there arrived, under contract with General Monk and to wild acclaim, the son of the Man of Blood, on the *Charles* (the *Naseby*, commemorating his father's final crushing defeat, hastily renamed).

The Monarchy was restored, under signed conditions, by what remained of the Rump of the Long Parliament and the Army, the City interests, the landed gentry. Much of its sacramental *mana* had been shattered, though rulers still 'touched' to cure the sick, attempting the miraculous, Queen Anne thus favouring the young Samuel Johnson. (She found the new Orangery at Kensington Palace served well for this ceremony, and the Palace's rooms were not made smelly by her subjects.) The constitutional settlement was more of a compromise than it appeared. The House of Lords, the Anglican Church were restored, some Royalists regained their estates; but the war casualities, his father's fate, his own escape after Worcester with a price on his head, and a large State debt inherited from the Republic debarred Charles II from the absolutist path followed by his cousin, Louis XIV. He was not naturally cruel, but felt entitled to give priority to policies for his own survival.

Revenge was inflicted on the regicides, those who had signed his father's death warrant, John Evelyn piously observing:

Scrot, Scroope, Cook and Jones suffered for reward of their iniquities, at Charing Cross, in sight of the place where they put to death their natural prince, . . . I saw not their execution, but met their quarters, mangled and cut, and reeking as they were brought from the gallows in baskets on the hurdle. Ah, the miraculous providence of God!

Pepys, in whom professional respectability amiably conflicted with more robust inclinations, saw Harrison butchered at the same spot, 'Looking as cheerful as any man could do in that condition, and expecting to shortly return and help Christ judge the Royalist judges.' Aubrey describes another regicide, Henry Marten, saved by the latest Lord Falkland, who pointed out to Parliament that under the Old Law, 'all sacrifices were to be without spot or blemish; now you are going to make an old rotten rascal a sacrifice!' This saved Marten's life, though not his liberty. Milton's books were publicly burnt, but a treason trial was vetoed by the King. 'He's old and blind and full of fleas,' Charles said, 'so let him be' – thereby securing *Paradise Lost.*

Freed from the Protector's protective eye, Londoners reverted to type. Pepys made an entry in 1666: 'On Tower Hill saw about 3 or 4,000 seamen get together, and one standing on a pile of bricks made his sign with his handkerchief upon his stick, and called the rest to him, and several shouts they gave. This made me afeared, so I got home as fast as I could.'

Though martyrdom sanctified the old King, the new one was of different material. 'Above two yards high', with subtle Italianate features, married to a Portuguese, witty though over-repetitive, Charles II, despite his Merry Monarch and Old Rowley tags – Rowley was a celebrated stallion – seems inwardly melancholy, with a low respect for human motives. Clarendon credited him with 'an Aversion for speaking, with any woman, or hearing them speak, on any Business but to that Purpose He thought them all made for'. Steadfast in selfishness, outwardly genial, he compared well with the pompous Louis XIV who, when a minister once arrived with exemplary punctuality, merely remarked, 'I was within an ace of being kept waiting.' Rochester, who died before Charles, composed an epitaph:

> Here lies a Great and Mighty King,
> Whose Promise none relies on;
> He never said a Foolish thing
> Nor ever did a wise one.

Charles, unperturbed, agreed, adding that while his sayings were his own, his actions were his ministers'. This is probably apocryphal, yet characteristic.

Two other stories are both characteristic and well-attested. Preaching at Court, Bishop Stillingfleet, instead of speaking extempore, as he usually did, read from a manuscript. Charles asked why, and the Bishop replied that he did not trust his own ability to do otherwise before so illustrious a prince. He then ventured his own question: why did His Majesty read his own speeches to Parliament, being faced with no such superiority? 'Why, Doctor, your question is a very pertinent one, and so will be my answer. I have asked them so often, and for so much money, that I am ashamed to look them in the face.'

Colonel Thomas Blood, hitherto distinguished for his failure to kidnap and murder Irish notables, was arrested for an attempt to steal the Crown Jewels, and imprisoned in the Tower, where Charles, always curious, visited him and inquired why he had not completed the theft. Blood brazenly replied that he had been suddenly overcome by reverence for His Majesty; whereat the King, undeceived, connoisseur not of art but of people, pardoned him.

Cosmopolitan, Charles loved French music and old English airs and dances, had an English devotion to dogs, walking, tennis, horse-racing, fishing, and had early offended Scots divines by playing golf on the Sabbath. Devoted also to the sea and ships, he and his brother James supported Pepys's naval reforms and retained Cromwell's Navy as a permanent reserve of foreign policy, though frequently forced to leave sailors unpaid and ships in disrepair.

Holland, sometimes needing support against France (now replacing Spain as the Great Power), her ports still essential for England's trade, was nevertheless the prime commercial rival. Reflecting the political game of Balance of Power, dodge and re-dodge, Charles' illegitimate son Monmouth commanded English troops for Louis against Holland in 1672, winning praise for gallantry at Maastricht, where d'Artagnan was killed, then led Dutch against Louis in 1678.

Financial expedience long compelled Charles to rely on Parliament, where the Party System was now incipient, deriving from factions of exorbitant Tory Royalism, anti-Catholicism, anti-French Whig republicans, and a shifting crowd of idealists, schemers, rogues and nuisances. Finally, by secret agreements with Louis, dubious, perhaps crafty, involving an improbable pledge to restore Catholicism with French aid, Charles received sufficient French funds after 1681 to dispense with Parliament until his death in 1685. Whig and Tory were contemporary epithets of disapproval, the former denoting a Scottish Presbyterian freebooter, the latter an Irish bandit.

The King lived in nervy, restless Whitehall Palace, half a mile long, with its two thousand overcrowded rooms packed with fortune-hunters, intriguers, sightseers, crooks, courtiers and would-be courtiers, courtesans. France's status was symbolised by Louis XIV's palace at Versailles, ruinous to German princelings in their efforts at imitation; removed, unlike Whitehall, from the noisy, insolent capital; cruel in its expenditure, its fountains alone used more piped water than was allowed to Paris. It was the hub of tittle-tattle, boredom, intrigue, infantile practical jokes; while, in its inner recesses, men in baroque wigs, on high heels, gravely planned the French hegemony of Europe. Christopher Wren visited it:

> The Palace, or if you please, the Cabinet of Versailles call'd me twice to view it; the mixtures of Brick, Stone, blue Tile and Gold make it look like a rich livery; not an Inch within but is crowded with little Curiosities of Ornaments: the Women, as they make here the Language and Fashions, and meddle with Politicks and philosophy, so they sway also in Architecture; Works of Filgrand, and Little Knacks, are in great vogue; but Building certainly ought to have the Attribute of eternal, and therefore the only Thing incapable of new Fashions.

In his *Epistle to Augustus* of 1737, Alexander Pope reanimated the Restoration Court:

> In Days of Ease, when now the weary Sword
> Was sheath'd, and *Luxury* with Charles restor'd;
> In ev'ry Taste of foreign Courts improv'd,
> 'All, by the King's Example, liv'd and lov'd.'
> Then Peers grew proud in Horsemanship t'excell,
> New-market's Glory rose, as Britain's fell;
> The Soldier breath'd the Gallantries of France,
> And ev'ry flow'ry Courtier writ Romance.
> Then Marble, soften'd into life, grew warm
> And yielding Metal flow'd to human form:
> Lely on animated Canvas stole
> The sleeping Eye, that spoke the Melting Soul.
> No wonder then, when all was Love and Sport,
> The willing Muses were debauch'd at Court.

This was not refuted by the courtier Lord Rochester, no example of Cromwellian virtues:

I rise at eleven, I dine about two,
I get drunk before seven, and the next thing I do,
I send for my whore, when for fear of the clap,
I dally about her, and spew in her lap . . .

Of the Duchess of Cleveland, one of the more expensive Royal mistresses, Rochester was uncharitable, if observant:

Cleveland, I say, is much to be admir'd,
Although she ne'er was satisfied or tired.
Full forty men a day provided for this whore,
Yet like a bitch she wags her tail for more.

The theatres re-opened, at last permitting actresses to play female parts, in the new brittle, amoral Restoration comedies. Through skilled plotting they offered endless variations of the arts of seduction, portrayed by characters of scheming insolence and mannered wit. Dryden's satirical masterpiece *Absalom and Achitophel*, poised on Monmouth and Shaftesbury, Charles and the second Buckingham, expertly delineated the political factions slowly coalescing in the Whig–Tory divide.

The pillared harmonies of Wren's Naval Hospital at Greenwich and the chilly, unassailable grandeur of his St Paul's both undoubtedly shared the 'Attribute of eternal'. Here was none of the sprawling antiquity of the Gothic which, through centuries of additions, allowed for the wayward, mysterious, digressive and impish. In hard, chaste deployment of disciplined space St Paul's suggests both the reason and clarity of Newtonian analysis and strictly-costed enterprise, the structure of a Nation–State recovering from war and excess and stabilising its own Grand Design, of commerce, sea-power, Empire. With native eclecticism Wren incorporated England and Europe, Catholic baroque and Protestant sobriety, elegance and function.

Elsewhere, in family chapels or halls, in monasteries or centres of pilgrimage, in great metropolitan churches and palaces on the Continent, escaping from Protestant constraints, the baroque might curl and writhe in glistening waves of colour, clouds spread with ecstatic angels, their legs dangling over into the aether, faces straining to dissolve into souls, pools of emotion dripping from sensational heavens ablaze with haloes, whizzing putti, excited draperies, sunbursts, long golden trumpets, all sustained by some divine breath. It was as if these sublime heights had to be stormed in order to escape inner doubts and unease released by science and scholarship, the exposure of papal and legal fraud, new claims that in much old lore was demonstrable nonsense. Even in Protestant England, baroque floridity affected Vanbrugh and Gibbs; can be found at Chatsworth and Burghley, in domes, ceilings, staircases; in costume and horse-trappings; and in garden design.

Religious and factional animosities remained dangerous, sometimes fanatical. Emotions which could be deflected against Holland and France could as easily go against the English Catholics, particularly Charles's brother and heir James, denounced by the former minister Shaftesbury, now the Whig leader, manipulator of London crowds, his 'brisk boys' and Green Ribbon Club flaunting the Levellers' colour. Shaftesbury's clique sought the crown for Charles's favourite son Monmouth, 'Absalom', able soldier but gullible, beloved of the multitude as 'the Protestant Duke'. He always contested his illegitimacy, through a combination of ambition and loyalty to his mother, a pretty Welsh girl who died, as Monmouth's Wicked Uncle James wrote with laconic precision, 'of a disease incident to her profession' – as, in another way, did her son.

Shaftesbury, nicknamed 'Little Sincerity' by Charles, was Dryden's 'false Achitophel', 'For close designs and crooked counsels fit, Sagacious, bold, and turbulent of wit.' An admirer of Cromwell, and of Locke, Shaftesbury was clever and unscrupulous; for him kings were at best public employees, liable to dismissal. His republicanism was unemotional expediency, not an ideal nor the offshoot of personal liberalism. A dynamic campaigner for Liberty, he had slave interests and encroached on poorer neighbours' lands. He revelled in imbroglios, plots and conspiracies, some invented by flitting, subterranean minions like Major Wildman, who afterwards helped lure Monmouth to agonising death. Better remembered was Titus Oates: he was expelled from Merchant Taylors' School, then from both Caius and St John's, Cambridge; accepting several Anglican curacies, he was then ejected from a naval chaplaincy before adopting Catholicism, a misleading preliminary to promoting the most vicious anti-Catholic terrorism yet known in London. Such a man, Graham Greene wrote, 'occurs like a slip of the tongue, discharging the unconscious forces, the night-side of an age which might otherwise have thought in terms of Dryden discussing the art of dramatic poesy'. He is the antithesis of the English view of themselves, and even to foreign detractors is scarcely the typical Englishman.

Fanatic rumours spread like fleas from Oates and his like. English ironic scepticism was overwhelmed by credulity. Catholics were to murder Charles and install James; a French army, an Irish army would murder all English Protestants; Jesuits were swarming in vile disguises. Deranged voices threatened to impeach the Catholic Queen, denounced hundreds of innocent suspects, bawled for the exclusion of 'the Catholic Duke', whose protégés, such as Pepys, found themselves in the Tower. Perjurers and liars rode high, 'inconsiderable fellows' were hanged. An inscription on the Monument, erected in the City in memory of the Great Fire, attributed it to Catholics. Maddened by 'the Popish Plot', thousands of Londoners tramped to Smithfield behind a dummy Pope filled with live cats, and tossed it screaming into a bonfire. Daniel Defoe, familiar with sedition, distress and human variousness, rumoured to have been a Monmouth rebel in 1685 but carefully covering any tracks, remarked that a hundred thousand were always ready to fight Popery, without knowing whether this was man or beast.

Fed mainly by the disreputable to the ignorant, the Terror inevitably subsided, Charles outmanoeuvering the Whigs. Shaftesbury fled abroad, Monmouth was exiled. The exposure of another, probably equally imaginary conspiracy, the Rye House Plot of 1682, allowed Charles to rid himself of two other enemies of the Stuarts, though at the price of making of them martyrs to strengthen the Whig cause. Lord William Russell was beheaded, also Algernon Sydney, most high-minded of them all, a republican of civility and culture who in his time had been equally opposed to the dictatorship of Oliver Cromwell. He had put on a private performance of *Julius Caesar* at his family's town house in Leicester Square in the 1650s as an implied criticism of the Protectorate. He closed his scaffold speech with sentiments which Shaftesbury might have easily expressed, without feeling them; Monmouth was incapable of either.

> The Lord forgive these Practises and avert the Evils that threaten the Nation from them. The Lord sanctifie these my sufferings unto me; and though I fall as a Sacrifice unto Idols, I suffer not Idolatry to be established in this Land . . . Grant that I may dye glorifying Thee for all thy mercies; and that at last Thou has permitted me to be singled out as a witness to the Truth; and even by the Confession of thy opposers, for that OLD CAUSE in which I from my youth enjoyed, and for which Thou hast often and wonderfully declared Thyself.

Though the mercies were obscure, Sidney's resolution may have encouraged some who rallied two years later, for the Old Cause and the Protestant Duke, to be shot down at Sedgemoor, strangled at Bridgewater, Taunton,

Dorchester, enslaved in Barbados. Judge Jeffreys, who was the instrument of James II's vengeance against the Monmouth rebels, had also presided at the trial of Sydney. Monmouth, about to kneel for the axe in his turn, professed no thanks for mercies but spiritedly defended his mistress's reputation.

Oates, perhaps a frustrated comedian turned blackmailing criminal, a congenital misfit, was condemned to a crippling fine, thrashings, the pillory, and to life imprisonment – revoked by William and Mary, who gave him a pension. This was a perplexing award to the loudest slanderer of Mary's father, James II.

The passing in 1679, amidst an epidemic of perjury and wrongful imprisonment, of the Habeas Corpus Act – preventing prolonged imprisonment without trial – strikes an English note. Though easily, if not wilfully, suspended in a crisis, it was a momentous stage in the growth of European civil liberties, but it was passed only because the teller amused himself by counting a fat member as ten, a joke which might have perturbed the sticklers if not the Englishman at large. Though hailed as guarantee of individual freedom, and envied by Continentals subject to arbitrary Royal and ministerial decree, it was no protection against press-gang and secret repressions; but at least set a notable example to a world still racked by torture, bullying and arbitrary incarceration.

Fanatics, eccentrics and republicans were not the only menace to citizens. Courtiers usually expected exemption from Common Law. The young Dukes of Somerset, Albemarle and Monmouth murdered a beadle for rebuking their behaviour in a brothel, and satirists rhymed at Monmouth for paying others to slit the nose of a parliamentary opponent to the King.

Metropolitan savagery and alarm – the Dutch in the Medway, the French, Papists, plotters – could surge into national sentiment of a sort, chauvinistic, perhaps instinctive, mocked in Defoe's 'The True-Born Englishman':

> These are the Heroes who despise the Dutch,
> And rail at new-come Foreigners so much;
> Forgetting that themselves are all deriv'd
> From the most Scoundrel Race that ever liv'd.
> A horrid Crowd of Rambling Thieves and Drones,
> Who ransacked Kingdoms and dispeopled Towns:
> The Pict and Painted Briton, Treach'rous Scot
> By Hunger, Theft and Rapine hither brought;
> Norwegi'an Pirates, Buccaneering Danes,

Whose Red-Haired Offspring ev'rywhere remains;
Who joined with Norman-French compound the Breed
From whence your True-Born Englishmen proceed.

Rochester's improprieties, Monmouth's inappropriate antics, must have held secret allure for many true-born English men and women.

Society remained slashed with startling contrasts, like colours in a marble, like the traits in the character of Samuel Pepys: admirable Civil Servant of the integrity and efficiency of Thurloe, the Republican administrator, censorious of idleness and blatant corruption, reconciling moderate puritanism with incessant philandering, cruising Lord's Day services and assessing the preachers with the professional acumen he simultaneously applied to any pretty woman in a nearby pew. Deeply musical, widely read, self-important but conscientious, he lamented: 'Most men that do thrive in the world do forget to take pleasure during the time that they are getting their estate but reserve that till they have got one, and then it is too late for them to enjoy it with any pleasure.' He himself forgot little and, but for fear of the pox, would have neglected even less.

Eventually victorious over the Dutch at sea, the Crown continued its neglect of sailors. After a Dutch victory in 1667, Pepys was confronted by their wives bawling, 'This comes of not paying our husbands', and was soon hearing of English sailors serving on enemy ships, preferring honest Dutch dollars to English 'tickets' (IOUs). The call of Duty will seldom override administrative callousness or fraud: forty-two thousand sailors were estimated to have deserted during the critical Napoleonic wars. Patriotism was a fragile substitute for cash. Dr Johnson gave his opinion: 'Why, Sir, no man will be a sailor, who has contrivence enough to get himself into a jail: for, being in a ship is being in a jail, with the chance of being drowned.'

The recesses of England were stored with obsessed scholars, inventors, cranks investigating Stonehenge, local historians, Civil War veterans plagued with long memories: the world of Aubrey's *Brief Lives*. At the centre, there was a development of a very different kidney: the foundation, with support from Charles and his cousin Prince Rupert, both chemists and empiricists, of the Royal Society for the Promotion of Natural Knowledge, rivalling the Florentine Society, the Paris Academy of Sciences, and the four great Dutch universities. Here attended Newton; Wren, mathematician, astronomer, mechanical expert as well as architect; the astronomer Halley; the Irish philosopher and scientist Robert Boyle, of Boyle's Law, researcher into gases, hydrogen, mercury, crystals, pneumatics, atoms, final destroyer of Aristotle's doctrine of Four Humours; the botanist John Ray; Pepys; the collector Hans Sloane; the ubiquitous Buckingham, in Dryden's words,

> A man so various that he seemed to be
> Not one, but all mankind's epitome:
> Stiff in opinions, always in the wrong;
> Was everything by starts, and nothing long:
> But in the course of one revolving moon,
> Was chemist, fiddler, statesman, and buffoon.

At the Greenwich Royal Observatory John Flamsteed mapped the stars with precision hitherto unequalled, and discussed or corresponded about light, heat, gravitation, the elliptical course of planets with Robert Hooke and the Dutchman Christian Huygens.

In tune with exactitudes of time and space, clocks and watches were beginning to dominate lives and livelihoods, with England foremost in horology. Even Creation was being strictly dated, most famously by the Irish bishop James Ussher (1581–1656), who fixed it at 10.30 a.m. on Sunday 23 October 4004 BC. The clock was an effective instrument for discipline, even coercion. Mill owners were soon to forbid watches to their 'hands', and craftily prolong labour hours by manipulating public clocks. E.P. Thompson called the watch the Poor Man's Bank, to pawn or sell. Another outcome of this measuring age was the science of statistics, essential to the City's development of its insurance market, which took much business from Amsterdam.

In this ferment of ideas and experiment lay the basis for British rationalism, and Hobbes's view of the body as enveloping mechanical responses to biological necessity, survival tactics without soul or conscience. It validated Francis Bacon's insistence that Nature, once comprehended, could be harnessed to all human needs and beliefs. Newton and Descartes were not anti-religious but, deducing reality from mathematics and general laws, rested their case on a balance of matter and spirit; not on passive Faith but on trial, error, resolution, proof.

Newton (1642–1727) saw the universe as the logical outcome of permanent, inter-connected pressures of light, motion, electricity, heat, gravity – divine in origin but henceforward autonomous, ever-moving, assembling and reassembling, and available for objective scrutiny: 'God, in the beginning, formed matter in solid, massy, hard, inpenetrable, movable particles, of such sizes and figures, and with such other properties, and in such proportions to space, as most conduced to the end for which He formed them.'

Pure logic, serene objectivity, however, had their limits within the complexity even of Newton's brain; he could devote almost as much energy to biblical prophecy and mystic esotericism as to his differential calculus, binomial theory, and General Law of Gravitation. In the next century Swedenborg too was both scientist and visionary theologian, as well as a profound influence on William Blake.

John Locke (1632–1704) applied the new concepts to politics and government. Appropriate to an ambitious commercial oligarchy, Natural Law was incompatible with a personal God captiously responding to prayer, punishing, rewarding, dismissing. More *It* than He, the divine was submissive to energy and motion, which made no exceptions: it could be felt as a discharge of energy which could be tapped, utilised like laudanum, but experimental, not omnipotent, a symbol of Good and the readjustment of balance against Evil. Reason and business-like agreements, not Faith, loyalty, tradition, should be the magnetic or attractive principle: government, like gas and light, should be susceptible to dispassionate analysis. Bound by contract like manager and client, rulers and ruled were mutually dependent, their arrangements needing divine sanction no more than watch or compass. 'Good and evil, reward and punishment, are the only motives to a rational creature: these are the spur and reins, whereby all mankind are set on work, and guided.' He and his followers, in Britain, Europe, America, did not claim too much. The brain was finite, the Ideal often as preposterous as the Holy Grail. 'It is one thing to show a man that he is in error, and another to put him in possession of the truth': a very English observation.

Thomas Hobbes (1588–1679) had no regard for divine nature and very little for human nature, Euclid rather than Genesis being a formative influence. Personally acquainted with Galileo, Cosimo de Medici, Bacon, Jonson, Descartes, he had translated Homer, who seldom showed the world at its most refined. Hobbes would have known of Plato's omnipotent 'Guardians', wise, disinterested totalitarian supervisors of the Republic, selflessly protecting people from themselves and each other, like Jacobin committees and H.G. Wells's enlightened but unappealing 'Samurai'. Hobbes discountenanced belief in human perfectability, man's inherent virtue, the criminality within authority. A survivor of the Civil War (although he had spent it abroad, as tutor to the young Earl of Devonshire), a contemporary of Continental atrocities and of lawless, sometimes demented, urban crowds, he defined the human condition as the war of everyone against everyone. Sceptical that the removal of a Strafford, Laud, Cromwell or of the 'Norman Yoke' would restore a Golden Age, he taught, notably in *Leviathan*, that absolute authority, a Grand Judge, a 'Mortal God', was vital to control common impulses, the violent, insurgent, malicious. Locke's doctrine of peoples' natural and irrevocable right to Liberty was thus a password to chaos. Controlled like a machine by a master mechanic, by the very absence of Liberty, society could be productive, more genuinely human, rather than suffering the anarchic freedoms of beasts of prey. Reason itself, having to work on multitudes themselves brutish and unreasonable, could not (as the twentieth century so drastically proved) guarantee virtue, generosity, satisfaction.

Leviathan was never a popular handbook in England, where absolutism, as much as or more than any other public authority or source of power, was known to attract superstition, erratic behaviour, even madness. Hobbes demanded that his Grand Judge be allowed unquestioned obedience, provided he did his job (again the prevalent theme of contract), which made him distinct from hereditary monarchs. In England his role was soon to be appropriated by the all-powerful Lords and Commons: periodic elections by the propertied allowed a change of government, but never dissent from the authority of Parliament.

Hobbes himself was no potential Grand Judge. Examining his letters in 1995 Oliver Letwin, Cambridge-trained political philosopher, concluded that, more than previous thinkers, 'Hobbes peered into the abyss of man's loneliness'. In an indifferent or hostile universe, man is besieged by the flawed, dangerous and vengeful, his outlook sometimes is more pessimistic, even more than in the old Anglo-Saxon poems *The Seafarer*, *The Wanderer*. To a sensitive seventeenth-century intellectual, this could scarcely be gainsaid. The letters mix the elegant and ironical with the harshly factual. Letwin continues, 'depth and passion in the inner life, contrasting with outer self-possession, mark Hobbes as, above all, an Englishman in the tradition of Chaucer, Shakespeare, Hume (*sic*), Berkeley (*sic*), Jane Austen and Trollope, an Englishman for whom the human predicament is a fact to be reckoned with, but not an excuse for imposing on friends and acquaintances.'

It is hard to imagine Charles II poring over theories of natural rights and contractual obligations. His political creed was expediency, and by 1682 he had apparently recovered Royal supremacy, with the Whigs dispersed, Parliament dissolved. But Royal control, as Charles foretold, was lost by his

Catholic brother James II. After the savage suppression of Monmouth's rebellion he seemed poised, ignoring the advice of the Pope and Louis XIV, to move against the Anglican Church and the Universities, enforcing Catholic appointments, illegally imprisoning bishops. The birth of an heir after a succession of miscarried and still-born daughters was greeted with ribald incredulity, as a trick to ensure the Catholic succession. Tensions quickened, Civil War memories revived. Republicanism was not on offer but Whig leaders, some Tory grandees, City interests invited James's Dutch son-in-law William to intervene. William landed in force; unlike Monmouth, he found powerful support. Strangely unnerved, James gave no lead; his troops deserted, he fled to France and, after a failed attempt in Ireland, remained there, a pensioner of King Louis.

William III and Mary II, joint monarchs, accepted the Crown on conditions ennobled as the Glorious Revolution of 1688. It was neither very glorious, nor sensationally revolutionary. No lives were lost in England, though in Ireland and Scotland Boyne, Londonderry, Bonny Dundee, Glencoe still reverberate in folklore and resentments. An Act of Union with Ireland revoked her remaining political rights.

The Glorious Revolution represented little increase in freedom from injustice, the gallows, unstable market forces; it was unconcerned with a wider franchise, women's rights, the press-gang, or slavery. Rather, it has been argued that it ensured the completion of the oligarchic powers of unrestricted Capital. Henceforth, the City and emerging industrial Interests, through Parliament, would prevail: Banking, Insurance, Textiles, Printing, Brewing, Coal, Iron, Shipping, Slavery, Agriculture, Tobacco, Law. All these would be competing and negotiating with some Locke-like concern for moderation, while the signed contract replaced the more subjective oath. Burke, with some plausibility, could diagnose this collusion of factions – 'the English Party System', grouped around institutions with their sinecures and 'places' manned by nepotism, bribery, ambition and laziness – as the English genius 'to compromise, reconcile, balance'. *Perks* have a long and distinguished lineage.

Private property was further guaranteed against arbitrary Royal taxation; Parliament would meet in obligatory sessions independent of the Royal will, and was safeguarded from Jews, Catholics, atheists, the unpropertied, and women. There was some erosion of the Crown's control over the armed forces and foreign policy. Within a few years, the monarch ceased to preside in Cabinet. Henceforth, he was a politician operating among other politicians, though with considerable resources for patronage and bribery. The Crown was left a hinge of State, a constitutional mechanism whose significance fluctuated according to the ruler's personality. Though the Royal Veto survived, it remained unused after 1707, when Anne opposed the Scottish Militia Bill.

For the unfranchised, the Glorious Revolution and its Bill of Rights was mostly a subscription to some very distant freedoms. Bolingbroke, one of Queen Anne's ministers, enjoyed calling the English a free people. Relative to most of Europe, there was indeed considerable freedom of expression; William Congreve, writing to John Dennis in 1695, connected freedom with a sense of humour:

> I look upon humour to be almost of English growth; at least, it does not seem to have found such encrease on any other soil. And what appears to me to be the reason of it, is the great freedom, privilege and liberty which the Common People of England enjoy. Any man that has a humour is under no restraint, or fear of giving it vent; they have a proverb among them, which, may be, will shew the bent and genius of the People, as well as a longer discourse: *He that will have a May-Pole, shall have a May-Pole.* This is a maxim with them, and their practice is agreeable to it. I believe something considerable too may be ascribed to their feeding so much on flesh, and the grossness of their diet in general. But I have done, let the physicians agree that.

Opportunities for extending political democracy were not, however, matched by those for economic democracy. Private property rights, privileges, opportunities were not to be gainsaid. Charity, loans, benevolence might be granted to the deserving poor, but recognition of their equality with the rich and genteel was restricted to Sunday morning church readings. Freedom more generally meant freedom from French aggression, Catholic tyranny, Dutch rivalry. 'How is it', Johnson demanded, 'that we hear the loudest *yelps* for Liberty among the drivers of negroes?' Nevertheless, certain principles were established, still abstract or shallow, but sufficient to provide a stable platform for successful nineteenth-century demands and change. In Europe and America, meanwhile, the Enlightenment became besotted with the idea of written Constitutions, brimming with immaculate promises and inherent with disappointing results.

English Whigs and Tories, loosely gathered around Trade and Land, Non-Conformism and Anglicanism, would spontaneously unite against rebellion, street agitation, foreign threats. Locke had argued not for the sovereignty of the Crown, not for the sovereignty of Parliament, but for the sovereignty of the People, which elects and renews a Parliament responsible to the People alone. The People, however, with most men and all women disallowed the vote, must have thought that Parliamentary debates, ornamented though they were with Classical quotations and allusions, were more about the division of spoils than the righteousness of the spoils themselves, from war, sales, taxation, colonial plunder, skilful treaties, successful speculation. Disraeli would not have been singular in remarking in 1832 that Whig and Tory were two names with a single meaning: 'To delude you.' Palmerston, in 1852, reminded the Commons: 'You who are Gentlemen on this side of the House should remember that we are dealing with Gentlemen on the other side.' Almost all abided by

> The good old rule,
> The simple plan,
> That they should take who have the power
> And they should keep who can.

Nevertheless, since 1688 very few in Britain have openly accepted, as a programme, Lenin's dictum that 'Democracy is a state which recognises the subordination of the minority to the majority, i.e., an organisation for the systematic use of violence by one class towards the other, by one section of the population against another.'

The individualistic English, later the British, have tended to prefer exceptions to rules and idiosyncratic characters, racy outsiders, to the restrictions of class definitions. To praise a porter or labourer as 'proletarian' seldom guarantees a genial smile. After 1688, only Celtic minorities consistently used violence against the State.

By 1700, England, on the point of becoming Great Britain, enjoyed considerable status. Britain's most permanent contribution to civilisation could pose a provocative examination question. Language and Literature? Penicillin? Parliamentary Procedure? Empire? The Civil Service? Trial by Jury? The Secret Ballot? Trade Unions? Historians? Footballers? The Greenwich Observatory? The Cavendish Institute? Television? The BBC? The Battle of Britain? Ultra? The Beveridge Report, laying the foundations of the Welfare State? The peaceful absorbing of two hundred thousand Poles and Ukrainians between 1939 and 1945? The peaceful withdrawal from

Empire? George Bernard Shaw asserted that by far the most credible incident in English history was the Philharmonic Society of London's hundred pounds subscribed towards Beethoven's Choral Symphony. George Orwell, apt to denigrate England, praised her for bathrooms, armchairs, brown bread, marmalade, mint sauce, new potatoes, proper beer.

A counter-case can be mounted: against the Empire for being an Empire; against colonial genocide, 'clearances', massacres. Not forgotten are callous labour relations and industrial conditions; abuse of naval power; the despatch of thousands of anti-Communists to be slaughtered by Stalin and Tito; Munich, Yalta, Suez; the arms trade. Abuse of Great Britain usually assures a round of applause, particularly in Great Britain.

On behalf of Britain, an argument might be sustained favouring the unspectacular growth, from the seventeenth century, of legal, eventually paid, parliamentary opposition – Her (or His) Majesty's Loyal Opposition. It implies not only division of spoils but tolerance, even justice, in which the English, perhaps self-deceiving, take some pride. Legal, 'loyal' opposition spread throughout the British Dominions, the West Indies, the United States and Scandinavia, fitfully in Latin America, belatedly in Russia. It was denounced by Robespierre and Saint-Just; the thought of it made Napoleon summon Fouché, his Chief of Police. The Papal States discountenanced it; the Habsburgs came to accept it, without enthusiasm; the Anglophile Napoleon III adopted it, too late; Bismarck craftily allowed it; Lenin and Hitler outlawed it.

6

Great Britain

There is something altogether symbolic of the intellectual atmosphere of 18th Century Scotland that one of the most epoch-making inventions of the 18th Century (the steam-engine) came about through the meeting of an instrument-maker from Greenock (James Watt) with a chemistry lecturer from Belfast (Joseph Black) over a collection of astronomical instruments given to the college by a Glasgow merchant who had made his fortune in the West Indies.

T.C. Smout

The Notion of Liberty amuses the people of England, and helps keep off the *Taedium vitae*. When a butcher tells you that *his heart bleeds for his country*, he has, in fact, no uneasy feeling.

Samuel Johnson

No, Sir; to act from pure benevolence is not possible for finite beings. Human benevolence is mingled with vanity, interest or some other motive.

Samuel Johnson

Englishmen are distinguished by their traditions and ceremonials,
And also by their affection for their colonies and their contempt for their colonials.
When foreigners ponder world affairs, why sometimes by doubts they are smitten,
But Englishmen know instinctively that what the world needs most is whatever is best
    for Great Britain.
They have a splendid navy and they conscientiously admire it,
And every schoolboy knows that John Paul Jones was only an unfair American pirate.

Ogden Nash

The Scottish Parliament recognised William III in 1689, and by a Treaty of Union in 1707 attached itself to England and Wales, peacefully though undemocratically, sending sixteen peers to the Lords, forty-five members to the Commons. Thus was Great Britain created, the 'Great' being a geographical adjective, not a boast. Within a generation, one Scot was Prime

Minister, another Lord Chief Justice. Scottish Law, Kirk and universities maintained their individuality.

The island, with an Act of Union with Ireland finally enforced in 1801, thus became the largest free-trade area in Europe, with the capital and the energies to create the world's first major industrialisation, through steam, railways, water-power, still deeper mining, mechanical inventions for the mass-production of cloth, linen, clothes, leather, munitions. Agriculture improved; harbours and fishing prospered, also the trade, based on Bristol, Liverpool and Glasgow, in tobacco 'to chew, sniff, spit'. Scottish genius, in engineering, banking, medicine, physics, technology, philosophy, religion, literature, was as powerful as any in transforming western societies.

Many Scots deplored the Union as an oligarchic conspiracy, surrendering the poorer to the richer. Certainly, since William Wallace, Scots landowners had collaborated with the English as often as they fought them, though less spectacularly. The Glencoe atrocity in 1692 was largely conceived by one Scot, Campbell of Breadalbane, and enforced by another, Lord Stair, hater of the doomed MacDonalds. An order – 'To putt all to the sword under seventy' – was signed by a third, Robert Duncanson.

For the Union, English bribes, promises, cajoleries were plentiful. 'We're bought and sold for English gold,' Burns raged, and though Walter Scott personally appreciated the Union (never endorsed by popular vote) he recorded, in *Tales of a Grandfather* (1828–30), that it was regarded with 'an almost universal feeling of discontent and dishonour', professing to have heard nothing but lamentation that national identity and dignity were all that the poor possessed, and that they were being robbed even of these. These in fact remained, together with fierce feeling for landscapes, local traditions, loyalties, despite the divide between Highlanders and Lowlanders. Scott also asserted, in *Thoughts on the Proposed Change of Currency*, published in 1826 when Scottish violence was no longer an immediate hazard, that the new opportunities increased Scotland's prosperity 'in a ratio five times greater than that of her more fortunate and richer sister'.

Scottish risings for the Stuarts in 1715 and 1745 had elicited more Highland support than Lowland, and bred fear and hostility in England. The last verse of *God Save the King* (1745) is now neglected:

> God grant that Marshal Wade
> May by Thy mighty Aid

Victory bring.
May he sedition crush,
And like a Torrent rush,
Rebellious Scots to crush,
God save the King.

After Culloden, where Scots fighting for the union outnumbered those fighting for Prince Charles Edward, Westminster methodically destroyed Highland society, though glad to accept clansmen into the Army, which in 1830 was 42 per cent Irish, 14 per cent Scots, the rest English.

History had never overlooked Scotland. Its deep forests repelled the Romans; Celts from Scotland and Ireland had been early colonisers of ninth-century Iceland; Scots may have joined early Viking expeditions to North America, and certainly fought with the Norwegians against Harold II at Stamford Bridge in 1066. The eleventh-century St Margaret, consort of Shakespeare's 'Malcolm', mother-in-law of England's King Stephen, was a sophisticated, French-influenced cultural innovator and church reformer, vigorously encouraging trade with France, her humanity embracing serfs and war captives. She restored Iona, earlier sacked by Vikings. King David intervened at will in Stephen's civil conflicts, and knighted his great-nephew, Henry II. Claimant to the Northumberland earldom, he adopted many Anglo-Norman feudal practices. Complex relations with England forced William the Lion to become the vassal of Henry II, with lasting effect on English constitutional demands on Scotland when later it lacked a strong, centralised monarchy.

Scottish poetry flourished with such writers as Robert Ferguson and William Dunbar; Scottish theologians, notably Knox, dominated the northern Reformation; Scottish armies fought both King and Cromwell; Presbyterians were earnestly concerned with education, law, social justice, though earnestness could degenerate to fanaticism, the denunciations savage, the penalties worse.

England rated French-oriented Scotland a gaunt and unnecessary region, a debased Albion of witchcraft, anarchic clans, cattle-rustlers. Lord Arran, Royal favourite and murderer, married a witch who had been promised by 'weird warlocks' that she would become great and marry 'the highest head in Scotland'. She died, abnormally swollen by disease; and Arran, an unscrupulous betrayer, was himself betrayed, his head paraded high on a lance. Lord Drumlanrig was famed for killing and roasting a spit-boy. James

Starkie of Cameron made public repentence for hanging a dog on the Sabbath. English lawyers might have sympathised with the Scottish judge, Lord Newton: 'Drinking is my occupation, Law my amusement.'

Scottish witches risked fire, English witches the rope: one late burning was in 1723, when a woman was condemned for transforming her daughter into a pony. Scott, at the end of the century, saw Scottish miners and salters wearing iron collars stamped with their masters' names, and denied freedoms of bargaining and mobility enjoyed elsewhere. Some nineteenth-century Highland chiefs, exploiting their clans' loyalty, cleared them from the glens and hills, replacing them with sheep and game, leaving them to emigrate.

An imagination deeply felt but prone to understatement and resolutely insular was an English characteristic: though their borders marched with Wales and Scotland, the English remained ignorant of both, unable to quote Daffyd ap Gwilym or Dunbar, salute Llewellyn the Great or St Margaret. Very few English schoolboys knew anything very truthful of John Paul Jones (1747–92).

Born John Paul of Kirkudbright, gardener's son, he was early at sea, carrying slaves and other 'merchandise'. He adopted 'Jones' when on the run after killing a mutinous seaman in the West Indies. He settled in Virginia and in the War of Independence, as a commissioned captain, he bore the Stars and Stripes into British waters, raiding Whitehaven, stealing Lord Selkirk's silver teapot and burning some of the harbour. On a moonlit night off Flamborough Head, watched by a Yorkshire multitude, his own ship, supplied by Louis XVI, sinking beneath him, he outfought and sank the British flagship, allegedly having refused to strike his colours with the words: 'Surrender! I have not yet begun to fight!' This was quoted by A.V. Alexander, First Lord of the Admiralty, defiantly broadcasting to America after Dunkirk in 1940.

Indomitable, bad-tempered, provoking quarrels and betrayals, Jones later beat the Turks for Catherine the Great but feuded with his German co-commander, offended Potemkin, and was trapped in a sexual frame-up. He died listless and unemployed in Paris, attending the Revolutionary Assembly, and with talk of him leading an American expedition to sweep the Mediterranean free of Barbary pirates.

Rilke defined Fame as the sum of misunderstandings gathering around a single name. This fits Jones. To Carlyle, he was a hero: 'and lo, the desperate valour has suffocated the deliberate, and Paul Jones too is of the Kings of the Sea.' Catherine disposed of him as 'wrong-headed, most worthy of acclaim by a mob of detestables'. Lafayette and Benjamin Franklin admired him, F.D. Roosevelt contemplated writing his biography. He has affinities to Byron's 'Corsair', is caricatured in Scott's *Redgauntlet* as Nanty Ewart, decayed but expert pilot ready to support an argument with a cudgel, 'a human ship-wreck', pirate, smuggler, drunken son of the manse 'with the hue of death on his cheek and the fire of vengeance glancing from his eye'. Depicting Jones as 'Captain Paul' in *Israel Potter*, Herman Melville saw him as symbol of America itself, who in his small craft 'went forth in single-armed champion-ship against the English host. It is not easy, in the present day, to conceive the hardihood of the enterprise. It was a marching-up to the muzzle; the act of one who made no compromise with the cannonading of danger or death; such a scheme as only could have inspired a heart which held as nothing at all the prescribed prudence of war.' To English Tories Jones was a murderous slaver, rebel, traitor, 'the Devil in a Scots bonnet'. Thackeray's Denis Duval refers to 'the commodore of a wandering piratical expedition . . . known to be a rebel Scotsman who fought with a halter round his neck'. Kipling has 'the notorious Paul Jones, an American pirate'. An Oxford History of England calls him pirate and privateer on the same page, though he always refused Franklin's privateering offers. He lies in the Naval Pantheon at Annapolis in Maryland, but in England he remains virtually unknown.

The benefits of the Union may have appeared slow in coming to the Scots poor: families could lose eighteen out of twenty children from childbirth, malnutrition, disease. Scottish fortitude and ingenuity, however, persisted and over the centuries, through the vast opportunities offered by the Napoleonic wars, free trade, the Empire, altered the world. Bute, Aberdeen, Rosebery, Campbell-Bannerman, Balfour, MacDonald, Macmillan, Douglas-Home and, more marginally, Blair, entered Downing Street. Eugénie, Spanish Empress of the French, was proud of Scottish ancestry; the Russian poet Lermontov also had Scottish forbears.

Peter the Great particularly valued Scots, as advisers, technicians, strate-gists: Patrick Gordon, student of Royal Society reports, a Catholic soldier, saved Peter's throne from revolt in 1689. James Bruce, cartographer, physi-cist, astronomer, mathematician, diplomat, Field-Marshal, commanded the artillery at Poltava against Charles XII of Sweden, of whom Johnson said he was extraordinary without being great. Bruce's brother became first Mayor of Petersburg. For Catherine, Charles Cameron designed Tsarskoe Selo, in Classical style, and was senior Naval Architect to Alexander I. Catherine's private banker was Robert Sutherland, and she invited the physician James Whiley to Russia, where he built a hospital at his own expense. Barclay de Tolly, of Scottish descent, commanded Russian armies against Napoleon in 1812.

Like Dublin and London, eighteenth-century Edinburgh attained international repute as a centre of scholarship, law, discussion, libraries, publishing, art. David Hume excited the Enlightenment with his *History of England* but, more profoundly, with his rationalism. His relating of human nature and behaviour, not to the soul and original sin but to physical analysis, sensation, environment, was welcome to a western culture valuing research, debate, friendship, free association of the sexes, literature, and disinclined to priestcraft and kingcraft.

Robert Burns, beloved in Russia, was a genuine national Laureate, articulating many submerged hopes and fears, grievances, regrets, lusts, laments, intemperance and swagger. Hating hypocrisy, snobbish illusion, injustice, he compressed resolution, radicalism, wit, broad humour and lyricism with a simplicity that appears easy yet baffles most imitators:

> The wan moon is setting ayont the white wave,
> And time is setting with me, O.

More easily translated than Burns, as a founder of the western short story and historical novel Walter Scott coloured and deepened the imagination – for which Mark Twain held him responsible for the American Civil War, in fostering the romanticism of 'Southern Gentlemen'. He delineated many eras, many classes, retrieving obscured lives, customs, memories, beliefs, ballads, and almost single-handedly dispelled the woeful ignorance and some of the superiority which the English displayed towards the Scots. His impact on the Continent was equalled only by that of Shakespeare and Byron.

Adam Smith's theories were well attuned to Reason, and to a small country of harsh necessities, deprivation, raw conflict. He saw economic self-interest as central to human motivation and social cohesion. Creating wealth and its cultural subsidiaries, the successful benefited society by increasing its resources, providing employment and patronge, keeping beggary and degradation at bay. In France, where a weak monarchy was losing an empire to Britain, such theories seemed pertinent, though over-looking the role of the unconscious impulse, divided personality, individual and unconsidered loyalties, which the French Revolution, like the English Civil War, was to demonstrate. Humanity is lumbered with the manic factor: will commit atrocities in order to be talked about, and reign supreme in the weird empire of dream.

Scots achieved reputation in all directions: Tobias Smollett, as historian and novelist; Allan Ramsay, a better portraitist, on his day, than Reynolds. Scottish architects abounded. James Gibbs from Aberdeen built the Cambridge Senate House, St Mary-le-Strand and St Martin-in-the-Fields; William Chambers the Pagoda at Kew as well as the solid, masterful Somerset House. Once almost next to it, the Adam brothers' vanished Adelphi is testimony to London's penchant for demolishing elegance and the human scale, though there is much of Robert Adam's work to enjoy at Syon House and Osterley Park.

Religious barbarities declined, freeing the imagination of gifted Scots for medicine, economics, philosophy, scientific research. Watt, Kelvin, Robert Ross, Rutherford the New Zealander, Clerk-Maxwell, Fleming, Watson-Watt, a sprinkling of names covering scores of others. Energetic Scots, men and women, purposefully voyaged into all continents. The explorations of Alexander Mackenzie laid the foundations for a united Canada, of which John Buchan became an almost visionary Governor-General; William Mackenzie led the Upper Canada rebellion in 1837. Scots dominated New Zealand as the Irish did Australia. Dr Rae charted the Arctic. James Grant, Joseph Thomson, James Bruce ranged Africa. Bruce's discovery of the Blue Nile in the eighteenth century was followed in the nineteenth by David Livingstone's discovery of Lake Nyasa, as he searched for the headwaters of the same river. William Mackinnon was a founder of the British Steam Navigation Company and the Imperial British East Africa Company.

By the end of Marlborough's wars, and with the succession to Anne, the last of the Stuarts, by George, the first of the Hanoverians, Britain's prospects were tempting. Spain, Holland and France were weakening, Russia remote, Germany and Italy still a motley of competing states, Austria and Prussia no threat, the Turks receding, though still holding Greece and the Balkans. Well might Britons read with some complacency James Thomson's bombastic 'Britannia's Empire' (1729):

And is a Briton seiz'd? and seiz'd beneath
The slumb'ring Terrors of a British fleet?
Then ardent rise! Oh, great in vengeance rise!
O'erturn the Proud, teach Rapine to restore;
And as you ride sublimely round the World,
Make every Vessel stoop, make every State
At once their Welfare and their Duty know.
This is your Glory; this your Wisdom; this
The Native Power for which you were design'd
By Fate, when Fate design'd the firmest State,
That e'er was seated on the subject sea;
A State, alone, where *Liberty* should live
In these Late Times, this Evening of Mankind.

As the century progressed, Westminster played a calculating hand, financing coalitions, fighting with opportunistic determination to correct the Balance of Power, gain markets and raw materials, promote investment, forestall rivals, winning the soubriquet 'Perfidious Albion' in tactical changes of alliance. The Peace of Paris in 1763 was mocked by John Wilkes, that ugly, squinting, intelligent thorn in the flesh of the administration, as the Peace of God, because it passed all understanding. The eighteenth-century Britain of Sir Robert Walpole, a very English type though not of the finest quality, the first 'Prime Minister', understood it perfectly, having acquired French Canada and India, together with Senegal, Grenada, Malta, Gibraltar, Louisberg, Florida – great land masses and small vital commercial and strategic pivots: London, first modern metropolis, having displaced Venice and Amsterdam, was now the world's securest bastion of Capital, conducting loans, pioneering marine insurance, colonial projects, foreign schemes with a finesse usually irresistable, unshaken by such eruptions as the South Sea Bubble in 1720 and the earlier collapse of the Darien Scheme. Foreign States bought British Government stocks.

Britain's pre-eminent war-leader, dominating King, Cabinet, Parliament, Treasury, War-Office with resourceful acumen and astute appreciation of sea-power, was Pitt, Lord Chatham, who conducted world war with imaginative energy, on the scale of Lloyd George and Churchill.

The wars were as barbaric as most. The courtesy of Lord George Hay to his enemy at Fontenoy in the War of the Austrian Succession – 'Gentlemen of the French Guard, you fire first' – is misleading. Marlborough's earlier triumph at Malplaquet, over France, was an abattoir. At the end of the Seven

Years' War Saxony's population had been reduced from two million to four hundred thousand, Frederick the Great needlessly bombarding Dresden in a foretaste of the Strategic Bomber Offensive in 1945. After rescuing Berlin from a wild Russian occupation, Frederick forecast that the Russians were digging the grave of mankind. He himself, after Zordorf, allowed his troops to bury Russians alive. The Christian rulers of Prussia, Austria and Russia dismembered, then absorbed, Christian Poland. 'She protested, she wept, and she took': so Voltaire summarised Maria-Theresa's theft of Galicia in 1742. Such treatment was again a foretaste, of Poland's betrayal to the Russians by the Allies at Yalta in the Second World War.

Britain was the ultimate winner in all this Continental hooliganism: it afforded a major distraction, under cover of which she was able to accumulate the colonies that later coalesced into an Empire.

The British Empire praised itself for aspiring to the virtues of Rome and avoiding the vices of Carthage, Assyria, Spain. It was idealised as a pattern of public-spirited proconsuls responsible to Westminster ruling peoples grateful for western religion, judicial systems, trade, communications, public works, for salvation from war-lords and bandits. This was not altogether false. Conquering French Canada, the British gave the French equal rights. In India the Mogul Emperors, themselves foreign conquerors, had decayed into a benign stupor while free-booting warriors ravaged the countryside. Only Britain could spare it the prospect of unending pillage and rapine.

The process of acquisition was often more abstruse than mere robbery. From small starts momentum would gather pace, often unplanned. A garrison protected a trading-mart, which grew, needing a larger force; traders, looking for new openings, were soon testing frontiers; frontier disputes, contrived or accidental, caused further expansion, dictated more by local opportunities than by any overall London vision. Tribal feuds could be exploited, missionary zeal provoke crises to be settled by troops who tended to remain, alliances be made with native rulers, ostensibly on equal terms but which could go awry through guile, mistranslation, personal weaknesses, legal obfuscation. Local rulers very easily got into debt with the British; it was natural for the British to instal a Resident or a small force to ensure the servicing of the debt. Western concepts of religion, property, promises, logic could seem startlingly grotesque or irrelevant to alien ears. Law courts were exported, providing Common Law, as against traditional customs such as female infanticide, the burning of widows; harsh provisions about property and debt were introduced; trousers were prescribed, enriching Yorkshire and Lancashire mills but absurd to Polynesians and Africans – one tribe used them as turbans.

Britain, like Rome, accumulated client-states and protectorates. By 1800 the Empire, despite the American Revolution, was as large as any in history, and more widespread, with British rule scattered through five continents. Unparallelled chances opened for farmers, technicians, miners, adventurers, exploiters. In most colonies, the State was expected merely to hold the ring, allowing entrepreneurs less fair play than free play, though immoderate officials could be recalled for prosecution, even impeachment. 'Free Enterprise' included slavery, indentured labour, genocide, strike-breaking, extortion. The profits underwrote the serene country house architecture of Wyatt, Adam and Paine, the decorum of Beau Nash's Bath, the improper hilarities of the Hell Fire Club at West Wycombe. East Indian nabobs, West Indian sugar planters initiated exotic or vulgar flourishes: peacocks, turbaned pages, an imitation of the Taj Mahal at Sezincote in Gloucestershire, which then spawned the Royal Pavilion at Brighton with its minarets, domes, lattices, fanciful glass, dreamy convolutions of dragons and palm trees. Sydney Smith said it looked as though St Paul's had gone down to the sea and pupped. Sugar money paid for William Beckford's Gothick extravaganza at Fonthill.

Victory on land and sea, the trader's competitive zest for survival, excited a rough nationalism. Though the term 'Patriot' was usually applied to themselves by opponents of the government, a more general fervour inspired odes and vainglorious songs, to Old England, Roast Beef and Hearts of Oak, military music, and heroic inn signs: Marquis of Granby (portrayed with a bald pate because he lost hat and wig charging at the head of the cavalry at Dettingen), Admiral Benbow, Lord Cornwallis, the George, the Hero or England's Hero – Nelson. Tankards were raised to Portobello, Quiberon Bay, the Saints, 'The Glorious First of June', victories over the Spanish and French. Whiggish dissidents also raised them to 'Saratoga', where Cornwallis surrendered to the Americans.

'Englishness', however defined or concocted, robustly resisted Spanish hauteur, Dutch fastidiousness, French scents and frippery, though not smuggled French brandy. Whatever the *ton* demanded, it enjoyed Thomas Arne's tunes, Gay's romanticised criminals and tavern ballads as much as Handel's Italianate arias. It approved both the sober, industrious adaptability of *Robinson Crusoe* and the scapegrace gusto and irresponsibility of

Fielding's *Tom Jones*, as well as the sentimentality of Richardson's *Pamela: or Virtue Rewarded;* absorbed the moral didacticism and earthy realism of Defoe and Hogarth, the platitudes of Gray's *Elegy*, Johnson's pugnacious moralising and hefty individuality; the fixed, clean landscapes behind Gainsborough's placid gentry, and those romantically evocative, idealised countrysides peopled by rustic archetypes which he summoned up from his imagination as a relief from endless 'face painting'; the posturing historical panoramas of Benjamin West; the landscape drawings and water-colours of Alexander Cozens and his more brilliant son, J.R. Cozens, whom William Beckford took on his Grand Tour as a kind of animated camera to record the sights for him. It also relished the sturdy if menacing hymns of Watts and Wesley, while shrugging off miracles, saints, reputations as readily as Gibbon, who obviously rejoiced in the tale of Baldwin II of Byzantium cashing in on his sale of the supposed Crown of Thorns to Louis IX of France: 'The success of this transaction tempted the Latin Emperor [Baldwin] to offer with the same generosity the remaining furniture of his chapel: a large and authentic portion of the True Cross; the baby linen of the Son of God; the lance, the sponge, and the chain of His Passion; the rod of Moses; and part of the skull of St John the Baptist.'

Complementing this, the Dandies' droll inconsequence was as English as *Tristram Shandy* and *The Newgate Calendar*. Paradox, contradiction, muddle, inconsistency and humour proved as necessary to the social psyche as fortitude, forbearance, decency, relative honesty. One strand was symbolised, from 1772, by 'John Bull', florid, jovial, coarse-grained, ponderously judicial and fair-minded; four-square in feature and posture, hard-drinking, hard-swearing, friendly if addressed courteously, otherwise blasphemous; respectful but not obsequious to superiors; with common sense rather than intellectual convictions and artistic insight: he expressed natural appetites more graphically than colourless 'Britannia'. Socially below 'Sir Roger de Coverley' but sharing a sturdy scorn of beliefs thrust upon him by others, he is imaginable singing in Henry Fielding's play, *Don Quixote in England* (1733):

> When mighty Rost Beef was the Englishman's Food,
> It ennobled our hearts and enriched our blood;
> Our soldiers were brave, and our courtiers were good.
>   Oh the Rost Beef of Old England,
>   And Old England's Rost Beef.
> Then Britons, from all nice Dainties refrain,

Which effeminate Italy, France and Spain;
And mighty Rost Beef shall command on the main.

In a letter about his engraving, *The Roast Beef of Old England,* Hogarth wrote in 1749:

The first time an Englishman goes from Dover to Calais, he must be struck with the different face of things at so little distance. A farcical pomp of war, pompous parades of Religion, and much bustle with very little business. To sum up all, poverty, slavery and innate insolence covered with an affectation of politeness, give you even here a true picture of the manners of the whole Nation. Nor are the Priests less opposite to those of Dover than the two shores. The Friars are dirty, sleek and solemn; the Soldiery are lean, ragged and tawdry; and as to the Fish-women – their faces are absolute leather.

In 1995 John Major wrote in the Madrid newspaper *ABC*: 'The German forests play a special part in her national life. For France, it is her language and cultural traditions. For Britain, our seas and the roast beef of Old England matter more deeply than the simple, bald, economic figures say.'

John Bull was to be confronted in 1793 with 'Mrs Grundy', who imbibed the sourer English juices, embodying Macaulay's suggestion that Puritans objected to bear-baiting not out of compassion for the bear but because of the pleasure it gave to spectators. Her image was of pursed lips under a black bonnet, button-eyes glowering at taverns, music-halls, sexual delight, dancers, human beauty and life after dark.

Augustan civilities did not reach the bottom of the heap, or extend to the 'Black Merchandise' safeguarded by British sea-power. Irish starvelings complained of being treated worse than serfs. English authorities transported a hundred 'derelict' children to Virginia in 1618. A consortium of court ladies headed by the Queen sold Monmouth rebels to Caribbean plantations. Children were sold or abducted to mill and mine well into the nineteenth century, and, until 1908, lacked legal rights. The pregnant servant was hustled from the back door, the ploughboy press-ganged for the Fleet. In 1844 Palmerston mentioned that higher insurance was paid on a sick black slave tossed overboard than for one who died on board.

Lord James Altham, born in Ireland in 1715, was so neglected at home that he deteriorated into a Dublin street-arab. When he was twelve his father died, and after several vain attempts he was abducted by hirelings of his uncle, Lord Anglesey, who coveted his heritage. Thrust on a ship, the *Games of Dublin,* he was sold as a slave to a Caribbean plantation, where he remained for thirteen years before escaping. Befriended by Admiral Vernon, the hero of Portobello, he returned to Britain, where Anglesey had usurped his property and title. Accidentally killing a poacher, he was arraigned for murder at the Old Bailey. Acquitted, he successfully prosecuted Anglesey, exposing him as an abductor and a perjurer in the matter of the poacher, a witness testifying that he had been promised £10,000 as an accomplice to get Altham hanged.

Reacting from seventeenth-century fanaticism, the Enlightenment did not concern itself with sin, redemption, sacred texts; instead, it earnestly researched light and gas, physics, genetics, sociology, economics. All this was deplored by Blake as surrendering emotion to intellect. He attributed some of his artistic ability to Joseph – whose wife, the Virgin Mary, was considered at Versailles to have been not of the very best society.

Diderot's and d'Alembert's giant *Encyclopaedia* was modelled on that of Ephraim Chambers, published in Edinburgh in 1728, followed by *Encyclopaedia Britannica* (Edinburgh, 1768–71). In Venice, Coronelli outlined but never completed his *Bibliotheca Universale* (1701–6). Encyclopaedia, dictionary, thesaurus, handbook, universal recipes satisfied British curiosity and delight in the practical results of knowledge. Libraries and publishing–printing shops multiplied; John Murray, founding his house in 1768, remarked: 'Many blockheads in the Trade are making fortunes, and did we not succeed as well as they, I think it must be imputed only to ourselves.' It was the success of Mrs Rundell's *Domestic Cookery* which allowed John's son to back his hunch and publish Byron's *Childe Harold* in the next century.

Encyclopaedias strove not to parade virtuoso brilliance of language, metaphysics, scholasticism, nor to finalise Truth, but to establish provisional verdicts, substantiated by all available evidence, thus providing the wherewithal to work towards further truths. This outlook upheld the dignity of society, its opalescent potential when liberated from arbitrary and dogmatic indexes and censorship, nationalism, State academicism, convention. Intelligent discussion, the tabulation of proved facts, speculations far-reaching but not far-fetched were preamble to such sober, even legalistic, but humane statements as the American Declaration of Independence, the French Declaration of the Rights of Man, Lincoln's Gettysburg Address, the Atlantic Charter signed by Churchill and Roosevelt, and the United Nations Declaration of Human Rights.

To the Europe of 'Enlightened Despots' – Catherine, Frederick, Maria-Theresa, Joseph II, Gustavus III, the young Louis XVI, and such liberal ministers as Struensee and Pombal – British institutions were illuminated as if by stage lighting, unreal but not fantastic. Voltaire, who knew England but not Ireland, rhapsodised in 1764:

> The English Constitution has in fact arrived at the point of excellence, in consequence of which all men are restored to those natural rights of which in nearly all monarchies they are deprived. These rights are: Total Liberty of person and property; freedom of the press; the right of trial in all criminal cases by an independent jury; the right of being tried only according to the strict letter of the law; and the right of each man to profess any religion he desires.

Spirited heirs of Lilburne and Winstanley, young Byrons and Shelleys, Jews and Catholics would have glowered or winced at every second word, mindful of corrupt MPs, drunken magistrates, tithe-hungry parsons, the prosecution of printers, and theatrical censorship; the Licensing Act imposed by Walpole, incensed by the satirical venom of Fielding and Gay, endured until 1968. Voltaire may have been obliquely attacking the French establishment rather than rigorously analysing British arrangements, but his encomium had some substance.

Beethoven did more than write variations on 'God Save the King', 'Rule Britannia!' and Scottish dances: he studied Westminster parliamentary reports. International thought absorbed *The Idea of a Perfect Community*, by the portly Hume, viewed by Talleyrand as 'the Word made Flesh' but whose book contained more common sense, less schematic rigidity than More's *Utopia*, and fitted French metropolitan scepticism of a persecuting and incredible religion and an incompetent monarchy presiding over a shrinking empire, State bankruptcy, quasi-independent provinces, obstructive privilege, periodic famine. Utopias published in Spain, Holland, Italy, France were countered by Hume's dispassionate contemplation, derived not only from insight into human feelings but from knowledge of history. Great ideas should be tried against practical experience. Human behaviour can sometimes change drastically, as would soon be proved; human nature, however, does not, a lesson to be disregarded at peril. Wise teaching does not, as Rousseau, Condorcet, Robespierre supposed, axiomatically make people wise: good laws are easy, morals are not; a pious and decent family can breed a monster. Hume lacked waffle, that bane of philosophy. 'All plans of government, which suppose great reformation in the manners of mankind, are plainly imaginary. Of this nature, are the *Republic* of Plato and the *Utopia* of Sir Thomas More.' The path to Utopia would lead to cattle trucks, death camps, pistol shots in cellars with enlarged drains.

Much of this was plain to Samuel Johnson, like Sophocles and Shakespeare thoroughly aware of the bubbling lava beneath restrained society, the universality of 'the dread of unconscious powers'. His aphorisms were as sophisticated as those fluttering in cosmopolitan salons and, though often caustic, lacked Napoleon's cynicism: 'Anxiety wears man out in schemes to obviate evils that never threatened him' or 'Abundant charity is the atonement for imaginary sins.'

Meanwhile, the French *philosophes*, debarred from government, could only hone their wits. 'Nothing', Talleyrand continues, 'eases the strain of obedience as readily as an epigram.' Analysis was increasingly scientific, analytical. Unabashed by Voltaire's epigram that history is a bundle of tricks played on the dead, Hume, Vico, Montesquieu, Voltaire himself were founding historical materialism, incorporating the effects of climate, soil, forest, mineral deposits, disease, geography, the migrations of fish, animals, peoples on social habits, class, change, thus reducing the role of heroes and villains. Morality and ideas were more closely related to struggle and necessity.

Free Will battled with Determinism, with appeals to Newton, to Descartes, and a motto minted by J.O. de la Mettrie in 1748: 'Man is a Machine, and in the entire Universe there exists but one substance, variously tempered.' The American Benjamin Franklin, student not only of Montesquieu but of Tacitus and Defoe, in *Observations on Electricity* (1753) scared some, thrilled others – like the young Robespierre – with his promise of a fifth element to be added to those of earth, air, fire and water. Blake had another apprehension, teaching that civilisation was repressing physical and spiritual energies capable of recharging humanity, particularly if unobstructed by clothes.

In 1770 the future appeared stable, despite the losses and resentments left by the European wars, and restlessness in British America. Château and schloss, palazzo, hall and park glowed with paintings and sculpture, carpets and upholstery, porcelain and silver; they resounded with music and song, while their library shelves filled with books. Increasingly they opened their doors to scholars, philosophers, wits, eloquent charlatans. Some objectivity was being attained, some control over elemental passions exercised, notions of *Progress* very clearly enunciated.

The eighteenth century remains deeply alluring, through the harmonious proportions of a Georgian frontage, bland scenery perfected by a temple glimmering above a lake, the continuous inventiveness of a Haydn quartet, the gracious line of a Sheraton chair, the sharply chiselled couplets of Pope, the structure of Gibbon's sentences, sonorous yet imbued with wit. It attracts with rumbustious novels, generous philosophies, Dresden, Sèvres and Wedgwood, enamelled snuff-boxes, the soufflé, the human scale of market-towns, its eccentrics.

Few epochs are easier to sentimentalise. Augustan elegance could disguise the gambler's ruthlessness or despair; outward deference be decoded into sly insolence; a loyal toast contain a sardonic insult. The protocol of Royalty, the reasoned if not always sober debates at Westminster and in American State Assemblies strove to restrain seething streets, ill-lit, unpoliced. Official deportment was more stately, wigs more elaborate, heels loftier, silks more transparent, brocades plushier, so that lords and ladies might appear higher, remoter than they actually were. Private carriages, running footmen, outriders and flunkeys never meant you were wholly safe from highwaymen, criminal gangs, and crowds. Petty crooks like Dick Turpin and 'MacHeath' were transfigured into heroes of folk-tale and ballad. The Ballad, Edwin Muir reflected, grew perfect by a kind of forgetting: just as the Irish famine of 1739, in which one in five perished, has been obliterated by the potato famines there in the 1840s. London, in the first half of the century, seemed at times as if it would be engulfed in a tidal wave of gin.

In northern and midland Britain, despite the deepening glow of blast-furnaces, the darkening of urban skies, the whirr of power-looms, the menacing tread of jobless machine-breakers, English moderation still held, thanks in part to the influence of Methodism, which blunted much sedition.

The Hanoverian State and Church were languid, conniving more than initiating. Enclosures were still sapping many villages, industrialism dislocating cottage livelihoods. The riches of Empire did not filter down very far. E.P. Thompson, historian of the emergent working class and champion of the poor, nevertheless substantiates an impression of social balance, brief yet fruitful, between Crown and Parliament, faith and scepticism, land and trade, street and mansion, custom and law; a considerable humanity within all classes. Time was not yet wholly money, the Clock not quite omnipotent. When Parliament was seeking remedy for catastrophes due to lost bearings at sea, in 1714 it offered £20,000 for a method of more exactly plotting longitude. This was won, only after many decades, by a self-taught carpenter and choirmaster, John Harrison (1693–1776), whose chronometer, against university and City apathy and hostility from the Astronomer Royal, was adopted by the powerful East India Company, followed by the rest of the world, permanently reducing wreckages and helping consolidate the Empire. Hodge was still free of Gradgrind and the hegemony of mass media and compulsory schools. Law might be tempered by public opinion, though crowds were manipulated as easily for King and Church as for Wilkes and Liberty.

Thompson does show patrician culture increasingly alienated from mass culture, itself deep-rooted, outspoken, bawdy, with its own bacchanalia, wakes, street-songs, caricatures, factional colours and ribbons keeping alive ancient resentments, its own mutinous riddles, effigy-burnings, clandestine meetings and prolonged, blood-chilling oaths. But each culture was conservative, tied, however unwillingly, to English Common Law, its precedents and antique rights. Agitation ensured the survival of London parks which foreigners were to praise as the capital's glory. In a famous dispute over Richmond Park, Royalty was defeated in open court, which would have been unthinkable in Russia, Spain, Prussia, France, or Naples. Civil law tended to be thought fairer than criminal law; 'Fair Play', easy to understand, difficult to define, impossible to translate, was deemed superior to either. Law, though, was ever a 'mystery', sustaining *Them* against *Us*, very seldom refuting Shakespeare's distinction between rich man's and poor man's justice:

> Plate sin with gold,
> And the strong lance of justice hurtless breaks;
> Arm it with rags, a pigmy's straw does break it!

With scant State provision for the poor and neglected, of necessity parsonage and manor house distributed charity, with allowance made for family temperament, women's energy, the parson's morality and the squire's gout. Their inhabitants exercised snobbery, if not as an art, at least to give an airing to minor prejudice, callous conceit, diverting absurdities. Yet they could maintain recognisable life-lines to those below which the caste-bound

French nobility would soon have urgent cause to envy. Classes could unite in love of gaudy parades, rhetorical ceremonies – a coronation, victory celebration, raucous election, hanging – and of sport.

One English custom, barbaric to Hanoverian gentry as to the present century, was public wife-sale, still famous through Hardy's *The Mayor of Casterbridge*. Yet Thompson suggested that it 'performed a function of ritual divorce both more available and more civilized than anything the polite culture could offer'. He logged 218 such sales between 1760 and 1880. The wife herself might initiate the transaction; one thrashed her mate with his wooden leg until she had procured her sale to her lover.

It has been suggested that industrialism, out-matching cottage crafts, weakened many women's position by submerging them as 'hands' in mill, factory, mine. But, particularly in fishing and clothing communities, they need not have been domestic and marital slaves, and could display contempt for law and conventional assumptions about sobriety, child-rearing, story-telling. They were adept, and probably did not forget it, at baking, bottling, pickling, bee-keeping, gardening, stitching, weaving, teaching, tending animals, painting, attending sick or maltreated neighbours. Women led certain food riots; one at Stockton was captained by 'a woman with a stick and horn using very ill language'. J.B. Priestley remembered his pre-1914 youth:

> It was still the custom in some Bradford mills, for the women to seize a newly-arrived lad, and 'sun' him, that is, pull his trousers down and reveal his genitals. But all this not unwholesome and perhaps traditional bawdiness – there was a suggestion of mythology, ancient worship, folklore, about that queer 'sunning' ritual – was far removed from cynical whoring. There was nothing sly, nothing hypocritical, about those coarse dames and screaming lasses, who were devoted to their own men, generally working in the same mill, and who kept on 'courting', though the actual courtship was over early, for years and years, until a baby was due, when they married.

Women, admittedly, frequently had a raw deal, and men's interests lay in making it rawer. They still had no access to Parliament, Church, Law, the armed forces, seldom to Education. Egypt and Russia each had a woman cabinet minister before the first woman, an American, Nancy Astor, was elected to Westminster in 1919. Annual pregnancy, early death, tuberculosis, 'the vapours' blighted many, though a few pushed into history. The partnership of Queen Anne and the gale-force termagant Sarah

Marlborough carried political weight. Females of rank dispensed advice, patronage, hospitality. Women could defy what might appear to be their fate. Mary Anne, 'The British Amazon', youngest of Lord Talbot's sixteen illegitimate children, enlisted in male uniform as a regimental drummer and then, as a powder-monkey, cabin-boy, second mate, in British, French and American ships before, in a manner, settling down, being jailed for debt, accepted as a goldsmith's assistant, an actress, and (understandably) a best-selling author. Mary Reed and Ann Bonny were pirates, estimated, though by men, as of inferior quality. Bonny, daughter of an Irish lawyer, married another pirate, 'Calico Jack' Blackham, and escaped hanging by opportune pregnancy. In 1809 HMS *Dreadnought* carried 800 seamen, 813 prostitutes. The Maritime Penitent Refuge for Poor Degraded Females would not have been under-used.

Morals were usually enforced not by the State but by public opinion, by social blackmail of scolding wives, brutal husbands, adulterous couples, sexual deviants, thieves, on whom were practised the 'shaming rituals' of ostracism, ducking, effigy burnings, prolonged noise from tongs, horns, pots and pans, and the skimmity rides, the dragging about in public of effigies of the proscribed couple, described by Hardy and seen in Somerset by Dr Andrew Morland who, as a young doctor, attended the dying D.H. Lawrence.

Different modes were expected from grander establishments. The patrician Henry James thought the Country House a characteristic English invention, illustrative of social genius and manners and, in its administration and achievements, 'the one great thing they have mastered completely in all its details'. He was supported by a plebeian republican, unpatriotic internationalist – H.G. Wells, bitterly caustic about 'above stairs' life at Uppark which he had seen from 'below stairs', angered by his mother's hands, once beautiful but ruined by drudgery. Wells knew the sub-regions where old servants coughed out their lives, the lonely terrors of pregnancy, children swindled out of education by parson and squire, meekly recruited for service among the higher 'quality'. Wells nevertheless asserted that 'The English Country House created the first museums and laboratories, gentle manners, good writing, and nearly all that was worthwhile in contemporary civilization.' It was hub of a paternalist realm, self-sufficing, dispensing employment and patronage for tenant-farmers, keepers and ostlers, craftsmen, smiths, builders, artists. This, and the care for the landscape, set some proportion to local anxieties. Friendship, if on peculiar terms, could exist between the servers and the served, hereditary loyalties could be deeply grounded. Imperfections were undisguised: over-long hours of under-paid work for families who had, in much-repeated phrase, merely taken the trouble to be born. Perhaps, however, the loss of America and the divisions in the governing class about rebellion and defeat, together with the retention of Canadian ties, by forcing the British to consider the issues more sharply, assisted feelings of national identity, even social cohesion.

French aristocrats still abandoned their châteaux for opportunities at Versailles. Their British counterparts were more concerned with local profits. Estates, as Jane Austen's Mr Knightley insisted, should be kept moving. Landowners planted unusual vegetables, improved livestock, encouraged the development of novel implements, to feed a swelling population. The Duke of Bridgewater not only demanded from Turner a companion-painting to a Van de Velde but, as 'Father of Inland Waterways', subsidised Brindley's canals.

Inside the country houses mannered voices chattered about India, a capsized warship, a St James's scandal, a murder in Hyde Park. In long galleries and orangeries, flounced ladies sauntered during bad weather. Chocolate, China tea, coffee were taken, as well as laudanum – tincture of opium – as a cure-all. In the next century, at Stratfield Saye, Wellington was said to employ an elephant to crop the grass. Square card tables were set, at which estates were lost in a session. From beneath other tables drunken diners were hauled away by collar-boys, and in the ballroom, a-shine with flaring candelabra, quadrille and minuet had not yet been overtaken by the waltz.

Pope, in his 'Epistle to Lord Burlington' (1731), described 'Timon's Villa'. Having discovered an opulent library, the books outdated and unread, he continues:

> And now the chapel's silver bell you hear,
> That summons you to all the Pride of Pray'r:
> Light quirks of Music, broken and uneven,
> Make the soul dance upon a Jig to Heaven.
> On painted Ceilings you devoutly stare,
> Where sprawl the Saints of Verrio, or Laguerre,
> On gilded clouds in fair expansion lie,
> And bring all Paradise before your eye.
> To rest, the Cushion and soft Dean invite,
> Who never mentions Hell to ears polite.

Of Pope, Wilde considered that there are two ways to dislike poetry: one is to dislike poetry, the other is to read Pope.

'The World', wrote Saint-Just, very young, very foolish, 'has been empty since the Romans.' The eighteenth century was almost suffocated by Classical enthusiasms. Polite society, Janus-like, saw progress as movement forward to further knowledge, innovation, refinement, yet also as recession to Athens and Rome, the radicals more devoted to the latter's republican than to its imperial era, some even favouring the extremism of Sparta. The ancient languages and literature remained paramount in English universities, just as the Classical orders of architecture dominated the thinking of most patrons and practitioners. Only on southern American plantations like Jefferson's Monticello could the full flavour of Classical Rome be recreated, with its domed villa – and hundred and fifty slaves. Marble Neptunes haunted English lakes, lead gladiators postured on lawns; carefully-crafted ruins, grottoes, pavilions, temples, groves, fountains, obelisks were a sigh for Theocritus and Virgil, for Arcadia. In his play of that name, Tom Stoppard pins down the sources of inspiration: 'English landscape was invented by gardeners imitating foreign painters who were evoking classical authors. The whole thing was brought home in the luggage from the Grand Tour. Capability Brown, doing Claude, who was doing Virgil. Arcadia!' Eventually, surfeited, the imagination sought further renewal in more tumultuous Romanticism or a revived Gothic, with its shadows and mysterious temptations. Younger, more earnest eyes could see sham-Classical statuary as but tasteful embellishment, empty abstraction, without *numen*. John Constable said, 'A gentleman's park is my aversion. It is not beauty because it is not nature.'

In France more than in Britain, misunderstandings of Classical republics and benevolent dictatorships were attracting intellectuals, who injected them into political theory. Jefferson, Frederick the Great, Catherine admired Plutarch's heroes; and Beethoven, in his deafness, confessed: 'I have often cursed my fate, but Plutarch taught me resignation.' Above Caesar, however, American democracy placed Cincinnatus, the hero who, his mission accomplished, quietly retired and went home to his plough. Houdon's famous statue of Washington (there is a copy outside the National Gallery in Trafalgar Square) has him standing, walking-stick in hand, his sword hung up, and a plough ready behind him. Indeed, Americans preferred *Republic* to *Democracy*. Britain seldom delighted in either.

Napoleon had been elected First Consul, with Senate and Tribunate, before grasping more grandiose status. Earlier, Robespierre was likened to Cato, Danton to Hercules, Saint-Just to the ruthless Spartan law-giver Lycurgus, Barère to Anacreon, Napoleon to Alexander. John Paul Jones, like Washington and Lafayette admitted to the Order of Cincinnatus, thought himself a Scipio, and on his ship *Ranger* carried two ex-slaves, Cato Carlile and Scipio Africanus. Diderot, with grammatical accuracy but poor observation, had assured Catherine the Great that she possessed the soul of a Brutus and the charms of a Cleopatra.

Johnson's *London* and *The Vanity of Human Wishes* aped Juvenal's satires on Imperial Rome. Wilkes edited Catullus. Burke denounced the proconsul Warren Hastings in imitation of Cicero's diatribes against Verres and Catiline; Ciceronian counterpoint persisted through Gibbon. For disciplined virtue, Latin and Greek were flogged into young gentlemen, and the Prince Regent allowed that gentlemen 'need to have Greek'. Like religion, the rules of Classicism suggested that truth had been finalised – which often allowed clichés to be ignored – and that originality, spontaneity, were often suspect. International art and literature nagged at imaginations inclined towards the conservative, even static. Turner claimed, though surely with only partial truth, that Van de Velde's *A Gust of Wind* transformed him into a painter. The Welsh painter Richard Wilson admired not only Claude but the Dutch landscapers; Reynolds learnt from Rubens and Van Dyck.

A further balance was still evolving in Georgian Britain, between Nature and Society, most visible in parks and gardens, patrician and plebian. By 1800 Cobbett noticed that 'All through the country, poor as well as rich are very neat in their gardens, and very careful to raise a great variety of flowers.' English gardens of whatever size responded to new cravings for privacy, the satisfaction of *Private Property*. Allotments, a retort to enclosures, produced food and also made humble but solid male clubs, a relief from domestic tensions. Though not given statutory recognition until 1845, they were already established. At the other extreme, the landscaping of Brown and Repton was an art, approximating to the painter's blending of the artificial with the natural, pasture and woodland with lake and lawn, relating all to stone and marble, to statue, urn and mansion. Unlike Constable, Tennyson thought an English gentleman's park in May the most beautiful sight on earth.

Prosperity now harvested the largesse of Empire. Goldfish, chips of Asiatic glamour, made live mosaics within pools rimmed by nereids and tritons, to match apricots, nectarines, bright against russet walls.

British garden-designers had learnt from French, Italian and Dutch formalists, but now embraced the irregular, preserving some favourite though intrusive elm, and encouraged the serpentine at the expense of the straight line, natural growth in place of clipping and pruning. They recognised the quiet drama of setting geometrical against wild, through contrived vistas incorporating the distant with the immediate, like poets teasing imagination with the half-seen, the recollected, the expectant. Silent messages came from the skyline glimpsed through a hedge-gap, or from an obelisk on a knoll rising from the mists. The summer-house was redolent of tea-talk, soothing gossip, golden and painless sunlight, freed from servants' eyes, sometimes from decorum; the gazebo allowed one to 'gaze about', out of the wind, across the ha-ha to the carefully positioned clumps beyond, to 'rides' through solid woodland, to bridges, to arches, finally to the open country outside the boundary belts. Shrubberies too, closer to the house, dense with leaves and berries from four continents, were shelters for more covert assignations, and children's games.

Gardens discourage thrift. At Blenheim, where he was employed by the 4th Duke of Marlborough, Capability Brown was relatively modest in flooding a hundred acres for a lake to complete his effect. The 5th Duke once owed fifteen thousand pounds for plants, then a stupendous sum. In the jaunty Hanoverian way he was appointed Commissioner of the Treasury; his heir, while deploring Government (and doubtless paternal) expenditure, once lost £26,000 at Doncaster Races. Not all the family were devoted to flowers. Walking at Chartwell with Sir Winston, A.L. Rowse praised a sickle-shaped swathe of blue anchusa and white foxglove. Churchill allowed them a brief glance. 'Yes, that's Clemmie – now, with regard to the Battle of Blenheim . . .'

A serene park and garden might appear an argument for the benevolence of Nature, but weeds, cruelty, violence, lust, revolution, and indeed a sight of the nearest baby told another tale, even to ladies and gentlemen. A sense of green, doubtless more literary than natural, lingered in eighteenth-century England, in the light green of elms under summer rain from which ladies have just tripped away, in the green of pastoral verse and village pageantry; also in the hues within morgues, as if stricken souls still hover, and the baize of gaming tables; children whisper of Winnie with the Long Green Fingers, a stray from the eldritch territory of Green Chapel, Green Knight, surviving in nightmare tales of nurses sadistic or half-possessed. There was a Regency celebrity known as 'The Green Man', Henry Cope, wearing only green, eating only green food, possessing only green furniture and objects, though finally jumping off a white cliff. An 1802 print of him exists, titled 'The Bath Bugabo or the Widow's Terror'.

England was often scorned, not least by W.H. Auden, for provincialism; but the Milord and Gentleman, related though not identical, made the Grand Tour, deploring French inns, the rowdy bells at Bruges and Rome, Neapolitan filth, the 'stinking ditches' of Venice; they acknowledged the Alps, were condescending towards the yellow frontages of Parma, the legend-soaked Rhine, Bavarian palaces, and patronised opera houses and brothels. They were admired, exploited, slyly ridiculed, imitated, but their tailoring and their guineas were effective against mockery of their insobriety and pomposity. They assumed the aplomb of a satrap over a humbled nation, even though in England the dun might lurk in the shrubbery, the excise officer watch the back door.

At home, they retained considerable political power until, and even after, Parliamentary reforms. The Duke of Newcastle manipulated nine constituencies, Lord Lonsdale nine 'pocket boroughs, the 'Nine Pins'.

Their insouciance was renowned. In Paris Lord Thanet lost £120,000, twice his annual income, at a sitting; but, when informed that he had probably been rooked, merely thanked his good fortune in only losing half what he might have. Lord Alvanley, admirer of cold apricot tart, habitually extinguishing his candle before sleep by placing it under his pillow, bet three thousand pounds on a raindrop racing others down a window at White's. The aristocracy, however, did not survive only on its estates, gambling, and by marrying heiresses. A Shaftesbury had extensive interests in colonial enterprises and international trade, a Bedford in urban property.

Broad acres, long rent-rolls, a smallish population gave scope for individuality, not confined to one class though the nobility flourished it like a banner. Brutal boarding schools were survival courses, rites of passage in which the son of a Mincing Line tea-merchant, John Company nabob or Edinburgh lawyer might be more prestigious than an earl. At Harrow, a Duke of Dorset was beaten twice: first for his misdemeanour, then for being a Duke. A quirk of personality could outreach pedigree; Beau Brummell the dandy was praised by Byron as the greatest man of the century, followed by Napoleon, then by himself. Once, of the Prince Regent, Brummell asked Alvanley, 'Who's your fat friend?'; often, he could make the Prince quail by disparaging his coat; yet he was the grandson of a lodging-keeper. Imagination still feeds on tales of Mr Hervey keeping his father chained to a bear, and cutting off a nose whose owner said he smelled an Irishman; of

Squire Waterton visiting Italy with a retinue of owls; of Squire Mytton setting fire to his night-shirt to cure his hiccups; of Mr Small in a field, playing a double-bass, to pacify a bull.

Admiral Sir Home Riggs, twenty-first child of his mother, became a Red Indian chief; then, tattoed all over, Governor of Louisiana. Charles James Fox roused wonder and curiosity by marrying his mistress, Elizabeth Armistead. Colonel Mackinnon's mistress eventually demanded the return of the gift of a lock of her hair, and received a box of female hair of all colours, and an invitation to identify her own. In his London Journal for 1763 Boswell introduced George Selwyn, whose spirituality would have displeased Blake:

> He was a droll dog when at Oxford, and kept up a most earnest and grave correspondence with a reverend bishop on a point of controversial divinity: whether, after receiving the Communion before Confirmation, he was in a reprobate state or in a state of grace. He kept up the disguise of mystical religion long, and tormented the worthy prelate with his many grievous doubts. The letters he has by him. He was at last expelled [from] the University for a piece of gross profanity, giving the sacrament to a dog. He did it literally, to a degree of craziness. He cut his arm and made the dog drink his blood . . .

Avoiding Brummell's small, dangerous smile while hoping to be offered his snuff-box, more exclusive than most clubs, lordlings would have savoured, as pragmatic English juiciness, Lord Chancellor Thurlow, patron of Johnson and Crabbe, addressing a Nonconformist from the Bench: 'I'm against you, by God! I am for the Established Church, damme! Not that I have any more regard for the Established Church than for any other Church, but because it *is* established. And if you can get your own damned church established, I'll be for that too!'

The Norwich Bible Society was once foolish enough to approach Lord Orford, who responded: 'I have long been addicted to the gaming table. I have lately taken to the Turf. I fear I frequently blaspheme. But I have never distributed religious tracts. All this was known to your Society. Notwithstanding which you think me a fit person to be your president. God forgive your hypocrisy.'

Lords and gentry would gallop recklessly to battle or to hounds, exploit Ireland, conquer Bengal, seduce the coachman's daughter, tinker with sentimental verse, spar with Mendoza and Gentleman Jackson, and solemnly argue the merits of varied neck-ties: the Oriental, Mathematical,

Osbaldeston, Napoleon, Mail Coach, Trône d'Amour, Irish Ballroom, Horse Collar, Maharatta.

Lords did not seek but accepted attention, by right of being; were apt to overlook creditors though not gambling debts; served in Parliament or on the Bench as an inherited burden, privilege, or chance for plunder; they could be more wasteful than generous, their courtesy frequently a mode of indifference, their love sometimes given more to animals than to humans.

The Gentleman was less blatant than the Lord, more restrained. Lord Chesterfield defined him as a man who knows how to play the trumpet, but doesn't; his own letters to his son promote artificial standards, many of them unendearing today, reducing human relationships to sententious obligations of contract and caste, Academy regulations, draining common sense of common feeling, and encouraging the English reputation for reserve.

One product of their teaching was singled out by the Devil in Shaw's *Man and Superman*. He described a sterile Paradise where 'a number of people, mostly English, sit in glory because they think they owe it to their position'.

The Gentleman was steadfastly loyal, but unshowy, disinclined to demand extra for overtime. Like Viking and Teutonic *scalds*, he could find nobility, even moral victory, in defeat. Money, titles, loudness, the peremptory would not, however, console for cowardice, dishonesty, ill-repute. He could be more stoical than adventurous and, supported by relative prosperity, was disinclined to the utopian and visionary. He was undemonstrative: Talleyrand, member of the gentlemanly Reform Club in Pall Mall, glancing around, said that the English hate to be seen.

The Gentleman, however decent and charitable, at best preferring values to cash value, was often unimaginative in art, religion, politics, and the care of children, preferring Good Taste to obsession. A Rawdon Crawley, a Mr Dombey failed in almost all that was expected of him. Trollope's Sir Roger Carbury, in *The Way We Live Now*, is better. His virtues are unsensational – incorruptibility, moderation, conscience-abiding – but he is no stained-glass apostle, with his liability to anger, impatience with moral weakness and misplaced love. He is responsible rather than selfless, more long-suffering and affectionate than passionate, magnanimous but selective. No idealist, expecting no immediate Second Coming or Apocalypse, his English good sense amends the Sermon on the Mount, taking a longer view than Christ: 'Roger Carbury did not quite believe in the forgiveness of injuries. If you pardon all the evil done to you, you encourage others to do you evil. If you give your cloak to him who steals your coat, how long will it be before your shirt and trousers will go also?'

Even less than the nobility was the gentry a petrified caste, Defoe writing in 1736:

> Trade is so far here from being inconsistent with a gentleman that, in short, trade in England makes a gentleman, and has peopled this nation with gentlemen ... The Tradesman's children, or at least their grandchildren, come to be as good gentlemen, parliament men, privy councillors, judges, bishops and noblemen as those of the highest birth and the most ancient families.

The Gentleman was no less valued in America: Washington esteemed his ancestor who had fought at the Battle of Lewes in 1264. F.D. Roosevelt, patrician landowner, charming, courageous, was a remarkable late flowering of eighteenth-century panache; behind smiles and banter, he had a resolute shrewdness in the mould of Pitt and Palmerston; also, perhaps, a loneliness which, seldom darkening the outward ebullience, could deceive by suggesting a remoteness from sordid political dealings, conspiracies, betrayals, evasions. Versions of the Gentleman were staged in the Southern States, in Russia, and by the Anglo-Irish Ascendancy. Elizabeth Bowen, a distinguished representative, remarked that the Ascendancy was Irish when it suited, English when it did not.

English 'Society' never lacked a maverick, sometimes titled, never wholly part of it: a Beaverbrook, Birkenhead, Disraeli, Brougham – Mr Melmotte, Mr Merdle, Falstaff. George Bryan Brummell was no Milord, never wholly the Gentleman, though courted by both. He was the reverse of the flamboyant exhibitionist of popular fiction, demanding sartorial sobriety, black evening-dress; restyling the coat, replacing knee-breeches with trousers, inventing the high, starched cravat, perfecting its symmetries. In dress, deportment, facial expression he pruned the inessential, made cleanliness obligatory, and his posthumous influence on masculine styles gave London the lead over Paris. A curious footnote was added by Henry Poole of Savile Row, master tailor in the Brummell tradition. He helped finance the return to France from exile of a client, Louis-Napoleon, with on the whole detrimental results for European progress.

Like Wilde, Brummell pleased himself by giving unexpected answers to commonplace questions. Asked his favourite vegetable, he professed disapproval of that unassuming article, while denying that he had ever eaten any. 'No, that is not quite correct: I once ate a pea.' Lewis Melville related:

'Once, when the Prince of Wales had just received the present of a horse, he asked Brummell what he thought of it, and how old it was: instead of examining it in the usual way, the Beau went behind the animal and studied its tail for a considerable time. The Prince at last asked him what he was doing. "Sir," he answered, "you should never look a gift horse in the mouth."' Again like Wilde, he died, broken, in France.

Brummell pitched his supercilious coolness precisely between the tolerable and the unacceptable, a delicate balance maintaining him for many years. 'Some more of that cider!' he ordered a servant, commenting on his host's champagne. The self-dedicated Dandy makes a supreme art of pointlessness; his mere existence is the point. To saunter is existentialist fulfilment of being; Time is nothing, timing is all-important, to be seen is everything; he is unimaginable in solitude, except preparing his appearance – for others. He shrugs off systems, dogmas, all authority save his own. His flickering glance or bored appraisal ridicules public opinion. He rises above all occasions, for he is himself an occasion; he refuses a duel with pretended terror and underlying scorn, leaving his opponent baffled and worsted.

English nobility and gentry were part of an international society with distinctive bearing, dress, tone, unwritten rules, in which women of style and wit had considerable sway. It respected private property and courtesy, disliked tax officials, soldiers, nosey parkers. In the salons, people discussed Hume, the troubles of Poland, the *Encyclopaedia*, the Lisbon earthquake of 1755 which amused Voltaire by wrecking churches and sparing brothels. Admiration was extended towards China, envisaged as a society ruled by rationalist mandarins – something like Plato's Guardians – and wise, disinterested emperors. Deism was fashionable, eschewing miracles, false prophecies, mysticism, Other World fantasies. Science and philosophy were optimistic, in the spirit which made Nahum Tate gave *King Lear* a happy ending, as Catherine the Great gave one to *Timon of Athens*.

The monarchical Old World was moving towards reform of serfdom, law, taxation, and if Britain appeared languid, it had an advanced constitutional base from which improvements could be expected. Popular education was regarded more cautiously. 'The day when our peasants wish to become enlightened,' Catherine addressed the Governor of Moscow, 'you and I will lose our jobs!'

Cultural cross-currents suggested an international unity as promising as that of the later Dark Ages. The educated would have agreed with Georges Simenon (1978) that, while all people are alike, nationalities are unreal.

National boundaries certainly offered little obstacle to the enterprising. After the 'Glorious Revolution' of 1688, some thousands of Irish Catholics and Scots Jacobites retreated to France, becoming dockers, shipwrights, sailors, mercenaries; and in their descent was a Napoleonic Marshal, MacDonald, and a French Marshal, Duke and President, MacMahon. The Duke of Berwick, having commanded for James II in Ireland, subsequently fought for Louis XIV. Austria and the German states recruited Irish mercenaries, 'Wild Geese'; and thousands more Celts, driven out by Highland Clearances, Irish Famine, poverty, evictions, grievance, crossed the Atlantic.

Among Napoleon's generals were Germans, Poles, Italians, Dutch, Swiss. An Irishman, Mr Wall, became a Spanish minister; a Scot, Mr Law, a financial expert, with his deft miscalculations almost bankrupted France. The Duke of Brunswick, having led Allied armies to defeat at Valmy, was offered command of the victorious French revolutionaries. The Pole Thaddeus Kosciuszko, the Frenchman Lafayette, fought for Washington. The Dutch Prince Nassau-Siegen commanded a fleet for Louis XV, served him and Poland as diplomat, went to Russia to secure peace with the Turks, accepted Catherine's commission to fight them, co-operating (very badly) with John Paul Jones. As if in afterthought, the Prince claimed to have seduced the Queen of Tahiti. Necker, father of Madame de Staël and hope of Louis XVI's Treasury, was Swiss; Marat a Swiss–Sardinian with a Scottish medical degree who had also studied and practised in Bordeaux, Paris, Holland, London. David Williams and Tom Paine helped to draft the French Constitution in 1793. Cagliostro could be met throughout Europe, born, he said, of an archangel, witness to the building of the Pyramids, intimate with Jesus and with Roman empresses, creator of an Egyptian Masonic Order. He sold at some profit an elixir guaranteeing 5,557 years of life, was ridiculed in a play by Catherine the Great and conspired in the Diamond Necklace scandal, tainting Marie Antoinette. In 1795 Napoleon, impatient with the disreputable Directory, volunteered for the Russian army but was affronted by the offer of an inferior rank, and was rejected for a French-controlled job of modernising the Turkish artillery.

The reforming monarchs were easy targets for abuse and protest as the century aged, with bad harvests and rising prices. Frederick the Great himself described his crown as only a hat that let in water, though he would have resented any attempt to remove it. Academics were pondering Cato's remark: 'A King is an animal that exists on human flesh.' Young men like Tom Paine of Thetford, Robespierre of Arras, were scrutinising Monarchy, which Jefferson denigrated as all body but no mind. For Paine, it was 'a poor, silly, contemptible thing'. He believed in elections though was seldom satisfied with the results. His books, *The Rights of Man*, *The Age of Reason*, sold well in Britain and, more ominously, in America.

Many Whigs sympathised with new men; Tories were disinclined to dismantle the 1688 Settlement, to let in Catholicism or egalitarianism. Neither wanted a Frederick the Great or Joseph II. All respected the attractions of money. But encyclopaedias and well-reasoned political tracts were producing, besides the well-informed, the know-all and the virtuous self-deluded. Over-sophisticates applauded a Rousseau for condemning their civilisation. They credited mankind with perfectability, believed in wisdom overcoming institutions and laws grounded in self-interest. Without extravagant charity to the poor at their gates, they revered 'The People', and the ideal of a 'Constitution'. They hankered after a Golden Age inspiring though imaginary, older than Troy or Albion, where naked primitives lived in sexual simplicity, instinctive goodness, ignorant of property, cruelty, competition. It lacked immediate proof, though Cook found traces of it among the Polynesians, before they killed him.

Visions drifted through Europe of a New Society undebauched by priest-craft, monarchy, law, oppression, disease; almost within reach, it was delayed only by the ignorant, the vicious, the endowed boobies. Two remarks bred of the Enlightenment, which covered everything save elementary psychology, were of a kind to excite a young Shelley, Coleridge, Wordsworth, Southey, though not the more seasoned Pitts and Burkes. Mirabeau declared: 'The more I ponder social abuse, the more I am convinced that it needs only twelve principles expressed in twelve lines . . . to set everything right, and restore the reign of Solomon.' (Gibbon could have told him that the reign of Solomon was disastrous.) Saint-Just, who ended on the scaffold at twenty-eight, execrated by 'The People', claimed that 'most political errors come from regarding government as a difficult science'.

Unrestrained by Johnson's belief that no place affords a more striking conviction of the vanity of human hopes than a public library, the eighteenth century loved not only to converse but to write. From boudoir and prison, from coach, privy, and the captain's cabin streamed diaries, journals, pamphlets, fables, novels, verses to disobedient children, verses to the moon by a clergyman beginning 'How Brave a Prospect is a Bright Backside', verses about the soul, Judgement Day, lost causes, and Melancholy; an ode to a favourite cat drowned in a tub of goldfish; elegies on dying landscapes.

Women competed with men in the race for immortality on the printed page, Rousseau lamenting his constant misfortune in being associated with authoresses. Catherine the Great joked that she never saw a new pen without craving to use it; she was a prolific author.

In Britain Aphra Behn, friend of Nell Gwynne, had been the first independent woman freelance writer. Lady Chudleigh's 'To the Ladies' (1703) begins with feeling:

> Wife and servant are the same,
> But only differ in the name!

ending:

> Value yourselves and men despise;
> You must be proud if you'll be wise.

Johnson's friend Fanny Burney was a novelist of serious themes. Her *Evelina* (1778) at last makes a marriageable girl subject, not object. Elizabeth Inchbald was as famous as Burney; novelist, memoirist, diarist, dramatist, it was her translation of Kotzebue's play *Lovers' Vows* that was so abruptly interrupted in *Mansfield Park*. Lytton Strachey said she 'won for herself a position which can hardly be paralleled among the women of the 18th Century – a position of independence and honour, based upon talent and upon talent alone.' He then concluded by declaring her plays to be so bad that it was difficult to believe they had brought her a fortune. Like W.G. Grace, Jane Austen never strove to revolutionise the rules of the game, but chose rather to manoeuvre as adroitly as possible within them. She allowed her heroines not only to protect their gentility and secure their fortune, but to use their minds, distinguishing between 'a rational creature' and 'an elegant female'. Loathing gentility, wanting wholesale changes, Mary Wollstonecraft in *A Vindication of the Rights of Woman* (1792), a retort to Burke's *A Vindication of the Rights of Man*, made pungent demands for female needs, cultural, educational, social, political, and for belated release of potential.

Rivalling *Gulliver's Travels* and *Robinson Crusoe* in popularity, *Fanny Hill* appeared in 1749 and was considered by Boswell, who must eagerly have searched it, 'treacherous and inflaming'. Though narrated by a cheerful whore, it was written by John Cleland in the Fleet, a debtors' prison. He sold it for twenty guineas; the publisher netted ten thousand pounds, and acquired a Turnham Green mansion. The novel, while sexually candid, is not smutty, but a good-natured riposte to cant and sentimentality. Compared to the corrosive pornography of Paris, it healthily celebrates life, not as a glum penalty for sins but as a chance to be enjoyed and enlarged.

Children had to take their literature like laudanum, salts, cod-liver oil, to induce piety, patriotism, virtue, to assuage instincts, to ensure exclusiveness. Their books disguised or distorted life's freshness, vividness, spontaneity, while indulging in prolonged and mawkish death-beds. All ages and classes knew the truth uttered in Wordsworth's *The Excursion*:

> So fades and languishes, grows dim and dies
> All that this world is proud of!

Robinson Crusoe, affirmed by Stalin as the first socialist novel, though actually promulgating bourgeois values of profitable adaptability, self-help and white leadership, was deplored for possibly encouraging 'an early taste for a rambling life and love of adventure'. Against all this, Dr Johnson uttered a blast, though apparently not for girls:

> I am for getting a boy forward in his learning; for that is a sure good. I would let him read any English book which happens to engage his attention; because you have done a great deal when you have brought him to have entertainment from a book. He'll get better books afterwards.

It had little effect: in Mrs Sherwood's popular *The History of the Fairchild Family* (begun in 1818 and its third part published in 1847; described by Orwell as an evil book) children, as a punishment for quarrelling, having first been thrashed spend a few hours under a hanged corpse, as further punishment.

In the eighteenth century's Age of Reason there were also, in balance, morbidity, insanity, hell-fears; Cowper, Collins, Clare, Smart were mentally afflicted. Defoe died 'of lethargy', oppressed by creditors. Chatterton, a suicide, died destitute, like Savage. Dr Johnson, majestic, even overbearing, feared death and loneliness, also suffering remorse, 'vile melancholy', guilt for hidden cravings, though his utterance at the last could not have been bettered even by Beethoven: 'I will be conquered: I will not capitulate.'

Passive morbidity is rapidly diminished, however, once the attention is focused on the brutality to be met at every turn. A police force was resisted, because such bodies were associated with foreign tyrannies; so felons, if captured, could expect full retribution. Not until 1837 were defending counsel able to cross-examine witnesses and address juries; until 1898, the accused could not speak from the witness box. No appeal court existed, save Home Secretary and Monarch. Judges had crucial powers; juries could be weak, stupid, vindictive, corrupt or bemused. They could also be compassionate, using *ignoramus* verdicts, refusing to convict, in the spirit of Wellington's Duchess, victim of a marriage unhappy for both: 'I have read somewhere, I forget where, never to despair of any human creature while you can discover as much *Heart* as you can rest the point of a pin on.'

The gibbet, 'Albion's Fatal Tree' – there were a hundred on Hounslow Heath – threw lurid shadows over street, market, fairground, and into the imagination. Roaring, partisan crowds swarmed to a hanging as to a boxing match. Those who should have known better were often fascinated by violence. 'It is a curious turn,' Boswell ruminated in 1768, 'but I can never resist seeing executions.' In the Lords in 1812 Byron, in a brief radical phase, attacked political hangings, but could watch with detached curiosity an Italian beheading. Dickens, demanding cessation of public executions, nevertheless attended them, enamoured of 'the attractions of repulsion'. At sixteen Thomas Hardy contemplated Martha Brown, hanged at Dorchester in 1856: 'I remember what a fine figure she showed against the sky as she hung in the misty rain, and how the tight black silk gown set off her shape as she wheeled half-round and back.'

Among capital crimes were poaching with a blackened face, whitewashing farthings to resemble shillings, tree-felling, impersonating a Chelsea Pensioner. Seven thousand were hanged between 1770 and 1830. Mrs Needham, a procuress delineated by Hogarth, died in the pillory under mass pelting. James Walvin has traced 104 children sentenced to death at the Old Bailey between 1801 and 1836, though none was actually hanged.

John 'Half-Hanged' Smith *was* hanged, for burglary, in 1705. Alive on the rope for fifteen minutes, a foul medley of jerking limbs, jutting eyes and tongue, bloody froth, when a reprieve arrived he was cut down and revived, the *Newgate Calendar* reporting:

> When he was turned off, he, for some time, was sensible of very great pain, occasioned by the weight of his body, and felt his spirits in a very strange commotion, violently pressing upwards: that having forced their way to his head, he, as it were, saw a great blaze or glaring light, which seemed to go out at his eyes with a flash, and then he lost all sense of pain. That after he was cut down, and began to come to himself, the blood and spirits forcing themselves

into their former channels, put him, by a sort of pricking or shooting, to such intolerable pain, that he could have wished those hanged who had cut him down.

Within six weeks he was again arraigned for burglary, but the jury left his fate to the judges, who acquitted him. On his next arrest, still for house-breaking, the prosecutor died before the trial, which by custom freed Smith, and he was heard of no more.

Blackstone in his *Commentaries on the Laws of England* (1765) claimed that the burning of women and the disembowelling of traitors did not take place until the victim had been deprived of sensation by strangling.

Crime was never wholly due to want: aristocratic Mohocks and Macaronis maimed and gouged pedestrians, stole dogs from the blind, thrashed night-watchmen, pelted beggars with hot coals. Rank did not inevitably secure privilege. It saved the bigamist Lady Bristol from branding in 1776, but not Earl Ferrers, hanged for murder in 1760.

Justice met many set-backs through many generations, and made an occasional break-through. Dickens's Miss Flite, crazed victim of Law's inter-minable delays and obfuscations, is a figure for all times, naming her pet birds 'Hope, Joy, Peace, Rest, Life, Dust, Ashes, Waste, Want, Ruin, Despair, Madness, Death, Cunning, Folly, Words, Wigs, Rags, Sheepskin, Plunder, Precedent, Jargon, Gammon and Spinach.' Imaginations ignorant of Enlightenment, or bored by it, tried hero-worship of the criminal, as 'honest rogue', 'rascal', 'rapscallion', 'knight of the road'. Ballads, broad-sheets, novels, engravings, celebrated Turpin, Duval, Aram, and Jack Shephard, whose escapes from Newgate elicited work from Defoe, Hogarth, Thornhill, Ainsworth. Pirates too were absorbed in vulgar folk-lore: Kidd, Bart Roberts; 'Blackbeard' Teach, who was in collusion with a Governor of South Carolina, rich speculators being seldom averse to a covert investment in piracy.

> His good old father, his aged mother
> Oftimes told of his past life,
> Along with those flashing girls his money he'd squander,
> Along with those flashing girls was his delight.
> Now he is dead, and laid in his coffin,
> Six jolly sailors walk by his side,
> Each of them carry a bundle of white roses,
> That no one might smell him as he passes by.

The eighteenth century was the heyday of English smuggling – though in some years Queen Elizabeth had received less than half her wine dues. Many culprits congregated in Bristol and Barnstable. Old titled ladies traded not only in heiresses but as receivers, and are known to have employed contract killers. Tobacco, brandy, tea, silks, lace, Catholic books were lucrative. It was very professional, with jewels stuffed into prunes, ships built with secret compartments. Expensive wars demanded larger tax returns, and the struggle intensified: high profits against high gallows. A permanent army of 'honest thieves' was reckoned by Neville Williams at twenty thousand. A Selsey farmer made ten thousand pounds in six years, by part-time smuggling. In ten years, 192,515 gallons of brandy were impounded. The blind, crippled and timid were enrolled as Excise officers. Lord Chancellor Macclesfield brought his stores of illicit liquor up the Thames in a warship.

The slow extension of literacy and civility, as barriers against savagery, had not assuaged national antipathies. A Smollett character refers to 'chattering Frenchmen, an Italian ape, a German hog, a beastly Dutchman'. Anti-Jewish outbreaks occurred in the 1750s. George III's England chuckled at report of a monkey hanged at Hartlepool in 1805, mistaken for a French spy. Johnson called the French 'a gross, ill-bred, untaught people', and Goldsmith disliked them for being slaves and wearing clogs. A Swiss, César de Saussure, in London between 1725 and 1730, described Englishmen:

> They do not trouble themselves about dress but leave it to their womenfolk. When the people see a well-dressed person in the streets, especially if he is wearing a braided coat, a plume in his hat, or his hair tied in a bow, he will, without a doubt, be called a *French dog* twenty-three times before he reaches his destination. This name is more common, and evidently, according to popular idea, the greatest and most forcible insult that can be given to any man and it is applied indifferently to all foreigners, French or otherwise.

A toast offered by William IV would have been fully supported: 'To the land we live in, and let those who don't like it, leave it!'

Blacks had been landing from the sixteenth century, as a result of the slave trade and colonial plantations. Henry VII had a black trumpeter-herald in 1511. At first they were exotic novelties, but multiplying, some prospering, their scarcity value dwindled. In 1555, John Lok was importing ivory, spices, and 'certaine black slaves', who caused unease. Whites feared sexual rivals and cheap labour. In medieval art and literature, blacks had been kings and heroes equal with whites, but now they were too easily identified with the menacing, the diabolic. Travellers' tales broadcast blacks' sexual relations with apes. They were rated far below Arabs, Chinese, Indians, finding employment as 'perpetual servants', which outraged no one.

Blacks could be inherited, treated as livestock. Walvin instances the Solicitor-General defining them in 1677 as 'goods and commodities'. Charles II and James invested in the slaving voyages of the Royal Africa Company, one ship being loyally named the *Duke of York*. A late eighteenth-century estimation was that '£45 is a good price for an able stout fellow'. Gladstone's father reportedly owned 2,183 Caribbean slaves, and the Society for the Propagation of the Gospel had two Barbados slave plantations, the Baptist Church several others. 'Robinson Crusoe' was a slave-trader, and few thought the worse of him. Danes, Spanish, French, Portuguese, Dutch participated; Denmark was the first to propose Abolition. Such was the brutality towards slaves in Haiti that France had to replace fatalities with two hundred Africans annually. 'How can slaves be happy when they have the halter round their neck and the whip upon their back?' demanded Mary Prince, first black American autobiographer. Catherine the Great bought her slaves from London in 1769. Boswell attributed Johnson's disgust at slavery to prejudiced ignorance; he himself insisted that, sanctioned by the Bible, it benefited Africans by giving them true religion, and that Abolition would shut the gates of mercy on mankind.

In 1745 the *Morning Chronicle* estimated the black population of London at thirty thousand, probably a considerable exaggeration. In 1773 the *London Chronicle* was urging their deportation for stealing jobs from starving whites and, by inter-breeding, 'threatening the Natural Beauty of Brixton'.

Not all blacks remained submerged, though valued as menials, curiosities, entertainers, dockers, coachmen. Pepys had had a black cook 'who dressed our meat mighty well', also a black Admiralty clerk. The son of Dr Johnson's Jamaican servant, friend and heir, Francis Barber, was a Methodist preacher; the black son of a ducal butler was friend of Garrick and librarian to Sir Joseph Banks, the great naturalist. George Bridgetower, outstanding black violinist, knew Beethoven, who dedicated the Kreutzer Sonata to him and accompanied him in its first performance, in Vienna in 1803. Ignatius Sancho, admirer of Britain, was domestic, grocer, friend of Garrick and Johnson; his letters to Sterne were posthumously published, and his son became Britain's first black publisher. Olaudah Equiano, Nigerian former slave, himself a slave-owner, published his autobiography in 1789, an international best-seller; he died in London, a prosperous money-lender. The first black British autobiography seems to have been that of Ukrawsaw Gronniosaur, published in 1772. James Walvin, authority on black history, mentions a parson in 1765, though not whether he intoned a prayer designed especially for coloured workers: 'O Merciful God, grant that I may perform my duty this day faithfully and cheerfully; and that I may never murmur, be uneasy, or impatient under any of the troubles of this life.' Two black servants were leaders in assaulting Newgate Prison during the Gordon Riots in 1780.

Philosophers and dignitaries were adept at presenting excuses for the inexcusable. Aristotle had coolly asserted that 'barbarian' races were natural slaves. The Pope had pronounced that blacks lacked souls. Lord Justice Mansfield, famously granting freedom to a slave who had escaped to England, and himself with a black great-niece, Dido, nevertheless worried lest in freeing Mr Somersett he might be endangering property, thus society itself. Locke had no condemnation of slavery. Hume asserted in *The Gentleman's Magazine* that all civilisations were white, and Dr Walvin, inspecting the 1810 *Encyclopaedia Britannica*, read that 'for this unhappy race, idleness, treachery, revenge, cruelty, impudence, are said to have extinguished the principles of natural law, and to have silenced the reproofs of conscience.' Jefferson denied the black capacity for creative thought. Washington and Jefferson bred and sold slaves. Nelson defended slavers, angered by 'the damnable and accursed doctrines of Wilberforce'. In 1798 Pitt proclaimed that Britain's overseas trade had made one million pounds in profit, exclusive of the Slave Trade, which had netted five million pounds.

Eighteenth-century governments never felt entirely safe. From 1707, London weavers rioted against technology and for higher wages. Religious riots, 'Wilkes and Liberty' riots, like the St George's Field Massacre of 1768, necessitated military intervention. The Gordon Rioters burnt Lord Mansfield's library and collections in 1780, and much more. These last were no rational protest, with such sensible proposals as secret ballot, but another blank cheque for crime, with 'No Popery' as the excuse. Parliament was moving to abate Catholic disabilities, and this incited frenzied rumours. The government, superintended by the King, assembled ten thousand troops, double the number needed at Sedgemoor; more than three hundred rioters were killed, twenty-five hanged. Even Wilkes, who had at last managed to

enter Parliament – three times elected, he had yet been refused – Lord
Mayor in 1774, helped defend the Bank of England.

Little of this galvanised Reform. Parliament, with new Interests and
population centres rising everywhere, was even less representative than it
had been in 1673, when Pepys was elected by 29 against 7. A broken wall
could send members, an industrial town none. The vast majority, voteless,
must have thought it a licensed fraud. The Commons were lively,
authoritarian, but scarcely reverenced; yet despite oligarchies, Britain was
still not strangled by plutocracy. Younger sons, adventurers, the NCOs of
life, found signal chances at home and abroad. Cook, innovator of naval diet
and hygiene, mapping Pacific skies and waters, planting the flag, had his
officers outnumbered by surveyors, physicians, vets, chaplains, cartogra-
phers, botanists seeking plants for Kew, artists supplementing his own
paintings, drawings, journals.

Talent struggled out of poverty and underprivilege. Southey's father was
a linen draper, Samuel Palmer's a small bookseller, James Mill's a cobbler,
Turner's a barber; Gifford, editor of the *Quarterly Review*, was son of a
drunken plumber and glazier, Charles Cameron of a carpenter. James Cook
himself was the son of a labourer. Sir William Philips, American State
Governor, began as a shepherd; George Gully, professional bare-knuckle
boxer who fought the champion 'Game Chicken', entered Parliament.
William Kent began as a Yorkshire coach-painter; a blacksmith's son became
the great scientist Faraday. Burns, Stephenson, General Sir David Dundas,
Telford, McAdam showed that poverty could not always stifle talent. One
Archbishop of Canterbury was a grocer's son, a Lord Chancellor the son of
a coachman's apprentice. The song 'The Ploughboy' traced the rise of a
yokel to butler, steward, corrupt MP, finally peer:

> Whatever is good for me, sir, I never will oppose,
> When all my Ayes are sold off, why then, I sell my Noes.

Despite hangings, evictions, riots, the population was increasing – 8
million in 1760, 10 million in 1811, 12 million in 1821 – helped by agrarian
innovations rather than by any improvement in sanitation or medical
knowledge. The *Reading Mercury* catalogued a week's fatalities in 1763:
'Small Pox, 42; Chin Cough, 1; Ague, 30; Fever, 30; Scald Head, 1; Griping
in the Guts, 12; Stoppage i' the Stomack, 3; Teeth, 22; Suddenly, 1;
Convulsions, 134; Consumption, 56; French Pox, 1.' Infant mortality, in

rooms often shared with farm animals, had scarcely improved since medieval times, when several children might be identically christened, on the chance of one surviving, preserving the Name.

Boredom, fear, penury were resisted not only by drink, but by Methodism, with its demands for moral rectitude, its threats of damnation. On this, Hazlitt had reservations: 'They plunge without remorse into hell's flame, soar on the wings of divine love, are carried away into the motions of the spirit, and are lost in the abyss of unfathomable Mysteries . . . and revel in a sea of boundless nonsense.'

The gentry deplored religious fervour as ill-bred, uninteresting and noisy, preferring scraps of philosophy, literature, travel, gossip, the music of 'London' Bach, Haydn, Boyce. Squire Westons were plentiful; gross, lolling, snoring and over-fed, apt to refer to women in market terms: 'Fair creature . . . could be a hand taller. Goodish fetlock, buxom tail, trim muzzle. Neat enough. Her Sportsman's Gap . . . just so. Good stock.'

E.P. Thompson's 'plebeian culture' remained robust until the worst excesses of industrialism after the Napoleonic wars, while lacking the graces of Haydn, Sheridan, Gainsborough. A cheerful cynicism whistled through the streets:

> Here lies the body of Mary Charlotte,
> Born a Virgin, died a Harlot;
> Until fifteen she kept her Virginity,
> Which is a record in this Vicinity.

All sexes and children, in tavern, fairground, pleasure-garden, sang bawdy rhymes, often to hymn tunes. Street puppetry retold tales of St George, Henry II and Fair Rosamund, Edward IV and his lover Jane Shore. Mr Punch, of Continental extraction, was hugely popular irrepressible anti-Gentleman, callous to women and babies. Barnstormers' melodrama continued the tradition of strolling players and the rougher edges of Theatre. *Titus Andronicus* was enjoyed for its cannibalism and torture.

Richardson's novels were read aloud to illiterates; broadsheets and songs retailed news of wars and notables, and of localised boundary disputes, dishonest bakers, quacks, shysters, lustful ostlers, feuds, and the workshy: 'St Monday' was a much revered stolen holiday. Parish records at Stoke-by-Nayland show an expenditure of three shillings for 'whyppinge of Mary Notley and carrying her and her sister out of towne'.

Language and caricature were uninhibited by deference, to an extent that a Frederick or a Peter would not have tolerated, though the young Louis XVI was finding himself forced to. Juries disliked convicting for libel. Cartoonists showed the Royal favourite, Bute, trying to seduce the Queen Mother; George III and Queen Charlotte seated on close-stools while news of the assassination of the King of Sweden is brought to them. Gillray and Rowlandson were pitiless to authority: Hogarth lampooned charlatan doctors, lawyers, judges. Anonymous abuse was nailed to church doors: 'Do not suffer such damned fat-gutted rogues to starve the poor by such Hellish ways on purpose that they may follow horse-racing etc. and maintain their families in Pride and extravagance.' During the American war, satirists mostly favoured the rebels, like pre-war newsreel audiences regularly applauding Gandhi. To give him his due, George III showed magnanimity when receiving John Adams, the first representative of the American Republic:

> I wish you, Sir, to believe, and that it may be understood in America, that I have done nothing in the late contest but what I thought myself indispensably bound to do by the duty which I owed my people. I will be very frank with you. I was the last to consent to the separation, but the separation having been made, and having become inevitable, I have always said, as I say now, that I would be the first to meet the friendship of the United States as an independent power.

Decency was essential to British society, but in all ages was unreliable. It was withheld from the disgraced Wilde. Also:

> Those who continued to refuse orders were put in solitary confinement. One warder took particular pleasure in tormenting his captives; he had them stripped, beaten, dowsed, then subjected to 'shot drill', an hour-long rhythmic ritual involving a bag filled with thirty pounds of sand, from one point to another while wearing handcuffs . . . A sergeant in the military police had a cable of wire looped around Briggs' chest, harnessed three soldiers to the wire and ordered them to drag him for a mile across the wooden duckboards. The batons across the boards were jagged and filled with loose nails. Briggs lost his clothes, caught in the snags and torn off him. A wound in his back opened and soon filled with dirt. When this sorry little group, three heaving young soldiers and the filthy, almost naked body of a nearly unconscious man reached a shell crater, they simply went through it, and on up the other side. A witness added that, at the last crater, they took him by the shoulders and tipped him head over heels back into the water. Just as he managed to get his head above water and was trying to get his breath, the sergeant fired a handful of muck into his mouth.

Thus Caroline Moorehead, describing in 1987 how pacifists in the Great War were taken to France so that they could be charged with disobedience on active service.

Between the long idle moment of Time and the swift rush of events, the imagination can be traced mostly by hints and guesses, though many wished to leave at least a mark on the wall. Beliefs receding through the Middle Ages to Albion were scarcely shifted by science or formal religion, by a Faraday or Franklin, by bishops in the Lords. The Montgolfiers' flight over Paris in a balloon in 1783 was widely feared as a blasphemy akin to the Tower of Babel, though for ladies and gentlemen God could be at best an intermittent pressure towards charity, the Devil a besetting urge to excess. For scores of tenants, church attendance was still compulsory in 1914, encouraging whatever thoughts. But in small Scottish towns, Welsh valleys, in lonely English homes, forces were tapped older than Christianity, whatever the ridicule of science: terrors of darkness, ghosts, the Other World, belief in omens, curses, magic. Wives still pricked Henry VIII's imposing codpiece in the Tower to cure sterility. The Devil was known to rove Galloway as 'a very mickle rough black man'.

The average man, Chesterton thought, has always considered science a bit of a joke. Illiterate sailors, dependent on the latest scientific gadgets, repeated lore at odds with that of the Royal Society. A naked woman was thought to affront the sea, though it could also be calmed by a near-naked female figurehead on the prow. Friday, day of Crucifixion, was inauspicious, also the first Monday in April, Cain's birthday. A priest stepping on board in his black clothes foreboded misfortune for sailors, like hares for fishermen. A sailor, Simon Halley, gave Coleridge his great theme, having himself shot an albatross, thought to bear the souls of the dead. Navvies building canals and roads, falling sick, demanded to be shown sick children, thought to exude health and luck. Live snails were swallowed against tuberculosis.

Ned Ludd, perhaps-mythical machine-breaker, issued orders from 'Sherwood Forest'. Bishop Percy's *Reliques of Ancient Poetry* (1765) inspired Romanticism through ballads, as did Macpherson's alleged translations from the Gaelic Ossian, which entranced even Napoleon. All coalesced in the genius of Scott, who taught all Europe the torments, valour, hopes, legends of a vanishing Britain.

Great Britain and *Empire* were making some headway. 'Rule Britannia!' was sung lustily, even in conditions that would have disgraced hell. The Year of Victories, 1759, when Wolfe stormed Quebec and Hawke broke a French invasion fleet at Quiberon Bay despite pounding seas and a rocky coast, was commemorated by William Boyce and Garrick in 'Heart of Oak', and glasses were everywhere raised to 'The Eye of a Hawk and the Heart of a Wolfe'. At Vauxhall Gardens, amid fireworks, water pageants, hilarity, civilian voices bawled:

> Come cheer up my lads! 'tis to Glory we steer,
> To add something more to this wonderful year.

The second line was subsequently amended by Christina Rossetti:

> As the soldier remarked, whose post lay in the rear.

The Westminster Abbey celebration in 1785 of Handel's Centenary was staged with overtones deliberately nationalistic. The Commons surged into song, 'Britons, Strike Back', after an empassioned speech by Pitt the Younger in 1797. The ebullience scarcely improved the sailor's lot. Even two hundred years later there are ex-delinquents who remember having to choose between Borstal and Royal Navy.

Humour is a captious muse. The English found the antics of lunatics and cruelty to animals amusing, and much theatrical clowning was, like Chaplin's early films, based upon pain. Joking, however, like sex, was the poor man's opera, in slum, doss-house, tumbledown whorehouse, the forecastle, the front line. 'Bob Can't', the Crimean soldiers chuckled, hearing of their French ally, General Canrobert. 'Blimey!' the Great War Tommy remarked, receiving his bread ration, 'I thort it was 'Oly Communion!' All classes enjoyed reports of a London supper given by the duc de Chartres: napkins concealed 'English Overcoats', condoms, filled with oxygen, which, uncovered, floated round the room. Vincent Cronin relates how the duc, finally marrying, escorted his bride to the Opera to find, massed beneath their box, the Paris prostitutes, all in widow's weeds.

Considerable though irrational mystique accompanies the close of a century: expectancy, nervousness, awe, fear. By 1785, British skies seemed to be darkening. America was lost: here was Great Britain's first major defeat, a solace to France, Spain and Holland. The Elder Pitt, the great war-leader, had died in 1778. The Gordon Riots of 1780 were a reminder of brute force and destructiveness.

In a letter, Ignatius Sancho offers a weather-vane: 'Lord S.H. [Sandwich, First Lord of the Admiralty] has gone to Portsmouth to be a witness of England's disgrace – and of his own shame. In faith, my friend, the present time is rather comique – Ireland almost in as true a state of rebellion as America – Admirals quarrelling in the West Indies – and at home Admirals that do not chuse to fight – the British Empire mouldering away in the West, annihilated in the North – Gibraltar going, and England fast asleep.'

Britain's moral prestige was evaporating. The savagery of her German hirelings in America, the ravages and burnings in Virginia, scandalised international salons, though occasional instances of humanity occurred. Delacroix wrote in his journal in 1824:

> Read the following in *La Pandore* this morning. During the American war an English officer in one of the advance posts saw an American officer riding towards him, who seemed so absent-minded and intent on his observations that he did not perceive him, although only a short distance away. The Englishman took aim and was about to pull the trigger, but struck by the dreadful thought of shooting a man as though he were a target, he held his hand over the trigger without firing. The American spurred his horse and galloped away. It was Washington!

Machinery was further transforming work and status, but also despoiling landscapes and degrading workers: Birmingham brass-hands found their hair turning green. Joseph Priestley, Joseph Black and the Frenchman Lavoisier were experimenting with oxygen, and agreeing with Von Grim that physics and chemistry were procuring more miracles than those once taught by fanaticism and superstition. Mozart's acquaintance Dr Mesmer was practising hypnotic magnetism, and found his methods enlisted to help along the plot of *Così fan tutte*. John Wesley unexpectedly disclosed: 'There is a prodigious number of continual links between the most perfect man and the ape.' Louis XVI and Marie-Antoinette followed Catherine the Great in volunteering for inoculation against smallpox.

The Age of Reason, however, had its disclaimers. John Clare complained of scientists 'strangling beetles and gibbeting butterflies to keep us wise'. Joseph Priestley's experiments were execrated as black magic. For Blake, pristine simplicities were being corrupted: scientific rationalism was upsetting the psychic balance between intellect and emotion. His texts still ring: 'Improvement makes straight roads; but the crooked roads, without improvement, are the roads of genius.'

Scientific benefits depended on their practitioners. Cross Kirk, Caithness exhibited a memorial to Donald Robertson (1785–1848): 'He was a peaceably quiet man and to all appearances a sincere Christian. His death, very much regretted, was caused by the stupidity of Lawrence Tulloch of Clotherton, who sold him nitre instead of Epsom salts.'

Literature, philosophy, music, architecture, Grand Tour were indirectly opposing nationalism, war, sectarianism. By 1780, in library, study, boudoir, people may have envisaged international harmony, respecting the past, pursuing knowledge and planning peaceful reform. Gibbon and Jefferson each styled himself 'Citizen of the World', a persona which Goldsmith adopted as a literary device. Similar temperaments and virtues hoped to transcend race and local loyalties, though in crisis this aspiration proved no more substantial than Marx's text 'Workers have no country', shattered in 1870 and again in 1914.

Freemasonry, liberal and anti-clerical, claiming medieval and Egyptian 'Mystery' antecedents, announcing that Classical thought, the Enlightenment itself, derived from Egypt, was an international bond, enfolding Goethe, Mozart, Kosciuszko, the duc de Chartres, his son Philippe 'Égalité', Joseph Bonaparte, Lafayette, Marat, Couthon, Robespierre, Jefferson, John Paul Jones, Benedict Arnold, Mirabeau, Paul Revere, Paine, and the doubtfully sane Tsar Paul I. Mozart glamorised it in *The Magic Flute*, Catherine the Great disparaged it in her plays. Accusations that it incited the French Revolution are long since rejected.

The derelict and declassed, victims of labour dislocations, shabby 'truck', starvation wages, faced child slavery in shanty town and diseased slum, the poor-house, the asylum. Starved children, dispossessed labourers gathered outside the Great House. One of Disraeli's polarised *Two Nations* was assembling, and busy, practical Mr Gradgrind was preparing to testify that the Good Samaritan was a bad economist. Goldsmith could mourn, in *The Deserted Village* (1770):

> Sweet-smelling village, loveliest of the lawn,
> Thy sports have fled, and all thy charms withdrawn;
> Amidst thy bowers, the tyrant's hand is seen,
> And desolation saddens all the green . . .
> Ill fares the land, to hastening ills a prey,
> Where wealth accumulates, and men decay;
> Princes and lords may flourish or may fade;

A breath can make them, as a breath has made;
But a bold peasantry, their country's pride,
When once destroyed, can never be supplied.

Tom Paine, who had served on Washington's staff, published his disruptive *Common Sense* in 1777. Voltaire's *Candide* quietly mocked political confusion and irrational morality; Rousseau deplored inequality as un-Natural, and English patriots now recognised the irony of 'The Year of Victories'. Jefferson, minister in Paris between 1785 and 1789, attacked the 'absolute despotism' of Louis XVI, which must have astonished a monarch rapidly becoming helpless. Optimism, however, was considerable. Condorcet, respected scientist, mathematician, Encyclopaedist, in *A Sketch for a Historical Picture of the Progress of the Human Mind*, written in 1793/4 though published posthumously in 1795, expressed a comfortable and general conviction that history was a linear record of inevitable advance, proceeding to classless international fraternity, liberty, virtue, sexual equality, with Religion irrelevant, Reason unquestioned. This he probably modified before his suicide, when imprisoned by his intellectual pupils who had so exultantly declared the Rights of Man.

Their contemporary de Sade recognised that heroes were usually victims, that Law, Religion, Statecraft, Sainthood, even Rights of Man, contained criminal elements, that life is massed contradictions. Blake discerned sexual impulses within righteous wars and movements, 'the pompous High Priest entering by a Secret Place'; life holding mysterious regions barely accessible to Reason, statistics, analysis and expert forecasting. Hitler was to inquire: 'Why babble about brutality and torture? The masses want that.'

Unknown to milords and gentlemen, a conflict was looming on a scale unprecedented in their history. In 1779 the comte de Guibert, less famed than Jefferson and Condorcet, Hume, Blake, Godwin, wrote:

A man is going to emerge, hitherto lost in the obscurity of the crowd, one who has as yet established his name neither in speech nor writing, one who has pondered silently, one who, in fact, has been unaware of his own gifts, while actually exercising them, one who has studied very little. He is going to snatch opinions, circumstances, chance, and will inform eminent theoreticians what the practising architect said of the orator: 'All that my rival *tells* you, I will actually perform.'

The frail western unity was illusionary. Despite its exquisite flavours, the eighteenth century, too much like the twentieth, was to prove a century which, in E.M. Forster's words, practises brutality and recommends ideals. A travesty of federation was shortly to be established by a Corsican Italian masquerading as a Roman Emperor, placing unsuitable relatives on European thrones, until Britain, Prussia, Russia, Spain, Portugal disposed of him as a public nuisance.

7

An Imperial Age

... the French Revolution ... had no authors, leaders, guides. The seed was scattered by writers who, in an era bold and enlightened, overthrew the principles of religion and of social life, and by incompetent ministers who increased the embarrassment of the Treasury and the discontent of the People.

Talleyrand

The weakness of all Utopias is this, that they take the greatest difficulty of man and assume it to be overcome, and then give an elaborate account of the overcoming of small ones. They first assume that no man will want more than his share, and then are very ingenious in explaining whether his share will be delivered by motor-car or balloon.

G.K. Chesterton

The French Revolution, preserved in the British imagination by Carlyle, Dickens, and indeed by the 'Scarlet Pimpernel', began with debates about modernising society and replenishing the Treasury, but ended by convulsing Europe with Terror and imperialist aggression. The middle-class and aristocratic idealists and intellectuals of 1789 learnt from the Enlightenment, but learnt the wrong lessons. Convinced of the benevolence of Nature, including Human Nature, they banked on vast hoards of virtue, to be dispensed by Platonic committees. With the cheerful assurance of ignorance Camille Desmoulins, dedicated to the overthrow of stifling monarchical culture, dreamed of founding 'a new Tahiti'.

After Gordon Riots and American Revolution, British oligarchs were sceptical: on evidence, human nature was not a unity but a muddle of checks and balances, like much sensible government. Burke held that 'some are so taken up with their theories about the rights of Man that they have totally forgotten his nature'. Like Plato, like Goethe, they preferred injustice to disorder: too little government was as reckless as too much, bad rule better than no rule. Hannah More, no feminist, feared that French declamations about

186

the Rights of Man must induce demands for the rights of women: she was right, and French women lost.

Institutions are long in growing, easy to ruin, difficult to replace with the tough and organic. Westminster never desired the Perfect State, its adherents merely demanded better government. The visions of the young Catos – Desmoulins, Robespierre, Saint-Just – would have bored the Commons and bemused the City.

> When savages are cruel, they take the first steps towards civilization.
>
> When all are free, they will be equal, and, when equal, just.
>
> Happy is the country where punishment is a free pardon.

Pitt, Cornwallis, Burke would have objected that such a country would be very unhappy. The revolutionaries, ardent youths in a hurry, forgot (or did not realise) that Nature has no favourites, that people can enjoy pain, sometimes their own, find virtue tedious, and that wise laws and devout training unsupported by stable institutions cause despotism or chaos. Drunk on Classical precedents inadequately examined, the zealots yearning for human brotherhood were, for comfortable English gentlemen, Jack Frosts tracing patterns, icily beautiful but dissolving at a breath from the streets. They achieved much: centralised administration, a codified law, decimalisation. They modernised male education, liberated Jews and the peasants; but, foundering on the human nature they so trusted, they first created free political parties, then the one-party state.

'The People do not judge like the law-courts; they do not pass sentence; they hurl a thunderbolt.' The rhetoric of Robespierre and Saint-Just disguised the reality of September Massacres, inquisitorial tribunals, rigged juries, censorship, conscription, finally Hobbes's Leviathan, the 'mortal God' in charge. Having bloodily demolished the Monarchy the Republicans, fearful, even paranoiac, of enemies real or imaginary – Allied arms threatened Paris and almost detached royalist Brittany – struggled for survival, reducing politics to oratory, exploring the hypnotism of slogans: 'Liberty or Death', 'The Country in Danger', 'The People'.

By the standards of Mary Shelley, Mary Wollstonecraft, Robert Owen, John Stuart Mill, or William Morris, the Revolution was a disaster, reducing the liberties of women, children, universities, unions, guilds, literary academies, Church, provincial assemblies. Red Terror was then ejected by

White Terror, a profiteering Directory lapsed into an Empire crushing small nations, treating allies like victims.

The guillotine remains the Revolutionary symbol, though used long before 1789 in Yorkshire, Scotland and Italy. Douglas Johnson has suggested how appropriate to the new scientific age was its geometrical precision: upright rectangle, horizontal bar, semi-circular neck-rest, gleaming triangle, efficiently executing some seventeen thousand. Authoritarians like straight lines and clean shapes.

Jefferson remarked in 1789: 'What signify a few lives lost in a century or two? The Tree of Liberty must be refreshed from time to time with the blood of patriots and tyrants. It is its natural manure.' Intellectuals – Bernard Shaw, Ezra Pound – have propensities for others' violence, are adept at finding eloquent excuses for the inexcusable. 'Was ever', Jefferson reflected, 'such a prize won with so little innocent blood?' The prize was the Bastille, with scores of deaths following a broken safe-conduct.

For British radicals, to whom City and Parliament were despicable, the Revolution was, in Saint-Just's words, a thunderclap to the wicked. Humanity, he declaimed, was to drop anchor in the future. For many in Europe the National Assembly was the blink of a new planet, midwinter harvest, the unfurling of colours and music hitherto unknown. All was guaranteed by the King's execution and that panacea, 'the Republic', already so fruitful in France's godchild, America. Charles James Fox, Whig libertarian, supporter of Washington, opponent of slavery, foe of George III, greeted the Bastille's storming: 'How much the greatest event it is that has ever happened, and how much the best!' Sheridan exulted. Wordsworth exclaimed: 'Human Nature is reborn!' Coleridge hailed 'the banishment of Tyranny'. War and the French occupation of the Low Countries, Britain's gateway to riches, like the brief French invasion of Ireland in 1798, scarcely offended republicans, malcontents, United Irishmen, poets. Byron rejoiced in the wrecking of 'that dull and stupid old system, the Balance of Power – poising of straw on kings' noses'. Burns financed weapons for France.

Some French Revolutionary gyrations were impressive, others comic. To honour rural virtues St Cecilia's Day was renamed 'Day of the Turnip', St Catherine's 'Day of the Pip'. Montmartre became 'Mont Marat'; Queen Bee, 'Worker Bee'. Many British intellectuals were as awed by the Jacobins' *Despotism of Liberty* as their descendants were by Mao's assurance that childbirth entails no pain.

Edmund Burke drew attention to those favourite tools of the unscrupulous revolutionary, euphemism and the substitution of slogans for rational discourse: 'The whole compass of language is to find synonyms and circumlocutions for massacre and murder. Massacre is sometimes *agitation*, sometimes *effervescence*, sometimes . . . *an exercise of revolutionary fervour.*' France's greatest contemporary poet, André Chénier, executed in 1794 following her greatest scientist, Lavoisier, reiterated this: 'Called *usury* and *monopoly*, industry and trade are depicted as crimes . . . the most hateful suspicions and most headlong slanders are called *freedom of opinion*. If you demand proof of an accusation, you are denounced as a suspect, an enemy of the people. Women attend the Jacobin Club to applaud outbursts of sanguinary lunacy. They presume to confer *Certificates of correct thinking.*'

Pitt and his Tory diehards knew what the revolutionaries themselves began to recognise after remarkable military triumphs, that Nationalism would outbid Classical principles of fraternity and Enlightenment beliefs in equality. Robespierre gained frenzied approval when he enunciated: 'The French are two centuries ahead of all other peoples. It is tempting to see them as a species wholly unique.'

British republican fervour dwindled with the Terror, war with France and then Spain, the influx of refugees, the threat of invasion, the glamour of Nelson, Collingwood, Moore, Wellington. Fox, it is true, long thought Napoleon a meritocratic Washington, but it is difficult to imagine this amiable, dissolute gambler tolerating Robespierre's axiom that champagne is fatal to freedom, the Jacobin prospectus of the Republic existing to promote virtue and 'compel people to be free', or Napoleonic despotism. Saint-Just had no important British counterpart (certainly not Fox) in proclaiming that 'the Republic needs only the free, has resolved to exterminate all others'. Fox's ironic sense might have been tickled by the story of how, during a battle, a Revolutionary officer's order to charge was cancelled by majority vote. Shelley would not have conformed to republican proprieties, nor have applauded Fouché, ex-Jacobin, Napoleon's police chief, who boasted that he had achieved a *holocaust* in shooting several hundred young people at Lyon.

Napoleon's claim to have desired the United States of Europe was vitiated by his insistence on French overlordship. 'Never forget', he told his brother Jerome, when making him King of Westphalia, 'that your first duty is to me, your second to France.' No mention of Westphalia. He, like the Jacobins, echoed Cicero's 'The Public Safety is the Supreme Law', a justification for State absolutism. He strengthened and clarified Roman Law, its emphasis on masculine control of State, Family, Education, and the sanctity of contracts. Britain still preferred Common Law, and a system of education abhorrent to Latin tidiness in being no system.

Pitt had promised fifteen years of peace; then embarked on a war lasting some twenty years, the City financing coalitions involving, at different times, Spain, Portugal, Holland, Sweden, Naples, Russia, Sardinia, Prussia, Austria. The Navy, irresistible after Trafalgar, kept open the vital Atlantic trade and provided an effective riposte to Napoleon's attempted Continental Blockade. 'Wherever wood can swim, there I am certain to find the English flag,' the Emperor complained.

Women were well to the fore in repelling the last invasion of the British mainland in 1797, when 1,400 French, commanded by an American, briefly landed in Wales. Income Tax was imposed; the Irish rebellion was savagely suppressed, and the Irish and Westminster parliaments colluded in enforcing full Irish incorporation into Great Britain in 1800, when a hundred Anglo-Irish entered the Commons. Combination Acts proscribed radical clubs, newspapers, strikers, unions; government agents multiplied; aliens, free-lovers, Jacobites, political suspects were rounded up. The war itself lacked all romance. Turner's unpopular *The Field of Waterloo* was defiantly anti-heroic: in it the night is lit by a flare to repel robbers, out to strip the wounded. 'They plunder in all directions,' Wellington said of his Peninsular troops, who treated their allies almost as brutally as did the French, while he himself was regularly betrayed by anti-war Parliamentary factions. Corporal John Park of the 20th Foot, in the Peninsula, recorded in his journal in August 1813 the order to storm San Sebastian and bayonet every man, women and child: the town was found to be empty, save for a few derelicts of both sexes 'who were treated very badly, before brandy was distributed and the entire town fired'.

Kings returned after the French Empire dissolved, but Revolution and Napoleon enflamed the European imagination until 1870. In England 'The Corsican Ogre' had been feared, execrated as a bandit breaker of treaties, destroyer of freedom, devourer of children. His firing-squads, secret police, rapist troops had been set for the invasion of Britain, as Hardy wrote in 'One We Knew':

> Of how his threats woke warlike preparations
>   Along the southern strand
> And how each night brings tremors and trepidation
>   Lest morning see him land.

Yet when 'Old Boney' sailed captive into Plymouth Harbour and appeared on deck, show-piece of defeat and a cause apparently lost, the men in the great crowd removed their hats. This can be variously interpreted: evidence of English snobbery about titles, even the self-awarded; demonstration of republicanism; sarcastic comment on flimsy grandeur; sporting compassion for a loser. The Prussians might have shot him, the Russians have incarcerated him in an asylum. To the Regent he wrote: 'In giving myself up to England, I have surrendered to a nation with honourable and just laws, which afford protection to every person.' This opinion he may have revised, on St Helena.

> Boney broke his heart and died,
>   Away-i-oh;
> Boney broke his heart and died,
>   John François.

Napoleon's adventure transformed him into a figure of Promethean tragedy, a hero of lonely souls, ballad-mongers, old soldiers, setting bedrooms awash with dreamy, alternative selves. 'He was a glorious tyrant, after all,' Byron concluded, finding greatness in the opportunities created, and in the grandeur of the fall. Hazlitt and Hegel reverenced him. For Elizabeth Barrett Browning, he magnified the image of the freedom he denied. Victor Hugo called him the mighty somnambulist of a vanished dream. Freud, however, rated his career the indulgence of puberty fancies, Napoleon himself 'the classical anti-Gentleman'.

Britain had a very different hero, 'the Duke', never defeated, wittily laconic in his refusal to be Napoleonic: Milord and Gentleman, Anglo-Irish, country magnate and London clubman, stoical, magnanimous without self-righteousness, at ease with all classes without condescension, reluctantly marrying from good manners to avoid forswearing an early pledge. He gathered stories about him like victories – which, in a sense, they were. No democrat, disliking the populace as much as he did poets, he feared railways would induce unrest by increasing working-class mobility – Ruskin thought they might transform people into 'parcels' – and considered the unreformed Parliament the climax of political wisdom. Most of all, he possessed an unfailing sense of social responsibility, believing in an individual obligation to serve Monarch and community, that government, civilisation should in all circumstances be sustained, despite protests from saints or scoundrels.

He knew when to withdraw. 'A good government is more important than the Corn Laws,' he admitted in crisis, when forced to join the Tories in repealing them, against his inclinations. 'Right about turn. March!' he said when, most famous man in Europe, he was refused admission to a club for being incorrectly dressed. Dignified, he lacked pomposity: 'Mr Duke', children called him. He was English common sense incarnate, his understatements proverbial. When a shell dropped before General Sir William Stewart at Waterloo, he observed, 'A shell, sir. Very animating', and continued his talk. Stories of him are usually succinct, humane, engaging. 'Ten minutes' he replied to a parson, who asked him what he liked a sermon to be about. His chapel at Stratfield Saye exhibited a plaque to a cleric who 'for forty years was a most painful preacher'.

Abused by Wordsworth as a most desperate profligate, reviled by Byron and Shelley, Wellington issued two memorable orders: in India, 'Protect the inhabitants. Do not oppress them. Behave like gentlemen'; in rainy Belgium, 'Lord Wellington does not approve the use of umbrellas during the enemy's firing.'

If his troops did not love him, they trusted him. Admired by society, he knew the value of its affectations and shallowness. 'I love to walk alone.' In popular song, affection balanced respect:

> If France again should boast
> They'll soon invade our coast,
> They'll find British seamen are quite handy-O,
> For all the world knows
> In conquering our foes
> The Marquis of Wellington's the Dandy-O.

Britain, Russia, Prussia, Austria – the Big Four – met in Vienna to settle the Peace and, more realistic than the Allies in 1919, allowed the presence of the defeated, represented by Talleyrand, once Napoleon's Foreign Minister: 'A lump of dung in silk stockings,' the Emperor called him. The Vienna Congress offered the first chance since the Medieval Papacy of establishing, peacefully, an element of European unity; though this, in truth, was less its design than the restoration of pre-1789 conditions. No more than in 1919 and 1946 did Britain assume purposeful leadership of Europe. Any demands of nationalists and reformers were blocked by Metternich, Austrian arch-conservative, and by 'legitimate' monarchs. Though its provisions kept general peace for four decades, 'unity' dwindled into the 'Holy Alliance' of

Austria, Russia, Prussia, from which Britain, pursuing her fortunes else-where, kept stolidly aloof. The scared rulers resolved 'to love each other, and their subjects as children', an attitude unlikely to cope with strident German and Italian nationalism, middle-class political needs, the growth of an organised industrial working-class.

In *Don Juan*, with all the verve of genius without responsibility, Byron scorned the Congress, and Britain's 'Villainton':

> Never had mortal man such opportunity,
> Except Napoleon, or abused it more.
> You might have freed fallen Europe from the unity
> Of tyrants, and been blest from shore to shore.

Westminster and City were indisposed to curse victories, and hastened to capitalise on them. Returning heroes nevertheless found the Corn Laws keeping food expensive in the Landed Interest, jobs scarce, enclosure of commons and wastelands rampant, to Cobbett's fury. 'Wastes indeed! Give a dog an ill name . . . was it a waste when a hundred, perhaps, of healthy boys and girls were playing there on a Sunday, instead of creeping about almost covered with filth in the alleys of a town?'

Until 1832, the franchise of 1429 was still in force, restricted to some prop-ertied males, in constituencies that still ignored the new industrial towns, while the gentry pretended that their privileges rested on the assent of all free-born Englishmen.

With no immediate rival the Empire was expanding, territorially and economically, morally. A Scottish chapel was built in Jamaica in 1805; today, Jamaican missionaries land in Scotland, with purposeful mien. Countering Napoleon's occupation of Holland, Britain had taken Dutch South Africa. Wellington's elder brother, Richard Wellesley, who almost entirely lacked his brother's fund of common sense, had used his term as Governor-General of India to increase hugely the area under the control of the East India Company. Following the traditional policy of keeping the Channel and North Sea Coast in as many hands as possible, with men and loans Britain secured Belgian independence from Holland in 1830. She also backed inde-pendence wars in South America against Spain, and in Greece against the Turks. The career of Admiral Sir Edward Parry (1790–1855) illustrates Britain's maritime range. 'Parry of the Arctic' fixed his name on the globe and beyond it: there were named after him three islands, four islets, five capes, one mountain, a breed of kangaroo, and a crater on the moon.

At times, the modern world seems almost a nineteenth-century British invention. 'Properly speaking,' Disraeli wrote in *Coningsby* (1844), 'Manchester is as great a human exploit as Athens.' Thomas Brassey, protégé of Stephenson, was constructing European railways, employing eighty thousand – it has been claimed that railways, not revolutions, destroyed old Europe. The Welshman Thomas Hughes founded a Ukrainian mine. The Scots Clark brothers' chain-bridge joined Buda to Pest. Paxton's Birkenhead Park (1843–7) was a model for New York's Central Park. Britons supervised the building of Japanese warships. Europe would imitate the Crystal Palace, and Brunel's masterpieces: the Great Western Railway, the mighty yet graceful Clifton Suspension Bridge and the *Great Eastern*, until 1908 the world's largest ship. London was first with its underground railway. Bessemer taught Britain the conversion of iron to cheap steel, reinforcing the Industrial Revolution. Rothschilds, Goldschmidts, Barings taught money how to live. British investments developed Russian heavy industry, Latin American, Canadian, Egyptian, Chinese communications.

As the century aged Trollope, in *The Way We Live Now*, perceived a change from honest trading and endeavour to the opportunism of the gambler. An American cynic instructs an English novice about the profits available from an imaginary railway invented to attract gullible investors. 'Fortune! What fortune had either of us? A few beggarly thousands of dollars not worth talking of, and barely sufficient to enable a man to look at an enterprise. And now where are you? Look here, Sir – there's more to be got out of the smashing up of such an affair as this, if it should smash up, than could be made by years of hard work out of such fortunes as yours and mine in the regular way of trade.' Trollope's upright Prime Minister, Plantagenet Palliser, 'Planty Pal', opines: 'Civilization comes from what men call greed.'

Though Adam Smith considered that colonies, needing the expense of conquest and then subsidies, cost more than they return, fortunes both corporate and individual were undeniably acquired. Teak was profitably extracted from Burma, jute, tea, indigo and opium from India, rubber was planted in Malaya, cocoa in West Africa. Sassafras was thought to cure syphilis. Not all, however, was a naked search for dividends. Cook looked further than markets, raw materials, cheap labour, and boasted little racial superiority, finding some native Australians 'far happier than we Europeans', and recognising that native concepts of property, honesty, truth, exchange, though vastly different from his own, were not thereby invalid.

The Scots – Livingstone, Kirk, Gordon – fought Arab slaving in Africa,

Livingstone suggestively stating that the most poignant disease he had seen in Africa was the broken-heartedness afflicting ex-slaves. Such men, missionaries, doctors, adventurers, would not impress Diane Abbott, MP, who pontificated in 1996: 'The British invented racism. They built an empire in which racism was an organising principle.' This reveals some ignorance of India, where caste was no British invention, and of the Spanish, Portuguese and Dutch Empires, let alone of Antiquity. Slavery, female circumcision, crucifixions on ant-hills, human sacrifices to sacred crocodiles, preceded the Empire. More usefully, Alan Moorehead wrote in 1960 of 'Missionaries like Livingstone, scholars like Burton, soldiers and collectors like Speke, sportsmen like Baker', who did not see themselves as empire-builders in the later, more systematic and callous mould of a Rhodes. None died rich.

Livingstone, once a child factory hand, no bigot, was concerned with Africans as people, not statistics. He crossed an unknown Africa from west to east, two thousand miles, in 1853–6, an extraordinary achievement. If often unrealistic and incompetent, he left a reputation for courage and practical goodness; his heart remains literally buried in Africa, at the request of Africans. Not every imperialist was a mere plunderer. Like Cook in his response to Australasia, in India Chief Justice Sir William Jones and Warren Hastings fostered Sanskrit studies and a rediscovery of Indian classics; the missionary William Carey taught Sanskrit, translated Hindu scriptures into Bengali, introduced India to her past. Persian manuscripts were exhumed. The East India Company subsidised some Hindu temples. Burton was a Master Sufi; Kitchener, speaking Turkish and Arabic, had archaeological interests; Lord Curzon, praising Indian civilisation as 'earlier and superior to the British', when Viceroy founded an Indian Archaeological Department, restored Indian monuments, even wayside shrines, and was commended by Mr Nehru as a cultural benefactor. John Buchan's son, another John, taught art to Esquimaux, as they were then called.

In extent, the Empire exceeded those of Babylon, Carthage, Rome, Persia, Spain, Portugal, Holland. By modern values, its acquisition was a disreputable activity. Yet the creation of New Delhi, Sydney, Melbourne, Ottawa, Durban, Capetown, Christchurch, Singapore, Hong Kong, Karachi, the cure of diseases, the alleviation of famine, the building of roads, railways, irrigation schemes are not discreditable, however scarred by indentured labour, expropriations, diamond wars, gold wars, opium wars. Opium then carried no stigma: as laudanum, it was as legal as spirits, and cheaper; it fortified 'Mother Bailey's Quietening Syrup', poured into Victorian children; and, for de Quincey, wine destroyed self-possession while opium sustained and reinforced it.

Despite its *laisser-faire* outlook, Westminster was not immune to protest, often made from the most mixed of motives. Sir Thomas Picton, popular Governor of Trinidad, incurred Privy Council disapproval for too severe suppression of witchcraft and for maltreating a black who, as a subject of King George, could seek redress at Common Law. Picton redeemed his reputation by his death at Waterloo, leading a cavalry charge. Joseph Wall, a Colonial Governor, was hanged for causing the death of a disobedient soldier by an illegal flogging. British philanthropists bought Sierre Leone as a refuge for freed or fugitive slaves. The British built East African railways, opened the Nile for navigation from Central Africa to the Mediterranean, a gigantic achievement; overcame the slave trade in sub-Saharan Africa, south Egypt, Zanzibar. Lord Guilford founded the first Greek University, on Corfu, in 1824. The East India Company ended the Maharatta wars, which had emasculated the Moghul Empire. Conquering without gentle finesse the British, for reasons seldom altruistic, built public works, bridges, hospitals; reformed coinages; planted and preserved forests; spread English as a common language. Kipling's Raj enjoyed ludicrous snobberies, tea-party spite and intrigues, political busybodies, pathetic and secret inter-racial liaisons, alongside massive public projects, and selfless attempts to bring justice or tax fairly, on the part of district officers confronting disease, famine, water-shortages, discontent.

The British Empire's people were often treated similarly to boys at Victorian boarding schools. 'A good thrashing first, and great kindness afterwards' was recommended by Sir Charles Napier, conqueror of Sind, an acquisition which he called 'a very advantageous, useful, humane piece of rascality'. He, and others like him, put a stop to *suttee*, widow burning. Little, however, is final: in 1987 Indian women were marching on Delhi, protesting against the practice. The British prohibited Dyak head-hunting in Borneo, resisted the arbitrary mass killings practised by Ugandan monarchs, cleared the China seas of pirates. An entry of 1849 in the journal of Naval Surgeon Edward H. Cree discusses Tonquin pirates: 'They robbed the poor natives of all they possessed and killed those who resisted, and carried off many of the young women . . . the people went on their knees to beg us to go after Shap-'ng-tsai, who keeps the whole coast in a state of terror.' Within a week, Cree's force had destroyed 58 pirate junks and killed 1,700 pirates, rescued 49 prisoners, and captured 40 guns, which were then delivered to the local Chinese governor.

Captain William Sleeman calculated that Thugs, 'Deceivers', were annually robbing and strangling forty thousand Indians, nominally to gratify Kali (the Hindu counterpart of Badt, Celtic goddess of Destruction), thus assuring themselves of Paradise. The East India Company piously objected in principle to interference with native habits but, supported by the Governor-General, Sleeman captured three thousand Thugs, between 1830 and 1836, virtually extinguishing the sect. One captive, before execution, confessed to 719 murders and, like most of his fellows, could not be convinced of any irregularity in this. 'Does any man feel compunction in following his trade? Is it not the Divine that works through us?' Indians assembled in multitudes to wish Sleeman godspeed when he retired.

Few benefits were free. Local industries might be outsold, parasitic usurers condoned, taxes and fines imposed, all in the name of improvements seldom very heartily demanded. Education was neglected or left to missionaries. Nelson Mandela expressed gratitude to his missionary school; Kwame Nkrumah, student of the London School of Economics, taught in one.

A Persian saying goes: 'If you trip over a pebble, you can be certain that an Englishman put it there.' No Empire, Russian and American included, existed without the vile and intolerable: exploited peasantry, unnecessary violence, indentured labour . . . they fill the records. Thomas Kendall brought the Gospel to Maoris; also alcohol, and guns. The 1840 Treaty of Waitanga is regarded by Maoris as enshrining the theft of hundreds of square miles through one-sided 'negotiations'; Elizabeth II apologised for it in 1995, and financial compensation was completed in 1996. Reprisals for lawlessness, from Australia to Barbados, could be pitiless. A Quaker, Mr Wallace, was heard chanting a Psalm while bayonetting Indian mutineers:

> I love the Lord, for He has heard me,
> And listened to my voice and my supplications.

Nevertheless, unlike the Roman and Spanish, the British Empire was not thought eternal. A Macaulay, an Elphinstone envisaged India and Canada reaching independence, yet remaining friends with Britain.

British occupation of Ireland, however, was not thought temporary. Restless and unhappy, the least successful of British conquests, its inhabitants were feared or despised in England, save for certain members of the Anglo-Irish 'Ascendancy' – Wellington, Castlereagh, Palmerston; Berkeley,

Swift, Steele, Congreve, Goldsmith, Burke, Sheridan, Maria Edgeworth, Wilde, Shaw – few of whom spent much time in Ireland itself. Disraeli understood the anger against absentee but profiteering landlords, the alien Protestant church, the lack of political representation, yet found the Irish 'wild, reckless, insolent, uncertain and superstitious'. Carlyle saw them as 'the sorest evil this country has to strive with'.

British progressives, humanitarians, workers, unwavering in sympathy for Continental and American slaves, for the oppressed, and for struggling nationalists, were largely indifferent or hostile to the Irish, while grandees like Palmerston drew heavy incomes from Irish properties. When cholera swept Ireland in 1832, the English seemed to feel more indignation at looters of emptied homes than sorrow for the dead. Few remembered, or cared to, that Ireland was not, in Joyce's phrase, an afterthought of Europe, but had been a teacher and reviver of the post-Roman world, rivalling Byzantium. Queen Victoria visited Ireland only twice, an unwise neglect.

The Great Famine of 1847 never ceased to reverberate in Ireland and America. Though Peel bought a hundred thousand pounds' worth of Indian corn to relieve the 1845 famine, Victorian economic philosophy deprecated government interference with market forces, saw it as an infringement of natural law and Providence. Famine assisted population control: the economist Nassau Senior told Benjamin Jowett in 1848 that the million deaths were 'scarcely enough to do much good'.

Sir Charles Trevelyan, of the Treasury, is usually painted as the heartless champion of this approach. After ascribing the Great Famine to 'God's Providence', he added, 'The great evil with which we have to contend is not the physical evil of the famine, but the moral evil of the selfish, perverse and truculent character of the people.' But after what he actually saw for himself in Ireland in 1847 he called for 'the rich and highly favoured portions of the Empire' to come to the aid of the Irish, to 'tide over the shoals upon which they have fallen'. Private British charity, headed by the Quakers, by the rich and not so rich, and by Queen Victoria, did indeed try to ameliorate Treasury stinginess. Movingly, through Quaker agency the impoverished Choctaw tribesmen of Oklahoma sent a hundred and seventy dollars to the starving Irish. A sequel occurred in 1995, when the Choctaw painter Gary White Deer met the Irish Ambassador in London, bearing with him a tribal promise to collect a million pounds for the charity Concern World Wide.

*

After 1815, victorious Britain was accorded international respect, if not universal popularity, as it enriched itself thanks to foreign industrial backwardness. The Irish Romantic actress Harriet Smithson's portrayals of Ophelia and Juliet overwhelmed Berlioz. The Paris Salon of 1824 honoured Bonington, recognised a genius in Constable; Baudelaire was soon praising Lawrence and Reynolds. British painting met a desire for calm light and colour, eschewing the blood-clotted corpses at Wagram, the bodies frozen into boards on the Beresina.

Walter Scott's historical novels engrossed Balzac and an enormous European public. With him and Byron in the van, British Romanticism swept the Continent; he made Scotland comprehensible to Europe, and indeed England. For Lermontov, Goethe, Mazzini, Turgenev, Romanticism haloed Byron – proudly, scornfully independent, roaming bedrooms with slightly sinister panache, seeking worlds outside institutions and dying for Greek freedom, another defeated hero. Delacroix wrote in his journal: '. . . always remember certain passages of Byron, they unfailingly spur your imagination; they are right for you. The end of *The Bride of Abydos*; the death of Selim, his body tossed about by the waves as they break and spend themselves upon the shore. This is sublime, and it is his alone. I feel these things in the way they can be painted.' Romanticism could inspire militant nationalism, republicanism, anarchism, Satanism; find the wayward and irrational more alluring than the routine perfection of wheels and cogs, watches, looms, leaving it to Kipling to demonstrate that these were as romantic as any waterfall and peak. It could inspire individual violence, passionate revenge on whatever or whoever imperilled hope and ambition. Most commonly, it surged into love of Nature, and cries for Freedom, embodied in Shelley, with his demands for free opinion, free love, freedom at whatever cost to others. He too was an image for Europe, dramatically realised in 1931 by Lauro de Bosis, an Italian poet and scientist, son of Shelley's translator, who, with negligible experience, flew from Marseilles to drop leaflets over Rome, urging the King, Church, Business, the people, to overthrow Fascism, then vanished in the sea. Nearer home, the influence of Shelley helped ignite the social conscience of the young Bernard Shaw.

With towns darkly swelling, pit and mill smudging out lives, railways thundering and smoking, 'Nature' was becoming a necessity, as refuge from the gross and artificial, or as gateway both to Beauty and to moral and psychological truths. Landscape was now promoted to the foreground with its two accompaniments, the weather and the seasons. No social blue-print,

Romanticism was a retort to scientific chatter about inevitable Progress, and to deadened impulses which reduced thrilling experience to chemistry and statistics. Napoleon, no Shelley, had remarked: 'I have always enjoyed analysis, and if I were to be seriously in love, I'd analyse my love, bit by bit.'

Herbert Read could imagine no book so representative of English beauty as one containing Wordsworth's poetry, illustrated by Constable. Delacroix declared that, with Rubens, his mentors were Byron, Constable, Bonington. Constable he felt to be one of the glories of England, leading an English school which was in pursuit of Nature while the French were only imitating others. As Henry Fuseli, the Swiss painter, once remarked, 'I like the landscapes of Constable . . . but he makes me call for my umbrella and greatcoat.' Constable's misgivings about the Royal Academy, where the authority of Old or fashionable Masters could stifle free vision, are understandable.

That Debussy so admired Turner does not require analysis; it merely seems fitting. Lover of Dutch art, Turner anticipated many modern schools, refining light, fire, water, mist to essences almost metaphysical, pushing them further than traditional limits. Someone, sneering at Turner's work, neared poetic truth when he called it 'pictures of nothing, and very like'. His genius was acknowledged by the great French Impressionists more readily than by the British public and critics, save for Ruskin; though his destruction of some Turner drawings he thought morally unacceptable has nevertheless saved Ruskin from the gratitude of posterity.

At fourteen Samuel Palmer was exhibiting at the Academy. Devotee of Virgil and Milton, founder-member of The Ancients, honouring Blake; for a while, devoid of sentimentality and prettiness, he too evoked strangeness from the familiar in landscapes, as David Piper wrote, often drawn out of night or dusk, 'perhaps the densest paintings in England art . . . landscapes of contemplation and adoration'. He could have illustrated superbly the twentieth-century poets, Edward Thomas, Dylan Thomas, R.S. Thomas.

That these artists painted largely in oil must not detract from the British landscape water-colourists, led by Alexander and J.R. Cozens, Francis Towne, Thomas Girtin, John Sell Cotman, whose work is at last now recognised as a unique contribution to the corpus of water-colour art, unparalleled in any other country. England too often held water-colour painting to be a minor branch of a literature concerned more with plot and character than with theme, particularly in the Victorian period, but these artists proved the fallacy of such an outlook.

The venomous satirical prints of Gillray and Cruikshank spared no section of society, from Royalty and Parliament to urban mobs, rivalling in their unrestricted bites the indecency of pre-Revolutionary Parisian illustrated attacks on Court and aristocracy, and the republican journalism of the Second Empire.

Popular art was expressed in sporting prints, genre paintings, tavern signs, barge decoration, samplers, rag-dolls, mats, quilts, settles, spoons, cow-jugs, moulded fire-backs, horse-brasses, tongs, candlesticks, hinges curled, horse-headed, shaped like initials or geometrical abstracts. Mechanisation, standardisation had not yet emasculated village crafts, particularly in south and west. G.M. Trevelyan, whose histories were attacked by G.R. Elton as an insult to the intelligence, felt that '. . . the sense of beauty was perhaps best shown in the pleasure taken by all classes in a native music. Songs and airs, composed all over the country by persons of every walk of life, were constantly sung, whether by Bunyan's Pilgrim or Shakespeare's Autolycus, in roads, lanes and streets which their descendants traverse in noisy silence.' In such pleasures, pastimes, work, habits as the Sunday bonnet, the informal garden, Washing Monday, the scoured doorstep, people kept their independence.

As the conveniences of modern travel were introduced – hotels, restaurants, the first trains, steamships across the Channel, down the Rhine, Mr Murray's new guidebooks – British tourists made their presence felt. Lord Edward Seymour was influential in founding the Paris Jockey Club, Sir Richard Wallace, of The Collection, presented drinking fountains to Paris, Brougham and Queen Victoria popularised the Riviera. British global magnificence, however, assured resentments. In 1848, French revolutionaries eagerly attacked British commercial premises. Louisa M. Alcott, in *Good Wives* (1869), described Nice as crowded with haughty English, lively French, sober Germans, handsome Spaniards, ugly Russians, meek Jews, free-and-easy Americans. Maupassant's character *Miss Harriet* depicts another representative that could intrigue and sometimes offend foreigners, the English spinster:

> She was, truth to say, one of those bigoted fanatics, one of those obstinate puritans, whom England breeds in such quantities, those devout and intolerable old maids who haunt all the tables d'hôte in Europe, who ruin Italy, poison Switzerland, and make uninhabitable the charming Riviera towns, on all sides introducing their weird obsessions, their manners of vestal virgins turned to stone, their indescribable clothes, and a peculiar smell of rubber, as if they were nightly stacked in a waterproof case.

The West always oscillated between Classicism and Romanticism, between hopes of Paradise and temptations from Hell, between the world and Other Worlds, Voltaire and Blake. Beneath was the terror of Nothingness, not yet melted by Asiatic philosophies ennobling 'the Void'. Comedy, nonsensical or observant, relieved manifold tensions engendered by impersonal institutions, formalities, conventions, caste, adult behaviour. Understandably, Dickens and Lewis Carroll impinged upon Kafka, who was profoundly stirred by the tortuous and corrosive ramifications of the Circumlocution Office and the Court of Chancery, as well as by the metamorphoses in Carroll's stories. Scientific scepticism about the 'soul' could enlarge the popular need for mysticism, intuition, poetic deception. Keats's *Hyperion*, Swinburne's melodious paganism, while lacking the hard edge of true Classicism, assuaged much spiritual aridity.

Myth is rooted deep in the psyche, with patterns of thought and belief perhaps permanent. Beneath the crust of Victorian materialism, urban squalor, Chartist and early socialist ambiguities and riddles, Albion was reviving, with resplendent colours and intricate designs in art and literature; lost, probably imaginary moral codes; and in architecture. Cults of Arthurian romance and sanitised medievalism catered for nostalgia, wistfulness, creeds of national regeneration, most spectacular in the pinnacles, towers, windows of the 1834 Houses of Parliament, the ironwork of Paddington Station, the arches and spires of the Strand's Law Courts. They prompted such revisionist festivities as the sham-medieval and rain-drenched Eglinton Tournament in 1839 (dates, protested the courtesan Harriette Wilson, Wellington's mistress, make stories dry and ladies nervous), with lists and mounted knights; and the medieval ball at Buckingham Palace in 1842, to assist British exports, with Prince Albert clad as Edward III, Victoria as Queen Philippa, surrounded by clanking, bejewelled lords and wimpled ladies. Manly Lancelots, swooning Guineveres, crafty Merlins, solemn Arthurs gleamed in canvases of Burne-Jones and the Pre-Raphaelites. Antique values were enshrined in Trollope's portrayal of the Gentleman, who also had place in Tennyson's Camelot, affected too by a somewhat Germanic moral haze. William Morris strove to revive Guild standards and the essence of manual craftsmanship. His quasi-Medieval values foreran romantic elements in Kipling – who, like T.E. Lawrence, had Celtic forebears and traits – and Arthur, Mordred, Lancelot subsequently reappeared in narrative poems by Masefield, who also produced a play, *Tristan and Isolt*. At least one public school Boer War memorial was clustered with Arthurian imagery.

Albion, Merrie England, the Good Old Days touched one of humanity's most fundamental yearnings, for the Golden Age, peaceful, comradely, glittering with short-cuts of magic and heroism, infused with honour and pride of being, and where people lived as individuals, not as masses, 'hands'. Such concepts, or misconcepts, underlay Disraeli's 'Young England' movement, with its visions of a land lost but not quite dead, hierarchical, but with lords and yeomen fulfilling their obligations freely, uncontaminated by the thrusting greed and trickery of middlemen.

The British Novel was matched only in Russia and France. Narrative had been made more subtle by Sterne's innovations, then by Thackeray's irony, Wilkie Collins's inventiveness. Darker corners of the unconscious were exposed, a reminder that little is extraordinary save the ordinary. Readers saw themselves exhibited in circumstances far from their actual lives, from viewpoints now better balanced. The Brontës, Mrs Gaskell, Maria Edgeworth, Charlotte Yonge, Margaret Oliphant, George Eliot, Harriet Martineau – her dying words reported as: 'I see no reason why the existence of Harriet Martineau should be perpetuated' – were adequate retort to Southey's rebuff of Charlotte Brontë: 'Literature cannot be the business of a woman's life and ought not to be. The more she is engaged in her proper duties, the less leisure she will have for it.'

Novelists were treating of mill-burnings, drunkenness, drugs, Oriental secret gangs, sectarian hatreds, class divisions, Zionism, women's lot within and outside marriage; attitudes to governesses, children, bastardy, the poor; clerical jobbery, naïve adventurers and hardened seducers; the Empire. As in Shakespearian drama, heroes could be flawed, villains scented with charm, and public taste still demanded happy, usually unreal conclusions, pessimism being at odds with progressive and Imperial philosophies. Moral indignation should be tempered by humour; social enormities, being human-made, were redeemable. Mrs Grundy, too, was alert. Napoleon III's regime prosecuted *Madame Bovary* as immoral, but Victorian Britain was more consistently inquisitorial, translations enduring much bowdlerism. The National Vigilance Society denounced Flaubert, Maupassant, Zola, fortified by a Commons motion deploring their dangerous realism. The London translator and publisher Henry Vizetelly, of Italian descent, was jailed for three months for issuing Zola's *La Terre* in 1888.

Tolstoy revered not only Ruskin and Morris but Dickens, whose profiles flicker behind Conrad, Strindberg, H.G. Wells, Brecht, V.S. Pritchett. Dostoevsky was fascinated by such chilly Dickens women as Estella, called himself and his second wife Micawbers, and thought Mr Pickwick and Don Quixote fiction's greatest creations. Manuel Arzana, Premier of Republican Spain, translated Dickens. Joseph Brodsky, Nobel Laureate poet, who had learnt from Donne and Auden, claimed: 'I believe – not empirically, alas, but only theoretically – that for someone who has read a lot of Dickens, to shoot his like in the name of an idea, is harder than for someone who has read no Dickens.' For Chesterton in 1906, Dickens was 'the rousing English Radical of the great Radical age in England. That spirit of his was one of the things that we have had which were truly national. All other forces we have borrowed, especially those which flatter us most. Imperialism is foreign, socialism is foreign, militarism is foreign, education is foreign. But Radicalism is our own, as English as the hedgerows.' Orwell respected his generous anger and free intelligence, 'hated by all the smelly little ortho-doxies which are now contending for our souls'. It should be also recalled that he was a mingling of compassion and cruelty, of gusto with manic morbidities and sadness, self-pity and fury, more complex than many of his characters.

In America in 1842, a citizen told Dickens that a slave-owner would not mistreat his slaves. Dickens was scornful. 'I told him quietly that it was not a man's interest to get drunk, or to steal, or to game, or indulge in any other vice; but he did indulge in it for all that. That cruelty, and the abuse of irre-sponsible power were two of the blind passions of human nature, with the gratifications of which considerations of interest or of ruin had nothing whatever to do.'

Dickens was a world synonym for extravagant vitality, for life's habit of erupting into the ludicrous, the pathetic, the sentimental, the facetious, the terrible. Virtuoso public reader, actor, conjurer, hypnotist, skills which galvanised his books, Dickens could touch the national nerve, like Churchill. 'Mr Popular Sentiment', Trollope called him irreverently. For several generations, in many countries, he brought to life a London, an England, of bustling coaches and inns, menacing railways, pauper institu-tions, vicious schoolmasters, solitary zanies and vindictive grotesques, roisterers and virginal wives, doomed children, enigmatic criminals, strut-ting con-men, perky amiable youths, rotting mansions, large dwarfs and punctured giants, despotic landladies and spinsters, eccentric occupations, saints in unlikely places, the languishing, lachrymose, drunken, sportive, absurdly cheerful, and the whimsical selfish. Here, spiritual deadness needed awaking, humbug required demolishing. Masks were more mobile than faces, dead things could crush lives, furniture be active, people wooden. Metaphor was a ruling principle, often startling. Van Gogh's love not only of Bunyan and George Eliot but of Dickens can be well observed in the imagery of his letters: 'I saw a group of savoy cabbages standing stiff with cold which reminded me of a group of women I had seen standing in a basement hot-water-and-coal shop early in the morning, in their thin skirts and old shawls.'

Few British followed Tolstoy in wondering why people should persist in living a life so horrible. Dickens could usually detect some hopeful trend in common existence, seldom acknowledging the absolute reality of evil. 'Hogarth in words', he assailed a society blighted by heartlessness, to be rescued not by Napoleonic *ukase*, or by Parliament, Church, Trade-Unionism, but by individual charity, courage, raids on Bumbledom, Coketown, Chancery. He could be flagrantly unjust to missionaries, politicians, Catholicism, foreigners (particularly Americans), cultural snobs, fellow do-gooders. He feared the mob, like the Jacobins he supported only 'the deserving poor' and denied that gentler prisons would make prisoners gentler. He lacked sympathy for the Empire and was of the tribe of Kropotkin, Schweitzer, Gandhi, not the Webbs, Shaw, let alone Marx, never confining himself to the research bureau, or joining a party, but personally investigating the vile, malodorous, unjust and wasteful, publicising enormities through speeches, articles, novels and, with Baroness Burdett-Coutts, rehousing penitent prostitutes and enlivening general philanthropy.

A watchful youth from nowhere, unversed in the Classics but familiar with Fielding, Smollett, popular melodrama and music, with tedious Parliamentary wrangles, sensational trials, the crowded, often lurid Thames and the swarming urban menagerie, he has been seen as the first European novelist of Megalopolis, the Total City with its ferocious contradictions, bottomless depths, chirpy comedy, and what Angus Wilson described as vast monsters frozen in their loneliness.

The popular drama of the period lacked any of Dickens's subtleties. *Sweeny Todd* luxuriated in throat-cutting and cannibalism. *Maria Marten* still satisfies English taste for murder, the occult, the libidinous, and is based on real life. William Corder, of Polstead, having murdered a girl, buried her in the Red Barn and fled to Brentford where, under another name, he married, and started a School for Young Ladies. Meanwhile, Maria's mother had regularly dreamed of her daughter calling her from the Barn, which was finally dug up. Corder was hanged before ten thousand spectators, who bought pieces of the rope at ten guineas an inch – such rope was believed to possess serum properties – after a sensational trial, described in a book bound with his own skin, still extant at Bury St Edmunds; his abnormally large skull is a treasure of the Royal college of Surgeons.

'If you will meet me at the Red Barn, as sure as I have life,
I will take you to Ipswich Town, and there make you my wife.'
I then went home happy, and fetched my gun, my pickaxe and my spade,
I went into the Red Barn, and there I dug her grave.

Raffish, dandyesque, Dickens was accepted as a genius but not quite a gentleman: Victorian snobbery could reach remarkable proportions. Francis Place, radical reformer and tailor, owned a considerable library in his shop off Whitehall, where passing MPs could halt to browse and chat; however, he lost some wealthy clients who, glimpsing the library, resented a tailor possessing so many books, a phenomenon upstart and unnatural.

The Victorian temper remains controversial. Margaret Thatcher honoured its values of thrift, industry, enterprise, solid achievement: Neil Kinnock defined Victorianism as cruelty, misery, drudgery, squalor and ignorance. The energies were undeniable. Britain's manufacturing fervour initiated the Age of Exhibitions with the Crystal Palace in 1851, swiftly copied by America and France. But the pace exacted grim penalties for failure and misfortune. Carlyle castigated 'the Mammon of Unrighteousness', the grip of the cash-nexus. 'Let inventive men cease to spend their existence contriving how cotton can be made cheaper; and try to invent a little how cotton in its very cheapness could be more justly divided between us.' In *Past and Present* (1843) he raged that horses were well-fed and men were starved.

Food prices fell after the repeal of the Corn Laws in 1846; railways boomed, and periodically collapsed; urban crime was reported to be diminishing, but genteel streets remained close to danger. Pierce Egan's *Life in London* (1840) mentions 'a system of cowardly assault and treacherous revenge displayed in the murderous use of the knife-weapon, which is becoming almost as common in England as in Spain and Italy'. Medicine, Housing Acts, Clean Water Acts may by 1900 have mastered the worst of typhoid, typhus, cholera, malaria, tuberculosis, syphilis; but London, largest city on earth, still had foggy, no-go areas of crime, adult and child prostitution. In *Sybil*, Disraeli pictured families breathing air tainted by human and animal excrement, babies born surrounded by skeletal figures, foetid pits, stagnant pools, verminous walls. Pigs might sleep alongside infants, incest was inevitable, mortality and infanticide rates grim. General Sir Charles Napier wrote in 1839, when sent to the manufacturing districts at a time of great Chartist unrest, that Manchester was 'the chimney of the world. Rich rascals, poor rogues, drunken ragamuffins and prostitutes form the moral, soot made into paste by rain the physique, and the only view is a long chimney: what a place! The entrance is Hell realised.' He must have been relieved to be sent back to India to conquer Sind.

That prisons were no worse than elsewhere was, given Britain's moral pretensions, no commendation. Clapham prisoners staged a furious food riot in 1861. Prison hulks lingered on, dispiriting, foreboding. These had begun as a temporary expedient in 1776 and remained for some hundred years; the *Bellerophon* and Cook's *Discovery* were degraded to such floating bestialities, peep-shows for the salacious and sadistic. Boys and old men, the crippled, the syphilitic, were crammed together, some naked in midwinter having gambled away their clothing. A chronicler, W. Blanch Johnson, described 'a generation of dead men rising from their tombs, hollow-eyed, wan and earthy of complexion, bent-backed, shaggy-bearded, and of a terrifying emaciation.'

Yet little was static. Protests were not only academic. During the 1830s and 1840s rioters burnt Nottingham Castle, Bristol Mansion House, Customs House and episcopal palace, while Derby jail was sacked; some twenty died in the Newport riots of 1839; Bradford, Manchester, Liverpool were rocked by violence; eighty-five thousand volunteers, supervised by Wellington and allegedly including Louis-Napoleon, assembled against Chartist threats, mostly inflated, in revolutionary 1848. In London, Wellington once lost his windows, while Lord Londonderry was dragged from his horse. The unemployed smashed grandee club windows and Piccadilly stores in 1886: a man was killed in Trafalgar Square on Black Sunday in 1887; Anarchists and Irish and American Fenians bombed Clerkenwell Prison, Scotland Yard, the Tower, Westminster Hall. Thousands of devout citizens demonstrated against the Sunday opening of museums.

Whether because of or in spite of these disturbances, the period saw further reforms, on behalf of women, children, Jews, Catholics, public health, education, housing, prisons. The efforts of Tuke in Britain and Pinel in France were extended, so that lunatics were increasingly treated as patients, not criminals or butts.

In spite of reforms, the 'Mother of Parliaments' itself was no high-minded Senate of detached Ancients. In 1810 Heywood Thompson heard a Sussex member, Mr Fuller, very drunk, who mistook the Speaker, too audibly, for an owl in an ivy bush, next day receive from the Chair a rebuke, dignified but severe. The 1851 assembly was called 'the Bribery Parliament'. Lord Salisbury's last ministry was nicknamed 'the Hotel Cecil', from his relatives stacked within it: he later resigned in favour of A.J. Balfour, his nephew. Despite Party bluster, the divisions remained fluid; coalitions occurred, frequently including Palmerston, who might have approved of a remark by the socialist James Maxton: 'If you can't ride two horses, get out of the bloody circus.' Attlee, asked what were the differences between the Parties, replied: 'Jobs. That's what the difference is. Jobs.' Trollope, who sought election, defined himself as 'a fairly advanced conservative Liberal'. Dickens consistently berated Parliament; the socialist Cunninghame Graham, who had an Argentinian town named after him, thought it 'a society of incapables'. Shaw mocked the system as government of everybody by anybody, and A.J.P. Taylor was to reflect that the basis of modern democracy is that men do not mean what they say.

The secret ballot had replaced the hustings, despite Palmerston's objection that it was 'skulking and un-English'. The franchise was further extended, for propertied males. Local government was more objectively systemised while like the magistrature remaining mostly unpaid, a process unusual in Europe, though words in the right quarter could still be decisive. Its excellence might perhaps be squared with Northcote Parkinson's assumption that men enter local politics through being unhappily married. A passage from Dickens is probably still pertinent:

> 'How do you suppose he comes to be a magistrate?' said I. 'Oh dear me,' replied Traddles, 'it would be very difficult to answer that question. Perhaps he voted for somebody, or lent money to somebody, or otherwise obliged somebody, or jobbed for somebody who got the Lieutenant of the county to nominate him for the commission.'

Philip Guedalla could be relied upon for deft observations. He cited Lord Chelmsford receiving command of a British army, defeated by the Zulus in 1879, because he was the son of a distinguished lawyer whom 'the family incompetence' had compelled the Prime Minister to exclude from the

Woolsack eleven years previously. 'The cogency of the reason will be readily apparent to any student of the English system.'

Victorianism may suggest not only brutal individualism and colonial greed but a stiff and smug philistinism, prudery, hypocritical church-going. All these were present, though in the 1850s witnesses lamented the emptiness of Anglican pews; and the century was one of tempestuous religious controversies, scientific discoveries, moral searchings, fine art and outstanding literature, sporting prowess and outsize personalities. *Gladstone* is apt to suggest a humourless puritan, of whom Disraeli complained that he lacked a single redeeming defect. Complex and many-sided, he was indeed the earnest moralist, to mark whose centenary Bulgaria respectfully closed all schools for a day; but also a vigorous enjoyer of life. John Clive has a glimpse of Mr and Mrs Gladstone singing:

> A ragamuffin husband and a rantipoling wife,
> We'll fiddle and scrape it through the ups and downs of life.

Mark Pattison, head of an Oxford College, formidable theologian, Renaissance scholar, editor of Milton and Pope, was seen by Walter Pater 'romping with great girls in the gooseberry bushes'.

Flush with competitive energies, 'Mistress of the Seas', 'Workshop of the World', with India once more quiet after the Mutiny of 1857, Britain in 1860 had small misgivings of any threat from America or a united Germany. Together with Napoleon III she had, for better or worse, powerfully assisted the unification of Italy who would, presumably, feel grateful. State interference at home was invoked only reluctantly but generous impulses were unremitting, despite prejudice, suspicion, blatant obstruction. Palmerston's gunboats were negligible beside the work of his son-in-law, the seventh Earl of Shaftesbury (1801–85), upholder not of affable hedonism but of severely Christian responsibility and uprightness. Against resolute opposition in the Lords and the Treasury, from Bureaucracy and among Party Interests, he accomplished as much as Robert Owen, Hyndman, Keir Hardie, Dr Barnardo, far more than Shelley, Godwin, Fourier, Kropotkin, Tolstoy, in his campaigns for vagrant children, young prostitutes, climbing-boys, for 'Ragged Schools'. His Ten-Hour Bill salvaged women and children from seventeen hours' daily labour. In his activities he had no western counterpart. He fought for Saturday Early Closing, reform of prisons and asylums; for better housing, allotments; for the evangelising of costermongers, whores, Italian Catholics. Miss Nightingale praised his services to hygiene in the Crimea. He provided evidence for Prince Albert on the impact of bad housing on morals. He campaigned against the trade in slaves and opium, the overloading of ships and exploitation of seamen; rescued cricket clubs from builders, organised missionaries to the Far East, to assist the Second Coming which he felt was humanity's real hope, more reliable than laws and agitation.

He was less rigid, thus more useful, than Tolstoy in mistrusting the State. He used State machinery in helping establish the Board of Health and the public control of London's water; he admired Napoleon III's authoritarian urban planning, and supported the Married Women's Property Act, though with the reservation that it might cause 'insubordination, equality and something more'. Like Dickens, he was as infuriating to liberals and social-ists as he was to the Interests. No democrat, like the Fabians he preferred granting to sharing. Intolerant, he dismissed Hinduism as 'beastly non-sense', while Methodism was probably worse. His reliable biographer A.M. Finlayson reports him rebuking a woman as the incarnation of Satan for her High Church preference. He found Victoria and Albert lax in their morning prayers, which vitiated their social awareness. People should be Christians, not Levellers, Chartists, republicans, or liberals, and he was unable to con-ceive that Christianity was compatible with each. He opposed Church and Parliamentary reform, complaining after the 1832 Reform Act that he was now 'sitting with Jacobins, Atheists, radical Dissenters and Whig place-hunters'. Like Robespierre, he regarded joking as misuse of language and opposition as personal insult, virtual blasphemy. He was intemperate about Christian Socialism, Modernist theology, Irish Home Rule, the secret ballot – all would be irreligious indoctrination – strikes, and vivisection. As chair-man of the Lord's Day Observance Society he had art galleries and museums and park music forbidden on Sundays. He must have shuddered at Gilbert and Sullivan, Offenbach, music-halls, pubs, Sir Frederick Leighton's sham-Classical nudes.

Like Dickens, Nightingale, Elizabeth Fry, John Howard in striving for social change by personal efforts, Lord Shaftesbury was soon regarded as anachronistic. To the men of the future such efforts, by being piecemeal, actually prolonged the system, and his patrician commendation of the poor for their marvellous patience would have disgusted Shaw, Wells, Marx. Yet he could daily utter words to make all society flinch, citing the urban victims of want, hundreds dying weekly: 'Are we to call ourselves a Christian country, knowing that two thousand of our fellow creatures, *just as good as ourselves*, are doomed to the most excruciating agony?' The epitaph on his highly inappropriate Eros memorial at Piccadilly Circus, written by Gladstone, praises his devotion to God and his fellow-men, his example to his order, 'a blessing to this people and a name to be by them ever gratefully remembered'.

Another British answer to both *laisser-faire* capitalism and dogmatic socialism was earlier offered by a managerial professional, Robert Owen (1771–1858), who like his father-in-law Robert Dale recognised that machinery could enhance human possibility, raise material standards, yet also increase profits. No mystic, as partner in the New Lanark cotton mill from 1800 to 1825 he was both reformer and disciplinarian, demanding that workers should work, not fancy themselves a government. He proved his thesis by giving fair wages and hours, providing clean houses, play parks, a school, clinic, moderately-priced shops, pleasant working conditions through co-operative units. The fame of New Lanark, a forerunner of the Garden City, crossed Europe, itself racked by attempts to interpret the French Revolution: even the future Nicholas I, 'the Iron Tsar', joined the twenty thousand foreign pilgrims and sociologists.

Owen gave powerful support to the National Co-Operative Movement and to labour unions, founding the Grand National Consolidated Trade Union in 1834 and leading thousands in support of the Tolpuddle Martyrs. The witty and cultured Lord Melbourne had condemned unions for tampering with the laws of nature, but the Combination Laws were repealed in 1824, unions finally legalised in 1875. Politically averse to Shaftesbury, Owen held the General Strike, or 'National Holiday', to be the ultimate weapon. His own experiments in Britain and America ultimately failed, but much survived, in Chartism, co-operative retail shops, Mutual Aid and Friendly Societies, Mechanics' Institutes, reading groups, innumerable voluntary charities and clubs, and the London Working Men's Association of Francis Place and William Lovett. An American visitor, Price Collier, in his *England and the English* (1909), noticed that 'The enormous amount of unpaid and voluntary service to the State and to one's neighbours, in England, results in the solution of one of the most harassing problems in every wealthy nation.' 'Solution' seems extravagant, though his witness was accurate.

Charities were remarkable in their variety. A Bill 'To Prevent the Cruel and Improper Treatment of Cattle' was introduced in 1822; the Society to Prevent Cruelty to Animals was founded in 1824, to European bewilderment. Not until 1966 was there a successful French prosecution for ill-treating a dog.

In this humane regard, children lagged behind. British children had long been considered necessary nuisances, limbs of Satan, painful rewards of piety, clumsy slaves or favourite toys. Boasts about Britain being first to found a Society to protect children from cruelty (1895) might incite a foreigner to retort, erroneously, that it was the only country to need it.

From about 1780, despite Low Church anti-Pelagian obsession with sin and impurity, slowly more children, it would seem, were being valued for their own sakes. Rousseau had spoken for them: a Charlotte Brontë, a Dickens – himself, like Rousseau, no model father in his treatment of his own children – perceived them to be at the centre of vital and unlimited kingdoms where incessant transformations took place, from the grotesque to the absurd, from dross to gold, from smiles to inexplicable rage. A dead tree could be a jungle, a ceiling the Pacific, a mysterious rhyme a treaty with the unknown. The child Ford Madox Ford saw wolves in a firelit bedroom; Richard Hughes, in infancy, imagined the pulpit was a tiny hospital in which you cured your illness by shouting. Parents and teachers in Dickens have usually forgotten their own childhoods, becoming chilled, cautious, incomplete: the most amiable – Brownlow, Nancy, the Cheerybles, Pickwick, Betsey Trotwood, Jarndyce – are childless.

'Life', Dickens asserted, 'is given us on the definite understanding that we boldly defend it to the last.' Children must have felt this in their blood, in their daily encounters, though their defence was not always adequate. *The British Medical Journal* in 1868 declared: 'There is not the slightest difficulty in disposing of any number of children so that they may give no further trouble and never be heard of, at £10 a head.' Urban gentlefolk tried to ignore hordes of verminous 'street-arabs'. Mayhew reported a hundred thousand London children used in brothels. Infant mortality was gross, though often only the deaths of the baptised were registered. Hardy remembered a Dorset child, dead from starvation. A corpse might lie for days in a crowded room.

Any new understanding of children was not wholesale. Early nineteenth-century punishments embraced the pillory, suspension in baskets, locking in cupboard or cellar, dropping head first into a well or sewer, overdosing with emetics – sometimes, Shaftesbury discovered, 'for doing any frivolous thing such as cleaning their shoes or doing anything so as to go home decent at night'. Examining statutes concerning children between 1780 and 1914, Professor Walvin confirms a shift, nevertheless, from the child deprecated as a small, usually delinquent adult to the child as possessor of separate needs and insights, even though for many, perhaps the majority, retribution, even Hell, still awaited the liar, the masturbator, the independent.

Religious culture was seldom rollicking:

> There is a Fountain filled with Blood
> Drawn from Emmanuel's veins.

Numerous deathbeds strengthened forebodings and terror. Walvin mentions the Victorian *A Child's Picture Book*, still available in 1926:

> Ah, little one, 'tis so,
> We know that soon we all must go;
> And so we wonder, whispering low,
> Whose turn next?

British nannies and governesses were in demand abroad, with under-considered effect on the ruling classes. 'How delightful it would be to be a governess!' Anne Brontë ruminated in *Agnes Grey*. 'To go out into the world! To act for myself; to exercise my unused faculties; to try my unknown powers to earn my own maintenance . . . to make Virtue practical, Instruction desirable, and Religion lovely and comprehensible.' The outcome was more often drudgery, emotional and literal rootlessness, bitterness, perforce only a step away from prostitution, petty crime, suicide. In a fragmentary novel, *Cassandra*, the young Florence Nightingale complained that women's wasted or unused energy 'makes them feel every night when they go to bed as if they were going mad'.

English national education lagged behind Scottish, Prussian, Danish, French, and was compulsory only after 1870. It was feared that, like a national police force, it would impair liberty, and aggravate taxation. There were charity schools, Sunday schools, Church and Nonconformist schools, fee-paying, private, grammar and public schools, and unambitious though mercenary dame schools; but in 1833, only one child in eleven was attending one. Hampden Jackson refers to a Liverpool garret ten by nine feet, enclosing a cock, two hens, three terriers, one master, and with forty pupils on the roll.

Boarding schools competed to supply recruits for administration, Empire, the officer class, and 'Society'. An Eton housemaster complained that college routine was seriously disturbed by the Cecil brothers' insistence on regularly attending Communion. 'The best schools in the world', Talleyrand purred, 'are the English public schools, and they're dreadful.' The sink-or-swim adolescent chaos, expensive, barely supervised, responsible to no authority, shocked Brougham and fellow-reformers like Arnold of Rugby, who himself flogged a small, delicate boy to excess, for telling the truth. Cobbett raged at 'those frivolous idiots that are turned out from Winchester and Westminster School, or any of those dens of dunces called colleges or universities'.

Classics, hierarchy, the birch, dire food, bullying, homosexuality were commonplace, at least until the Clarendon Reforms of 1862. Dr Johnson was amply justified in saying of a headmaster that it was not his pupils' faces he remembered but their anatomies. 'Learning', Thring of Uppingham pronounced, 'is Pain.' At Winchester, tea was forbidden, beer obligatory. The world's leading industrial nation, unlike Prussia and America, injected its political leaders with unremitting Classics, virtually ignoring science and technology. At Shrewsbury, Darwin was admonished for studying 'useless chemistry'. Because of his deficiency in Latin, Churchill was placed in the bottom class at Harrow, to learn mere English, alongside the oafish, incapable, retarded, and hopeless. Only after 1945 did Classics dwindle, so that the Foreign Office was reported in 1996 to have banned the use of Latin and Greek quotations, to avoid embarrassing more ignorant colleagues. Lewis Carroll recollected that, at Rugby, he was 'not secure from annoyance at night'. In *Bleak House*, Dickens was sarcastic about the Winchester curriculum as unreal, useless, ultimately harmful, neglectful of the boys' basic needs, though he sent a son to Eton and praised the public schools for manliness, and as more disdainful of rank and riches than any other English institution.

E.M. Forster indicted public school products as possessing well-developed bodies, fairly developed minds and undeveloped hearts. But, until the end of the nineteenth century at least, to accuse public schools of breeding conformity seems unfair. At Eton Gladstone wrote a subversive *Ode to Wat Tyler*, and eccentricity, whether among masters or boys, was no bar to esteem. One Eton beak preached to his class, 'My brothers', on the Duties of the Married State; another tried to comfort Swinburne by reading him psalms. A new headmaster, after his first flogging, presented the victim with a case of champagne. Even in 1934 a Haileybury master, C.W. Adams, a mathematicial near-genius, liked to begin a lesson by being pelted with waste paper.

'Robustness' was general. A Shrewsbury boy was permanently disfigured for defending the headmaster's translation of Aeschylus. At Marlborough an eight-year-old was branded. Shaftesbury's brother Francis died at Eton after a fight lasting more than three hours, a mishap accepted by his family without writ or reproach but with stoic forbearance. In 1820 eight Eton masters, wretchedly paid and dependent on pupils' tips, were grappling with more than five hundred boys: snakes and rats might be released in chapel; one pupil stoned a four-year-old townee, another challenged the headmaster to a duel. Dr Keate's mass floggings, his regular howling-down at prayers, the glue poured on his chair, attained national celebrity. Elsewhere, after a boy's suicide to escape three bullies he had earlier reported, the headmaster requested a verdict of insanity, as the only plausible explanation of *sneaking*, dishonouring the code. Pupil power engulfed Harrow in 1771, the rebels demanding rights in appointing headmasters; troops suppressed a Winchester riot; Shrewsbury boys used knives against the headmaster's hired posses, and in 1871 turned pistols on the villagers.

Dr Arnold's conviction that schools should mould character surprised most masters and pupils, to whom the eighteenth century was preferable to the nineteenth though they were supposedly dedicated to the ideal of the Gentleman. Keate feared that railways would discourage the English love of adventure; his reaction to Mayhew's account of London children using trains to get to Wolverhampton races would have been interesting. As so frequently, what should have been often was not. Boys and Old Boys resented outsiders' attention, even attempts to abolish flogging. Keate was popular, perhaps due to the stubborn English preference for 'a character' over an example of rectitude.

Eventually the Civil Service, the War Office, the growing Empire demanded Benthamite utilitarianism, Gladstonian meritocracy, the onus of public examinations, less nepotism, more talent, better-paid masters, better diet, more restrained punishments. Organised field sports ousted loose 'country rambles', prefects were chosen for 'character', as against thuggery. The schools had their subsequent defenders, but detractors remain vehement.

The prep. school, the public school's junior accomplice, a Victorian institution, has attracted a reputation at worst evil. David Niven enjoyed remarking that only the English and the Chinese sent their sons off to homosexual schoolmasters precisely when they most needed parental love. Hugh Walpole shuddered at memories of his Marlowe school: 'The food was inadequate, the morality was "twisted", and Terror – sheer, stark, unblinking Terror – stared down every one of its passages.' Pathological and cruel teachers feature in his novels *Fortitude* and *Mr Perrin and Mr Traill*, the latter set in a public school masters' common-room. Lord Edward FitzMaurice, researching a Beaconsfield prep. school, found no evidence of class privilege. 'Lord Russell recounted how, having a great dislike for the mutton fat which every boy was ordered to eat with his meat, he had succeeded, as he hoped unobserved, in dropping it under the table. Having been discovered, he was compelled by a clerical pedagogue to sweep it up off the floor and eat it, dirt and all.' At Temple Grove a headmaster, having thrashed a boy, would then kiss him, to convince him that all was forgiven. *Brother where-art-thou?* was the synonym for bread-and-butter pudding, lacking currants. Other common dishes were *Hard-Baked Tombstone, Cat's Illness, Worms, Dead Man's Leg, Leprous Toenails, House on Fire, White Baby* and *Stuff*. Comedy intruded. One headmaster, informally known as the Actor-Manager, would regularly accost a new boy: 'Brat, the Vice-Captain wasn't too pleased with what you were doing yesterday when you thought no one could see you.' Or, 'Brat, the Vice-Captain was rather keen on the way you went for that goalkeeper.' By half term, the novice would realise that the Vice-Captain was Jesus.

A newspaper advertisement in 1879 must have attracted a considerable if murky response:

> Boarding schools wanted in London for a boy, nine years, and two boys, six and seven years old, requiring firm discipline, having become wild and unruly, through neglect occasioned by family misfortune. No holiday could be given, as holidays destroy any good effected at school. The father, quite a gentleman, can only pay 20 guineas each. This advertisement is only intended for schools of pre-eminent efficiency for such cases, and prosperous enough to be able and willing to accept such terms and undertake the needful taste of reformation for the sake of the schools' additional credit of success.

The faults of the system meant not only neglect and swindle, but the waste of young brains, grace, spirit. In 1936, H.G. Wells at seventy was still infuriated: 'Seven-eighths of the hideous killing going on in the world is being done by young people under thirty, youngsters fed on stale old dogmas or not fed at all.' The bravery of thousands of British victims at

Gallipoli, the Somme, Ypres, was balanced by the herdish principles on which they were raised.

Science with all its wonders was frequently despised as 'stinks', taught by young men with curious accents and stained hands. Even in 1934, science for younger pupils at Haileybury was a mere alternative to geography. A few authors attempted to induce scientific awareness: Samuel Smiles, with his *Lives of the Engineers* (1861–62), Conan Doyle, Kipling, Wells himself. The better (or more expensive) schools remained bound to Roman concepts of duty, leadership, team spirit, formalised religion; to gentlemanly Honour and Fair Play; to avoidance of Celtic spontaneity and candid exuberance or anger. Raised on patriotic songs and undemanding sermons, the Old Boys could be relied upon to fear God, honour the King, administer Cheshire or Bengal. Their cult of the amateur remained pre-eminent until about disastrous 1916.

Following the 1870 Education Act, there was a flood of cheap literature. For boys, the extrovert *Chums* and *Boys' Own Paper* competed with penny dreadfuls, Baden-Powell's Scouting yarns and exhortations, and many adventures derived from the Empire. There were also the reports of those new adventurers, the War Correspondents, stemming from William Russell's despatches for *The Times* from the Crimea in 1854: Archibald Forbes of the *Daily News* galloped a hundred and twenty miles in fifteen hours to report a battle; G.W. Steevens of the *Daily Mail* was named by Churchill as the greatest contemporary prose-writer, which would have aggrieved Henry James. Churchill was perhaps flattering Steevens in so saying, since he too was a war correspondent, escaping Boer captivity with a price on his head, which he complained was too low. Edgar Wallace was private soldier, Reuters' correspondent in South Africa and sub-Kipling versifier.

The most indefatigable of the breed was G.A. Henty (1832–1902), Crimean volunteer, reporter of Garibaldi's 1867 anti-Papal campaign, a Balkan War, an Ashanti War where the nubile girls among his supplies were resented. He also covered wars in Spain, India, Abyssinia; the Franco-Prussian war and the Paris Commune; Dreyfus's retrial in 1899; a Fenian outbreak in Ireland, a Welsh miners' riot. He was colourful and graphic, though largely ignoring the sub-world of field-punishments, executions, torture, mobile brothels, gangrene.

Henty's was a type which, in Imperial Britain, Imperial Germany, easily attracted hero-worship. Confessing himself the worst of marksmen, he was an expert swordsman, Garibaldi's boxing instructor, had farmed in South America, worked as an engineer in the Habsburg Empire, edited the *Union Jack*, written a dozen 'adult' novels from 1868; after his first story, *Out in the Pampas*, he published some eighty more adventure books for youth – *Under Drake's Flag, With Clive in India, With the Allies in Pekin, The Young Buglers, The Young Franc-Tireurs* . . . all sharing courage, ambition, exotic challenges; contempt for cowards, barrack-room lawyers, stay-at-homes, trade-unionists. An American tourist demanded to see the Abbey, the Tower, Mr Henty and all his books. He was in strong opposition to another literary celebrity, H.G. Wells, loather of kings, bishops, military heroes, childish wars, churches, conventional morals and outlooks, and of Carlyle's belief that world history was a biography of Great Men.

National complacency was unconducive to universal popularity. In children's geography manuals, James Walvin discovered such dicta as 'The English are kind to other people in distress; industrious and active; fond of liberty themselves and willing to allow it to others.' Or, 'England, as a nation, stands without a rival; the intelligence, the industry, and the enterprise of her people have raised her to a pitch of greatness enjoyed by no other Power.'

Yet imaginitive sturdiness could weather tawdry and pandering reading distributed to youth. As described in *Lark Rise to Candleford*, Flora Thompson escaped her humble Victorian cottage and school through *The Royal Reader* and such contributions as 'The Skater Chased by Wolves', and 'The Siege of Torquilistone', from Scott's *Ivanhoe*; Fenimore Cooper's *Prairie on Fire*, Washington Irving's *Capture of Wild Horses*. 'There were fascinating descriptions of such far-apart places as Greenland and the Amazon; the Pacific Ocean with its fairy islands and coral reefs; the snows of the Hudson Bay Territory and the sterile heights of the Andes.' Verse was popular: *The Slave's Dream*; Tennyson's 'The Brook', and 'Ring out, wild bells'; Byron's 'Shipwreck'; Scott's 'Young Lochinvar'; Hardy's grandmother, a yeoman's daughter, was familiar with works of Addison and Steele, Fielding and Richardson; with *Paradise Lost* and *Pilgrim's Progress*.

Taste and education perhaps do not wholly depend on limitless expenditure, tiny classes, busy unions, the latest technology, even mechanical transport. Schooling at Lark Rise necessitated lengthy daily walks, with opportunities for gang-bullies, developing friendships, observation,

> plenty of shouting and quarrelling, and often fighting. In more peaceful moments they would squat in the dust of the road and play marbles, or sit on

a stone heap and play dibs with pebbles, or climb into the hedges after birds' nests or blackberries, or to pull long trails of byrony to wreath round their hats. In winter, they would slide on the ice on the puddles, or make snow-balls – soft ones for their friends and hard ones with a stone inside for their enemies.

Most children abandoned school at eleven – more waste – 'with an interest not in books but in life, and especially the life that lay immediately before them'. Thousands of the barely seen, seldom heard, still managed to accumulate a mosaic of human variousness. Joseph 'Posh' Fletcher, of Suffolk, scarcely literate but intimate with Edward FitzGerald of *Rubáiyát* fame, cherished words, not least his own:

> Man that is born of woman,
> Has very little time to live,
> He comes up like a fore-mast top-sail
> And down like a flying jib.

An element of national cohesion was fermented by love for sport. Chesterton once dismissed socialism by observing that the English were more interested in the inequality of horses than in the equality of Man. The Parliamentary parties were manipulated by 'Whips': on the north-west frontier of India undercover missions to outwit Russian incursions there were christened 'the Great Game', a phrase popularised by Kipling; reprisals after the Indian Mutiny in 1857 were described in hunting and shooting terms. Montgomery promised to 'hit Rommel for six'; headlines, CLOSE OF PLAY, announced Britain's successive withdrawals from Empire.

Britain invented or developed Association and Rugby football, cricket and baseball – both are early mentioned in *Northanger Abbey* – lawn tennis, golf, hockey, squash, rackets, Eton and Rugby fives, bowls, curling, darts, badminton, table tennis, netball, rounders, pigeon-racing, and devised world rules for boxing, rowing, horse racing, lacrosse. Eton fives, first improvised between the chapel buttresses, then spread to Switzerland, Nigeria, Argentina, Nepal. Polo (and chess) derived from Asia. Mary Outerbridge brought lawn tennis to America in 1874, after watching British officers playing in Bermuda. J.D. Forbes, John Ball, Edward Whymper were famous Victorian Alpine climbers: Whymper was first to scale the Matterhorn in 1865, and Leslie Stephen, founder of the *Dictionary of National Biography*, father of Virginia Woolf and Vanessa Bell, first conquered the Schreckhorn, and was President of the Alpine club from 1865 to 1868. Mrs Aubrey Le

Blond, first President of the Ladies' Alpine Club, climbed the Zinahothorn – over 13,000 feet – and repeated the feat the same day, to recover her lost skirt.

Earlier sport was vigorously unsporting. Labourer and squire, milord and groom jostled to goad forward dog-fights, cock-fights, bare-knuckled boxers slamming each other into insensibility. Old England rejoiced in badger-baiting, hare-coursing, fox-hunting, shin-hacking, head-butting, shooting, wrestling. English love of sport was inseparable from indulgence in gambling. A cricketer, C.W.L. Bulpett, won two hundred pounds in 1881 for walking a mile and running a mile in eighteen minutes, next year rather more for repeating it in less. Eighteenth-century cricket had provided income for Lord Frederick Beauclerk and his like, who rigged games, bribed players.

The young Charles II was rebuked by Scottish Presbyterians for over-attention to golf. P.G. Wodehouse dedicated a book of golfing stories to 'the immortal memory of Henry and Pat Rogie who, at Edinburgh in the year AD 1593, were imprisoned for "Playing of the Gowff on the links of Leith every Sabbath the time of the sermones". Also of Robert Robertson, who got it in the neck in AD 1694 for the same reason.' Swapping Wodehouse quotations is in itself a minor sport. His foreign admirers included ex-Emperor Wilhelm II, who allegedly, when in ill-temper, would read him aloud to his suite. Wilhelm also much praised Kipling's 'If', for its laconic catalogue of the Stoic virtues.

The world's oldest sporting fixture is the Doggett's Coat and Badge sculling race, from London Bridge to Chelsea, continuous since 1715. The Royal Yacht Squadron, sustaining the enthusiasm of Charles II and James II, is the oldest sailing institution. The Derby was first run in 1780, Cabinets never meeting on Derby Day, to allow ministers' attendance, a habit now rescinded.

Soccer, the most universal sport, perhaps began in a primitive rough-and-tumble for a sacrificial head. Medieval kings forbade it, as a street nuisance and a distraction from archery. Traditionally, Oliver Cromwell was a keen player. It was often castigated for violence, 'knavery', even 'vile murder'. The Football Association was supervising more orderly league competitions from 1863, and England first played Scotland in 1872, when the first Cup Final was won by Wanderers, public school Old Boys, who had four subsequent wins.

Cricket is the distinctive English – not British – national game. In

Europe, only Holland and Denmark have many players, though Corfu (British-run for a few decades) has four teams: Phaex, Gymnasticos, Ergaticos and, appropriately, Byron, who played for Harrow against Eton. The Bastille riot prevented an inaugural match in Paris in 1789, sponsored by the British ambassador, the Duke of Dorset, admirer of Marie-Antoinette. In 1829, when a game was staged at Dieppe to entertain a French royal duchess, one player, after an innings had been completed, was asked by a Frenchman when the game was to start. Napoleon III saved Paris cricket when the municipality tried to ban it as dangerous. In final exile, he would watch games on Chislehurst Common and once, after a spectacular catch, sent out a message requesting the fielder to repeat it forthwith. Like chess and fishing, the game is subtle, with much movement within the seemingly static. A German, playing at Munich in 1996, considered that the essence of it is invisible from the boundary. That a draw can be as purposefully dramatic as victory or defeat may reflect an English love of compromise, not timid, but civilised.

The length of a match allows observation of character; and with its eccentrics, statistics, tall stories, pastoral associations, cricket too has produced a considerable literature, though this can falter, as an article in *Perception* (1996) reveals: 'Slow bowlers may manipulate the flight of the ball so as to induce the batsman to supplement his inadequate retinal image information with inappropriate prior knowledge and thus to misinterpret the vertical angular speed of the retinal image of the ball.' Cricket is mentioned in John's reign. 'Krickett' was played at Aleppo in 1676, by English sailors. Players in hats and waistcoats moved through the eighteenth century. The Regent played on his private ground at Brighton, and village cricket was spreading, with its auxiliary pleasures of ale, exasperating umpires, amiable ladies, periodic clapping, still heard by the journalist Dexter Pedley, 'like a handful of wooden bricks gently toppling over'.

Wellington judged that there was 'nothing the people of this country like so much as to see their great men take part in their amusements; the aristocracy will commit a great error if they fail to mix freely with their neighbours.' The head gardener of Knole captained Kent against All England in 1746, the team including his employer's son Lord John Sackville, father of the Duke of Dorset who tried to introduce the game to Paris. The Dukes of Richmond played with servants and tenants; one of them, a Governor-General of Canada who fought a duel with the Grand Old Duke of York, had played for Surrey. The gentry, however, preferred batting to bowling, and around 1850 the exclusive I Zingari Club was refusing to hire professionals merely to relieve richer players of this chore.

Anecdotes, however apocryphal, help distinguish flavours untasted by those seeking the impersonal and determinist. Cricket allows disparate temperaments to join in competitive unity, outside politics and, often, class, but well within everyday habits.

The game produced personalities still remembered. James Dean would bowl at one end, then keep wicket at the other. The patrician Lord Harris selected his team for Australia, grandly forgetting its need for a wicket-keeper. He could have invited an amateur keeper, Queen Victoria's grandson, Prince Albert Ludwig Ernest Anton Christian Victor of Schleswig-Holstein. The founder of modern English cricket was the Victorian W.G. Grace, of Gloucestershire, all-round sportsman, who captained England at cricket and bowls, and once left a cricket match to win a foot race, then returned. He was a doctor, too, but when a patient desperately knocked at his door: 'Is the Doctor in?' 'Yes, of course he's in. He was Not Out last night and was still batting at lunch.' No addict of English ironic understatement, a deprecator of books, Grace drew no fine line between sharp practice and adolescent exuberance, though an old professional expostulated at suggestions of dishonesty. 'The Old Man cheat? No, sir, never. He was too clever for that.' One legend is typical. Grace was captain against a university team. The day was very hot, and Grace had no wish to field first. He loomed up, huge, bearded, resourceful, before the young and respectful undergraduate. 'Better toss, eh? I'll call. *Monkey.*' The coin rose, glittered, fell. Grace scarcely glanced at it. 'Ah, yes, *Monkey*. We'll bat.'

Rules could be slapdash. William Midwinter played for Australia in 1876–7, for England in 1881–2, for Australia in 1886–7. His biographers add: 'Half-way through the 1878 tour of England, he was persuaded (by Grace) to leave the touring party and appear for Gloucestershire.' *Persuaded* might have been amplified.

Cricket was, nevertheless, associated with ethics: 'Playing the Game', 'Fair Play', 'A Straight Bat', 'It's not Cricket'. A novel, *Baxter's Second Innings* (1892), asserts that 'Life is simply a cricket match – with Temptation as the Bowler.' In her biography of Evelyn Waugh, Selina Hastings quotes a letter from Arthur Waugh to his other son, Alec, then a schoolboy, recommending that, if tempted to masturbate, he should think of cricket, of the day's game and of the probable team for next week. Gerard Manley Hopkins wrote, in a manner not associated with his maturity:

Where is the field I must play the man on?
O welcome there their steel or cannon.
Immortal beauty is death with duty
If under her banner I fall with honour.

The ideals of the Gentleman Amateur, and of the Sporting Spirit which prefers honourable defeat to tawdry triumph, were incorporated into the deaths in the Antarctic of Captain R.F. Scott and his companions, out-matched in a race to the Pole by the more professional Norwegian, Amundsen. Scott's last diary entry, on 29 March 1912, though unimaginable from the pen of Dr Grace and now easy to deride, appealed to British sto-icism: 'I do not think we can hope for better things now. We shall stick it out to the end, but we are getting weaker, of course, and the end cannot be far. It seems a pity, but I do not think I can write more. For God's sake look after our people.' Other passages were read aloud in British homes and schools, respectfully received in Europe: 'I do not regret this journey, which has shown that Englishmen can endure hardship, help one another, and meet death with as great a fortitude as ever in the past.'

Here was the ethos still recalled by such figures as Henty, Kipling, W.E. Henley, Rider Haggard, P.C. Wren, A.E.W. Mason: such words somehow made Amundsen's superior methods appear unsporting, particularly when people heard that the Norwegian had ordered the eating of his dogs. With Europe lurching imperceptibly towards catastrophic war, such noble unre-alism, the treatment of almost any activity from marriage to one's life's work as sport, carried dangers.

8

Towards the Somme

The optimism that filled the air of Bernard Shaw's London was as little justified as that of Croce's Naples or Bergson's Paris. It was the dusk of a civilization, which they mistook for the dawn of a new era.

Gerhard Masur

By now the Admiralty wireless whispers through the ether to the tall masts of ships, and captains pace their decks absorbed in thought. It is nothing. It is less than nothing. It is too foolish, too fantastic to be thought of in the twentieth century. Or is it fire and murder leaping out of the darkness at our throats, torpedoes ripping the bellies of half-awakened ships, a sunrise on a vanished naval supremacy, and an island well-guarded hitherto, at last defenceless? No, it is nothing. No one would do such things. Civilization has climbed above such perils. The interdependence of nations in trade and traffic, the sense of public law, the Hague Convention, Liberal principles, the Labour Party, high finance, Christian charity, common sense, have rendered such nightmares impossible. *Are you quite sure?*

Winston Churchill

In the late 1880s Liberalism and Fabianism appeared equipped to defuse discontent, and tackle foreign competition. Only Ireland was continually poised for violence, even civil war. Maude Gonne, W.B. Yeats's muse, scorned Victoria as 'The Famine Queen'. A Fenian 'Jubilee Address' began, with vicious sarcasm:

> Madam, you have done well! Let others with praise unholy,
>   Speech addressed to a woman who never breathed upon earth,
> Daub you over with lies or deafen your ears with folly,
>   I will praise you alone for your actual imminent worth.
> Madam, you have done well! Fifty years unforgotten
>   Pass since we saw you first, a maiden simple and pure;
> Now when every robber landlord, capitalist rotten,
>   Hated oppressors, praise you – Madam, we are quite sure!

Unlike Karl Marx, few British were inclined to march over corpses to attain a distant ideal. The Institutions, political, legal, social, were adapting to change without totally relinquishing the old. *Either–Or* was generally distrusted. Appearances had to reflect inner decorum. Prince Albert addressed the Prince of Wales in 1858:

> A gentleman does not indulge in careless, self-indulgent lounging ways such as lolling in armchairs or on sofas, slouching in his gait, or placing himself in unbecoming attitudes with his hands in his pockets . . . He will borrow nothing from the fashions of the groom or the gamekeeper, and whilst avoiding the frivolity and foolish vanity of dandyism, will take care that his clothes are of the best quality.

In 1912 Ben Guggenheim and his valet, standing starched and trim on the deck of the sinking *Titanic*, having changed into evening dress, announced, 'We've dressed in our best and are prepared to go down like gentlemen.'

Modesty and restraint were still respected, Conan Doyle writing that the monologue man, however clever, can never be a gentleman at heart. Restraint, though, could be overdone. J.S. Mill wrote of his father that he resembled almost all Englishmen in being ashamed of the signs of feeling and, 'by the absence of demonstration, starving the feelings themselves'. Marriages blighted by power-conflict, lovelessness, disillusion, silence, were not inventions of Tolstoy and Ibsen, Galsworthy and Lawrence. H.G. Wells described the civilisation around him as that of a sexual lunatic.

In rebellion, Havelock Ellis, Edward Carpenter, youngsters in progressive summer schools, queried sexual restrictions and emotional tepidity. Robert Skidelsky has suggested that the most striking revolution in the West has not been the socialist revolution that the Fabians wanted, but the sexual revolution they feared.

From 1760 the Crown, gradually though not continuously, was shedding political power; was looked on variously with reverence, indifference, and contemptuous anger. In 1776 Paine indicted it as the Master Fraud that sheltered all others. Fox protested it to be intolerable that one blockhead (George III) should have the power to do so much mischief. The Prince Regent, opening Parliament in 1817, had his coach pelted by crowds roused by 'Orator' Hunt and, as George IV, was an expensive and unpopular bigamist. William IV attracted more mirth than awe. *The Times* obituary of the bankrupt Grand Old Duke of York in 1827 was unexpectedly moderate, praising his kindliness and popularity, though adding that he had been what was termed a good liver. 'He liked wine – he loved play – and he had other tastes – unfortunately too often indulged in by men of all professions.' Greville in 1829 had no favourites: 'Good God, what a set they are! We talked about the Royal Family, and we agreed that the three kingdoms cannot furnish such a brood, so many and so bad, rogues, blackguards, fools and whores.'

Victoria and Albert made a curious pair, unglamorous beside Franz-Josef and Elizabeth, Napoleon III and Eugénie, though behind their official dignity ardent, even romantic. Victoria declared that her wedding night had been most gratifying and mysterious, Albert took care always to lose when playing chess with her during their first few years of marriage. He suffered public abuse as a drain on the Treasury, a German spy, prig, busybody. She was sensible, even far-sighted about education and, the mother of nine, deplored the ugliness of babies. Patron of Landseer, Tennyson, Mendelssohn, and enjoying drawings of nude males, she also warned her children against artists: 'You don't know where they have been.' Susceptible to gross flattery from the rakish Disraeli and Napoleon III – of whom the Goncourts wrote that his head seemed to have fallen between his shoulders from a great height – she also appreciated the coarser addresses of John Brown. Unpredictable, she supported Dreyfus, pleaded for humanity towards Indian mutineers and dismissed the Boers as 'a horrid people, cruel and overbearing'. In 1871, though emphatically insistent on her own prerogatives, she wrote to Theodore Martin about the need to check 'this mad, wicked folly of Women's Rights! . . . It is a subject which makes the Queen so furious that she cannot contain herself . . . Tennyson has some beautiful lines on the difference between men and women in *The Princess*. Woman would become the most hateful, heartless of human beings were she allowed to un-sex herself.' She rated highly the novels of Marie Corelli. Though conventionally pious, she disliked bishops and was impatient with cant, enscribing 'That is what I call twaddle' on the letter from a future archbishop, at Albert's death, telling her to remember that henceforth Christ would be her husband. Albert's death she once diagnosed as due to lack of 'pluck'.

Physically, unlike such contemporary rulers as Alexander II, Wilhelm I or Mr Lincoln, she was unimpressive. The French General Canrobert compared her to an untidy cabbage, while praising her military knowledge. Wagner called her a silly old frump, whose abdication was overdue. A Danish diplomat mentioned in 1879: 'I am agreeable to see that the Queen dances like a pot.' In the *Arts Gazette* in 1919, however, Shaw wrote that she had great decision of manner, a beautiful speaking voice, and carried herself extremely well.

> It was part of her personal quality that she was a tiny woman, and our national passion for telling lies on every public subject has led to her being represented as an overgrown monster. The sculptors seemed to have assumed that she inspired everything that was ugliest in the feminine fiction of her reign. Take Mrs Caudle, Mrs Gamp, Mrs Prig, Mrs Proudie, and make a composite statue of them, and you will have a typical memorial to Queen Victoria.

Victoria's popularity could be low, especially during her reclusive though well-endowed widowhood after Albert's death in 1861. *Reynolds News* assailed her in 1877 as 'a horse-leech', and she was mocked as 'Mrs John Brown'. But by the mid 1880s she had pulled herself together and Brown was dead. She re-entered the world on a tide of imperial sentiment which coincided with her own feelings about her country's rapidly accumulating possessions. The Golden Jubilee of 1887 loosed an outpouring of affection for her which continued to feed on itself until it reached little short of hysteria at the 1897 Diamond Jubilee.

Letters, conversations, anecdotes, reveal much common sense, contrariness, considerable ungraciousness, and indomitable personality. 'These are trying moments,' she wrote, 'and it seems to me a defect in our much-famed Constitution to have to part with an admirable govt: like Lord Salisbury's for no question of any importance, or any particular reason, merely on account of the number of votes.'

Nevertheless, R.C.K. Ensor considered her influence, based on the application of horse-sense to hard work, far above that of the vivacious but lazy Edward VII, and of her energetic but erratic grandson Wilhelm II, who telegraphed congratulations to Paul Kruger, Boer President of the Transvaal, after the defeat of the opportunistic incursion – known as the Jameson Raid – of some Britishers into his territory. 'As late as 1896 the incident of the Kruger telegram had illustrated the difference between the attainments of mother and son. The Prince of Wales's reaction was to join in the general indignation and call for "a severe snub". The Queen's was to compose a consummate letter to the Kaiser which no diplomat in history could have bettered. By the side of her ripeness in counsel and unruffled skill, her son's quality seemed that of a crude beginner.'

Prince Albert was under-valued, for being both foreign and un-English in manner and outlook, too professional. Practising sport only as a duty, he was politically astute, artistic, conscientious. Himself a composer, he too venerated Mendelssohn, and was an early connoisseur of Italian Primitives, presenting twenty-two to the National Gallery. His range of interests – artistic, scientific, sociological, diplomatic, philosophical – allowed Robert Rhodes James to compare him to Jefferson. Awkward with fox-hunting hearties, he had some humour. 'Richard Coeur de Cotton' he dubbed the Free Trader and Cotton Interest MP, Richard Cobden. Social reform engrossed him, though Shaftesbury had misgivings. 'The Prince is a literary character, I fear, with a turn for science: these tastes may lead him into very pernicious society.' Undeterred, Albert campaigned for workers' dwellings, model villages, savings banks, allotments, benefit societies; for schools and industrial training. His memoranda were voluminous: on the evils of military duels, the duties and limitations of bishops, on slavery, Cleopatra's Needle, the Royal Gallery frescoes, the renovation of Buckingham Palace, rewards for gallantry. As Chancellor he galvanised a drowsy, Classics-based Cambridge into accepting modern languages; was an active first President of the scientific Imperial College; was a founder of the Royal Society of Chemistry, and encouraged scientific agricultural methods. He dominated the Great Exhibition and, before his premature death in 1861, may have averted war with America. He had envisaged a peaceful, liberal, philosophic Prussia ruled by his son-in-law, whose death from cancer in 1888 after three months as German Emperor ushered in his grandson, the very different Kaiser Wilhelm II.

Parliament, Bureaucracy, Church, Law continued to evolve alongside the Crown, weathering frequent discord and scepticism. The Irish Famine, the Indian Mutiny, the Boer War did not result in permanent dislocation. Organised labour accepted constitutionalism, but Britain was still disfigured by the Two Nations, blatant even in 1939 when their involuntary rural hosts were appalled by the verminous clothes, poor teeth and skins, the language of urban child refugees. Victorian Forsytes too easily overlooked the pregnant skivvy in the canal.

Fabian socialism was aristocratic and patient, wishing to raise the masses to its own level, not sink itself further. The London School of Economics, adult education, parliamentary representation, union power would in time oust the Liberals as the motor of progress: infiltration into local government, law, even the Church, offered a better prospectus than any more exciting movements abroad. British socialism largely disengaged itself from beloved

Continental abstractions – 'The Proletariat', 'Class-War', 'The Revolution', 'The Red Dawn' – working for accessible improvements, not to destroy government but to become The Government. Attlee, a Fabian, less full-blooded than the great French demagogue Jaurès, nevertheless accomplished more, changing the lot of millions.

Two Fabians acquired world status, 'HG' and 'GBS', becoming Institutions themselves. Wells soon abandoned the Fabians, as he abandoned much else, including many women. 'A romancer spoilt by romancing,' Beatrice Webb remembered. Wells had no respect for her conviction that socialists should be respectable, and displeased two important Fabians by seducing their daughters. Always an individualist, he demanded fewer resolutions, more resolution.

> You cannot change the world, and at the same time not change the world. You will find socialists about, or at any rate men calling themselves socialists, who will pretend that this is not so, and who will assure you that some little jobbing about municipal gas and water is Socialism, and backstreet intervention between Conservative and Liberal is the way to the millennium. You might as well call a gas-jet in the lobby of a meeting-house the glory of God in heaven.

Chesterton reminisced: 'Whenever I met him, he seemed to me to be coming from somewhere rather than going anywhere. He always had been a Liberal, or had been a Fabian, or had been a friend of Henry James or Bernard Shaw. And he was so often nearly right that his movement irritated me, like the sight of somebody's hat being perpetually washed up by the sea and never touching shore.'

Though he enjoyed Great Houses, aristocratic ladies, Wells loathed the Institutions, advocating free love, world government, republicanism, atheism, and administration by scientifically-minded Platonic prefects. He loved games, but abhorred Playing the Game and the Team Spirit. He was mischievous, petty, large-minded, querulous, fun, always challenging, blazing away at anything in sight – Nationalism, Monarchy, Zionism, Catholicism, the Empire, the Party System – with a vituperation that entitled him to be vilified as cad, fascist, immoralist, anti-Semite, racist, male chauvinist, traitor. With the irresponsibility of genius he was, as he thought, betrayed by his own offshoots – the New Woman, the New Deal, the New Machiavelli, the Russian Revolution, the League of Nations, Mussolini, Science Fiction, the Century of the Common Man. His early titles were a clarion call to the world intellect, to the young, to the future: *The First Men in the Moon, A Modern Utopia, The Shape of Things to Come, The Research Magnificent, The New Republic, Anticipations, The Undying Fire, The Open Conspiracy, The Discovery of the Future, When the Sleeper Awakes, The New Accelerator, The War that will end War, The World Set Free, Men Like Gods, The Man Who Could Work Miracles.* In him were entwined Plato, Dickens, T.H. Huxley, Darwin.

In his first story, *The Time Machine*, Wells warned the literate world that civilisation could end in terrifying petrification, and he never ceased to exhort, insult, warn, reproach: 'Adapt or Perish', 'Learn or Suffocate', 'Unite or Collapse': 'Think globally'. Twice he was an unsuccessful Labour candidate for Parliament, and another of his titles may explain why: *Travels of a Republican Radical in Search of Hot Water*. No more than Shaw did he venerate the Common Man: both desired the Uncommon Man, for whom disease, poverty, crime were offensive to eye, nose and mind, and should be removed. His demands for a World Order saw abortive promise in the League of Nations, more substantially in the United Nations.

With a boozing reprobate for a father, and an uncle who thought himself the Holy Ghost, Shaw was different. Hard-working on committees, he served in local government, campaigning successfully for women's lavatories in north-west London. A gentlemanly charmer, with residues of Voltaire and Mr Punch, he incessantly taunted England, employing the nimble-witted privileges of licensed jester. Finally losing faith in Parliament, he also lost himself in admiration for his own Caesar, for Mussolini; with some reservations, for Hitler; and, unreservedly, for Stalin. With Irish opacity, he compared Hitler to a stage Bolshevik, Stalin to an English Gentleman.

GBS was more a 'character' than an effective fount of wisdom. Lenin dismissed him as a 'useful idiot'. A writer, Shaw considered, should discover what most needed saying, then say it with the utmost levity. In a solemn Fabian pamphlet of 1911 he suggested gassing incorrigible criminals. He too never ceased, more wittily than Wells, to harangue and irritate. His plays literally played with ideas, defusing any indignation in those he teased, berated, accused. Chesterton called him a tree with its roots in the air. Middle-class audiences from well-policed, well-armed Britain chuckled at his wit and departed undisturbed, having risked nothing by hearing or reading. Professional odd-men-out, sergeants in the socialist awkward squad, HG and GBS, while making fun of most of the world, made literacy, speculation, ideas, fun for a large part of the world.

Considered a saint by both Shaw and Yeats, William Morris (1834–96),

Old Marlburian, was communist, working capitalist; printer, book-designer, illustrator, calligrapher, painter; poet, novelist, journalist; public speaker, teacher; craftsman in wood, in glass; manufacturer, designer and weaver, of tapestry, carpets, tiles, wall-papers, furniture; a conservationist, a prophet, engrossed with attempts to educate working people, the philistine, the pig-stupid. In him met Scott and Keats, Carlyle, Ruskin, Rossetti, Proudhon, Marx. He strove to fuse literature and crafts and induce a sensibility of new standards, a new society in which riches meant not vulgar opulence but self-fulfilment. His name is still a synonym for the conjunction of idealism and practicality, beauty and utility, the nostalgic and programmatic, the passionate and fastidious; he was an exceptional individual within the collective, his further elements aligned with Kropotkin, Dickens, the Pre-Raphaelites, Cobbett. He was a visionary, for whom art and craft could transform industrial output from shoddiness to grace, a medievalist and futurist, author of *How We Live and How We Might Live*, a sworn enemy of the materialism corrupting the land, eroding the soul, humiliating the practitioner. Teaching was as vital to him as finding strange and alluring tints for a rug, as his superb edition of Chaucer, produced in collaboration with Burne-Jones: all were parts of a unity, a force to combat meanness, cruelty, sub-standards. Lord Londonderry's belief that 'not everyone is born to read and write' must have outraged him. He attempted to humanise the rigid, Teutonic schema of Marxism.

An extrovert, he loved English rain and the colour grey. He was an émigré from an often illusionary past, his imagination a compound of Albion, Scandinavian and Teutonic saga and myth, Icelandic harshness, medieval geste and ballad, the soft greens of Blatchford's *Merrie England*, near-Eastern austerity and Pre-Raphaelite brilliance, medieval cathedrals, the 'just price' and the guilds' insistence on a new member's presentation of a personal 'masterpiece'. He planned the Art Workers' Guild, urging that homes should be miniature universities and studios, helping redeem a polluted nation. Like Socrates, like Dickens, he believed that education, right knowledge, produced right people, since people instinctively demand the best: a conviction that sometimes faltered. He ransacked the past for examples to teach the present and confront not only Mrs Grundy but John Bull, though the title of his celebrated *News from Nowhere* was more apt than he may have thought.

Like Robert Owen, he disliked business failure: though championing Labour he did not eulogise his own employees, was infuriated by the slovenly, whining, apathetic, once hurling a clumsy workman into a vat of green dye. He was as wary of Institutions and the majority vote as were Shaw and Wells. Like Dickens, he felt Parliament a sham, a betrayer of the people: its reforms he associated less with Peel, Gladstone, Disraeli than with Bismarck. Like most of the great, he could be inconsistent. Disappointments, particularly after the shock of Black Sunday in 1887, threatened his energies: British socialism and trade-unionism remained stolidly in the Philistine van, but his English patchwork of romanticism, wishful thinking, philanthropy and seriousness never hardened into cynicism. He had to reconcile many contrasts. Nauseated by the profit-motive, his concerns depended on it: horrified by the rags and boils of the poor, he had to provide silks and settings for rich patrons. Like Gladstone and Dickens he strove to redeem prostitutes. His wife, an ostler's daughter, beautiful as a figure from a Rossetti painting, he painted as Guinevere, and then endured with magnanimity some of Arthur's marital tribulations. His struggles against mass-production failed, but much of him lingered, in his works, his beliefs in art and history as springboards for action, and in the necessity for individual independence in an era of standardised thought and of public opinion, in the socialism of a Tawney. Wilfrid Scawen Blunt, no socialist, thought him 'the most wonderful man I have ever known, unique in this, that he had no thought for anything or person, including himself, but only for the work in hand.'

Rural Institutions remained in place; neighbourliness and Big House perforce supplied the social services, while the Workhouse loomed as a perpetual threat; the Church confronted the indignant tithe-protester, and the tavern. Crafts still catered for diminished markets; not yet finally swamped by print, memory brooded over ancient wrongs, disasters, exploits, freaks, characters:

> Here Lyeth Thomas Pierce whom no man taught,
> Yet he in Iron, Brasse and Silver wrought.

Sentimentality was a later invention. Sherlock Holmes rebuked Watson's rhapsody on meadowland peace: 'The lowest and vilest alleys in London do not present a more dreadful record of sin than does this smiling and beautiful countryside.' Tennyson was more laconic:

An' I thowt 'twur the will o' the Lord,
But Miss Annie she said it wur drains.

In 1884, Lady Portsmouth showed Hardy where bastard babies had been drowned, almost until then. Men might still daily walk seven miles to work, and back. As neighbour, not as Queen, Victoria complained of an absentee Highland landlord ill-treating his tenants, which gave a Liberal politician the chance to say to her, 'Well, ma'am, you've admirably described a state of affairs whose existence in Ireland has made me a Home Ruler.' George Coleman in 1929 remembered his Norfolk childhood, when failing to raise his hat to the parson might lose the family its coal allowance from the railway. Fred Kitchen, dying in 1969, wrote of his youth on a Yorkshire farm: 'Hiring fairs! To me it always seemed a wretched business, especially for a lad of 13 or 14, to be taken like a calf to market and sold to the highest bidder.' But Flora Thompson's seemingly over-roseate memories of village life must have some validity: 'The community was largely self-supporting. Every household grew its own vegetables, produced its new-laid eggs and cured its own bacon. Jams and jellies, wines and pickles were made at home as a matter of course. Most gardens had a row of beehives . . . even the poor enjoyed a rough plenty.' *Beehives* recall a belief reminiscent of Albion that bees are always the first informed of a villager's death.

The ancient cycles still prevailed: Monday washing, Tuesday baking, Plough Monday, Candlemas, Shrove Tuesday, All Fools' Day, Easter, St George's Day, Whitsun, Midsummer, Lammas, Harvest . . . later joined by Empire Day, and Armistice Day. An Islington mother, when asked in 1995 by her daughter, during the Two Minutes' Silence on the last, why no one was talking, explained: 'It's to remind the world that the aristocracy sent the working classes to die for them.'

A feature of the village – and the town, for that matter – was the Parson, often what Wodehouse terms a stately procession of one, supposedly above Class or Party. Absence of 'enthusiasm', spiritual intensity, after the Restoration could benefit local goodwill, appealing, if not to the soul, at least to the charitable conscience, suggesting that good living need not be godly living, that aimlessness was un-Christian. The Parson, as against pastor, minister, elder, was an English compromise between mysticism, austerity intolerant or intolerable, and jovial or reclusive bone-laziness.

Literary men, scholars, indigent younger sons, unfulfilled geniuses, could be slid into livings by private patrons. Tennyson's father was forced into holy orders to save the family estates from his incompetence. The parson's social standing could be ambiguous, often midway between the gentleman and the upstart farmer or lawyer, his own personality the final determinant of how often he was invited to dine at the Big House or town mansion. Within village life, Thomas Hinde adjudicates,

> Taken as a whole, country parsons suggest some sociological experiment: give a reasonably-educated middle-class Englishman a modest income, a house in the country, and job security for life, and see what he will do. He does remarkable things; he invents a theory of history which makes the Druids a tribe of Phoenicean pre-Christian Christians; he plants 5,000 roses in his garden and the surrounding countryside, runs his own foxhound pack, makes his rectory into a monastery, collects folk-songs, breeds winning race-horses or green mice, rides from Land's End to John o'Groats.

Much can be added for a catalogue of ordained worthies. John Skelton, Henry VIII's Laureate, venomously satirical against Wolsey, was poignant and tender in religious verse, and grandly exhibited his bastard baby from the pulpit. William Lee devised a mechanical stocking-frame, though dying in want in 1610. Dr Dodd, Royal Chaplain, linguist, compiler of *Thoughts in Prison* and *The Beauties of Shakespeare*, whose translations introduced the latter to a number of undiscerning Germans, was hanged for forgery in 1777, despite a growling plea from Johnson. Among parsons were Sydney Smith, George Herbert, Robert Herrick, Laurence Sterne, George Crabbe, Charles Kingsley, Andrew Young, R.S. Thomas. There were Marxists, like Conrad Noel who flaunted the Red Flag above Thaxted Church, and Hewlett Johnson who advertised Stalin's Russia as 'that new and richer freedom that all the world's great minds looked for and prayed for'. Francis Kilvert's famous diary logs a frog-woman; Sabine Baring-Gould of Lew Trenchard was essayist, novelist, mythologist, folk-lorist, anthropologist, historian, travel-writer and authority on Devonshire churches: he wrote 'Onward, Christian Soldiers', and investigated 3,600 saints, many imaginary. Hugh Eyton-Jones preached at Cowes in 1972 on 'British Sea-Power Decisive in Recent Wars'.

Physical prowess was not neglected. J.H. Parsons, E.T. Killick, D.S. Shepherd were notable cricketers; K.R.G. Hunt played in the 1908 Cup Final. James Adams won the VC in Afghanistan; J. Bradford roamed the countryside seeking someone to wrestle with. William Wilkes of Shirley spent a decade perfecting the Shirley Poppy. Elisha Fawcett, dying in the Admiralty Islands, had his wooden leg buried with him; it took root, and gave abundant material for cricket bats. Harold Davidson, of Stiffkey, was known as the Prostitutes' Padre; ejected from his parish he was prosecuted for obstructing the highway, financed his costs by exhibiting himself at fairs in a barrel, then in a glass-topped coffin. Defrocked, assaulted, he made public fasts, was unsuccessfully charged with attempting suicide, addressed crowds from the lions' cage in a circus before fatally allowing a lion the last word.

Theological niceties could be inexact. A Victorian cleric jibbed at embarking on HMS *Infernal* but accepted HMS *Destruction*. Nevertheless, the saintly are recorded amid the humdrum or bizarre. John Stevens Henslow of Hitcham championed many popular rights. Once Cambridge Professor of Botany, admired by Darwin, in 1837 he found Hitcham in Suffolk famous for violence, arson, harassment of rectors, sheep-stealing. He cured this by fostering local pride, founding a school, clubs, allotments, against landowners' opposition, and transforming village shows into great social occasions. What Britain absorbed from pre-1914 pulpits and ceremonies is hard to fathom. Many parsons must have respected Christ's ethic but, in the age of Darwin, Huxley, Spencer, German Higher Thought, Comte . . ., dispensed with supernatural dogma. Hardy's 'God's Education' has God muttering:

> Forsooth, though I men's master be,
> Theirs is the teaching mind.

General Baden-Powell's Scout Movement was one attempt to reconcile town and country, rich and poor, less militaristic than Continental youth organisations but unlikely to recruit a young Shaw, Wells, Russell, Churchill, Asquith. It was Baden-Powell's response to his open-air adventures in India, Afghanistan, West and South Africa, his witness of endurance of disease and famine while he defended Mafeking against the Boers. He judged there was a flaccidity among British civilians, believing, as Kipling wrote:

> That the sunshine of England is pale,
> And the breezes of England are stale.
> An' there's somethin' gone small with the lot.

To withstand class divisions, undernourishment and dirty streets breeding socialism, strikes, atheism, vice, the General began his movement for boys (later for girls) in 1907, and it expanded throughout the Empire and beyond. He wanted a scout to be, like Kipling's Kim, a 'friend to all the world . . . friends don't fight each other'. Scouting collected the last shreds of Chivalry and the Gentleman, 'Honour and Courtesy', with team spirit, hierarchical order, 'Fear God and Honour the King', respect for Nature, practical skills, resourcefulness, truthfulness. The oath to be Clean in Thought, Word and Deed was, predictably, rescinded in 1966. Scouting, whatever its actual influence, was thought to be of such stature that dictators banned it.

Undernourishment was the fault of short commons, not of English cooking, stable as the alphabet, equivalent in foreign esteem to the English Sunday, and associated with underdone beef, boiled mutton, rainy cabbage, soggy potatoes, suet, steak pies, and rancid game. 'The worst part', Zola lamented, 'is their recipes: for a French person, they spoil everything.' Belated praise came in 1980 from Kenneth Lo, Chinese diplomat, tennis champion, author, restaurateur, chef, who loved English pork pies, bread-and-butter pudding, sausages with mustard, and 'an outstanding culinary invention', bubble-and-squeak.

British drinking habits also had a European-wide reputation. King Edgar ordained standardised measurements in 875 to curb excess, probably ineffectively. The Red Lion or Dog and Pheasant are as rooted as the Abbey. 'The Tippling Philosophers' was a favourite melody of Jane Austen's. Crabbe saluted the pub:

> All the comforts of life in a tavern are known,
> 'Tis his home who possesses not one of his own.

Hardy's *Far from the Madding Crowd* nets the unctuous English habit of reconciling physical appetite with morality:

'Of course you'll have another drop. A man's twice the man afterwards. You feel so warm and glorious, and you whop and slap at your work without any trouble, and everything gives on like sticks-a-breaking. Too much liquor is bad and leads us to that horned man in the smoky house; but after all, many people haven't the gift of enjoying a wet, and since we be highly favoured with a power that way, we should make the best o't.'

'True,' said Mark Clarke. ''Tis a talent the Lord has mercifully bestowed upon us, and we ought not to neglect it. But what with the parson and clerks and school-people and serious tea-parties, the merry old ways of good life have gone to the dogs – upon my carcase, they have!'

Towards the Somme

Pubs could be unwelcoming, exclusive, quarrelsome, violent. Until recently their Public Bar, Saloon Bar, Private Bar, Snug, Coffee Room reflected strict divisions of class and purse, and the English love of forming clubs. But they did give outlets for the social cement of gossip, yarning, scandal-mongering, news, their atmosphere dependent on the host's personality. In Bethnal Green is buried a Victorian publican who was also a protection-racketeer, brothel-keeper, churchwarden, promoter of dog-fights and bullock-hunts; a human envelope of crossed wires. His was one of the nine thousand pubs enlivening Victorian London.

Taverns spawned yet another, though shorter-lived, Institution, the music-hall: open to all generations, classes, sexes, most temperaments, a sanctuary of Old England, ribald liberties, lost causes, and bad taste. Part of the culture of brass bands, piers, children's 'comics', vulgar postcards, the music-hall covered the common lot of crime, distress, satire, physical oddity; its repertoire embraced Jingoistic patriotic songs, Dickensian sketches, sub-literary monologues, political lampoons, stock jokes about lodgers, parsons, Jewish moneylenders, Scots misers, mothers-in-law, viragos. Women impersonated men, clowns sublimated pain and grief, and aroused the mirth which Hobbes defined as sudden glory at the sight of an inferior.

'The halls' originated in eighteenth-century tavern back-rooms, evolving into separate theatres, bars still essential, and a promenade for sexual transactions. Gold and crimson splendours parodied the Baroque, the Oriental. Dickens, Kipling, Max Beerbohm, T.S. Eliot, even the severe Wittgenstein, were fans. Churchill maintained that his first public speech had been at the Empire, Leicester Square, protesting against a female prude's attempt to 'purge our Music-Halls'. For the young James Joyce, 'the music hall, not poetry, is a criticism of life'. John Masefield enjoyed

> Don't put your feet in the port wine, Joe,
> There's plenty of stale old beer.

Here were trained the balletic inventive genius of Chaplin, the simpler, perhaps purer art of Stan Laurel, the thoroughly impure charm of Marie Lloyd and Max Miller. Patronage by the Prince of Wales, later Edward VII, overcame some reservations of the snobbish, themselves zestfully teased:

> How d'ye like the la-di-dah, the toothpick an' the crutch?
> How d'ye get those trousers on, an' did they hurt you much?

John Bull could rout Mrs Grundy and Sabbath gloom with mockery of hypocrisy, class affectations, loose-living statesmen. Artistes were rueful, self-mocking, maudlin, steeped in innuendo, targeting the pompous, the aesthetic, the sanctimonius, fully appreciating the Idle Apprentice and St Monday.

> On Monday I never go to work,
> On Tuesday I stay at home,
> On Wednesday I don't feel inclined,
> Work's the last thing on my mind.
> Thursday's a half-holiday
> And Friday I detest,
> Too late to make a start on Saturday,
> And Sunday is my day of rest.

Gus Elen, in 'It's a Great Big Shame', mused over the trials, real or imagined, of Jim, six foot three, henpecked by his four foot two wife. In joyous chorus, all could telescope a distant, almost mythical figure into the everyday:

> I'm 'Enery the Eighth, I am,
> 'Enery the Eighth I am, I am.
> I got married to the widow next door,
> She's bin married seven times before.
> Every one was a 'Enery,
> She wouldn't have a Willy or a Sam.
> I'm 'er eighth old man named 'Enery,
> I'm 'Enery the Eighth, I am.

The parade of comics, singers, dancers, acrobats, performing seals, conjurers, ventriloquists has subsided, bequeathing Champagne Charlie, Burlington Bertie, One of the Ruins that Cromwell Knocked abaht a Bit, My Old Dutch, Mary from the Dairy, the Man who Broke the Bank at Monte Carlo. They were sung by singers with reddened noses, blackened faces, gilded hair, sparkling tights, tinsel jackets; singers in kilts, in tattered shawls, with glittering monocles, with shimmering hats; singers with gigantic voices, or ones worn to a hoarse rattle. One voice could enrapture the multitude, another invite a gale of hoots, bad eggs, cabbage stalks. Performer and audience were in familiar intimacy with the grandiloquent chairman or watchful orchestra conductor striving to assure equilibrium.

In song, superior hopes might be toppled, violent turnabouts endured, with gleams of wistful dignity, a flake of barely remembered lyricism, or the indomitable acceptance of a bad job.

> He only fought a round or two, an' he felt queer,
> And his teeth were missing an' 'alf an ear.
> Lying in the gutter, blind to the world,
>   That's where Love lies Bleeding.

Humour, Freud was teaching – what Euripides, Plautus, Shakespeare had already demonstrated – is easily first of the methods of self-defence. Crowding the halls, the British poor scoffed at lordly rituals, but also accepted deprivation and injustice with a wry shrug, a lewd joke, with some of the grinning fortitude of a plumber during a freeze-up, an attitude which, for better or worse, mitigated class antagonisms and even some of the horrors of war. National animosities were neutralised.

'Wot's diff'rent between Irish and Welsh?'
'Irish know between Right and Wrong but prefer Wrong: Welsh don't know the diff'rence!'

Topical comment was not neglected, ribald, sardonic or raucously patriotic. In 1910, all England knew that Mrs Belle Crippen, a minor music-hall singer, wife of a London doctor, had been killed by her husband and buried in their coal cellar. Crippen and his lover Ethel le Neve, disguised as a boy, fled to America, but in vain; Crippen was caught and swiftly hanged, and audiences cheered lustily at

> O Miss Le Neve, O Miss Le Neve,
> Is it true that you are sittin'
> On the lap of Doctor Crippen
> In your boy's clothes,
> On the *Montrose*,
>   Miss Le Neve?

Resonances quivered with 'Only a Violet Plucked from my Mother's Grave', heard sung on her last night alive by 'Marie-Jeannette' Kelly in 1888, last victim of another Londoner of international standing, hero of European opera, verse, fiction – Jack the Ripper. An occasional Edwardian song, heard in an old folks' home or decayed pub, can still stir:

Sunlight may teach me forgetting,
    Noonlight bring thoughts that are new;
Twilight brings sighs and forgetting,
    Moonlight brings sweet dreams of you.

Changing tastes and media destroyed the last halls after 1950. John Osborne uttered their requiem in *The Entertainer* (1957): 'The Music Hall is dying, and with it a significant part of England has gone, something that once belonged to everyone, for this was truly a folk-art.'

The music-hall had thrived on national affection for the outsize, the vulnerable, the eccentric. Dickens has been rebuked for inventing caricatures rather than characters but, a great journalist, he knew how to use his eyes and ears. Standardisation resulting from education and cheap print had not decimated the oddities visible on every street, in any village: Squire Waterton riding a crocodile and designing a stable-yard for horses to exchange talk; Dr Porson, mighty scholar, wearing brown paper on his nose and drinking ink. Dickens noticed a teacher wearing onions in his ears; Lady Cardigan, widow of the Light Brigade commander, had tenants buried upright so that their graves should provide jumps for her when she was out riding. At Hubbersholme, a man insisted on his wife and himself being buried with a stream flowing between them. Gordon, besieged in Khartoum, shared his plate with a mouse. An Oxford Vice-Chancellor and official of the University Press, in one version, embezzled the profits of an edition of Clarendon's *History* and, to help him meet the repayments, was made Professor of Divinity.

Consistency was not a pronounced English failing; Richard Burton loved animals and with his wife Isabel started an SPCA outpost in India, yet enjoyed cock-fighting: explorer, geologist, botanist, erratic Imperial official, an authority on bayoneting, falconry and farting, he had himself circumcised to complete his disguise as an Arab when pursuing Islamic culture. When a Doctor Bird inquired how he felt after killing a man, he retorted: 'Quite jolly, Doctor. How do you?' Engrossed with dervishes and sufis, deserts and secret cities, bazaars and brothels, he was mocked as 'the white nigger', but for Arabs, after his pilgrimage to Mecca, he was Hajj Abdullah. He translated Catullus and Camoëns; his racy and accurate version of *The Arabian Nights* has not been superseded by Isabel's edition, 'Prepared for household reading'.

Like Dickens, Fry, Nightingale, the Anglo-Irish Conan Doyle championed the declining belief that resolute amateurs could effect social change. His defence of unpopular legal victims was in part instrumental in establishing the Court of Criminal Appeal. He was President of the Divorce Law Reform Union. He defended Sir Roger Casement, hanged for supplying German arms to Irish rebels in 1916: Casement, like himself, had earlier publicised Belgian Congolese atrocities, and the brutality towards Mayans of British and European South American rubber cartels. Doyle himself had served on the Congo Reform Association which exposed King Leopold's hangings and mutilations, and impelled E.D. Morel to write the powerful *The Black Man's Burden*. Doyle quixotically, eloquently, though foolishly, pleaded for the captain of the *Titanic*, against the caustic anger of Joseph Conrad and George Bernard Shaw, to such effect that an editorial suggested right-thinking Englishmen would prefer to be wrong with Sir Arthur than right with Mr Shaw. His amateur spiritualism enticed him into being gulled by a faked photograph of two fairies. He was creator of Brigadier Gerard, Professor Challenger; of Sherlock Holmes, whose methods influenced those of the French and Egyptian police. Like many contemporaries – A.E.W. Mason, Rider Haggard, Buchan – he easily mixed private hobbies with public concerns, good humour with good causes. He promoted Norwegian skiing in Switzerland, played cricket for the MCC, football for Portsmouth, was a heroic doctor in the Boer War, and in the Great War urged a reluctant War Office to adopt the steel helmet and mechanical caterpillar.

Aubrey Herbert and C.B. Fry – Classicist, English cricket captain who, casually, broke the world long jump record, a feat which then stood for two decades – are the only Englishmen known to have refused the Albanian crown. Herbert once dropped from a tree onto a tea-party 'because I was ripe'. In 1914, rejected for the army because of his near-blindness, he purchased a uniform and mingled unnoticed among Irish Guards as they marched to the embarkation train. Later in the war he used his fluent Turkish to negotiate with the enemy from the trenches at Gallipoli to enable both sides to bury their dead. An MP, he risked his career by supporting General Maurice's accusation that Lloyd George had lied to the Commons about British defeats and casualties, telling indignant members and constituents that on certain occasions he chose to behave as a gentleman. John Buchan wrote in 1923 that Herbert 'was the most delightful and brilliant survivor from the days of chivalry . . . the most extraordinary combination of sweetness and gentleness with insane gallantry that I have ever known. I drew Sandy in *Greenmantle* from him.' General Sir Archibald

Hunter, 'Kitchener's Sword-Arm', a hero of the Sudan, Egypt, South Africa, retired after four years in the Commons, because he wanted to die an honest man.

English history is a lengthy process of immigration and integration, with a counterpoint of emigration. A graffito once scrawled on the American Embassy in London read: 'Remember, Yanks, if it wasn't for us you'd all have been Spanish.' Medieval immigration was constant. Matthew Paris, in his *Chronica Magna*, wrote of Henry III:

> At this time the King daily, and not just slowly, lost the affection of his natural subjects. For like his father [John], he openly attracted to his side whatever foreigners he could and enriched them, introducing aliens and despoiling Englishmen . . . and so in England there arose many kings to carry off carts and horses, food and cloths and all necessities. Moreover, the Poitevins occupied themselves in oppressing the nobles of the land and especially the monks in a thousand ways.

Henry III was a discerning and spendthrift lover of European styles, an artistic patron, enlarger of Westminster Abbey in Anglo-French Gothic. His French poets helped beflower the English lyric, religious and secular, French fashions elaborated heraldic design, fusing the clannish and boastful with the mythological and ornate. Henry's tastes were repeated by Edward II, lover of the Gascon Piers Gaveston, 'sweet brother Piers', though Edward I had shown a xenophobic streak in expelling the Jews in 1290.

Civilisation results from cultural interchange, and Britain owes much to immigration. Hans Holbein and Anthony Van Dyck transformed English portraiture. Van Dyck's master, Rubens, extolling the new Stuart line, gave the Banqueting House in Whitehall a painted ceiling of baroque grandeur which, accepted too personally, perhaps nudged them towards tragedy.

Henry Bessemer, whose innovations underlaid Victorian prosperity, was French-born, as was Isambard Kingdom Brunel; Pugin, contriver of the multitudinous Gothicisms of the Houses of Parliament, was son of a French émigré. The Dutchman Vermuyden added many square miles to England by draining the Fenlands, though he failed in the Somerset Levels. Wilde had Dutch forbears, as had Betjeman. Germans were influential among medieval English armourers, pioneered Tudor industrialism in mining, iron, brass, and served as mercenaries in the French and American wars. Alfred

Milner, British imperialist, 'almost an ideal' to John Buchan, was of German stock. Sickert's father was Danish. The Italian Gabriele Rossetti, father of Christina and Dante Gabriel, settled in England, teaching, painting, talking. Sebastian Ferranti, of Venetian descent, built the first British power-house, gave London electricity.

Flemings were arriving in the fourteenth century, quickly establishing themselves at Southwark as weavers, painters, glaziers, brass-engravers, masons, sculptors, and in land-management. Deeply musical, they were able constructors of all stringed instruments, and elaborated the fifteenth-century madrigal. As portraitists, they were foremost in Tudor courts. Welcome was stingy. 'The English', Froissart attested, 'are affable to no nation but their own.' Fierce professional competition contributed to the massacre of London Flemings in 1381, remembered by Chaucer as akin to a fox-hunt. A plot to mutilate and kill Southwark Flemings was frustrated in 1468.

More Flemish Walloons, Dutch and French Protestants, 'Huguenots', escaped to English from French and Spanish Terror, numbering some four thousand in Norwich by 1570. Colchester still has its 'Dutch quarter'; a Flemish dialect developed in Kent. Again, benefits were substantial. French and Dutch engravers gave Stuart coinage a finer cut. Engineers – Salomon de Caus – transformed English gardens with fountains, artificial pools and waterfalls. Huguenots were active in glassware, textiles, paper-making. Led by Burghley, the Privy Council recognised their value, planting settlements in Canterbury, Colchester, Norwich, according to local needs – and restricting their size. They attracted some religious sympathies; charity, Royal and private, was generous; the last Huguenot pensioner died in 1874.

Terror resumed under the bigoted Louis XIV, followed by sporadic persecutions, Huguenots fleeing, sometimes with infants hidden in donkey-panniers and hogsheads. About fifty thousand reached England between 1670 and 1810, their craft secrets and European contacts helping the Anglo-French trade balance in England's favour, particularly in clock-making, carpets, silks, velvets, calico, soap. They introduced rainproof hats and oxtail soup. They were foremost librarians and etymologists. Their silk market at Charing Cross received considerable support from Nell Gwynne:

> All matters of state from her soul she doth hate,
> And leaves to the politic bitches.
> The whore's in the right for 'tis her delight
> To be scratching just where it itches.

Recognising his mistake, Louis vainly despatched agents to London to bribe, blackmail or scare the exiles into repatriation. By 1800 the red hats of Vatican cardinals were made by Wandsworth Huguenots. Seven Huguenots were among the original twenty-four directors of the Bank of England, and there were sixty-five Huguenot members of the House of Commons between 1734 and 1832. They were early promoters of English insurance. William III's troops in Portugal were commanded by Henri de Massue de Ruvigny, Earl of Galway; at the Boyne he commanded Irish, English, Danes, Norwegians, Italians, Swiss, French, Germans, Huguenots organised by his senior General, a German, facing James II's army commanded by a Frenchman. Another Huguenot, Field-Marshal Jean-Louis, Earl Ligonier, was cavalry commander under Marlborough, and led infantry at Fontenoy; Admiral James Gambier, a Lord of the Admiralty, commanded the Channel Fleet in 1807. Huguenot blood ran in Garrick, Sydney Smith, Samuel Courtauld, the Nobel physicist E.D. Adrian, and Henry Tizard, whose researches in radar and thermodynamics helped save civilisation from Hitler. Sheridan Le Fanu, Harriet Martineau, Walter de la Mare, Roget, F.R. Leavis – all these are Huguenot names. B.J.T. Bosanquet upset English cricket by inventing the 'googly', a slyly deceptive delivery.

Onwards from the Regency, a swarm of illustrious Continentals, many of them Jewish, illuminated British culture and benefited the economy: Conrad, Ford, Belloc, Vinogradoff, Richter, Hallé, Delius, Barbirolli, Gerhardie, Namier, Popper, Hayek, Berlin, Ayer, Korda, Gombrich, Mayer, Elton, Pevsner, Dahrendorf, Kedourie, Hobsbawm. The actor Leslie Howard, quintessential Englishman in wartime patriotic films, was Hungarian. Cromwell had first sanctioned the return of the Jews who prospered in the succeeding centuries.

Nineteenth-century British merchant banks of global import were galvanised by Europeans and Americans; Rothschilds, Barings, Brandts, Lazards, Warburgs, Schroders, Hambros, Morgans. British science was impregnated by a Mond, Brunner, Lindemann, and many refugees worked at crucial, cipher-breaking Bletchley Park, its most essential machine smuggled from Poland; others sat on the Maude Committee, making Britain an atomic power.

In Victoria's time Chinese, Lascars, Jews, Slavs, Italians crowded the East End of London, more leisured exiles and voyagers the West. From Soho, Orsini assembled his bombs to murder Napoleon III: 'The risks of our trade,' the Emperor murmured to his wife, both blood-bespattered amid the surrounding carnage. This aborted a Channel Tunnel plan, approved of by Napoleon, Albert and Victoria. Londoners rapturously greeted Garibaldi and Kossuth. Mazzini was intimate with the Carlyles. Herzen and Kropotkin came from Russia. Marx attended the 1st International, in Greek Street; Lenin, at revolutionary congresses, mostly in Charlotte Street, conferred with Trotsky, Martov, Plekhanov, Vera Zasulich, Gorky and Stalin; studied at the British Museum almost alongside Masefield. Shaw admired Kropotkin as much as he did Morris: prince and anarchist, the Russian advocated the mutual aid he had observed in animals, and indeed in English history, as against Marxist one-party dictatorship, while idealising the Jacobin terrorist Marat. Though mass immigration from Eastern Europe prompted a restrictive Act in 1905, Herzen wrote that 'In England the policeman at your door adds a feeling of security', and the Marxist capitalist Engels, himself of German origin, admitted: 'England is the only country which has never expelled a refugee, and where juries have never let themselves be dictated to by a foreign despot.'

From 1850 Britain's artistic and intellectual ferment quickened. Towering physicists like James Chadwick and J.J. Thomson were uncovering the patterns of matter. Faraday's electronic studies prepared to transform the entire world, as Lenin readily understood. W.T. Kelvin pioneered laws of thermodynamics, introduced underwater cables, a magnetically-protected compass, a quadrant electrometer. From the time of James Lind's revolutionary discovery in 1753 of fruit juice as a cure for scurvy, scourge of sailing, diseases were being overcome, populations expanding, through such men as Lister, with his great work on antiseptics; Ross and his discovery of the mosquito's role in malaria; and Jenner's vaccinations against smallpox. No region was exempted from objective scrutiny. Geology was undermining Biblical accounts of Creation, forcing the mind to examine millions of years of evolution. T.H. Huxley described God as a 'gaseous invertebrate', then Freud's disciple, Ernest Jones, analysed the Holy Ghost, which proved to be the sublimated sensation of infantile flatus.

All this did not, however, induce a general scientific consciousness. Science seemed vaguely un-English, enthusiasm for its enthralling promise that everything could be discovered, nothing was forbidden, something best left to the Germans. Prince Albert's death removed a very considerable official support.

Until the 1920s print was not rivalled by cinema or radio. Writers were supreme, but few were scientifically inclined, and only Wells, Conan Doyle and Kipling positively acclaimed science: railway engines and steamships, astro-physics and telepathy were enthralling clues to a novel romanticism, a purposeful awareness. But they were not hypnotised into facile optimism about Progress. Wells, not only in *The Time Machine* but in a fearful picture of misapplied science in *The Island of Dr Moreau*, warned against it: Kipling wondered whether, 'when Rome began to flop, her people had reached our stage of possessing most of the emotions and few of the capacities'.

Yet for many in late-Victorian Britain, capacities seemed limitless; the future was ascertainable, exciting; humanity was getting a grip on Nature. Disease was vanishing, engineering could bridge the widest river, the City guaranteed peace, the Empire was quiescent, a generation of schooling would abolish ignorance and satisfy curiosity. A phial here, a lens there would eliminate mystery, illuminate the dark corners.

For others, members of a country at root conservative, territorially surfeited, slow-moving though not slow-witted, the new could be disconcerting. Science was undermining the reassurances derived from a personal God susceptible to small prayers, willing to change the weather or provide cake, and unlock the Other World. Doubts about free will were majestically delineated in Hardy's *The Dynasts*, reducing Napoleonic pyrotechnics to the blunderer caught in timeless and unknowable cosmic processes.

Atheism offered a bracing but bleak alternative. Slightly preferable to it was the impersonal but pliable Life Force, 'Creative Evolution', propounded by Nietzsche, Lamarck, Schopenhauer, Shaw, with variations. Capable of clumsy mistakes like Neanderthal Man, succeeding with a Jesus or Buddha, a Leonardo or Goethe, it demanded assistance from human genetic control, medicine, tribal responsibility and will. It had been conceived by Classical thinkers, acknowledged by Alexander Pope, enunciated by Berkeley as a pure spirit or invisible fire present throughout Earth and Cosmos. The soul could be reinterpreted as consciousness surviving through the genes, plasmic metamorphosis; conscience as the outcome of clan training, or biological survival tactics.

Orthodox religion, Other World premises, might be quickened by intellectual challenge or continue, sluggish and defensive, expert in a narrowing dimension. Another avenue, unwelcome to most churches, was spiritualism, justifying the establishment of the Society for Psychical Research in 1882. Its membership included such respectable names as William James and Oliver

Lodge, though its seances, with mediums and unappetising fluids in dark-ened rooms, were generally inconclusive, occasionally startling, sometimes fraudulent though hilarious.

Further conclusions emanated from belief in the survival of the fittest, evolutionary theories commandeered by practical 'Social Darwinism'. Eurocentric admiration for achievements in science, art, politics, colonisa-tion fortified theories of Natural Selection in which the weaker were super-seded by the healthier. Thus Britain, Prussia, America, the strongest Great Powers, best merited survival. Race was thought vital to evolution, certain races being relegated as lost causes. Carlyle espoused this and, following a Jamaican rising in 1865, concluded in *The Nigger Question* that Natural Law showed work-shy blacks had no rights to sustenance, but an indisputable right to work competently. Cecil Rhodes ascribed imperial triumphs in Africa to White virtues, primarily to those of 'God's Englishman'. Joseph Chamberlain, Imperialist statesman, believed that of all known governing races, the British were the best. Ruskin informed youth that the English were still undegenerate in race, compounded of the richest northern blood. He thought it urgent for civilisation that 'the British Race' should colonise everywhere possible. Richard Burton wrote of the African: 'He seems to belong to one of those child-like races which, never rising to Man's estate, fall like worn-out links from the great chain of animated Nature.' Samuel Baker, another African explorer, told compatriots: 'However we may condemn the horrible system of slavery, the results of emancipation have proved that the negro does not appreciate the blessings of freedom, nor does he show the slightest gratitude to the hand that broke the rivets of his fetters.'

T.H. Huxley, a leading western scientist, champion of Darwin, mentor of Wells, deplored the native Australians as 'hopeless, irreclaimable savages, whose elimination from the earth's surface can be viewed only with satisfac-tion as the removal of a great blot from the escutcheon of our common humanity.' Trollope agreed: 'Of the Australian black man we may certainly say he has to go. That he should perish without unnecessary suffering should be the aim of all those concerned with the matter.' Arnold of Rugby earlier deplored genocide in Tasmania, where five pounds were paid for a dead adult, two pounds for a child, because natives 'worried sheep'. Cook had found them trustful and gentle, their wars ceasing at the first fatality. Victorian settlers clubbed them to death, hurled them against rocks; they castrated, beheaded, hanged.

Kipling, in contrast, often exalted Indians above white missionary bigots, ignorant MPs, snobbish and prejudiced British wives; and his 'lesser breeds without the Law' seems to refer to Germans, who were to kill his son at Loos in 1915.

Darwin's cousin Francis Galton, anthropologist, explorer of central Africa, codifier of finger-printing methods, once compared his estimates of the annual density of prayers for the Royal Family with the ill-fortune of many individual members, but is better remembered as the founder of the study of eugenics. He proposed the breeding of physical and intellectual élites. In a famous exchange Isadora Duncan, anti-Classical dancer, proposed that she should have a child by Shaw: it would surely be a prodigy, combining her looks and his brain. Shaw demurred, holding it just as probable that the child would exhibit his looks and her brains.

In the hectic climate of change and revelation, notables flirted with these simplistic notions: the Webbs, Shaw and Wells, Havelock Ellis, the young Churchill and, decades later, Aldous Huxley. The socialist writer Jack London lauded Anglo-Saxon superiority, deplored 'mongrelisation'. Fabians discussed sterilisation of 'the unfit', or their isolation in prison camps. The Webbs thought Natural Selection would 'shred' them 'without killing', without 'lethal chambers', and by 1905 were opposing segregation in favour of carefully-planned mating, birth control, sexual education. Wells was thinking in 1901: 'Those swarms of black and brown and yellow people who do not come into the needs of efficiency, well, the world is not a charitable institution, and I take it that they will have to go.' In 1907 Sidney Webb bemoaned the fact that while birth control was increasingly regulating the more civilised British, 'children are being freely born to the Irish Catholics and the Polish, Russian and German Jews on the one hand, and to the thriftless and irresponsible . . . on the other', forecasting that Britain would be over-run by Irish, Jews, and perhaps Chinese.

Novelists accepted rather casually an anti-Semitism more snobbish than racist, denoting a dislike of cosmopolitanism, upstart South African millionaires, a suspicion of insider rings and foreign conspiracies. Trollope's honourable Mr Brehgert was more typical than a Shylock or Fagin: 'He seldom or never came to his office on a Saturday, and many among his enemies said he was a Jew. What evil will not a rival say to stop the flow of grist to the mill of the hated one?' J.M. Keynes in 1913 desired that birth control be strictly applied to the 'drunken and ignorant' working-classes.

Kaiser Wilhelm II, Victoria's grandson, was agitated by the Asiatic 'Yellow Peril', and thus exhorted German troops in China during the Boxer

Rebellion: 'Give no quarter! Take no prisoners! Kill the foe when you capture him! Even as a thousand years ago the Huns under their King Attila made such a name for themselves as still resounds in terror through legend and fable, so may the name of Germans resound through German history a thousand years hence.' For Wilhelm, 'the principles of democracy can only create weak and often corrupt social institutions. A society is strong only if it recognises the fact of natural superiorities, in particular the superiorities of birth.' In common with much of the French and Russian intelligentsia he was anti-Semitic, telling Edward Grey that Jews were far too numerous in Germany. 'They need stamping out.' He also referred in 1905 to 'the pathetic and degenerate Latin races . . . eunuch peoples bred from the ethnic chaos of ancient Rome'. Bismarck's constitution had left too much responsibility and too heavy a crown for those likely to wear it. As sovereign of Britain's chief European competitor in commerce and arms, Wilhelm would continually address the Continent, possibly with bluster, possibly with intent, but scarcely in the language of Salisbury and Balfour, Asquith and Grey: 'The Press, the Jews, and mosquitoes are a nuisance that humanity must somehow get rid of. I think the best method would be gas.' Gorged with their own conquests, the British listened without pleasure to the 'Supreme War Lord' of the latest Empire: 'God has summoned us to civilise the world. We are Missionaries of Progress.' It should be added that Germany's last Kaiser survived to declare that the Nazi *Kristallnacht* pogrom in 1938 made him ashamed to be German.

By 1870 women were rebelling against annual pregnancies, male despotism, and the view that marriage gave women opportunity for mere devotion. The Married Women's Property Act of 1882, though in advance of anything similar in the world, scarcely liberated British women, who were only gradually admitted to universities, the professions, and senior union and Party status, the Suffragettes agitating with increasing violence until the Great War. Literature had force: Ibsen's plays, confronting masculine harshness, sexual disease, provincial neurosis; Mill's *On the Subjection of Women*; Hardy's insistence that his murderess, Tess, was a pure woman; the New Woman – Tolstoy's Anna, Wells's Ann Veronica, Bennett's Hilda Lessways, Grant Allen's 'Woman who Did'. Marie Stopes's books and clinics combated sexual ignorance, and a public opinion scandalised by birth control and the adulteries of Parnell, Dilke, Wells himself.

The New Woman joined unions, practised medicine, rejected what Allen called 'the Great Taboos' and the unreal belief in female sexual passivity: she could take the sexual initiative, supervise great schools: or, like Gertrude Bell, roam wild Arabia; like Mary Kingsley, stroll through Africa. Through New Woman's writings men found some inklings of what women really were, or likely to become. She was not morally superior to Tess, but better equipped in education, security, hard cash.

British men and women responded briskly to international developments not only in science but in art, music, urban development, psychology and journalism. Shaw was propagating the New Realism of Ibsen, the Music of the Future, of Wagner, the New Economics, of Marx. The Impressionism of Degas and Manet was infiltrating the Slade and the New English Art Club, encouraged by Sargent and the half-Danish Sickert. Sickert, disrespectful to 'George Bernard Cocksure', learnt not only from Degas but from Zola, both manifest in his canvases of minor London music-halls, gloomy bedrooms, soiled maltreated bodies, apprehensions of murder. Sickert seldom lost interest in the passing scene. Hearing in 1909 that Hugh Lane had been knighted for admiring Manet, he wondered whether he would have been so honoured for merely buying Manet.

Wyndham Lewis emerged, modernist in paint and words, whose harsh, sometimes menacing canvases bore the metallic upthrust of an industrial age, while his magazine was aptly named *Blast.* Posters, shop displays, lettering, illustrations were more varied and adventurous, while Roger Fry prepared to offer an unwilling public the startling angles and juxtapositions of Post-Impressionism, over which an English visitor hooted so strenuously that he had to be hauled away, to secure his life. After Edward VII's accession the sculptor Jacob Epstein began his long career of disturbing, horrifying and bewildering the public, which found more to delight and stimulate in the Russian Ballet. The French Symbolist poetry of Baudelaire and Rimbaud was absorbed by Wilde, translated by Arthur Symons. In France, Proust was translating Ruskin; with an exhilaration he later, though slowly, relinquished, he wrote: 'The universe suddenly regained pricelessness in my eyes, my admiration for Ruskin invested whatever he had made me love with so great an importance that they seemed to possess a value greater than life itself.'

Art nouveau was indebted both to Scots and English, its sinuosity reminiscent of Celtic and Old English love of line, the serpentine, in flame and wave, foliage and blossom, spirals and gyrations. Kenneth Clark taught the impact of Beardsley's fluidity, his somewhat ominous drawings, on Klee and

Kandinsky, Munch and Picasso. A Scottish counterpart of William Morris, Charles Rennie Mackintosh, was an early practitioner of art nouveau, painter, architect, interior designer. A perfectionist, he conceived his buildings as wholes, with carpets, panels, fabrics, furniture, ornamentation conforming to his central design, backed by innovations of colour, shadow, light that gave varying moods to particular areas. Long undervalued since, his ideas were vehemently debated at the time, not only in Glasgow but in Vienna.

Despite periodic jingoism, some literary fervour about national and imperial matters, and a cult not of militarism but of individual generals, Britain never quite succumbed to the hypnotic perils of raw, aggressive nationalism. The Queen–Empress herself visited the Riviera, but not her Empire. Indeed, the young Disraeli had observed that 'The people of this country have ceased to be a nation.' Later, possession of Empire and affection for 'the Flag', though scarcely a cult, may have helped to remedy any lack of national cohesion, assisted by social and parliamentary reform.

The Empire widened, less often deepened, the imagination. The Pole Joseph Conrad, assailed today by the Nigerian writer Chinua Achebe as a thorough-going racist, though horrified by Belgian cruelties in the Congo, declared: 'There was a vast amount of red – good to see at any time, because one knows that some real work is being done.' The socialist Sidney Webb joined Ruskin, Disraeli, Chamberlain in similar approval. Shaw, Webb and Russell supported Britain in the Boer War, bitterly attacked by many socialists as a stampede for gold, diamonds, and land. Chesterton and Belloc inveighed against the many Jewish and cosmopolitan South African speculators, plutocratic conquistadores with their corrupt mining companies, and the entwining of naked money-power and racketeering politics of Rhodes, Beit, Lugard, Barnato. 'Barney' Barnato, former conjurer and music-hall artiste, transferred his gifts to the Kimberley diamond fields, banking, 'development', puffing the boom of the mid nineties. Investors profited by his advice, were destroyed by his collapse, and doubtless rejoiced when he threw himself off a ship in 1897. Bits of Belloc's invective in *The Modern Traveller* survive; during an African mutiny his William Blood, 'who understood the Native mind', remained unperturbed:

> He stood upon a little mound,
> Cast his lethargic eyes around,

And said beneath his breath:
'Whatever happens, we have got
The Maxim Gun, and they have not!'

Many who slighted 'the Colonies' boasted of 'The Empire'. Gladstone, who presided over the occupation of Egypt, once remarked, 'And so, gentlemen, I say that while we are opposed to Imperialism, we are devoted to the Empire.' Contradictions and disputes were plentiful. E.J. Eyre (1815–1901), Australasian explorer, Governor of New Zealand, was known for his kindness to Australian aboriginals, yet as Governor of Jamaica his pitiless suppression of the 1865 rising had divided Britain on a Dreyfus scale, Carlyle, Dickens, Ruskin, Tennyson, Kingsley supporting him; Mill, Huxley, Darwin, Thomas (*Tom Brown's Schooldays*) Hughes opposing.

Wordsworth had lamented British 'tyranny over India's patient millions' and would have deplored the building of 23,000 miles of road. Wilfrid Scawen Blunt, poet, ardent for Irish and Egyptian freedom, baiter of officialdom, sang gleefully when Gordon was speared at Khartoum though he himself, a sexual tyrant, was accused of savagely thrashing intruders on his Egyptian estate. Kipling saw the Empire less in terms of Rhodes's 'Philanthropy plus five per cent' than as an opportunity to extend 'the Law' through under-paid engineers, doctors, district officers, the Army. He certainly cherished the 'Anglo-Saxon' virtues, more poetically than Rhodes who insisted: 'We are the first race in the world, and the more of the world we inhabit, the better it is for the human race. I contend that every acre added to our territory provides for the birth of more of the English race who otherwise would not be brought into existence. Added to which, the absorption of the greater part of the world under our rule simply means the end of all wars.' He even entertained hopes for the recovery of the United States. As someone said, 'All men have foibles, and Rhodes's is *size*.' Meanwhile, annexations could be extraordinarily casual. By 1914, in Kenya, over four million acres of the best land had been distributed to some thousand whites.

Curzon considered that a decree of Providence had summoned the British to India for the lasting benefit of millions. John Buchan wrote: 'Imperialism is a spirit, an attitude of mind, an unconquerable hope. You can phrase it a thousand ways without exhausting its content. It is a sense of the destiny of England. It is the wider patriotism which conceives our people as a race and not as a chance community.' For others, the Empire was a mass of dirt which could be transformed into property. The Salvation Army's founder William Booth published *In Darkest England and the Way Out* in 1890, in which he proposed large-scale colonial emigration to relieve massive poverty and distress.

The reality of Empire could be boredom, early death from disease or suicide, the corruptions of power and materialism. Rider Haggard's Allan Quartermain, Great White Hunter, reflects on Africa at the end: 'Well, it's not a good world – nobody can say that it is save those who wilfully blind themselves to the facts. How can a world be good in which money is the moving power, and Self-Interest is the guiding star? The wonder is not that it is so bad, but that there should be any good left in it.' Haggard was a busy imperialist between 1875 and 1885, the first to raise 'the Flag' in the Transvaal, and himself substituted for a drunken hangman in the execution of a Swazi Chief for murder.

By 1900 the Empire represented an imposing façade, bound by nominal or perhaps genuine loyalty to the Crown, guarded by the largest Navy in the world and a few thousand military and civilian officers: at Embu in Kenya the District Commissioner superintended half a million people spread over eight thousand square miles, with one District Officer and thirty-two native policemen. Regulated by an intricate mixture of direct and indirect rule the Interests, British and Native, enjoyed huge markets, limitless raw materials and, for the moment, docile labour. One-third of British goods were being absorbed by imperial territories still profiting from free trade, though Germany and America were set to profit still more by tariffs. From 1903, clamour began in Britain to imitate this; Joseph Chamberlain proposed emphatic privileges for Empire goods, but the issue was postponed until 1931.

Generalisations about the Empire are continuously offered, sanctioned by political and moral pressures, but they generally mislead. It was never, like the Continental empires, a genuine unity: Canada, South Africa, Australia, New Zealand swiftly evolved into Dominions, self-governing, what Wells called Crowned Republics. Blacks and whites socialised in West but less in East Africa: British would foregather in African homes in Christian south Nigeria, not in the Moslem north. For some missionaries, the Empire could be a racecourse, rival sects competing in conscienceless rancour; for others it was an allotment to be planted with literacy, hygiene, moral instruction and Truth.

British power, festooned with complacency and moral precepts, neither pleaded for nor received foreign goodwill. When Harold Nicolson, on a pro-paganda mission to the USA during the Second World War, was heckled with 'What about the Indians?' he justifiably inquired, 'Do you mean our Indians or yours?' Sadistic British reprisals after the Mutiny, hanging parties at Benares, were swiftly notorious, while their immediate suppression by the Governor-General, derided as 'Clemency' Canning, received less notice. Few remarked when Sir Francis Piggott was appointed Legal Adviser to the Japanese Government, tribute to his own integrity and to a certain admira-tion for British Common Law and alleged impartiality. The better-disposed might have pondered some words of Gandhi, himself periodically in British captivity:

> An Englishman never respects you until you stand up to him. Then he begins to like you. He is afraid of nothing physical, but he is very mortally afraid of his own conscience if you ever appeal to it and show him to be in the wrong. He does not like to be rebuked for wrongdoing at first but he will think it over and it will get hold of him and hurt him till he does something to put it right.

King Mutesa of Buganda burnt alive his sixty brothers, and subsequently indulged in beheadings and clubbings to death for such offences as cough-ing in his presence. Europeans, themselves reprehensible for introducing guns, liquor, smallpox, syphilis, found Mutesa's successor, Mwanga, had burnt alive thirty Christian children, having already tortured to death several boys for their dislike of his predilection to sodomy. The British may appear arrogant in later ruling Uganda with only 640 of them on the ground in a country of 2.8 million, but at least they put an end to such casual butch-ery.

Unlike the Portuguese, Belgians, and Germans – latest invaders of Africa, whose General von Trotha, after armed retaliation by the Hereros in South-West Africa in 1904, killed sixty-five out of eighty thousand – the British were beginning to train Africans for administration. Africans, Indians, Arabs were to sit on provincial councils, though Independence found too few experienced and honest civil servants, teachers, doctors. National boundaries were often fixed to suit European powers, irrespective of ethnic distribution, tribal custom, popular wishes.

Macaulay, member of the Supreme Council of India in the 1830s, looked forward to the proudest day in British history as that when India voluntar-ily adopted British institutions. To some degree this hope was fulfilled when the Indian Republic opted for an elected Parliament, secret ballot, free press, retention of the British civil service apparatus, legal codes, language, and Commonwealth membership. Earlier, in prison for sedition and, like Raleigh, writing a history of the world, Nehru received better treatment than he would have from the Germans, Japanese, or Indian Moslems.

The British, with their smiles and ironies, did not avoid the superior attitude once enjoined by Dr Johnson: 'Don't cant in favour of savages.' Westerners were over-confident in their enormous vocabularies, religion, technology and sciences. Europe failed to perceive that through throne and altar, titles, oaths, it too had amassed superstitions. European authority protected itself with gold and feathers, jewelled wands, elaborate chant and ceremonial, ritual slogans. Whites prayed for rain, feared ghosts and vampires, described the After Life, credited magic numbers.

Conquerors mistook military victory for essential, self-fulfilling virtue, dismissing the defeated as fuzzy-wuzzies, heathens, primitives, even when these possessed the sophisticated nuances of organisation and culture necessary for survival, a profound indentification with Nature. Condescension and ignorance could cause fatal misunderstandings. Taboos and fetishes were ignored or trampled on by invaders seldom instinctively cruel, but unimaginative, and anthropologically illiterate. The Ashanti Gold Stool, symbol of the people's soul, was commandeered as a mere throne. Throwing a spear could be a Maori offer of truce, spitting in a stranger's face an African gesture of trust. Though the Empire's Moslems outnumbered the population of Arabia and Turkey, few British ministers or officials studied the Koran and exceptions like Gordon and Burton were usually unpopular in Whitehall.

C.E. Carrington, from New Zealand, an Imperial historian, Great War veteran, biographer of Kipling, considered the American colonists had been infuriated not by British oppression but by neglect, and because London Society was unwilling to believe that Washington could be a gentleman or that Franklin should not be patronised. Field Marshal Lord Wavell, penultimate Viceroy of India, argued that the Empire was lost not because of cruelty or exploitation but through the bad manners of the British overseas who, Wells complained, strutted like owners rather than administered as trustees. From a different podium, Lady Maud Cecil pronounced: 'Of course, the best class of English don't come out to the colonies, and those that do are apt to be bounders.'

An Indian prince once asked Somerset Maugham if he knew the

difference between the Bengal Yacht Club and the Bombay Yacht Club. Maugham did not, and was told that in Calcutta, members barred dogs and Indians, in Bombay they allowed dogs. 'I couldn't for the life of me think of an answer to that, and I haven't thought of one since.' A South African factory order was: 'Before starting the winch, operators must ensure that neither men nor natives are in the vicinity.' In 1899 the Queen–Empress referred Lord Salisbury to 'the snobbish and vulgar overbearing and offensive behaviour of many of our Civil and Political agents in India', while adding that the Indians 'must, of course, feel that we are the masters, but it should be done kindly and not offensively, which alas is so often the case.' She was disgusted by Kitchener in Khartoum collecting the dead Mahdi's head as a souvenir. Visiting India in 1906, the future George V deplored racial arrogance: 'Evidently we are too much inclined to look upon them as a conquered and down-trodden race, and the native, who is becoming more and more educated, realises this.'

Those who first brought back ethnic art tended to see it as loot; only a Burton, a Curzon, cared to recognise that Saharan paintings were millennia older than Lascaux, that Timbuktu pre-dated Oxford as a centre of learning, that Ceylon had three thousand years of intricate history, far older than Rome. The Fauves, Post-Impressionists and Cubists then started borrowing freely from African and Pacific art.

Preening themselves for their work in eradicating trachoma, cerebral malaria, enteric yellow fever, spotted and black fever, in spelling out the Gospel, introducing sport, the whites could be grossly intolerant of the witch doctor, who at best understood the psychic elements within certain sicknesses, and whose elimination could cause social dislocations similar to those following the removal of priests at the Reformation.

Much still festers. Anxious to conciliate the defeated Boers, the British ignored the blacks, some of whom remember the Afrikaaner's whip or boot as they crawled to receive orders or punishment. A Zulu revolt in 1906 cost thirty white dead, three thousand black. Cheap Chinese labour was imported, regardless of African, Caribbean and Malayan sensibilities. Benefits to Egypt given by Lord Cromer, in more honest administration, public works, anti-drug enforcements, were almost vitiated by inattention to Egyptian self-respect.

Malevolent images linger. After the Mutiny, General Neill ordered Indians to lick British blood from the ground. The Amritsar Massacre is part of diabolic folklore. In the Sudan, Kitchener's order 'Loot like blazes', though in the established mould of western behaviour, was no tribute to it. His defeat of Emir Mahmoud on the Nile on Good Friday in 1898 was celebrated like a Triumph in ancient Rome. Alan Moorehead described it:

> Kitchener rode forward on a white horse, to take the salute. At the head of the parade came the defeated general, Mahmoud, a proud and handsome young man in his early thirties. Chains were riveted round his ankles, a halter was passed round his neck, and his hands were tied behind his back. In these bonds he was made sometimes to walk, sometimes to run, and when he stumbled the guards drove him on. The inhabitants of Berber and the camp followers of Kitchener's army jeered at the prisoner and pelted him with rubbish.

Newspapers polished the reputation of generals. From Sir Garnet Wolseley Gilbert and Sullivan concocted 'the Modern Major-General', and *all Sir Garnet* became a synonym for success. Wolseley campaigned in Burma, witnessed the Relief of Lucknow, commanded in Canada, Ashantiland, Sudan. For him, a nation without glory was like a man without courage, a woman without virtue: 'Those who in youth learn to value it as a holy possession are, as life goes on, inspired by its influence. It becomes eventually a sort of national religion.'

Despite Wells's strictures, the British tended to display more self-assurance than swagger, their aloofness comparable to that of the Brahmin, the Mandarin, certain African statesmen, senior bureaucrats everywhere. Policies required a balance between Moslems and Hindus, Malay and Chinese, whites and non-whites, Boer and British: apologists called this 'Holding the Ring'; detractors, 'Divide and Rule'. Individuality could survive 'the System'. Francis Younghusband, who ruthlessly conquered Tibet, later supported Indian independence and became absorbed in mysticism. Leonard Woolf resigned as a civil servant in Ceylon in 1912, finally unwilling to administer alien laws to a subject people. In 1960 he revisited the country, now independent, rather uneasily, even with expectations of hostility, through feelings of guilt for imperialism. Everywhere he was greeted with respect, even affection. *The Ceylon Daily News* embellished the visit:

> Immediately one remembers . . . others who, like Woolf, not only worked conscientiously at their day-to-day tasks, but found time through their 'extra-curricular' research to make an essential contribution to such fields as history, literature and oriental studies. One quality characterises the public service in

their period – the ideal of service to the community. The public servants of this era were not afraid to move among and with the people. In this they provided a striking contrast to their successors of today. The latter have built a wall between themselves and the people they are meant to serve.

Less satisfactory than Woolf, Lord Beauchamp was gazetted Governor of New South Wales at 23, but was recalled following his speech assuring Australians that, considering their convict past, they had done jolly well. Dr James Cobb, an alcoholic, supervisor of Mathari Mental Hospital in 1927–8, was famed for attempting to sodomise lions.

Women can be overlooked amid the showy panoply of Viceroys, Governor-Generals, Field Marshals, Chief Justices; or abused for racism, snobbery, intrigue; but many possessed distinction. Emily Hobhouse exposed to an indignant world the squalor of Kitchener's 'Concentration Camps' for Boer women and children though, like everyone else, she was unconcerned with those for blacks. In Malta, Mabel Strickland was a courageous liberal and anti-Fascist, editor of *The Times of Malta* which staunchly helped public morale under incessant wartime bombings; as a farmer, she was prominent in developing the avocado pear: all-round, formidable, her influence extended far beyond the parochial. For nearly forty years Mary Slessor worked for Nigerian health, for women's and children's welfare. Another English woman started a clinic in Malawi which markedly reduced infant mortality, though after Independence she was not allowed by the Director of Agriculture to feel complacent: 'What on earth do you think you are doing, keeping more and more people alive to live on less and less land?'

Adrian Davies, an ex-colonial administrator, said in 1983: 'I honestly felt we were doing something; we were helping, in a way. I know that the popular image of the old colonial is a dead-beat, gin-swilling so-and-so, who's out there for what he can get out of it. It's not so, it wasn't like that at all. We felt we were making a contribution to the country and helping them in their development.' Or, as Laurence James put it in his book on the Empire (1994): 'Few empires have equipped their subjects with the intellectual wherewithal to overthrow their rulers. None has been survived by so much affection and respect.' However, the last word must be Kwame Nkrumah's in newly-independent Ghana in 1957: 'It is far better to be free to govern or misgovern yourself, than to be governed by anyone else.' The words of the masses are generally left unrecorded.

The ending of Empire did not end all British interest – as against Interests

– in it. Joy Bath worked as a nurse for ten years in independent Africa before dying of Aids in 1995, after having cut her foot on a hospital floor damp with contaminated blood. 'I knew the risks. I'd do it again. I'm grateful for all the time I've been able to spend helping other people.'

In 1897, Victoria celebrated her Diamond Jubilee: Monarch, Nation, Empire blended in what appeared the apex of British world power. Britain could claim to be the world's most prosperous State, its Empire and sea-power the foremost, its constitution the most unshakeable, its trade unions the least restricted. Fifty thousand troops escorted the Queen–Empress to St Paul's through a roaring capital, certainly the largest, richest, most powerful city in the world, amid fervid shouts of 'Go it, old girl'. Crowds saw a jostling panoply of plumes, helmets, turbans, multi-tinted sashes, jewelled stars, golden chains, ornate epaulettes, ribbons, medals; kilts, cloaks, scarlet liveries; lancers and hussars, riflemen and guards, Australian seamen, Canadian cavalry, Dominion premiers, Indian grandees; Cypriots, Dyaks, Rhodesians, Gurkhas, Sikhs, Jamaicans, seemingly half the world. Only Ireland struck a dissenting note. In a single year, 1880, arson attacks there had numbered five hundred: in 1882 there had been ten thousand evictions, and the murder of the Irish Secretary, stabbed in Phoenix Park in Dublin.

In retrospect, the Jubilee appears like a company report, dramatically presented: not fraudulent, but misleading. British strength was suspect, despite the magnificent externals. The collapse of France in 1870 had drastically shifted the European Balance: Germany stood alongside Britain as a Great Power, together with America and a newcomer, little-known and thus romantic – Japan. The Empire itself was still loosely-organised, the Dominions, the 'crowned republics', increasingly pursuing social and economic policies at odds with London's. Yet all must have seemed well enough to those in straw hats, light bonnets, blazers, bright cheap frocks, lounging on piers, drowsing on sands, listening in parks to Strauss and Suppé, Lehár, Offenbach, Sullivan; and comfortably day-dreaming to the melodies, lulling, nostalgic, vaguely reassuring, of Edward German's *Merrie England* (1902). Norman Angell's *The Great Illusion* (1910) showed that the international economy had rendered war impractical and unprofitable. Competition for markets, materials, colonies made exciting headlines and fostered a Great Power arms-race; scare-stories of spies and invaders were popular (*The Riddle of the Sands* is still read), but presumably the Royal Navy kept ahead; dividends were regular, the pound stable.

Abroad, treaties were being signed, alliances proclaimed, declarations of peace publicised. An International Court of Justice was established at The Hague, an international Trades Union Conference promised a General Strike if war threatened. Few bothered with Hobbes's warning that covenants without the sword are but words, and of no strength at all to secure a man. And actually Europe was littered with the swords, rifles, artillery of vast conscript armies.

The social routine was perfected: Henley, Lord's, Derby Day, Royal Ascot, Cowes, grouse moors were undisturbed by hatreds in Ireland and the Balkans, and proudly survived Lloyd George's 'Soak the Rich' Budget and the attentions of suffragettes. Parliament, Labour safely incorporated, was more representative; Common Law was being amended faster than Continental law. Edward VII, 'Tum-Tum' – never one to toy with his food, an obituarist wrote in 1910 – had outlived scandals and acquired popularity at home and abroad. A visitor in 1907, Chulglonkorn, modernising King of Siam, thought that it must be pleasant to be a British king, 'so long as one does not want to have too much one's own way. One must let others do the work. They usually come and tell you about it before, and, if you have any ideas of your own, you can state them. But if they persist in having their own way, you must let it go, otherwise, it may lead to a disastrous quarrel. This system works very well in England, and this King knows very well how to make it work.'

Leonard Woolf, assessing the period in 1969, thought that people might have been on the point of becoming civilised. The world's conscience had been aroused not only by the Congo atrocities and British military arrogance in Egypt, but by German brutality to a single Alsatian cobbler. Gas, electricity, and the by-products of coal; anaesthetics, X-rays, radium: all promised comfort and relief from pain far superior to those of the ancients. Few doubted H.G. Wells's vision of men stepping from star to star as now they stepped from stone to stone across a stream. Trains, trams, motor-buses, motor-cars, bicycles were transforming lives, and horizons. Shaw taught Bertrand Russell to cycle, and at weekends thousands rode out to unravaged countrysides and inexpensive inns.

Havelock Ellis, like Marie Stopes, was propagating women's rights to sexual pleasure, and his *Studies in the Psychology of Sex*, from 1897, must have reassured the ignorant, the confused, the lonely, by exposing symptoms, perplexities and myths common to all, though many of the middle class and 'chapel' folk flinched at such knowledge. Ellis belonged to the Order of Chaeronea, dedicated to the needs not only of women but, with a candour lost since the eighteenth century, of male homosexuals. Shortly after Oscar Wilde's imprisonment Mrs Grundy enforced police confiscation of Ellis's *Sexual Inversion* (1897), as 'lewd, wicked, bawdy, obscene libel'. An early Fabian, Ellis espoused Ibsen's social realism, advocated a national health service, wrote on Shakespearian drama, dance, dreams, experimented with mescalin. He recognised that a society which banned Shaw's *Mrs Warren's Profession* and Wilde's *Salomé* (in which Sarah Bernhardt had promised to appear), and which shied from the open discussion of sex to be encountered in Zola, Ibsen, Brieux, was here lagging behind metropolitan Europe. The music-hall was less squeamish:

> My first was a cornet
> In a regiment of dragoons;
> I gave him what he didn't like
> And stole his silver spoons.

Otherwise, reform continued, amid spirited controversy. Death Duties helped finance Old Age Pensions, industrial innovations, Unemployment Relief – and Dreadnoughts. The power of the House of Lords, mostly the hereditary Landed Interest, was diminished – though not the Honours System, which prospered as at no time since the needy James I. Edward Hamilton, Gladstone's secretary, commented on the Prince of Wales's list: 'The recommendations have rather an ugly air about them.' When he became King as Edward VII, his City share-tipsters jibbed at no title within their reach. A price-list existed when Lloyd George was Prime Minister, with the proceeds meant for Liberal Party funds. One rubber manufacturer was awarded a baronetcy for purchasing Edward VII's love-letters to Lady Warwick, thus saving George V embarrassment by their publication. Honours were a perpetual source of profit, snobbery, pride, and general amusement. Lord Melbourne had earlier refused a Scottish peer the Order of the Thistle, on the grounds that he might eat it.

Country gentry reliant solely on agricultural rents might have been hard up, but many others were affluent, and this encouraged excess. The half-imaginary Golden Edwardian Afternoon also meant Mammon-worship, plutocracy, ostentation. Town House revels, Country House field sports and adulteries were luxuriant and long remembered. Powerful hostesses vied to entertain the King; the hot-house boilers were stoked, the strongly-scented flowers banked high, competing with the aroma of cigars as the quails, the ptarmigan, the gulls' eggs, the aspic-covered confections were cleared away, along with the empty magnums of Krüg and Bollinger. Guests had small chance to remember the Hungry Forties. Expenditure on flowers for a ball could exceed a miner's annual wage.

Nature itself merely served to gratify human appetites. American bison were almost extinguished, to feed Kansas railway workers and to starve unruly Red Indian tribes. Whales were slaughtered wholesale for oil and corsets. Lions, elephants, moths, butterflies were recklessly squandered. More than a million sealskins were wrenched annually from the Arctic. A marble slab commemorated Wilhelm II's fifty-thousandth victim, an albino cock pheasant. Before he was himself shot, Archduke Franz Ferdinand had killed more than a quarter of a million birds and beasts. In 1913 George V, his heir and five others shot 3,945 birds in one afternoon. 'Perhaps we went a little too far today, David,' the King admitted. Even Queen Mary was enlisted as a beater at Sandringham sometimes: 'Rattle your brolly, May. Rattle your brolly,' the King told her. Ruskin had already raged that English rivers had become sewers. Collieries had blackened entire landscapes, the towns were polluted by industrialism; the new motor-car would sicken the country air, end the silence. The process was unabated by war, protest, anger. 'The real tragedy of England, as I see it,' D.H. Lawrence wrote in 1929, 'is the tragedy of ugliness. The country is so lovely; the man-made England is so vile.'

The United Kingdom was not, in spirit, wholly united. Ireland was verging on civil war, Asquith greeting the European hostilities of 1914 with: 'This will take the attention away from Ulster, which is a good thing.' Class divisions, if less disruptive, indeed bloody, than in Russia, Spain, Mexico, were disagreeably patent: rags seldom led to riches, and Asquith's daughter Violet Bonham Carter was puzzled and querulous about the 1912 Transport Strike: 'It is impossible to believe that such a collection of commonplace, insignificant, respectful beings can have this power to upset the whole scheme of our lives.' The dead Victoria, remote from Ireland, slums, district visiting, had been guilty of some self-deception when she wrote: 'The division of classes is the one thing which is most dangerous and reprehensible, never intended by the law of nature and which the Queen is always labouring to alter.'

Society, as always, had its misfits. Young hooligans terrorised urban streets, arousing the clamour that in Germany such outrages were prevented by traditional disciplines and by conscription. Women, if still sexually and politically under-privileged, retained muscle, the suffragette violence reaching ample proportions until war imposed truce.

Foreign influences, however, were incessant: breezy American know-how, French Post-Impressionism, Debussy and female chic, German music, the Russian Ballet with its startling colours and dissonances, electric rhythms and unearthly performers. The British themselves, in the mass, clung to insularity and condescension to foreigners. Though Cook's Travel Agency was replacing the Grand Tour with everyday tourism, this had small effect on what Wodehouse discerned as 'that shifty, hangdog look which announces that an Englishman is about to talk French'. Chesterton remarked that the Englishman abroad was for all serious purposes the Englishman at home.

Without being cosmopolitan, military castes shared an international code of values and a conviction that officers were a superior breed, governed by considerations of honour, loyalty, contempt for the unconventional in thought, art, behaviour. It seems outrageous that German officers expected civilians to step off the pavement to let them pass, and had a monopoly of first-class railway carriages to Potsdam; but British Guards officers were forbidden to carry parcels, smoke Virginian rather than Turkish or Egyptian cigarettes, or reverse when dancing the waltz. To many, the prospect of an age of peace was unwelcome, since it would provide no opportunity for promotion, glory, no justification of privileges, their very existence. Not only German officers would have been interested in the thoughts of the German Crown Prince, as confided to the American ambassador in 1913: 'he hoped war would occur while his father was alive; but, if not, he would start a war the moment he came to the throne.'

Successive distant international crises were interesting or dramatic for the British public, but scarcely serious. The momentum of industrial America and Germany might increase demands on the labour force and on taxpayers, but bloodshed could be left to foreigners. Wilhelm II was a volatile irritant, indulging in theatrical scares and poses but barely conceivable as a serious part of the modern world. He had been genuinely moved by the death of his grandmother, Victoria, measuring her for her coffin at Osborne, then riding through London at her funeral in dignified finery, momentarily seeming one of the national family. Years afterwards, William Gerhardie assessed him as 'interesting because of his colourful insignificance; all his life he darted backwards and forwards between St Petersburg and London, Rome and Vienna, to consult his fellow monarchs on how to keep the peace of Europe which he alone was disturbing.'

From the thrones, chancelleries and war offices, the deeper tides were often imperceptible. People, largely restraining from extravagant demands, trusted their rulers to assure peace and prosperity, though occasionally the pact faltered. Strikers were killed at Louvain, Nantes, Liverpool, Llanelli. Political assassinations increased: there was also fiercer competition for colonies, markets, oil, nitrates, cheap labour. British coal was threatened by foreign oil: the need for oil necessitated complex, perhaps dangerous British and German designs in the Middle East. The sinking of the Tsarist fleet by 'brave little Japan' at Tsu-Shima in 1905 was welcomed by the liberty-loving British, careless that a new naval power had joined Germany and America, challenging British maritime assumptions.

European intellectuals, seeking the course from Nothing to Being, tended to disparage peaceful evolution as a betrayal of 'Destiny': as spiritual torpor, racial degeneration, slothful materialism. The State should chasten and deflect the hedonistic, visionless surge of democracy. Though unread by the British, Hegel, Nietzsche, Wagner, Treitschke, Sorel, von Bernhardi justified violence, gave a metaphysic to war, Nietzsche committing himself to the proposition that a good war justifies any cause. In language cruder but more comprehensible Wilhelm II, who owed his imperial crown to the 1870 war, lectured the effete and moderate: 'The only nations that have advanced to greatness have been those which do not flinch from wars.' This was not the language of Liberal or, indeed, Conservative Britain, though occasionally something like it was used by Churchill, who was both in his time. A different vocabulary but similar vehemence was deployed by Lloyd George against the Landed Interest.

The rapid progress of modernity, in science, art, surgery, architecture, induced a complacency more evident to hindsight than to those living before 1914. One dreadful warning is now part of legend. In 1906 a seasoned Atlantic professional, Captain E.J. Smith, spoke from on high: 'I cannot imagine any condition which would cause a ship to founder . . . Modern shipbuilding has gone beyond that.' Six years later, he sailed in command of the latest technological masterpiece, the SS *Titanic*. Professional incompetence, individual vanity, a certain lingering mystery ensured that the Great Unsinkable sank in three hours with fifteen hundred dead, leaving only a grin of oil on the freezing water. The last survivor died in 1997, remembering her father, glass in hand, smoking a cigar, on the stern of the sinking liner. An official Inquiry in America elicited a remarkable exchange:

'Mr Lowe, what is an iceberg made of?'
Fifth Officer H.G. Lowe: 'Ice.'

The Feminist Interest was upheld by the American Anna Shaw and the British Fabian Millicent Murby, resenting 'Women and Children First'. Some American blacks approved of the disaster, as an affront to white conceit. So did the Russian poet Alexander Blok, who feared that technology would obliterate Nature. 'The sinking of the *Titanic* has made me indescribably happy: there is, after all, an ocean.'

Scepticism about progress was not confined to socialists, pacifists, mystics, underpaid workers, over-cerebral philosophers. Grand Respectables had misgivings. Victoria had deplored the 'Society' in which her heir was so conspicuously spendthrift. She pronounced that danger existed, not from 'the *Lower Orders*', rapidly improving, but 'in the conduct of the *Higher Classes* and of the *Aristocracy*'. Garnet Wolseley, now Field Marshal and Viscount, much fêted, before his death in 1913 confided to his wife:

To the man whose first thought is England, and who feels that she must sink or be saved by her gentlefolk, the contemplation of English Society is painful. I feel that a country whose upper classes live as a certain set of men and women do, can only be saved from annihilation by some such upheaval as a great war which will cost all the best families their sons, and call forth the worst animal passions and the noblest of human virtue and for the time place the very existence of the kingdom in danger.

Edgell Rickword, gifted Marxist poet, critic, editor, wounded in the Great War, recalled in 1940:

It is doubtful if the younger generation today, familiarised for years through the news-reels and illustrated papers with the destructiveness of modern warfare as practised on the bodies of Jonah-countries, can realize the virgin ignorance of their counterparts in 1914–15. We were inured to colonial wars, pacifications of backward peoples, our toy soldiers had significantly bright armaments, which only differed from the more risky and expensive forms of sport in the degree of hardship involved.

Peter Parker, a masterly researcher into the public school, discovered that at pre-1914 Uppingham, shooting ability was required before acceptance of an academic prize or membership of a team. He aptly cites Ian Hay, Old Fettesian, author of *The Lighter Side of Public School Life* (1921), who distinguished between 'funny peculiar' and 'funny ha-ha'. Hay was rated by Orwell an exponent of the clean-living Englishman tradition at its silliest. He wrote:

> For officers, Britain turned to her Public Schools. When the great call came, those young armies of course were officered without difficulty by many thousand competent cadets furnished by this system. They were pathetically young, but they possessed two priceless qualifications: they knew their job and they played the game. They never asked men to go where they would not go themselves. So, children as they were, their men followed them everywhere.

Acceptance of war, passive, unreflective, or romantic, certainly dogged much of the social and even intellectual élite, less emphatically than in Austria, Germany and France, but strongly enough for an enthusiastic rush to the Colours from all classes in 1914. Orwell, at prep. school, displayed a conditioned response:

> Awake, O you young men of England,
> For if, when your Country's in need,
> You do not enlist in your thousands
> You truly are cowards indeed.

This pales beside the words of the German Ernst Jünger, aged a hundred and one in 1996, writing in his book *Storms of Steel* in 1920: 'We had set out in a rain of flowers to seek the death of heroes. The war was our dream of greatness, power and glory. It was a man's work, a duel in the fields where flowers would be stained with blood. There is no lovelier death in the world . . . Anything rather than stay at home.'

Britain, in truth, was the least warlike of the great Powers, though indolent in her desire for peace. Churchill reflected in 1911: 'We have got all we want in territory and our claim to be left in unmolested enjoyment of vast and splendid territories, mainly acquired by violence, largely maintained by force, often seems less reasonable to others than to us.' J.B. Priestley, pugnaciously not Public School but the epitome of growling, unshakeable English common sense, explained in 1964 his reasons for volunteering in 1914, which were unconcerned with heroism, nationalist indoctrination, mass-hysteria, Belgium. 'There came out of the unclouded blue of that summer, a challenge that was almost like a conscription of the spirit, little to do really with King and country and flag-waving and hip-hip-hurrah, a challenge to what we felt was our untested manhood. Other men who had not lived as easily as we had, had drilled and marched and borne arms – couldn't we?' Classical epic, chauvinist housemasters, the boredom of the over-leisured and frustrations of the romantic contributed to recruitment. Also poverty.

Europe, like the *Titanic*, was speeding, all lights blazing, with engines too powerful for its own good, towards a New World, but a world not of its choosing. Officers and crew remained preoccupied with the new machinery, the gadgets and refinements, the sheer size of it all, the wonder, and did not notice the paucity of lifeboats, the possibility that alliances might drag one down rather than buoy one up.

A few historians might have recalled that in January 1870 Napoleon III had announced that the year could only increase peace and civilisation; his Prime Minister stated that at no time in history had the maintenance of European peace been more certain. In July 1870 he was telling Europe that France entered the war against Prussia with a light heart – a war that destroyed the dynasty and 141,000 men, and united Germany.

Similar satisfactions were rife before 1914. Lord Harcourt informed Winston Churchill in 1895 that the experience of a long life had convinced him that nothing ever happens. John Morley, pacific Liberal statesman who resigned in 1914 in protest against Britain entering the war, had praised Germany as high-minded, benignant and virile, a guardian of the European peace. Mrs Asquith asserted that Churchill, First Lord of the Admiralty, should not be allowed too much money, now that all foreign nations were peaceful. Lloyd George, in January 1914, professed gratification that the sky had never been more perfectly blue. The Governor of the Bank of England said: 'There's talk of war. It will never happen. The Germans haven't the credits.' After Franz Ferdinand's murder, Russian mobilisation, Vienna's ultimatum to Serbia, an Eton master assured his pupils, among them Anthony Eden: 'There won't be any war, the City would never allow it. Even if fighting did break out, it couldn't last more than a few days, the money would run out.' The young Bernard Montgomery, future Field Marshal, reckoned the war would last three weeks. The credulous re-read *The Great Illusion*. International trade union delegates renewed their pledge to forestall war by a general strike. None of them could stop the Kaiser signing his country's declaration of war, seated at a table made out of some timbers from HMS *Victory*.

Britain's entry into the Great War was controversial: Morley and Burns left the Cabinet in protest; Bertrand Russell feared that war would endanger civilisation itself, which was more valuable than national interests; Ramsay MacDonald courageously opposed the conflict throughout. Norman Angell wrote to *The Times*:

> We can best serve civilization, Europe – including France – and ourselves, by remaining the one power in Europe that has not yielded to the war madness. This, I believe, will be found to be the firm conviction of the overwhelming majority of the English people.

The Asquith Government, while civilised and reforming, was unlikely to accept this, though not from any romantic heritage of Albion, which might indeed have affected the populace with images of Arthurian chivalry riding out to succour gallant little Belgium, her steadfast King and immaculate Queen ravaged by the Hunnish giant. More decisive were informal understandings with France and the centuries-old policy of keeping the Low Countries, so vital to British interests, free from an aggressive Great Power. The Cabinet scarcely envisaged the fateful consequences of European war.

The Great War shocked the British as earlier wars, fought without military conscription, had not. Perhaps the Indian Mutiny and its savage aftermath came nearest. Today, despite the Nazi and Soviet atrocities, images of 1914–18 persist, in print, on film, in family and regional memory. Writing in dire 1917, John Masefield left an abiding prose-picture of the upheaval that destroyed monarchical Europe, questioned the validity of many hallowed British institutions, while offering hopes to submerged classes, particularly among the defeated. He describes a monstrous gap in nature, after a huge mine exploded at Beaumont Hamel on the Western Front, another lasting synonym of the vile and barely endurable. In its way, Masefield's paragraph is an epitaph of collapse of reason, order, style which had been advancing, with periodic set-backs, since the eighteenth century.

> It is like the crater of a volcano, vast, ragged and irregular, almost one hundred and fifty yards long and twenty-five yards deep. It is crusted and scabbed, with

yellowish tetter, like sulphur or the rancid fat on meat. The inside has rather the look of meat, for it is reddish and all streaked and scabbed with this pox and with discoloured chalk. A lot of it trickles and oozes like sores discharging pus, and the liquid gathers in holes near the bottom, and is greenish and foul and has the dazed look of eyes straining upwards.

The crowds roaring at Victoria's Jubilees or acclaiming George V after the German collapse in 1918 could scarcely have foreseen the subsequent hatreds, 'ethnic cleansings', even cannibalism, which were to sweep the Continent on a scale unknown since the Thirty Years' War.

Soldiers of all ranks had displayed traditional traits of stoicism, tolerance, loyalty, unless outraged by unfairness or outsize incompetence. Grumbling was incessant but mutiny, which had demoralised the French and destroyed the Russian Tsar in 1917, surfaced only after victory, through tardy demobilisation and fears of unemployment. Music-hall humour had assisted morale amid atrociousness and bewilderment. In post-war tensions, however, would such qualities survive – and were they indeed required for new, perhaps unprecedented challenges? Statesmen would have to find unusual resources to grapple with republican Germany and Russia, the League of Nations, slumps, ethnic minorities, African, Indian, Arabic, and Caribbean nationalism, and with brash, wealthy, inventive America, where half a million patents had been registered as early as 1879.

Victory could be almost as perilous as defeat. Possession, or apparent possession, of the largest, most varied Empire in history entailed debate, persistent and ever-noisier, about the legal, moral and economic justifications of imperialism. Being the first nation to have become industrialised meant the possibility of being the first to be outdated, become complacent, resting on laurels once refulgent but now fading. Beset with post-war difficulties, Britain risked being deceived by externals grandiose but corrupt, and by unconsciously relying on national myth and wishful thinking. Younger, more competitive empires were alert for British weaknesses.

In the global web of supra-national commerce, finance, transport, communication, ideas, national independence itself might prove to be less authentic than flags, Foreign Office communiqués, City reports suggested. Certainly the gifted amateur must be replaced by more professional technology, political procedure, and by statesmen familiar with foreign languages, traditions, sensitivities.

Other challenges could be less neatly analysed: the menace of swollen cities confused by half-knowledge, declining certainties and Other World beliefs, the resentment of the unemployed, the plight of women now granted the vote but with their men killed; together with startling, not very reassuring diagnoses of mind, nature, sexuality disclosed by the new psychology, in which even Humour could be analysed in terms of envy, fear, vengeance, sadism. Under the colossal shadows of the dead, Britain might not be immune to the lure of quacks and saviours, to self-doubt, more sternly organised social conflicts, loss of identity.

The twentieth century would be convulsed in crises more dangerous to Britain than the post-Reformation conflicts, the aggressions of Spain and France, the loss of America, the equivocal returns of Empire and of victory in two world wars. With the revival of Celtic demands, Englishness itself might be revoked as mere sham, the product of propaganda, credulity, misunderstanding and brute force, English History a record of exploitation, violence, opium wars, betrayals, and unequal treaties. Deploring the Empire, Dennis Potter was roundly applauded when he asserted: 'Perhaps the noblest task of the popular historian should be to make us ashamed of our forefathers.' This does not tempt me, but I agree with Eric Hobsbawm that getting History wrong is an essential part of being a nation. This of course includes Albion, the detritus of which is now left to literature, antiquarianism, Hollywood, and commercials. However, even if most of our popular history is a self-regarding tall story, I like to think that the gist of it was worth the telling.

Bibliography

Peter Ackroyd, *Blake* (Sinclair-Stevenson, 1995)
Joan Alexander, *Voices and Echoes* (Quartet, 1983)
——*Mabel Strickland* (Progress Press, 1996)
Michael Alexander: see *Earlier English Poems* (Penguin, 1966)
Geoffrey Ashe, *King Arthur's Avalon* (Collins, 1957)
——*From Caesar to Arthur* (Collins, 1960)
——*Kings and Queens of Early Britain* (Methuen, 1982)
Richard Barber, *The Knight and Chivalry* (Longmans, 1970)
——(trans.), *Bestiary* (Folio Society, 1992)
Frank Barlow, *William Rufus* (Metheun, 1983)
——*Thomas Beckett* (Weidenfeld and Nicolson, 1986)
——See also *The Norman Conquest* (ed. C.T. Chevallier) (Eyre and Spottiswoode,
    1966)
Henry Batsford and Charles Fry, *The English Cottage* (Batsford, 1950)
Georgina Battiscombe, *Shaftesbury* (Constable, 1974)
H.S. Bennett, *Life on the English Manor* (Cambridge, 1937)
Henry Bett, *English Legends* (Bastford, 1950)
Bruno Bettleheim, *The Uses of Enchantment* (Thames and Hudson, 1976)
Peter Hunter Blair, *The World of Bede* (Secker and Warburg, 1970)
Robert Blake, *Disraeli* (Eyre and Spottiswoode, 1966)
Lesley Blanch, *The Wilder Shores of Love* (John Murray, 1954)
T.C.W. Blanning, *The French Revolution* (Macmillan, 1987)
Harold Bloom, *Omens of Millennium* (Fourth Estate, 1996)
Ronald Blythe, *Akenfield* (Allen Lane, 1969)
E.W. Bovill, *The Golden Trade of the Moors* (Oxford, 1958)
Brian Branston, *The Lost Gods of England* (Thames and Hudson, 1957)
Christopher Brookes, *English Cricket* (Weidenfeld and Nicolson, 1978)
Arthur Bryant, *Samuel Pepys: The Years of Peril* (Collins, 1936)
——*English Saga* (Collins, 1942)
John Buchan, *These For Remembrance* (Buchan and Enright, 1987)
M. St Clare Byrne, *Elizabethan Life in Town and Country* (London, 1925)
Neville Cardus, *Cricket* (Longmans, 1930)

Bibliography

C.E. Carrington, *The British Overseas* (Cambridge, 1968)

Noel Carrington, *Popular English Art* (Penguin, 1945)

Richard F. Cassady, *The Norman Achievement* (Sidgwick and Jackson, 1980)

David Cecil, *The Cecils of Hatfield House* (Constable, 1973)

John Chandos, *Boys Together* (Hutchinson, 1984)

G.K. Chesterton, *Heretics* (Methuen, 1905)

——*Charles Dickens* (Methuen, 1906)

Winston S. Churchill, *A History of the English Speaking People* (Cassell, 1956–8)

Gregory Claeys (ed.), *Utopias of the British Enlightenment* (Cambridge, 1994)

Joseph R. Clancy, *Medieval Welsh Lyrics* (Macmillan, 1965)

John Clive, *Not by Bread Alone* (Collins Harvill, 1990)

Lady Chudleigh, *Poems on Several Occasions* (London, 1703)

Linda Colley, *Britons: Forging the Nation, 1707–1837* (Yale, 1992)

Olive Cook, *The English Country House* (Thames and Hudson, 1974)

Vincent Cronin, *Louis and Antoinette* (Collins, 1974)

J. Mordaunt Crook, *The Greek Revival* (John Murray, 1995)

Kevin Crossley-Holland and Bruce Mitchell, *The Battle of Maldon and other Old English Poems* (Macmillan, 1963)

John Cummins, *Francis Drake* (Weidenfeld and Nicolson, 1995)

Harold S. Darby, *Hugh Latimer* (Epworth Press, 1953)

Basil Davidson, *The Search for Africa* (Currey, 1994)

A.R. Davies, *The Revolt of Owain Glyn Dŵr* (Oxford, 1995)

Daniel Defoe, *The Complete English Tradesman* (London, 1736)

Eugene Delacroix, *Journal* (Phaedon, 1951)

Michael De-la-Noy, *The Honours System* (Allison and Busby, 1985)

Frank R. Donovan, *The Vikings* (Cassell, 1965)

David C. Douglas, in *The Norman Conquest*, ed. C.T. Chevallier (Eyre and Spottiswoode, 1966)

Georges Duby, *The Age of the Cathedrals* (Croom Helm, 1981)

——*William Marshal* (Faber and Faber, 1986)

Anthony Eden, *Another World: 1897–1917* (Allan Lane, 1976)

Michael Edwardes, *The Last Years of British India* (Cassell, 1967)

Peter Beresford Ellis, *H. Rider Haggard* (Routledge, 1979)

G.R. Elton, *Policy and Police* (Cambridge, 1972)

D.J. Enright, *Fields of Vision* (Oxford, 1988)

R.C.K. Ensor, *Oxford History of England* (Oxford, 1969)

Dennis Farr, *English Art, 1870–1940* (Oxford, 1984)

Christina Fell, and others, *Women in Anglo-Saxon England and the Impact of 1066* (British Museum and Blackwell, 1986)

Geoffrey B.A.M. Finlayson, *The Seventh Earl of Shaftesbury* (Eyre Methuen, 1981)

Ruth First, and others, *The South African Connection* (Temple Smith, 1972)

Bibliography

Antonia Fraser, *The Weaker Vessel: Women's Lot in 17th Century England* (Weidenfeld and Nicolson, 1984)

—— *The Gunpowder Plot* (Weidenfeld and Nicolson, 1996)

George MacDonald Fraser (ed.), *The World of the Public School* (Weidenfeld and Nicolson, 1977)

Anne Geneva, *Astrology and the 17th Century Mind* (Manchester University Press, 1995)

Ian Gentles, *The New Model Army in England, Ireland and Scotland, 1645–53* (Blackwell, 1994)

Gretchen Gerzina, *Black England* (John Murray, 1995)

Michael Gilbert (ed.), *Prep School* (John Murray, 1991)

David Gilmour, *Curzon* (John Murray, 1994)

Antonia Gransden (ed.), *Historical Writing in England c. 550 to c. 1307* (Routledge, 1974)

—— *Historical Writing in England c. 1307 to the Early Sixteenth Century* (Routledge, 1982)

Michael Grant, *The Civilization of Europe* (Weidenfeld and Nicolson, 1965)

—— *The Dawn of the Middle Ages* (Weidenfeld and Nicolson, 1981)

Robert Graves, *The White Goddess* (Faber and Faber, 1952)

—— *The Greek Myths* (Penguin, 1955)

Graham Greene, *Collected Essays* (Bodley Head, 1969)

—— *Lord Rochester's Monkey* (Bodley Head, 1974)

John Guy, *The Tudor Age* (see *Oxford Illustrated History of Britain*, Oxford, 1984)

Peter Gwyn, *The King's Cardinal* (Barrie and Jenkins, 1990)

Robin D. Gwynn, *Huguenot Heritage* (Routledge, 1985)

John Hale, *The Civilization of Europe in the Renaissance* (Harper Collins, 1993)

Elizabeth M. Hallam, *Domesday Book Through Nine Centuries* (Thames and Hudson, 1986)

F.E. Halliday, *Cultural History of England* (Thames and Hudson, 1967)

Evelyn Hardy, *Survivors of the Armada* (Constable, 1966)

Jose Harris, *Private Lives, Public Spirit: A Social History of Britain, 1870–1914* (Oxford, 1993)

J.F.C. Harrison, *The Common People* (Croom Helm, 1984)

Patrick Hastings, *Famous and Infamous Cases* (Heinemann, 1950)

Selina Hastings, *Evelyn Waugh* (Sinclair-Stevenson, 1994)

Ronald Hayman, *The German Theatre* (with contributions from Gertrude Mander, H.M. Waidson and T.M. Holmes) (Wolff, 1975)

John E.N. Hearsey, *London and the Great Fire* (John Murray, 1965)

Vera and Helmut Hell, *The Great Pilgrimage of the Middle Ages* (Barrie and Rockcliff, 1984)

Christopher Hibbert, *The Virgin Queen* (Viking, 1990)

Bibliography

Christopher Hill, *The Century of Revolution* (Nelson, 1961)

——*A Turbulent, Seditious and Factious People* (Oxford, 1992)

Gertrude Himmelfarb, *The De-Moralization of Society* (Institute of Economic Affairs, 1995)

Thomas Hinde, *A Field Guide to the English Country Parson* (Heinemann, 1983)

Charles Hobday, *Edgell Rickword* (Carcanet, 1989)

Eric Hobsbawm, *On History* (Weidenfeld and Nicolson, 1997)

Christina Hole, *English Folk Heroes* (Batsford, 1948)

Henry Holorenshaw, *The Levellers and the English Revolution* (Gollancz, 1939)

Michael Holroyd, *Bernard Shaw*, Vol. 1 (Chatto and Windus, 1988)

J.C. Holt, *Robin Hood* (Thames and Hudson, 1982)

Roger Hudson, *The Jubilee Years* (Folio Society, 1996)

James W. Hulse, *Revolutionaries in London* (Oxford, 1970)

Archie Hunter, *Kitchener's Sword-arm* (Spellmount, 1996)

J. Hampden Jackson, *England since the Industrial Revolution* (Gollancz, 1936)

Lawrence James, *The Rise and Fall of the British Empire* (Little, Brown, 1994)

G. Jekyll and S.A. Jones, *Old English Household Life* (Batsford, 1939)

Paul Johnson, *The Offshore Islanders* (Weidenfeld and Nicolson, 1972)

W. Blanch Johnson, *The British Prison Hulks* (Christopher Johnson, 1957)

Gwyn Jones, *A History of the Vikings* (Oxford, 1970)

Denis Judd, *Empire* (HarperCollins, 1996)

John Keane, *Tom Paine* (Bloomsbury, 1995)

Anthony Kenny, *Thomas More* (Oxford, 1983)

Charles Kightly, *Folk Heroes of Britain* (Thames and Hudson, 1982)

Mary Kingsley, *Travels in West Africa* (Folio Society, 1976)

David Kynaston, *The City of London*, Vol. 2 (Chatto and Windus, 1995)

Margaret Wade Labarge, *Medieval Travellers* (Hamish Hamilton, 1982)

Paul Henry Lang, *Music in Western Civilization* (Dent, 1963)

Ronald de Leew (ed.), *The Letters of Vincent Van Gogh* (Macmillan, 1996)

Brendan Lehane, *The Quest of Three Abbots* (John Murray, 1968)

Patience Leith-Ross, *The John Tradescants* (Peter Owen, 1984)

Oliver Letwin, in *The Times*, 1996, reviewing Hobbes's *Letters*, ed. Noel Malcolm

Shirley Robin Letwin, *The Gentleman in Trollope* (Macmillan, 1982)

Michael Levien (ed.), *The Cree Journals* (Webb and Bower, 1981)

Jack Lindsay, *Arthur and his Times* (Muller, 1958)

Elizabeth Longford, *Wellington: The Years of the Sword* (Weidenfeld and Nicolson, 1969)

Lord Longford, *A Vowed Intent* (Little, Brown, 1994)

Angela M. Lucas, *Women in the Middle Ages* (Harvester, 1983)

Fiona MacCarthy, *William Morris* (Faber and Faber, 1994)

Kirsty McCleod, *The Last Summer* (Collins, 1983)

Bibliography

Jock McCulloch, *Colonial Psychiatry and the African Mind* (Cambridge, 1995)

H.B. McNicol, *History, Heritage and the Environment* (Faber and Faber, 1946)

David Mannix and Malcolm Cowley, *Black Cargoes* (Longmans, 1963)

Philip Mansel, *Royal Guards* (Quartet, 1985)

Victoria Manthorpe, *Children of the Empire* (Gollancz, 1996)

Richard Marius, *Thomas More* (Dent, 1984)

Jean Markdale, *Women of the Celts* (Gordon Cremonesi, 1976)

P.J. Marshall (ed.), *Cambridge Illustrated History of the British Empire* (Cambridge, 1996)

John Masefield, *The Old Front Line* (Heinemann, 1917)

W. Somerset Maugham, *A Winter's Notebook* (Heinemann, 1949)

Tom Mayor, *Thomas Starkey and the Commonweal* (Cambridge, 1990)

Dudley Miles, *Francis Place* (Harvester, 1988)

Giles Milton, *The Riddle and the Knight* (Allison and Busby, 1996)

Alan Moorehead, *The White Nile* (Hamish Hamilton, 1960)

—— *The Fatal Impact* (Hamish Hamilton, 1996)

Caroline Moorehead, *Troublesome People* (Hamish Hamilton, 1987)

Kenneth Q. Morgan (ed.), *The Oxford Illustrated History of Britain* (Oxford, 1984)

Jan Morris, *Heaven's Command* (Faber and Faber, 1973)

John Morris, *The Age of Arthur* (Weidenfeld and Nicolson, 1973)

Norma Myers, *Reconstructing the Black Past* (Cassell, 1996)

Helen G. Nussey, *London Gardens of the Past* (Bodley Head, 1930)

Roland Oliver and J.D. Fage, *A Short History of Africa* (Penguin, 1962)

Iris Origo, *A Need to Testify* (John Murray, 1984)

Valerie Pakenham, *The Noonday Sun: Edwardians in the Tropics* (Methuen, 1985)

Peter Parker, *The Old Lie* (Constable, 1987)

Anne Parry, *Parry of the Arctic* (Longmans, 1959)

Lindsay Paterson, *The Autonomy of Modern Scotland* (Edinburgh, 1991)

Margery Perham, *East African Journey* (Faber and Faber, 1976)

Maria Perry, *The Word of a Prince* (Boydell Press, 1990)

Dexter Petley, *Little Nineveh* (Polygan, 1995)

John Peters, *A Family From Flanders* (Collins, 1985)

Caryl Phillips, *Extravagant Strangers* (Faber, 1997)

Steven Pincus, *Protestantism and Patriotism* (Cambridge, 1996)

David Piper, *Painting in England, 1500–1870* (Book Society, 1960)

Sir Hugh Plat, *Delights for Ladies* (1609: ed. G.E. and K.R. Fussell, published by Lockwood, 1948)

J.H. Plumb, *Men and Places* (Cresset Press, 1963)

J.B. Priestley, *Margin Released* (Heinemann, 1964)

V. S. Pritchett, *London Perceived* (Chatto and Windus, with Heinemann, 1962)

Frank Prochaska, *Royal Bounty* (Yale, 1995)

Bibliography

Jack Ravensdale, *The Domesday Inheritance* (Souvenir Press, 1986)

Herbert Read, *The Meaning of Art* (Faber and Faber, 1936)

John Rex, *Race, Colonialism and the City* (Routledge, 1973)

Edgell Rickword, *Essays and Opinions* (Carcanet, 1974)

Jasper Ridley, *Lord Palmerston* (Constable, 1970)

—— *Henry VIII* (Constable 1984)

—— *Elizabeth I* (Constable 1987)

—— *The Statesman and the Fanatic: Thomas Wolsey and Thomas More* (Cambridge, 1995)

Charles Ross, *Richard III* (Eyre Methuen, 1981)

A.L. Rowse, *Tudor Cornwall* (Cape, 1941).

—— *The England of Elizabeth* (Macmillan, 1950)

—— *Eminent Elizabethans* (Macmillan, 1983)

—— *Reflections on the Puritan Revolution* (Methuen, 1986)

—— *Court and Country* (Harvester, 1987)

George Rudé, *The Crowd in History: 1730–1848* (John Wiley, 1964)

M.L. Ryder, *Sheep and Man* (Duckworth, 1988)

Marshal Sahlins, *What Natives Think* (Chicago, 1995)

Anne Salmond, *Two Worlds* (Viking, 1992)

Jonathan Saurday, *The Body Emblazoned* (Routledge, 1995)

John Saville, *1848: The British State and the Chartist Movement* (Cambridge, 1995)

Ronald Segal, *The Black Diaspora* (Faber and Faber, 1995)

Martin Seymour-Smith, *Hardy* (Bloomsbury, 1994)

Sacheverell Sitwell, *For Want of the Golden City* (Thames and Hudson, 1959)

Robert Skidelsky, *Interests and Obsessions* (Macmillan, 1993)

Edwin Smith, Olive Cook, Graham Hutton, *English Parish Churches* (Thames and Hudson, 1976)

T.C. Smout, *A History of the Scottish People* (Collins, 1968)

Alfred P. Smythe, *King Alfred the Great* (Oxford, 1995)

Mary Soames, *The Profligate Duke* (Collins, 1987)

Dava Sobel, *Longitude* (Fourth Estate, 1996)

Pauline Stafford, *Queens, Concubines and Dowagers* (Batsford, 1983)

Suzanne J. Stark, *Female Tars* (Constable, 1996)

Lawrence Stone, *The Past and Present Revisited* (Routledge, 1987)

Lytton Strachey, *Characters and Commentaries* (Chatto and Windus, 1941)

Roy Strong, *The Renaissance Garden* (Thames and Hudson, 1979)

—— *Henry, Prince of Wales* (Thames and Hudson, 1986)

John Sugden, *Sir Francis Drake* (Barrie and Jenkins, 1990)

Peter D.G. Thoms, *John Wilkes* (Oxford, 1996)

E.P. Thompson, *Customs in Common* (Merlin, 1992)

Nikolai Tolstoy, *The Quest for Merlin* (Hamish Hamilton, 1985)

Bibliography

——*Victims of Yalta* (Hodder and Stoughton, 1997)

G.M. Trevelyan, *English Social History* (Longmans, 1944)

Barbara Tuchman, *The Proud Tower* (Hamish Hamilton, 1966)

——*A Distant Mirror* (Macmillan, 1978)

Peter Vansittart, *Worlds and Underworlds* (Peter Owen, 1974)

Hugh Walpole, *Fortitude* (Martin Secker, 1913)

——*The Crystal Box* (Privately Printed, 1924)

James Walvin, *Black and White* (Allen Lane, 1973)

——*A Child's World* (Penguin, 1982)

Colin Ward and David Crouch, *The Allotment* (Faber and Faber, 1988)

C.V. Wedgwood, *Oliver Cromwell* (Duckworth, 1939)

——'Poetry and Politics in Baroque England', in *Penguin New Writing*, ed. John Lehmann (1944)

Gavin Weightman and Steve Humphries, *The Making of Modern London* (Sidgwick and Jackson, 1987)

Stanley Weintraub, *Victoria* (Unwin, Hyman, 1987)

H.G. Wells, *The Time Machine* (Heinemann, 1895)

——*A Modern Utopia* (Chapman and Hall, 1908)

——*The Work, Wealth and Happiness of Mankind* (Heinemann, 1932)

Rebecca West, *Black Lamb and Grey Falcon* (Macmillan, 1944)

Jennifer Westwood, *Albion* (Granada, 1985)

Laurence Whistler, *The English Festivals* (Heinemann, 1957)

Neville Williams, *Contraband Cargoes* (Longmans, 1957)

John Dover Wilson (ed.), *Life in Shakespeare's England* (Pelican, 1944)

P.G. Wodehouse, *The Heart of a Goof* (Herbert Jenkins, 1926)

Charles L. Wood, *The Age of Chivalry* (Weidenfeld and Nicolson, 1970)

Leonard Woolf, *Downhill All the Way* (Hogarth, 1967)

Virginia Woolf, *The Second Common Reader* (Hogarth, 1932)

Joyce Youings, *Sixteenth Century England* (Allen Lane, 1984)

Anthea Zeman, *Presumptuous Girls* (Weidenfeld and Nicolson, 1977)

Acknowledgements

Thanks are due to my editors, Gail Pirkis, Roger Hudson and Liz Robinson, for their hard labour on the many yards of the original manuscript, and, once again, to Douglas Matthews for his usual impeccable Index, and adroit queries. My typist, Terry Jordan, deserves high praise.

P.V.

Index

Index